Decision

Decision

HOW THE SUPREME COURT
DECIDES CASES

Bernard Schwartz

NEW YORK   OXFORD

Oxford University Press

1996

Oxford University Press

Oxford   New York
Athens   Auckland   Bangkok   Bombay
Calcutta   Cape Town   Dar es Salaam   Delhi
Florence   Hong Kong   Istanbul   Karachi
Kuala Lumpur   Madras   Madrid   Melbourne
Mexico City   Nairobi   Paris   Singapore
Taipei   Tokyo   Toronto

and associated companies in

Berlin   Ibadan

Published by Oxford University Press, Inc.
198 Madison Avenue, New York, NY 10016

Library of Congress Cataloging-in-Publication Data
Schwartz, Bernard.
Decision : how the Supreme Court decides cases / Bernard Schwartz.
p.   cm.
Includes index.
ISBN 0-19-509859-5
1. United States.   Supreme Court.   2. Judicial process — United
States.   I. Title.
KF8742.S323   1996
[347.30735]   95-16119

AC-CENT-TCHU-ATE THE POSITIVE
Lyric by Johnny Mercer
Music by Harold Arlen
©1944 (Renewed) HARWIN MUSIC CO.
All Rights Reserved

9 8 7 6 5 4 3 2 1

Printed in the United States of America on acid-free paper

For Aileen
and all we have had
together

Preface

During the past decade and a half there have been unprecedented revelations about the Supreme Court's decision process. According to Anthony Lewis in the *New York Times*, they have resulted from a "new genre of books penetrating the Court's secrecy," starting with *The Brethren* by Bob Woodward and Scott Armstrong in 1979. The situation has changed completely from that of only a few years earlier, when Nina Totenberg wrote that there was "no more secret society in America than the Supreme Court." In those days, what went on behind the red velour curtain was as removed from the public gaze as the decision process in Stalin and Brezhnev's Kremlin.

As described by Erwin Griswold, former solicitor general and Harvard Law School dean, the revelatory type of book "tells you just what the justices said in the conference room, as they entered the elevator and to their law clerks—how they pulled, hauled, schemed, battled and traded until somehow or other they got all those cases decided, some of them of supreme importance."

In her 1975 article, Totenberg stated, "It is unheard of for a Justice to reveal anything specific about the Court's case work; law clerks, too, are sworn to secrecy." To the contrary, the recent revelations about the Court's decision process have been based upon information provided by Justices and law clerks, as well as material from Court files provided by them. The present book has been made possible by the willingness of some of the Justices to speak to me, not only generally about the Court's operation, but also about how specific cases were decided. They have given me virtually unlimited access to their files, containing conference notes, draft opinions, letters, and memoranda. Likewise, former law clerks have furnished me with information on the Court's work during their years of service.

In addition, the papers of many of the Justices are available in collections open to the public or to serious researchers. I have been afforded generous access to the papers of Chief Justice Earl Warren and Justices Hugo L. Black, Harold H. Burton, Tom C. Clark, William O. Douglas, Felix Frankfurter, Robert H. Jackson, John Marshall Harlan, and Thurgood Marshall, as well as to earlier papers in the Library of Congress.

This book's discussion of the Supreme Court's decision process is thus based upon both documentary and oral sources. The documentary sources are of two kinds: (1) the conference lists and notes and the docket books of the Justices. The conferences themselves, at which cases are discussed and the votes taken on decisions, are, of course, completely private — attended only by the Justices themselves. The secrecy of the conference is, indeed, one of the great continuing Court traditions. I have tried to reconstruct the conferences in most of the cases discussed. The conference discussions, which are given in conversational form, are reconstructed from notes made by at least one Justice who was present, including, but not limited to, the notes of Justices William O. Douglas, Felix Frankfurter, Harold H. Burton, Tom C. Clark, John Marshall Harlan, Thurgood Marshall, and Chief Justice Earl Warren; (2) the correspondence, notes, diaries, memoranda, and draft opinions of members of the Court, including, but not limited to, the papers of the same Justices and Justice Hugo L. Black. The documents used and their locations are identified, except where they were made available upon a confidential basis. In the latter case, I have tried to identify the documents, usually by title and date. I have personally examined every document to which reference is made.

The oral sources were, as stated, personal interviews with Justices and law clerks. Every statement not otherwise identified was made to me personally. I have tried to identify the statements made by different people, except where they were made upon a confidential basis. In the latter case, I have given the position of the person involved, but not his name.

In a review of my biography of Chief Justice Warren, Anthony Lewis noted, "Schwartz reconstructed what purported to be verbatim quotations from the justices' conferences. In important instances he did not disclose his sources, making it difficult to judge the fairness of the accounts; might they have come from one side in a hotly disputed case?" The conference discussions in this book, as well as in that reviewed by Lewis, are, as stated, reconstructed from notes made by at least one Justice who was present. It is true, as Lewis points out, that the conference notes used have not normally been identified. That is because they were supplied on a confidential basis. It is also true that the notes may "have come from one side in a hotly disputed case." It should, however, be stressed that these were notes taken during the conference by the Justices concerned for their own use. Their purpose was to provide a summary of what was said to help in their own consideration of the case. It is most unlikely that the Justices' own biases would color notes taken for that purpose — notes that are only a sketchy summary by active participants in the conference, who are at best amateurs in transcribing each Justice's presentation.

This book may, however, be the last of its kind—for some time at least. The type of access I have had to Justices and their papers may now be a thing of the past. A major reason for the lifting of the Court's curtain of secrecy has been the willingness of Justice William J. Brennan to make his papers available to serious researchers. Most of the published revelations on what goes on during the Justices' deliberative process have been based upon materials obtained from the Brennan files. The members of the Rehnquist Court have, however, been disturbed by Brennan's actions in this respect. Justice Brennan responded to their concern in a December 19, 1990, Memorandum to the Conference circulated both to the other Justices and to retired Chief Justice Warren E. Burger and Justice Lewis F. Powell.

"Sandra and the Chief," began the memo, referring to Justice Sandra Day O'Connor and Chief Justice William H. Rehnquist, "have expressed to me the concern—shared, they tell me, by others of you—that researchers who examine my official papers thereby gain access to memoranda written to me by other Justices. They have suggested that, to avoid embarrassment to any of our colleagues, I should not grant access to files that may include any written material from Justices who are still sitting on the Court." According to Brennan, "As I interpret this suggestion, it would require that I close all of my files for the years following 1962, when Byron [White] joined the Court."

The memo confirmed that the Justice had, indeed, given researchers access to "my collection of official papers in the Manuscript Division of the Library of Congress. . . . These papers consist primarily of case files from previous Terms." The memo stated, "About a decade ago, I began to grant permission to study these files to certain academic researchers, and that practice has continued. . . . Virtually all of the researchers who received permission have been affiliated with an institution of higher learning (typically, a law school or political science department)."

Though, as will be seen, Justice Brennan defended the opening of his files, the concern expressed by Chief Justice Rehnquist and his colleagues led Brennan to modify his practice. "When I became aware of your concerns," Brennan wrote, "I reviewed with the Library of Congress the procedures governing access to my papers." Applicants would be screened more carefully and "I have also imposed a time limit on such research."

More important, Justice Brennan has refused requests for access to his files on cases decided since Chief Justice Rehnquist has headed the Court. This has not, however, prevented me from including substantial unpublished material on the decision process in the Rehnquist Court. The material thus disclosed was obtained from the Thurgood Marshall papers in the Library of Congress, which contain files on the cases decided through June 1991 (the end of the 1990 Term). In view of the opposition of the present Justices, however, it is unlikely that comparable files will be made available for later terms—at least in the foreseeable future.

This is underscored by Justice O'Connor's statement, in a letter to me, that she "removed a number of items in [her] files in the aftermath of the Library of Congress' handling of Justice Marshall's files." Nor has Justice O'Connor been alone. She told a Drake law faculty luncheon that, because of the controversy over the Marshall papers' release, other Justices, too, "stripped" their files of provocative material—exactly the kind of material needed for a book such as this. A more significant question is whether any confidential Court files should be made public. "One wonders," wrote Erwin Griswold about one of my books describing the inside workings of the Warren Court, "what effect this sort of presentation of documents, interviews and so on, so soon after the events, has on freedom of exchange, frankness, trust, common understanding, even bonhomie, among present and future justices." Griswold then posed the question: "Is there not an appreciable risk that there may be a . . . chilling effect in interchange even among Supreme Court justices? Sunshine can be carcinogenic as well as antiseptic." Griswold concluded, "Many people think we are confronted with more knowledge about the U.S. Supreme Court than is good or really useful."

Needless to say, I do not agree with the Griswold critique. In an age of open government and sunshine laws, it has been anomalous that almost nothing was known about the internal functioning of the fulcrum on which the entire constitutional system turns. This book is an attempt to help change that situation—to lift the Court's curtain of secrecy somewhat so that the Justices and their work may be better understood.

But what about the effect of revealing the Court's internal operations on the Justices themselves and the freedom of their deliberations? In his already-quoted review, Anthony Lewis voiced a concern similar to that expressed by Griswold: "Will the justices be able to argue among one another with the candor that may change minds if they think their words will soon be retailed to the public? Or will their conferences degenerate into posturing, like most Congressional debates?"

The Griswold-Lewis criticisms are based on an a priori assumption that may or may not be consistent with the facts of judicial life. Is it proved that the Justices will be less candid if their decision process is no longer completely sealed? Will a conscientious judge really be affected by the possibility that the position he takes in a conference or a draft may someday see the light of day? The nine Justices, after all, are not mere friends exchanging gossip at a social gathering. They are deciding the most vital questions that arise in our society and they are deciding them conclusively, because there is no way that the Court's decisions can be overruled except by constitutional amendment. One is reminded of Justice Jackson's famous statement some years ago, "There is no doubt that if there were a super-Supreme Court, a substantial proportion of our reversals of state courts would also be reversed. We are not final because we are infallible, but we are infallible only because we are final."

It is important that we know as much as possible about how people placed in such a position of infallibility exercise their awesome power. Lord Acton's dictum that great men are almost always bad men does not necessarily apply to Supreme Court Justices. But our attitude toward them should still be based on some such assumption. Today, we must not judge those in possession of public power by the maxim that the king can do no wrong. On the contrary, if there is any presumption it should be the other way, against the holders of power, and it should increase as the power increases.

Are the Court and the country harmed by learning what a sitting Justice reveals in conference — for example, that had he been on the Court in 1954 Justice White would not have agreed with *Brown v. Board of Education*'s famous footnote 11 because he feels modern sociological and psychological data do not support the notion of stigma relied on by Chief Justice Warren's *Brown* opinion? Or if a letter of Chief Justice Burger is published which contains an animadversion on "women's lib"? Or even if it is made known that Justice Frankfurter wrote about Justice Frank Murphy, "you would no more heed [his] tripe than you would be seen naked at Dupont Circle at high noon tomorrow"?

Is the public interest really served if such things are kept behind a veil of secrecy? If possible disclosure may lead to more restraint by the Justices, that is not necessarily undesirable. It is hard to see how the work of the Court will be hurt if the decision process is purged of the intemperate type of comment that Court revelations sometimes bring to light.

I have always seen my role in writing about the Court's decision process as that of a reporter who describes what went on in the cases under scrutiny. My function is to tell what happened, not to shield the Court's inner processes from public view. I have been fortunate in having documents made available to me, such as those used throughout this book. But the decision to make them available, as well as to discuss the cases involved, was not made by me but by people within the Court community — particularly by Justices who believed that the claims of history were more important than those of judicial secrecy.

The documents published in this book — the drafts and internal memoranda, the extracts from letters and conference notes — these all help to explain the workings of the Court: how the Justices vote and change their votes and how opinions are drafted and redrafted before they are finally issued. The Court's decision process is made clearer by this sort of material than it possibly can be by analysis, acute though it may be, of only the opinions published in the *United States Reports*.

The bottom line, however, is ultimately to be found in the claims of history — even vis-à-vis the highest court. The right of the people to know does not degenerate into a mere slogan where the work of the Justices is concerned. The country has the same right to information on how the Supreme Court operates that it has with regard to other governmental institutions. As Justice Brennan put it in his 1990 memo, "My decision to allow selective access to my papers was not taken lightly, but I ultimately concluded that scholarly examination of the Court's workings would serve the public interest."

It should not be forgotten that the Court is, to quote Alexander Hamilton, "the weakest of the three departments." The Justices themselves have recognized this. In Justice Frankfurter's words, "The Court's authority—possessed of neither the purse nor the sword—ultimately rests on sustained public confidence in its moral sanction." The authority of the Court is moral, not physical. It operates by its influence, not by its power alone. The Justices must depend on public support for the ultimate efficacy of their judgments.

Public support depends on an informed public opinion. "What strikes me increasingly, in writings on the work of the Court," Justice Frankfurter once complained, "is their unrelatedness to actuality." For the country to find out how the highest bench actually operates can only increase understanding of the Court's crucial role in guarding "the ark of the Constitution." It must be admitted that my intention was not to solidify popular support for the Court, but to tell what actually happened in these cases and let the chips fall where they may. In fact, they do fall in a way that reflects favorably on the Court. One is constantly impressed by the willingness of Justices to change their views owing to the intellectual arguments made by their colleagues. No other governmental institution could be subjected to comparable scrutiny of its internal processes and come out so well.

The public may conclude from this book that the Court does not work at all in the cold, purely logical way that most people think it does, but that it does work—through the constant give and take between the Justices—in a way that ultimately serves the best interests of the country. Surely, it is better for Court and country that this be made known by what the Brennan memo termed "responsible scholarship about the Court" than for it to be kept concealed behind the red velour curtain.

Tulsa   B. S.
September 1995

Contents

Decision

Introduction

In 1788, an opponent of ratification of the Constitution, who wrote under the pseudonym of Brutus, asserted, "I question whether the world ever saw . . . a court of justice invested with such immense powers" as the Supreme Court. In such a tribunal, Brutus declared, the Justices would "feel themselves independent of Heaven itself."

The power peremptorily to define the Constitution makes the Supreme Court unique among governmental institutions. To it alone is assigned the function of guarding the ark of the Constitution. Through the exercise of its constitutional role, the Court has wielded power far beyond that assumed by any other judicial tribunal. "In no other nation on earth," caustically commented a critic, "does a group of judges hold the sweeping political power — the privilege in practice, not just in theory, of saying the last governmental word — that is held by the nine U.S. Supreme Court Justices."

Authority such as that exercised by our highest court is not inherent in judicial power. On the contrary, as the experience in other countries amply demonstrates, the judiciary is normally the weakest branch of government. "The judiciary," wrote Alexander Hamilton in *The Federalist*, "is beyond comparison the weakest of the three departments of power. . . . [It] has no influence over either the sword or the purse; no direction either of the strength or the wealth of the society; and can take no active resolution whatever. It may truly be said to have neither FORCE nor WILL, but merely judgment."

Despite the inherent weakness of its original position, the Supreme Court has managed successfully to assert its power as authoritative expounder of the Constitution. Though it possesses neither the sword of the executive nor the purse of the legislature, its judgments are normally adhered to without question by those who direct the strength and the wealth of the society.

The Supreme Court is far more than the usual law court. It is primarily a political institution whose decrees mark the boundaries between the great departments of government. Upon its action depend the proper functioning of federalism and the scope to be given to the rights of the individual. A judge on such a tribunal has an opportunity to leave an imprint upon the life of the nation as no mere master of the common law possibly could.

Only a handful of men in all our history have made so manifest a mark on their own age and on ages still to come as did Justices such as Oliver Wendell Holmes and William J. Brennan. The same cannot be said of even the greatest of modern English judges. To be a judge, endowed with all the omnipotence of justice, is certainly among life's noblest callings; but the mere common-law judge, even in a preeminently legal polity like that in Britain, cannot begin to compare in power and prestige with a Justice of our Supreme Court. A judge who is regent over what is done in the legislative and executive branches — the *deus ex machina* who has the final word in the constitutional system — has attained one of the ultimates of human authority.

HISTORICAL PERSPECTIVE

One who is familiar with the manner in which the highest court has operated is struck with the generally successful way in which it has exercised its awesome authority. The Court's jurisprudence has illustrated the antinomy inherent in every system of law: the law must be stable and yet it cannot stand still. The essential outlines of the constitutional system are still those laid down in 1787; there is here a continuity in governmental structure that is all but unique in an ever changing world. But the system still proves workable only because it has been continually reshaped to meet two centuries' changing needs.

There have been aberrations, but in the main the Supreme Court in operation has reflected the history of the nation: the main thrust has been to meet what Justice Holmes called the "felt necessities" of each period in the nation's history.

At the outset, the primary needs of establishing national power on a firm basis and vindicating property rights against excesses of state power were met in the now classic decisions of the Marshall Court. A generation later, the needs of society had changed. If the Court under Chief Justice Roger B. Taney was to translate the doctrines of Jacksonian Democracy, and particularly its emphasis on society's rights, into constitutional law, that was true because those doctrines were deemed necessary to the proper development of the polity. In addition, they furthered the growth of corporate enterprise and prevented its restriction by the deadening hand of established monopoly.

If in the latter part of the nineteenth century the Court was to elevate the rights of property to the plane of constitutional immunity, its due-process decisions were the necessary legal accompaniment of the industrial conquest of a continent. The excesses of a laissez-faire-stimulated industrialism should not lead us to overlook the vital part it played in American development. Nor should it be forgotten that the decisions exalting property rights may have been a necessary accompaniment of the post–Civil War economic expansion.

The picture has been completely altered during the present century. The Court has come to recognize that property rights must be restricted to an extent never before permitted in American law. At the same time, unless the rights of the person are correlatively expanded, the individual will virtually be shorn of constitutional protection — hence the Court's shift in emphasis to the protection of personal rights. The Justices, like the rest of us, have been disturbed by the growth of governmental authority and have sought to preserve a sphere for individuality even in a society in which the individual stands dwarfed by power concentrations.

One must, however, concede that despite the Court's efforts the concentration of governmental power has continued unabated. The second half of the century has, if anything, seen an acceleration in the growth of such power. Indeed, the outstanding feature of the late twentieth century is the power concentrations that increasingly confront the individual. Even a more conservative Court may find it necessary to preserve a sphere for individuality in such a society.

NINE LITTLE LAW FIRMS

This book will examine the way in which the Supreme Court decides cases.

The decision process begins after the oral arguments when the Justices meet in conference to discuss the cases. The conference is led by the Chief Justice, in what is perhaps his most important function as Court head. How a great Chief Justice can lead the Court is shown by the experience under Earl Warren. As we will see in Chapter 4, Warren led both the conference and the Court as effectively as any Chief Justice in our history. When we speak of the Warren Court, we speak of a Court led to most of its important decisions by the Chief Justice in its center chair.

We will, however, also see that a Chief Justice can lead the Supreme Court but cannot dominate it. The most effective Court leader was, of course, our greatest Chief Justice, John Marshall. Marshall's preeminence rests upon two things. The first, we will see in Chapter 3, is the quality we call leadership. Whatever that elusive quality may mean, we know leadership when we see it; and we know that Marshall was the most effective leader any court has ever had.

Just as important, however, was that the principal Marshall decisions corresponded to Justice Oliver Wendell Holmes's "felt necessities" of the developing nation. The other Justices came to see this as clearly as Marshall himself. In a day when, to most Americans, one's state was still one's country, all the Justices understood the need to assert national power and the need for a powerful Union.

Even the strongest Chief Justice, however, cannot lead the Justices to decisions that do not, in their view, meet the Holmes criterion. The following chapters will show that the Chief Justice is unable to secure a decision with which the others do not agree. The Court head may be primus inter pares (first among equals), but in the decision process it is the *pares* that should be emphasized. Aside from his designation as Chief of the Court and the attribution of a slightly higher salary, the Chief Justice's position is not superior to that of his colleagues. As Justice Felix Frankfurter strikingly put it in a letter to another Justice, "He is not the head of a Department; not even a quarterback."

A story is told at the Supreme Court that Justice James C. McReynolds was once late to conference. Chief Justice Charles Evans Hughes told a messenger, "Go tell him we're waiting." The testy McReynolds sent word back: "Go tell the C.J. I don't work for him."

The key thing to remember about how the Supreme Court operates is that the Justices operate, as a number of them have said, as "nine little law firms." To this, one commentator adds, "Little is right: two secretaries (the Chief needs and gets three), a messenger and three to four law clerks."

The nine little law firms are completely autonomous. "The Court," said Justice Lewis F. Powell, "is perhaps one of the last citadels of jealously preserved individualism." Their individual independence is underscored by the fact that it is the votes of the individual Justices, not the will of the Chief Justice, that are decisive in the Court's operation. Coming out of a heated conference, Justice William J. Brennan was once heard to mutter, "Five votes can do anything around here." Five votes could change even long established procedures at the Court: the Rule of Four which governs the grant of certiorari (the Court's decision to hear a case), the rule that only the Justices are present during conferences, and even the practice that the Chief Justice leads the conference and assigns opinions.

In fact, of course, the established practices and procedures are unlikely to be altered by the Justices, though some of them have advocated changing the Rule of Four to require five votes for the granting of certiorari. But the Justices do use their voting power to resist decisions with which they do not agree.

Nevertheless, the Court's decision process works because it is essentially a cooperative process. The nine little law firms are wholly independent of each other, yet they must work together for the Court to be able to decide a case and, more important, to explain the decision that has been reached.

The cooperative process begins after the oral argument, when the Justices meet to discuss the case in conference. There the Justices learn how each of the others believes that the given case should be decided and why. Even though the discussions now are less freewheeling than they once were, the conferences do reveal how each Justice stands on the cases discussed.

After the conference discussion shows the Court's consensus on the case, the opinion is assigned to an individual Justice. Here, too, however, the opinion-writing process is anything but an individual performance. "Of course," Justice Frankfurter once wrote to Justice Stanley Reed, "the writer of the Court's opinion . . . is not singing a solo, but leads the orchestra to wit, the Court." The opinion may bear the name of the Justice to whom it was assigned; more often than not, all the same, it is a collective product. The opinion writer prepares a draft that is circulated to the other Justices. Their replies play a crucial part in the decision process.

The exchange of memoranda that occurs after the draft opinion of the Court is circulated is so great at times that a Justice could refer to "the deluge of memoranda of December" in the landmark 1978 *Bakke* affirmative-action case. Memos are sent back and forth as the Justices seek to deal with the issues raised in the circulated draft, as well as in any prior memoranda that have been circulated, and to persuade each other to adopt their authors' views. In particular, there are efforts to reach the Justices who are seen as the swing votes in a case.

One familiar with the work of the Warren Court cannot help but note an important difference in this respect between that tribunal and its successors. In Warren's day, as we will see in Chapter 2, a major part of the exchanges between the Justices was oral, especially in the form of Justice-to-Justice politicking designed to obtain votes for a given point of view. Chief Justice Warren was notably effective in such efforts, and his persuasive powers enabled him to secure key votes in a number of important cases. Several Justices have recalled how hard it was to withstand the Chief Justice when he was able to operate in a one-on-one setting.

In the Burger and Rehnquist Courts, the situation has been different. Neither Chief Justice has been able to the catalyze the decision process the way their predecessor could. Moreover, the characterization of the Justices as operating like nine separate law firms has been particularly appropriate for the Burger and Rehnquist Courts. In them, the Justices have tended to exchange their views in writing. There has been much less of the kind of personal give-and-take that played a crucial role in the Warren Court's decision process.

In part this has been a natural consequence of technology, such as the Xerox copier, first installed in the Court soon after Chief Justice Warren E. Burger took office, and the individual word processors installed more recently. It is so much easier now to exchange memos that it is not necessary to have as much discussion among the Justices on cases before the Court. "I had thought of the Court," Justice Powell once said, "as a collegial body in which the most characteristic activities would be consultation and cooperative deliberation. . . . I was in for more than a little surprise . . . a justice may go through an entire term without being once in the chambers of all the other members of the Court."

Whether through personal contacts or the circulation of draft opinions and memoranda, the post-draft-opinion exchanges are pivotal in the decision process. It is at this point that votes may be switched (with the result an entirely different decision) or the language and even the rationale of the draft opinion of the Court drastically changed. It is at this stage, too, that the cooperative process weeds out potential errors and even blunders such as those discussed in Chapter 9.

When the decision comes down, the opinion issued is the product of the collaborative process. The nine "law firms" have worked together and the opinions issued are not the solo product of their named authors but the handiwork of all the Justices. Sometimes, to be sure, this situation is carried to the extreme of the "opinions by committee" discussed in Chapter 6. After he had read the *Swann* opinion dealt with in that chapter, Judge Griffin B. Bell of the U.S. Court of Appeals for the Fifth Circuit told a *Newsweek* reporter, "It's almost as if there were two sets of views laid side by side."

Judge Bell spoke more accurately than he knew. As we will see in Chapter 6, the final *Swann* opinion was a composite, containing both the lukewarm views of the Chief Justice in whose name it was delivered and the strong views in support of desegregation advocated by the other Justices. The result, as the *New Republic* put it, was "a negotiated document looking in more than a single direction."

In the important cases, the opinions issued by the Court are, as often as not, also "negotiated documents" — the result of a cooperative process in which nine supreme individualists collaborate to bring about the desired result — a result that is the joint work of the Justices rather than the product of the named author alone. The case is decided by the Court — once again, "Five votes can do anything around here" — not by the Justice who delivers the opinion of the Court.

The cooperative nature of the Supreme Court's decision process is what makes it work effectively. Indeed, one must conclude that in most respects the Court's decision process does work effectively. That conclusion is, if anything, reinforced by the following chapters, which provide a behind-the-scenes look at how the court decides cases. In its essentials, the decision process in the Court is a *political* process (in the nonpejorative use of that word). Yet all the lobbying and efforts at persuasion that go on — the sometimes petty infighting, the drafts and memoranda going back and forth among the Justices, the changes made in opinions as part of the bargaining process — all this is done for the purpose of reaching what the individual Justice considers the best result. There is, to be sure, politicking, compromises, and horsetrading in the often complex negotiations needed to attain a working majority, yet all for the purpose of advancing not the Justices themselves but the judicial doctrines in which they believe.

Cases Covered

Access to the Justices and case files has enabled me to describe what happened behind the scenes in the cases discussed in the following chapters. The cases in the book have been chosen to illustrate different aspects of the Supreme Court decision process — aspects that are not revealed at all in the public documents available on each decided case, that is, the briefs, oral-argument transcripts, and published opinions.

The cases chosen illustrate, first of all, the role of the Chief Justice in the decision of cases. The Chief, as he is usually called within the Court, plays a crucial role in the decision process. He leads the conferences at which cases are discussed and voted on and he assigns the opinions in most cases (the exception is when he does not vote with the majority — in which case the senior Associate Justice in the majority assigns the opinion). These are the only formal powers of the Chief in the decision process. In the hands of a strong Chief Justice such as Earl Warren, however, they enable the Chief to lead as effectively as a strong President or military leader.

As the cases discussed show, however, the Chief Justice can only lead, he cannot dictate. As Justice Felix Frankfurter once wrote to Justice William J. Brennan, the notion "that he [the Chief Justice] is the boss . . . must be rigorously resisted." Basically, as Justice Tom C. Clark summarized it in a 1956 article, "The Chief Justice has no more authority than other members of the Court."

The point just made is illustrated dramatically in the *Webster* abortion case in the first chapter. There were few cases that Chief Justice William H. Rehnquist felt more strongly about than *Roe v. Wade*, the 1973 decision establishing a constitutional right to abortion. He had dissented from the decision and strongly opposed it in later cases. In the 1989 *Webster* case, Rehnquist made a major effort to have *Roe* overruled and, we will see, even wrote a draft opinion of the Court accomplishing that result. He ultimately failed in his effort, because Justice Sandra Day O'Connor switched her vote and refused to discard *Roe*. Though the overruling of *Roe* was high on the Rehnquist judicial agenda, he was not able to accomplish it in *Webster* or the other abortion cases decided by his Court.

As Chapters 3 and 4 show, however, the strong Chief Justices have effectively led their Courts during their tenure. We know relatively little of the decision process in earlier Courts. What little we know is summarized in Chapter 3, where illustrative cases point up the roles of Chief Justices Morrison R. Waite, Edward D. White, and Charles Evans Hughes in the decision of important cases, as well as the differences between Chief Justices in presiding over Court conferences.

Chapter 4 summarizes the leadership of the Super Chief (as Earl Warren was affectionately called by his closest colleague, William J. Brennan). Why Warren deserved his encomium is shown by the illustrations in the chapter—not only the great cases discussed, such as *Brown v. Board of Education* (1954), the school segregation case, *Reynolds v. Sims* (1964), the legislative apportionment case, and *Miranda v. Arizona* (1966), the Warren Court's most important criminal-law decision, but also the lesser cases covered, most of which are known today only to students of Supreme Court arcana.

We come back to the theme illustrated by the *Webster* case in Chapters 5 and 6. There we see again the inability of the Chief Justice to dictate decisions—first of all in the rebuff to Chief Justice Warren E. Burger in *Bowsher v. Synar*, the 1986 case striking down the Gramm-Rudman Act, as well as the cases in Chapter 6, where the Court refused to follow the Chief's lead and forced him to go along with the majority consensus. Particularly striking was the majority's rewriting of the Burger draft opinions in the 1971 *Swann* and 1974 *Nixon* cases and the abdication of the Chief Justice's function of assigning cases in favor of an "opinion by committee" in *Buckley v. Valeo* (1976), the leading case on election contributions and expenditures.

Chapter 7 shows how individual Justices can play a key role in the decision process. This has been true from the earliest Courts, as the 1852 *Cooley* case will illustrate. That leading decision on state power to regulate interstate commerce was largely the result of Justice Benjamin R. Curtis's lead. Other similar cases are discussed, but the focus is on Justice William J. Brennan, who, in his role in the decision process, was the most influential Associate Justice in the Court's history. The cases covered show dramatically that Brennan played a crucial part in setting the pattern in the Warren, Burger, and Rehnquist Courts—more "a lawgiver" (as the British magazine the *Economist* called him) than the typical judge. Particularly striking was the Justice's hitherto unknown role in overruling the Clear and Present Danger Test—one of Justice Oliver Wendell Holmes's major contributions to Supreme Court jurisprudence.

Chapter 8 discusses cases that show that the Court engages in a continuing deliberative process, even in cases where the Justices have reached a conference decision. The conference votes are anything but etched in stone. On the contrary, more cases are ultimately decided by vote switches than those outside the Court have realized. This has been true from the earliest days, as the discussion of the 1857 *Dred Scott* case and 1895 Income Tax case will show. More recent illustrations are drawn from the Warren and Burger Court jurisprudence in areas as diverse as expatriation, criminal law, and freedom of the press.

The vote switch theme is continued in Chapter 9, with illustrative cases involving sodomy, broadcasting, and legislative apportionment. In addition, there are cases to show some of the Court's near misses—cases where the Justices came close to committing serious blunders. These cases include some of the most significant cases decided by the Court, from the 1954 case on school segregation in Washington, D.C., to *Roe v. Wade*, the landmark 1973 abortion case. Only last-minute changes enabled the Justices to avoid grave judicial blunders in the cases covered.

The themes discussed above are renewed in the Rehnquist Court cases in Chapter 10. First, there is a reprise of the *Webster* theme of Chapter 1—this time to show how Chief Justice Rehnquist was unable to secure the overruling of leading civil-rights decisions, even though a vote switch in the 1989 case of *Patterson v. McLean Credit Union* did lead the Court to construe a civil-rights statute more narrowly than the original draft opinion of the Court had done. Other Rehnquist Court vote switches are dealt with in the remainder of the chapter. They show that the decision process in the Rehnquist Court is basically similar to that of the earlier Courts already discussed.

It should be emphasized again that this book's consideration of cases is based upon materials that, in the main, have not before been made public. Discussion is based less on the published opinions than on interviews and the documents (docket books, conference notes, letters, memoranda, and draft opinions) made available to me. The aim in revealing these materials has not been to publish a Court exposé, but to inform the public of how the highest court actually operates, warts and all. The hope, once more, is to make a significant contribution to the "responsible scholarship about the Court."

1

Rehnquist and Roe

Justice Harry A. Blackmun was livid as he read Chief Justice William H. Rehnquist's May 25, 1989, draft opinion in the case of *Webster v. Reproductive Health Services*. If it came down as the opinion of the Court, he felt, it would undo his own *Roe v. Wade* opinion, which he considered the Court's greatest modern contribution to our constitutional law—"a landmark in the progress of the emancipation of women," Blackmun had termed *Roe* in a 1986 speech.

Justice Blackmun himself was known as the slowest author on the Court. In the famous 1978 *Bakke* affirmative-action case, he had held up the decision for months until near the end of the 1977 Term, while he agonized over his posture in the case. But now he answered the Rehnquist draft in what for him was record time, with a June 21 draft dissent. The Blackmun draft was an impassioned cri de coeur which mourned the majority interment of *Roe v. Wade*. "The simple truth," the draft dissent declared, "is that *Roe* no longer survives. . . . the majority discards a landmark case of the last generation, and casts into darkness the hopes and visions of every woman in this country who had come to believe that the Constitution guaranteed her the right to exercise some control over her unique ability to bear children."

Under the Rehnquist draft opinion of the Court, the Blackmun dissent asserted, "The pendulum swings, as it always has, and we move a very long step backward." As Justice Blackmun saw it, what was happening in *Webster* was very clear: "Let there be no misunderstanding: the two isolated dissenters in *Roe*, after all these years, now have prevailed, with the assent of the Court's newest Members, in rolling back that case and in returning the law of procreative freedom to the severe limitations that generally prevailed before January 22, 1973."

HOW THE COURT OPERATES

To understand how the Supreme Court dealt with the *Webster* case, one must understand how the Court itself operates. The Justices sit from October to late June or early July, in annual sessions called terms, with each term designated by the year in which it begins. Cases come to the Court from the lower federal courts and the highest state courts — usually by petitions for writs of certiorari. The Justices have virtually unlimited discretion in deciding whether to grant certiorari (or cert, as it is usually called in the Court). Each year the Justices decide to hear only a fraction of the cases presented to them. Thus, in the 1993 Term, the Court reviewed and issued opinions deciding 84 cases out of 7,786 on its docket.

In a handwritten note to Justice John Marshall Harlan, Justice Felix Frankfurter wrote, "In my old age, when I shall have attained wisdom, I plan to write a book entitled 'The Calculus of Certiorari or How the Supreme Court determines when to grant and when to deny.' " In a 1955 letter Frankfurter stated his own calculus, "Wouldn't you gladly settle for one in ten — such is my proportion — in granting petitions for certiorari?" By the 1990s, the proportion granted had become closer to one in one hundred.

Following an unwritten rule, when at least four of the nine Justices vote to take a case, certiorari is granted or the appeal is taken. However, if the case elicits fewer than the required four votes, the case in question is over and the last decision of the state court or lower federal court becomes final. In recent years some Justices have urged that changes be made in the Rule of Four, on the ground that it results in the Court agreeing to hear too many cases.

Thus, Justice John Paul Stevens has proposed that five votes be required to grant certiorari. That would certainly cut down on the number of cases taken by the Court. But it would also eliminate important cases which the Court should decide. If a five-vote rule had been in effect during the Warren Court years, at least one of that Court's most important decisions, *Baker v. Carr*, the famous legislative apportionment case that Chief Justice Earl Warren once described as "the most important case of my tenure on the Court," would never have been decided. Though it was not made public by the Court, only four Justices voted to hear that case.

For those few cases the Supreme Court agrees to take, written briefs will be submitted by the opposing lawyers, and then the attorneys for both sides will appear for oral argument in which they present arguments in favor of affirming or reversing the lower court decision. The arguments are presented publicly in the ornate courtroom. Each side usually has half an hour, and the time limit is strictly observed — though in important cases some additional time may be allowed.

It is said that Chief Justice Charles Evans Hughes was so strict in enforcing the time limits that he cut off an attorney in the middle of the word "if." Chief Justice William H. Rehnquist has a similar reputation; he, too, has been known to stop counsel in the middle of a word when the red light goes on signaling expiration time. Once counsel saw the light come on and stopped on his own. Justice Antonin Scalia interposed, "He wasn't watching. I think you could have gotten away with the end of that sentence." Chief Justice Rehnquist then noted, "Even Homer nodded."

What makes argument most difficult for counsel is the fact that the sessions are characterized by incessant interruptions from the bench. The days of the great advocates of the past, when Daniel Webster or William Wirt would give virtuoso performances extending over several days, have long since been gone. Supreme Court arguments now are less solo presentations than Socratic dialogues in which bench and bar play an almost equal part.

All too often, indeed, the bench may virtually take over the argument. This has been notably true of former law professors, such as Justices Antonin Scalia and Felix Frankfurter. The latter in particular used to treat oral argument as the equivalent of a Harvard Law School class, with himself displaying the professor's mastery of the Socratic method. "Some of us," wrote Justice William O. Douglas in his *Autobiography*, "would often squirm at Frankfurter's seemingly endless questions that took the advocate round and round and round." Above all, Justice Frankfurter could never shed the professorial need to get in the last word, whether in conference or repartee from the bench. About the only time he failed to do so occurred when a lawyer from the Midwest arguing his case did not answer a series of Frankfurter questions to the Justice's satisfaction. His patience exhausted, Frankfurter testily asked, "Counsel, before you go any further, I want to know how did you get to this Court?" The answer came back, "I came on the Pennsylvania Railroad." For once, the normally irrepressible Justice was speechless.

In the Rehnquist Court, the participation by the Justices in oral arguments has, if anything, intensified. There are times, in fact, when the Justices have so much to say that the attorneys can hardly get a word in edgewise. In a 1993 argument, as soon as counsel began her case, Justice Scalia interrupted. Before she could reply, other Justices chimed in. The exchange between them went on until the red light on the lectern flashed, signaling that the attorney's thirty minutes were up. "Thank you Ms. Foster," said Chief Justice Rehnquist, "I think you did very well in the four minutes that the Court allowed you."

The *Webster* argument took place on April 26, 1989. Like all Supreme Court sittings, the session began at precisely 10 A.M. When the hands of the clock behind the bench indicated the hour, the nine black-robed Justices stepped through the red velour draperies and took their places. At the sound of the gavel all in the packed courtroom rose and remained standing while the Court Crier intoned the time-honored cry, "Oyez! Oyez! Oyez! All persons having business before the Honorable, the Supreme Court of the United States, are admonished to draw near and give their attention, for the Court is now sitting. God save the United States and this Honorable Court."

The Court Chamber itself is the most impressive room in the Supreme Court Building. It measures eighty-two by ninety-one feet and has a ceiling forty-four feet high. Its twenty-four columns are of Siena Old Convent marble from Liguria, Italy; its walls are of ivory vein marble from Alicante, Spain; and its floor borders are of Italian and African marble. Above the columns on the east and west walls are carved two marble panels depicting processions of historical lawgivers. Of the eighteen figures on the panels, only one is famous as a judge, and he is the one American represented: John Marshall. His symbolic presence strikingly illustrates the Supreme Court's role as a primary lawgiver in the American system.

The room is dominated by the Justices' long raised bench. It used to be the traditional straight bench, but in 1970 Chief Justice Warren E. Burger had it altered to its present "winged," or half-hexagon, shape. Like all the furniture in the courtroom, the bench is mahogany. In back of the bench are four of the room's massive marble columns. The large clock hangs on a chain between the two center ones. In front of the bench are seated, to the Court's right, the pages and Clerk, and, to the Court's left, the Marshal. Tables facing the bench are for counsel. Behind the tables is a section for members of the bar and a much larger general section for the public, with separate areas for the press and distinguished visitors.

Goose-quill pens are placed on counsel tables each day that the Justices sit, as was done in the earliest session of the Court. The practice had been interrupted by World War II, when the prewar supply ran out, and then again in 1961, when the quills were temporarily replaced by more modern writing instruments. But traditions die hard at the Supreme Court. The quills soon found their way back to the counsel tables, and there are still spittoons behind the bench for each Justice and pewter julep cups (now used for their drinking water).

The *Webster* argument began just after the Justices sat down in their plush high-back black leather chairs. The audience also sat down and Chief Justice Rehnquist began, "We will hear argument now in No. 88-605, *William L. Webster v. Reproductive Health Services*. By General Webster."

At this, William L. Webster, the Missouri Attorney General, who argued the case for appellant, stepped to the lectern and began with the traditional opening, "Mr. Chief Justice, and may it please the Court."

After the other attorneys had presented their arguments, the session concluded with a rebuttal by Webster. Chief Justice Rehnquist then leaned forward and said, "Thank you, Mr. Webster. The case is submitted."

"Whereupon," the official transcript concludes, "at 11:00 A.M., the case in the above-entitled matter was submitted."

CONFERENCE AND DECISION

Oral arguments in the Supreme Court are often dramatic events, participated in by leading attorneys. That was certainly true of the *Webster* argument, which had all the drama associated with the landmarks of Supreme Court juris-prudence. Yet it was not the headlined argument that played the significant part in the Court's decision. Indeed, it can be said that, like the reports of Mark Twain's death, the typical reports on the value of the Supreme Court oral argument are greatly exaggerated. True, virtually everyone who has written on the subject, including the Justices themselves, has stressed the importance of the argument to the Court's decision process. A lifetime's study of the high bench has, however, convinced me that the principal pur-pose of the argument before the Justices is a public-relations one — to com-municate to the country that the Court has given each side an open opportunity to be heard. Thus not only is justice done, but it is also publicly seen to be done.

But the cases are rare when the arguments of counsel — brilliant though they may appear to the courtroom audience — really influence the decision in an important case. The oral argument in *Webster* itself well illustrates the point. It may be doubted that the statements by counsel influenced even one vote on the Court. Instead, as Justice Robert H. Jackson once put it, the Court's argument begins where that of counsel ends. The crucial argument in a case takes place among the Justices in their conference that meets after the public oral argument is concluded.

As far as the public is concerned, the postargument decision process in the Court is completely closed. The next time the outside world hears about the case is when the Court is ready to announce its decision publicly; simul-taneously, the majority opinion and any dissents or concurrences are distrib-uted. But in that interim period between oral argument and the announcement of the Court's decision, much has gone on. First, the Justices have "confer-enced." These conferences used to be held on Fridays. More recently, Wednes-day sessions have been held as well. The privacy of the conference is one of the most cherished traditions at the Court. It began years ago when the Justices mistakenly thought that a clerk, secretary, or page had leaked a decision. Since then, only the nine Justices may attend. In addition to the conference discus-sion, ideas are exchanged by the Justices through the circulation of draft opinions and memoranda. Such a memo, sent to all the Justices, is usually titled Memorandum to the Conference.

The *Webster* conference, like all those held by the Justices, took place in the Court's conference room — a large rectangular chamber at the rear of the Court building, behind the courtroom. One of the longer walls has two windows facing Second Street. The other, with a door in the middle, is covered with bookshelves containing reports of decisions of the Supreme Court and federal courts of appeals, as well as copies of the *United States Code* and *U.S. Code Annotated*. Along one of the shorter walls is a fireplace, above which hangs a Gilbert Stuart portrait of Chief Justice John Marshall in his robes. During the Burger tenure, there was also a forest painting by John F. Carlson, as well as two landscapes by Lily Cushing, a beach scene and another forest scene. Chief

Justice Burger said that he originally had these paintings hung for Justice William O. Douglas, always noted for his love of the outdoors.

In the center of the conference room ceiling is an ornate crystal chandelier, and at one end of the room stands a rectangular table around which the Justices sit, with the Chief Justice at the head and the others ranged in order of seniority, the most senior opposite the Chief Justice, the next at the Chief Justice's right, the next at the Senior Associate Justice's right, and so on. In the ceiling above the chandelier are bright fluorescent lights — one of the improvements installed by Chief Justice Burger.

At the conference, the Justices discuss the cases that have been argued and decide how to dispose of them. The discussion sometimes becomes heated, reflecting the controversial nature of the case or personal differences among the Justices. The Warren years, for example, saw heated exchanges between Justice Felix Frankfurter and Chief Justice Earl Warren. According to one account, when Warren took exception in conference to a Frankfurter sermon, the furious Frankfurter retorted, "You're the worst Chief Justice this country has ever had!" The Justices who sat during the Warren years reported that no such Frankfurter outburst occurred. But none denies that Frankfurter came to have a poor opinion of Warren. Once, during a heated conference session, Frankfurter was overheard screeching at the Chief Justice, "Be a judge, God damn it, be a judge!" Use of the verb "screeching" is not an exaggeration. As Justice Potter Stewart described, once Frankfurter would "get going . . . his voice would rise to a pretty high decibel content and pretty high on the scales."

After the vote is taken at the conference, the case is assigned by the Chief Justice, if he is in the majority, either to himself or to one of the Justices for the writing of an opinion of the Court. If the Chief Justice is not in the majority, the senior majority Justice assigns the opinion. Justices who disagree with the majority decision are free to write or join dissenting opinions. If they agree with the result but differ on the reasoning, they can submit concurring opinions. Opinions are usually issued in the name of individual Justices. Sometimes per curiam (literally, "by the court") opinions are issued in the name of the Court as a whole. That is what happened in the so-called Pentagon Papers Case in 1971 — where the Burger Court refused to stop the *New York Times* and *Washington Post* from publishing a classified Defense Department history of the Vietnam war — though each of the Justices involved also wrote an individual opinion explaining the decision from his own point of view.

The last stage is the public announcement of decisions and the opinions filed by the Justices. The custom used to be to have decisions announced on Mondays (a tradition that began in 1857); hence, the press characterization of "decision Mondays." In 1958, this was changed to announcing decisions when they were ready.

When decisions are announced, the Justices normally read only a summary of their opinions, especially when they are long. But some insist on reading every word, no matter how much time it takes. On June 17, 1963, Justice Tom C. Clark was droning through his lengthy Court opinion in the case involving the constitutionality of Bible reading in public schools. Justice William O. Douglas, who could stand it no longer, passed Justice Hugo L. Black a plaintive note: "Is he going to read all of it? He told me he was only going to say a few words — he is on p. 20 now — 58 more to go. Perhaps we need an antifilibuster rule as badly as some say the Senate does."

JUSTICE AND CHIEF JUSTICE REHNQUIST

In his draft *Webster* dissent, Justice Blackmun asserted, "the two isolated dissenters in *Roe* . . . now have prevailed." The two dissenters in *Roe v. Wade* had been Justice Byron R. White and Justice Rehnquist. Their attitude toward that case was, of course, very different from that of Justice Blackmun. Indeed, Rehnquist, now elevated to the Court's center chair, must have felt a keen sense of satisfaction as he circulated his draft opinion of the Court in *Webster*. Just before he became Chief Justice, Rehnquist gave an interview to the *New York Times* in which he compared the Warren and Burger Courts. Justice Rehnquist stated that the impact of the Court had been diminished under Chief Justice Warren E. Burger. "I don't think that the Burger Court has as wide a sense of mission. Perhaps it doesn't have any sense of mission at all."

What he said of the Court then was emphatically not true of Justice Rehnquist himself. If any Justice had a "sense of mission" it was the Justice whom *Newsweek* had dubbed "The Court's Mr. Right." In fact, Rehnquist was one Justice who came to the Court with a definite agenda. In his *Times* interview he noted that he joined the Court with a desire to counteract the Warren Court decisions. "I came to the court," Rehnquist said, "sensing . . . that there were some excesses in terms of constitutional adjudication during the era of the so-called Warren Court." Some of that Court's decisions, the Justice went on, "seemed to me hard to justify. . . . So I felt that at the time I came on the Court, the boat was kind of keeling over in one direction. Interpreting my oath as I saw it, I felt that my job was . . . to kind of lean the other way." The Rehnquist agenda sought what his interview called "a halt to . . . the sweeping rules made in the days of the Warren Court" — and not only a halt, but a rollback of much of the Warren jurisprudence.

In his first years on the Court, however, Justice Rehnquist was scarcely able to fulfill his rollback agenda. On the contrary, the intended counterrevolution served only as a confirmation of most of the Warren Court jurisprudence. It can be said that no important Warren Court decision was overruled by its successor. Worse still, the Burger Court went even further than the Warren Court in some cases — notably in *Roe v. Wade* itself.

True, Justice Rehnquist had repeatedly spoken out against the Court's direction during the Burger tenure. During his early Court years, nevertheless, the majority remained largely unsympathetic to the Rehnquist entreaties from the right. It was then that he received a Lone Ranger doll as a gift from his law clerks, who called him the "lone dissenter" during that period. During his fourteen years as an Associate Justice, Rehnquist dissented alone fifty-four times a Court record.

His extreme views did not prevent Justice Rehnquist from being on good terms with the other Justices. Even his ideological opposites like Justice William J. Brennan have commented on their cordial relations with the categorical conservative. To his colleagues, Rehnquist was as well known for his good nature as for his rightist acumen. On a Court where, as Justice Blackmun once lamented, "There is very little humor," Justice Rehnquist stood out because of his irreverence and wit.

Rehnquist was the only Justice in recent memory to begin opinions with a Gilbert and Sullivan lyric and the limerick, "There was a young lady from Niger." In a December 1986 argument, counsel said that his opponent "wanted words to mean what he says they mean. That didn't fool Alice and I doubt very much that it will fool this Court." "Don't overestimate us," came back the Rehnquist riposte.

The Rehnquist sense of humor sometimes degenerated into practical jokes. On April Fool's Day 1985, Chief Justice Burger was the Rehnquist victim. Rehnquist had a life-size photo cutout of Burger produced and sent a street photographer to a corner outside the Court with a sign, "Have your picture taken with the chief justice, $1." To make sure he wouldn't miss Burger's reaction, the Justice called him at home, saying he needed a ride to Court on April 1. Rehnquist was laughing loudly when he drove past the scene that day with the overdignified Chief Justice.

Before his appointment as Court head, Rehnquist also had anything but the appearance of a Justice. Well over six feet tall, he still had the look of an overage college student—with his long sideburns and lumbering around the Court in his thick brown-rimmed glasses, mismatched outfits, and Hush Puppies shoes. As a recent book on the Court put it, "In the marble halls of the Court, he looked more like a refugee from a small college math department than a justice of the Supreme Court."

After becoming Chief Justice, Rehnquist curbed both his appearance and his wit. He has also acquired something of his predecessor's emphasis on the dignity of his office. In a February 16, 1990, memorandum on the instructions given to counsel arguing before the Court, he noted that "they are told: 'A member of the Court should be addressed as "Justice" — not judge.';" Rehnquist pointed out that "this is not, strictly speaking, correct so far as The Chief Justice is concerned." Therefore, Rehnquist wrote, "I suggest we replace this sentence with the following: 'A member of the Court should be addressed as "Chief Justice" or "Justice" as the case may be — not as "judge."' "

At times, however, the old Rehnquist appears beneath the Chief Justice veneer. In a May 2, 1991, memorandum transmitting a fourth draft opinion in *Barnes v. Glen Theatre, Inc.*, Rehnquist wrote, "it is my great hope that the enclosed draft will dispel some of the confusion about the case which has, unfortunately, been engendered by the dissenting and concurring opinions." The Chief Justice then asserted, "The theme of this fourth draft is a very positive one, and it can be summed up in the following verse from a once popular song:

> 'Accentuate the positive
> Eliminate the negative
> Latch on to the affirmative
> Don't mess with Mr. In Between.' "

A TOUCH OF GILBERT AND SULLIVAN

More recently there was the almost opéra-bouffe change made by Rehnquist in his robe. When the Supreme Court first met in 1790, Chief Justice John Jay wore a black robe trimmed with red. The other Justices followed Jay's example. According to *The Oxford Companion to the Supreme Court*, these "robes with a red facing [were] somewhat like those worn by English judges." The explanation is more personal to the first Chief Justice. Jay simply used his Doctor of Laws gown from the University of Dublin, which had conferred the degree upon him.

The members of the Court soon switched to plain black robes. An 1802 Senate speech referred to "six venerable Judges decorated in party-colored robes, as ours formerly were, or arrayed in more solemn black such as they have lately assumed." Since about 1800, the black robe has been worn by the Justices.

Almost two centuries of tradition has, nevertheless, recently given way. The first crack appeared in the Court attire of Sandra Day O'Connor and Ruth Bader Ginsburg. It was perhaps unchivalrous to complain when the first women Justices began to brighten their courtwear with what *Time* called "modish, attention-getting dickeys." But Chief Justice Rehnquist, rumored, according to the same source, "to be jealous of the court's female justices," went further so that, since January 1995, the high bench has had a new sartorial touch: four thick golden stripes on the upper part of each sleeve of the Rehnquist robe. "He designed the robe himself," the Court's public-information officer stated, "after having seen a performance of Gilbert and Sullivan's 'Iolanthe' last June in which the lord chancellor wore a similar robe." It was added that the stripes "very likely will be permanent." They have been worn by the Chief Justice ever since.

Rehnquist himself is a Gilbert and Sullivan aficionado, who once appeared in a production of *Trial by Jury*. Yet, even those masters of comic opera would have hesitated to attire a real Chief Justice in the robe used by one of their ludicrous characters. Chief Justice Rehnquist was quoted in the press as defending the new attire by saying that a British Lord Chancellor is decorated that way. The true Gilbert and Sullivan touch, however, is that that is not at all the fact. The British Lord Chancellor does have a gown that is embossed all over with ornamental gold stripes. According to Lord Woolf, a member of the House of Lords, "It appears that there are a few more stripes on it than your Chief Justice's new one!" But this is true only of the Lord Chancellor's dress robe which he wears on formal occasions, such as for the Queen's Speech which opens Parliament. When he normally presides over the House of Lords, he wears what Lord Woolf calls his "every day" robe of plain black. As for the other judges on the highest British court, their attire is even less formal than that of our Justices. "In the House of Lords," Lord Woolf writes, "we wear no robes or wigs — just crumpled suits!"

REHNQUIST AND COMPROMISE

As Chief Justice, Rehnquist has trimmed more than his sideburns. In a 1976 article, Justice Rehnquist had discussed the role of a Chief Justice, using Chief Justice Charles Evans Hughes as his model: "Except in cases involving matters of high principle," a book on Hughes points out, "he willingly acquiesced in silence rather than expose his dissenting views. . . . Hughes was also willing to modify his own opinions to hold or increase his majority."

Rehnquist too has realized that a Chief Justice who does not have a majority has failed in his primary function of leading the Court. More than is known, Chief Justice Rehnquist has modified his position to retain a Court, even though it meant compromising his extreme rightist views. Thus, in a November 28, 1990, letter to Justice White on *Cheek v. United States*, the Chief Justice wrote, "I believe I voted to affirm at Conference in this case, but in the interests of getting a solid Court opinion I am prepared to join your present draft vacating and remanding if you would make some minor changes."

Earlier the same month, on November 13, Chief Justice Rehnquist circulated a *Memorandum to the Conference* on *Irwin v. Veterans Administration*. In it, he informed the Justices, "Nino [Scalia] has shown me a copy of a proposed concurrence in this case which he will circulate this morning. The concurrence takes the position that the same presumption of equitable tolling should apply to statutes of limitations applicable to government suits as is applicable to private suits."

Rehnquist wrote, "I prefer the position taken in the most recent circulation of my proposed opinion for the Court, but want very much to avoid a fractionated Court on this point." Therefore, the memo went on, "If a majority prefers Nino's view, I will adopt it; if I can get a majority for the view contained in the present draft, I will adhere to that. If there is some 'middle ground' that will attract a majority, I will even adopt that."

In the end, Rehnquist did adopt the Scalia position. This enabled him to issue his opinion as that of the Court; a strong majority joined his opinion, including Justice Scalia, who withdrew his proposed concurrence.

REHNQUIST AND *ROE*

In his 1976 article quoted above, Rehnquist noted that Chief Justice Hughes was willing to suppress his own views in the interest of securing a majority— "Except in cases involving matters of high principle." For Chief Justice Rehnquist, *Roe v. Wade* was emphatically such a case. As already seen, Justice Rehnquist had been one of the two dissenters in *Roe v. Wade*. Moreover, the Rehnquist dissent had been an unusually strong one, which compared the Court's decision to one of its most discredited decisions—that in the 1905 case of *Lochner v. New York*.

The Court's *Roe* opinion was based upon two essential holdings: (1) "the right of privacy, however based, is broad enough to cover the abortion decision." It follows from this that there is a "fundamental right" to an abortion; (2) "Where certain 'fundamental rights' are involved, the Court has held that regulation limiting these rights may be justified only by a 'compelling state interest.' "

Justice Rehnquist, in his dissent, pointed out what the Court had done in its *Roe* opinion. According to Rehnquist, "The Court eschews the history of the Fourteenth Amendment in its reliance on the 'compelling state interest' test." The strict-scrutiny–compelling-interest approach had been developed to deal with equal-protection claims. Now, in *Roe*, the Court held that the compelling-interest test should be used when a statute infringing upon fundamental rights was challenged on due-process grounds. As the Rehnquist dissent put it, in *Roe* "the Court adds a new wrinkle to this test by transposing it from the legal considerations associated with the Equal Protection Clause of the Fourteenth Amendment to this case arising under the Due Process Clause of the Fourteenth Amendment."

In a December 14, 1972, letter to Justice Blackmun, Justice Potter Stewart had criticized the *Roe* opinion because of the "dicta [in the Court's opinion] being so inflexibly 'legislative.' " In his *Roe* dissent, Justice Rehnquist gave voice to a similar animadversion: "the Court's sweeping invalidation of any restrictions on abortion during the first trimester is impossible to justify . . . , and the conscious weighing of competing factors that the Court's opinion apparently substitutes for the established test is far more appropriate to a legislative judgment than to a judicial one."

More than that, as pointed out, the Rehnquist *Roe* dissent compared the decision there with one of the most discredited Supreme Court decisions. "While the Court's opinion," asserts the Rehnquist dissent, "quotes from the dissent of Mr. Justice Holmes in *Lochner v. New York* . . . , the result it reaches is more closely attuned to the majority opinion of Mr. Justice Peckham in that case. . . . As in *Lochner*," *Roe* requires "this Court to examine the legislative policies and pass on the wisdom of these policies."

Certainly, there is danger that the importation of the compelling-interest standard into the Due Process Clause will lead to a revival of the substantive due-process approach that prevailed in what Justice Stewart termed, in a

February 8, 1973, letter to Justice Lewis F. Powell, "the heyday of the Nine Old Men, who felt that the Constitution enabled them to invalidate almost any state laws they thought unwise."

From this point of view, there may be validity to the Rehnquist charge that *Roe* marked a return to the substantive due-process approach followed in cases such as *Lochner v. New York*, when, as the Court put it in a 1963 case, "courts used the Due Process Clause to strike down state laws . . . because they may be unwise, improvident, or out of harmony with a particular school of thought." According to Justice Rehnquist's *Roe* dissent, the adoption of the compelling-interest standard in due-process cases will inevitably require the Court once again to pass on the wisdom of legislative policies in deciding whether the particular interest put forward is or is not "compelling." As Rehnquist put it in a November 11, 1977, memorandum, "the phrase 'compelling state interest' really asks the question rather than answers it, unless we are to revert simply to what Holmes called our own 'can't helps.' " Just as important, in Rehnquist's view, under the *Roe* approach, the determination of what are and what are not "fundamental rights" is also left to the unfettered discretion of the individual Justices.

PARADISE REGAINED?

Justice Rehnquist continued to assert his opposition to *Roe v. Wade*, as well as efforts to expand its doctrine, in the Burger Court's later abortion cases. In particular, in 1980, he successfully fought efforts to hold that the right to abortion included a right to public funds for abortions for indigent women. On November 12 of that year, Justice Blackmun wrote to Justice Marshall, "I fear that the forces of emotion and professed morality are winning some battles. The 'real world' continues to exist 'out there' and I earnestly hope that the 'war,' despite these adverse 'battles' will not be lost."

Justice Rehnquist saw things differently. As he explained it in a 1977 dissent, a decision such as *Roe* "placed [the Court] in the position of Adam in the Garden of Eden . . . subjected to the human temptation to hold that any law containing a number of imperfections [is unconstitutional] simply because those who drafted it could have made it a fairer or a better law." To Rehnquist, *Roe v. Wade* was the Court's "original sin" which expelled it from the Paradise of proper constitutional construction — in the phrase of his same dissent, "a cat-o'-nine-tails to be kept in the judicial closet as a threat to legislatures which may, in the view of the judiciary, get out of hand and pass 'arbitrary,' 'illogical,' or 'unreasonable' laws."

Now, with the *Webster* case, Chief Justice Rehnquist sensed that he at last had the opportunity to win the *Roe v. Wade* "war" and regain judicial Paradise.

At issue in *Webster* was a Missouri law regulating abortions, which was characterized at the time as one of the most restrictive laws on the subject. It (1) specified that a physician, prior to performing an abortion on any woman twenty or more weeks pregnant, had to ascertain whether the fetus was "viable" by performing "such medical examinations and tests as are necessary to make a finding of [the fetus'] gestational age, weight, and lung maturity"; (2) prohibited the use of public employees and facilities to perform or assist abortions not necessary to save the mother's life; and (3) made it unlawful to use public funds, employees, or facilities for the purpose of "encouraging or counseling" a woman to have an abortion not necessary to save her life.

The lower courts had ruled that these provisions violated the Court's decisions in *Roe v. Wade* and subsequent cases. The Justices who supported the right to abortion feared that, under the new Chief Justice, the majority would use the case to strike at the *Roe* decision. "Taking this case," a December 29, 1988, memo on *Webster* to Justice Thurgood Marshall by his law clerk warned, "would pose a great threat that the majority on this Court would overrule or dramatically limit, Roe." Despite this, the Court voted on January 9, 1989, to take the case, with Justices Brennan, Marshall, and Blackmun voting the other way.

On April 28, two days after the oral argument, the Justices held their conference on the *Webster* case. Five of them voted to uphold the three restrictions in the Missouri law—the Chief Justice and Justices Byron R. White, Sandra Day O'Connor, Scalia, and Anthony Kennedy. Justices Brennan, Marshall, and Blackmun voted to strike down the law. The position of Justice John Paul Stevens was not clear; Justice Marshall's docket book, for example, contains only the scrawl, "On and off" next to the initials "JPS" on a blue-lined page of notebook paper attached to his tally sheet (used to track a case from the time it comes to the Court to its final disposition).

The sketchy Marshall conference notes on *Webster* indicate that Chief Justice Rehnquist stated that he "disagrees with Roe v. Wade," but would "not overrule as such." The phrase "as such" foreshadowed the debate among the Justices during the *Webster* decision process: Chief Justice Rehnquist would maintain in his drafts that his opinion would not "revisit the holding of *Roe* . . . and we leave it undisturbed," while the dissenters declared that it would all but dismantle the *Roe* ruling.

REHNQUIST DRAFT

Since he was in the conference majority, Chief Justice Rehnquist could, of course, choose the writer of the *Webster* opinion. On May 1, 1989, he assigned the opinion to himself, following the tradition that the Chief Justice should prepare the opinions in important cases. In addition, there is no doubt that Rehnquist wanted the opportunity to strike what could be a mortal blow against *Roe v. Wade*.

On May 25, the Chief Justice circulated the first draft of his *Webster* opinion. It consisted of twenty-three printed pages and was headed, "CHIEF JUSTICE REHNQUIST delivered the opinion of the Court." After the conference vote, Rehnquist naturally assumed that he was writing for a majority of the Justices.

The Rehnquist draft squarely upheld the Missouri law's abortion restrictions. The prohibition on the use of public employees and facilities for the performance of abortions was ruled consistent with the Court's prior abortion decisions. "Nothing in the Constitution," declared the draft, "requires States to enter or remain in the business of performing abortions." States "need not commit any resources to facilitating abortions." Similarly, the draft held that the prohibition on the use of public funds for abortion counseling did not impermissibly burden the right to an abortion. "If, as we have held, Missouri's policy of not using public facilities and employees to perform or assist in abortions is constitutionally permissible, we see no reason why the State may not also refuse to fund any speech-related conduct intended to encourage abortions." (The final Rehnquist opinion was to adopt Justice O'Connor's reasoning and avoid deciding the validity of this prohibition, holding that the controversy over it was moot.)

Chief Justice Rehnquist's draft also sustained the challenged law's requirement that a physician performing an abortion on a woman twenty weeks or more pregnant must first perform tests to determine if the fetus was "viable." This viability-testing provision was ruled valid as "promoting the State's interest in potential human life." Here the Rehnquist draft made a direct attack on the trimester analysis that was the foundation of the *Roe* decision. "We think," the draft declared, "that the doubt cast upon the Missouri statute . . . is not so much a flaw in the statute as it is a reflection of the fact that the rigid trimester analysis of the course of a pregnancy enunciated in *Roe* has resulted in subsequent cases . . . making constitutional law in this area a virtual Procrustean bed."

The draft recognized that, though stare decisis (requiring the following of precedents) was "a cornerstone of our legal system," it should give way in a case involving "a prior construction of the Constitution that has proved 'unsound in principle and unworkable in practice.' " That was the case here: "We think the *Roe* trimester framework falls into that category."

The Rehnquist draft called the *Roe* framework "rigid" and asserted that it "is hardly consistent" with a Constitution such as ours. Here the draft quoted the landmark 1937 opinion of Chief Justice Hughes in *West Coast Hotel Co. v. Parrish*, which overruled the cases that had applied the doctrine of freedom of contract to strike down laws protecting labor, on the ground that freedom of contract was not contained in the Constitution. Similarly, the *Webster* draft pointed out, "The key elements of the *Roe* framework—trimesters and viability—are not found in the text of the Constitution or in any place else one would expect to find a constitutional principle. Since the bounds of the inquiry are essentially indeterminate, the result has been a web of legal rules that have become increasingly intricate, resembling a code of regulations rather than a body of constitutional doctrine."

Instead of the *Roe* framework, the Rehnquist draft offered a new test for the abortion restriction at issue: whether it "reasonably furthers the state's interest in protecting potential human life." This was, of course, a far less restrictive review standard than the "compelling interest" test that *Roe* required abortion restrictions to pass — at least during the first and second trimesters of pregnancy.

At the end of his draft opinion, Chief Justice Rehnquist noted that the Court had been urged to "overrule our decision in *Roe v. Wade*." The draft ostensibly declined the invitation, saying of *Roe* that "we leave it undisturbed." All that the draft opinion did was to state, "To the extent indicated in our opinion, we modify and narrow *Roe*."

THE JUSTICES' REACTION

The disclaimer at the end of the *Webster* draft opinion of the Court could scarcely disguise the potentially fatal effect it might have upon *Roe v. Wade*. Though the Chief Justice received memos on May 30 from Justices White and Kennedy joining his opinion, other Justices indicated dissatisfaction with the draft. The day after the draft was circulated, on May 26, Justice Blackmun sent around a memo, "I shall be writing something in this case." This foreshadowed a dissent by the author of the *Roe* opinion, as well as a joinder in it by Justices Brennan and Marshall, who wrote on May 30 that they would wait to see the Blackmun opinion.

On the same day, Justice Stevens, who had been undecided at the conference, sent a two-page "Dear Chief" letter, in which he challenged the Rehnquist repudiation of *Roe*. In particular, he rejected what he termed "your newly minted standard of 'reasonably further[ing] the state's interest in protecting potential human life.'" Stevens complained that, in the draft, "you make no attempt to explain or justify your new standard."

Under the new review standard, Stevens wrote, "If a simple showing that a state regulation 'reasonably furthers the state interest in protecting potential human life' is enough to justify an abortion regulation, the woman's interest in making the abortion decision apparently is given no weight at all."

In addition, the Rehnquist test would uphold virtually all abortion restrictions. The Stevens letter gave the following illustrations: "A tax on abortions, a requirement that the pregnant woman must be able to stand on her head for fifteen minutes before she can have an abortion, or a criminal prohibition would each satisfy your test." In fact, Stevens went on, "the same result could be accomplished by requiring tests of the woman's knowledge of Shakespeare or American history."

Justice Stevens asserted that the test in the Rehnquist draft "really rejects *Roe v. Wade* in its entirety" and it did so without acknowledging its fatal effect. "I would think," Stevens wrote, "that it would be much better for the Court, as an institution, to do so forthrightly rather than indirectly with a bombshell first introduced at the end of its opinion." As this passage indicates, Justice Stevens strongly objected to the manner in which the Chief Justice had accomplished "your somewhat gratuitous rejection of the trimester approach."

The Stevens letter clearly indicated that its author would not join the Rehnquist draft. "As you know," the letter mockingly concluded, "I am not in favor of overruling *Roe* v. *Wade*, but if the deed is to be done I would rather see the Court give the case a decent burial instead of tossing it out the window of a fast-moving caboose."

BLACKMUN DISSENT

Justice Blackmun followed up his May 26 memo, indicating that he would write separately, with his draft dissenting opinion, which he circulated on June 21. As indicated at the beginning of this chapter, the Blackmun draft was a passionate dissent that mourned what it termed "*Roe*'s passing."

> Today, a bare majority of this Court disserves the people of this Nation, and especially the millions of women who have lived and come of age in the 16 years since the decision in *Roe v. Wade* . . . recognized that the constitutionally guaranteed right to privacy encompasses a woman's right, with her responsible physician, to choose whether or not to terminate a pregnancy. To those women, and to all others, this Court owes an essential duty of explanation — a duty of candor and forthrightness, a duty to interpret the Constitution and our past decisions in a reasoned and honest fashion. The majority mocks this duty. At every level of its review, from its effort to read the real meaning out of the Missouri statute to its evisceration of precedents and its deafening silence about the fundamental constitutional protections that it jettisons, the majority labors to obscure what is at stake in this monumental case and to cloak what it actually has decided.

Justice Blackmun referred to the "feigned restraint" of the Rehnquist draft when it stated that *Roe* was not overruled. "This disclaimer," Blackmun asserted, "is totally meaningless." Instead, the draft dissent declared, "The simple truth is that *Roe* no longer survives, and . . . the majority provides no substitute for its protective umbrella."

The Blackmun language was unusually strong: "I rue this day. I rue the violence that has been done to the liberty and equality of women. I rue the violence that has been done to our legal fabric and to the integrity of this Court. I rue the inevitable loss of public esteem for this Court that is so essential. I dissent."

The draft dissent was caustic in its reaction to the review standard stated in the Chief Justice's draft opinion. "There," Justice Blackmun wrote, "tucked away at the end of its opinion, the majority works a radical reversal of the law of abortion." What the Rehnquist draft had done was "to throw out *Roe*'s trimester framework." In its stead, "In flat contradiction to *Roe*, the majority concludes that the State's interest in potential life is compelling before viability, and upholds the testing provision because it 'reasonably furthers' that state interest."

The Blackmun draft complained that the Rehnquist opinion did not explain why *Roe* was wrong: "The majority does not bother to explain [the] alleged flaws in *Roe*. Bald assertion masquerades as reasoning. The object, quite clearly, is not to persuade, but to prevail." Later, after analyzing *Roe* and its reasoning, Blackmun asserted, "The new majority today advances not one reasonable argument as to why our judgment in that case was wrong and should be abandoned."

The draft dissent referred again to the Rehnquist review standard, saying, "the majority casually upholds the testing provision because it 'reasonably furthers the State's interest in protecting potential human life.' In keeping with the rest of its opinion, the majority makes no attempt to explain or to justify this newly minted standard, either in the abstract or as applied in this case. But the meaning of the standard is clear enough: for all practical purposes, *Roe* is overruled."

Justice Blackmun used and adapted the mocking examples in the Stevens letter: "A tax on abortions or a criminal prohibition would both satisfy the majority's standard. So, for that matter, would a requirement that a pregnant woman memorize and recite today's majority opinion before seeking an abortion."

The Rehnquist test, Blackmun urged, would uphold virtually all abortion restrictions. "It is impossible," declares the Blackmun draft, "to read the majority's penultimate paragraph without recognizing its implicit invitation to every State to enact more and more restrictive abortion laws, and to assert their interest in potential life as of the moment of conception. All of these laws will satisfy the majority's non-scrutiny, until sometime down the line, the new regime of old dissenters and new appointees will summon the courage to say what will have been true from this time forth: that *Roe* is no longer good law."

The Blackmun draft categorized the Rehnquist opinion's result as "its revolutionary revision in the law of abortion." Indeed, declared Blackmun, "With *Roe*'s passing, a political revolution in the law takes hold." Justice Blackmun then made his already-quoted statement about the swinging of the pendulum and the Court's "very long step backward." He stated that the pendulum would swing again one day. "In the meantime, though," his draft dissent concluded, "the liberty of women to control their own destinies, despite our Bill of Rights, will be subject to the vicissitudes of political controversy. In a Nation that cherishes liberty, this should not be."

REHNQUIST'S MAJORITY CANNOT HOLD

As soon as Justices Brennan and Marshall read Justice Blackmun's draft, they sent memos joining it. The Brennan memo called Blackmun's opinion "magnificent."

The next day, June 22, Chief Justice Rehnquist circulated a scheduling memorandum that told the Justices that he would announce the *Webster* decision on June 29 — then designated as the final day of the Court's term. Presumably the Chief Justice believed that he still retained his majority for what the Blackmun dissent had termed the "deceptive" overruling of *Roe*.

On June 23, however, Justice O'Connor circulated a sixteen-page printed opinion headed, "JUSTICE O'CONNOR, concurring in part and concurring in the judgment." The O'Connor opinion indicated for the first time that the *Webster* majority was not holding.

In her opinion, Justice O'Connor concurred in the Rehnquist opinion in refusing to strike down the challenged statute's public-funding provision as well as the provision prohibiting use of public funds, employees, or facilities for abortion "encouraging or counseling" (though she dealt with the latter provision on the ground of mootness, rather than on the merits, as the Rehnquist draft had done — an approach that, as already noted, the Chief Justice was to follow in his final *Webster* opinion).

However, the O'Connor draft categorically refused to agree with the portion of the Rehnquist draft repudiating *Roe v. Wade* and concurred only in the judgment upholding the "viability" test provision of the Missouri law. "Unlike the Court," Justice O'Connor wrote, "I do not understand these viability testing requirements to conflict with any of the Court's past decisions concerning state regulation of abortion." That being the case, "there is no necessity to accept the . . . invitation to reexamine the constitutional validity of *Roe v. Wade*." In such a case, the Court should follow the "venerable principle" that a constitutional question should not be decided "unless absolutely necessary to decision of the case." Referring to the Rehnquist draft, O'Connor wrote, "No reason is offered for departing from this 'fundamental rule of judicial restraint,' . . . and I would not do so in a case of such constitutional moment. When the constitutional invalidity of a State's abortion statute actually turns on the constitutional validity of *Roe v. Wade*, there will be time enough to reexamine *Roe*. And to do so carefully."

Justice O'Connor contended that the viability test requirement could be upheld "even apart from *Roe*'s trimester framework which I continue to consider problematic;" she had written "outmoded" in the typed draft of her opinion, but now replaced it with the less pejorative "problematic." Either way, she concluded, "It is clear to me that requiring the performance of examinations and tests useful to determining whether a fetus is viable, when viability is possible, and when it would not be medically imprudent to do so, does not impose an undue burden on a woman's abortion decision. On this ground alone I would reject the suggestion that 188.029 as interpreted is unconstitutional."

In the O'Connor view, this meant that this case "cannot provide a basis for reevaluating *Roe*." On this — the crucial aspect of the Rehnquist draft — the Chief Justice's opinion had now apparently lost its majority.

FINAL MANEUVERING AND DECISION

On June 26, the Rehnquist draft received a further blow. Justice Scalia circulated an opinion "concurring in part and concurring in the judgment." The Scalia draft agreed with Justice Blackmun that the Rehnquist opinion "effectively would overrule *Roe v. Wade.*" Scalia wrote, "I think that should be done, but would do it more explicitly." The Rehnquist draft was "finessing *Roe,*" and on this Justice Scalia refused to go along. "I concur in the judgment of the Court," the Scalia opinion concluded, "and strongly dissent from the manner in which it has been reached."

Assaulted from the left (by the Blackmun draft dissent, joined by Justices Brennan and Marshall), the center (Justice O'Connor), and the right (Justice Scalia), Chief Justice Rehnquist now struggled to secure a majority. First, he sought to answer the Blackmun dissent. A third Rehnquist draft, circulated June 26, conceded, "Our holding today will allow some governmental regulation of abortion that would have been prohibited." On the other hand, the Chief Justice asserted, the Blackmun warning that the states "will treat our holding today as an invitation to enact abortion regulation reminiscent of the dark ages not only misreads our holding but does scant justice to those who serve in such bodies and the people who elect them."

On June 27, Chief Justice Rehnquist sent around a fourth draft designed to attract Justice O'Connor. Rehnquist incorporated some of the points in O'Connor's draft—particularly, as indicated, the O'Connor refusal to rule on the abortion-counseling provision because of mootness. "Sandra has indicated that she had no objection to such modest plagiarism," Rehnquist wrote in his covering memo.

The Rehnquist fourth draft still was headed "the opinion of the Court"— indicating that the Chief Justice had not yet given up his hope of getting a majority behind his opinion. The draft also contained the June 29 scheduled announcement date—another suggestion that Rehnquist thought that the decision process was nearing its end.

But the Chief Justice could not reconstitute his majority. A Rehnquist memo to the Justices postponed the *Webster* announcement until July 3. Then, on June 28, Justice O'Connor circulated a new draft that was the first opinion referring to the Rehnquist opinion as a plurality opinion, rather than that of the Court or of a majority. The same day, the final Blackmun dissent was sent around. It changed the word "majority" to "plurality" some forty-five times.

Now Justice Blackmun abandoned his draft's alarmist tone. In his final draft, Blackmun wrote that the plurality opinion did not make "a single, even incremental, change in the law of abortion." The Blackmun final dissent retained much of his sharp draft language, but he deleted the words, "*Roe* no longer survives." And, instead of the passage beginning, "I rue this day," he now wrote, "I fear for the future. I fear for the liberty and equality of the millions of women who have lived and come of age in the 16 years since *Roe* was decided. I fear for the integrity of, and public esteem for, this Court."

The Blackmun dissent's conclusion also deleted the phrase about the "revolution" created by "*Roe*'s passing" and the Court's "very long step backward," Instead, the final Blackmun dissent concluded, "For today, at least, the law of abortion stands undisturbed. For today, the women of this Nation still retain the liberty to control their destinies. But the signs are evident and very ominous, and a chill wind blows."

By this point, even Chief Justice Rehnquist recognized that his opinion's "wind" would not blow away *Roe v. Wade*. On June 29, the Chief Justice circulated his fifth and last draft. Recognizing reality, he finally headed the draft, "Chief Justice REHNQUIST announced the judgment of the Court . . . and an opinion with respect to" the portions that challenged *Roe* in which Justices White and Kennedy alone joined. The Rehnquist opinion was thus announced on July 3 only as the opinion of a plurality. In his published opinion, the Chief Justice had to modify his earlier draft statement that "we modify and narrow *Roe*." Instead, the final plurality opinion concluded, "To the extent indicated in our opinion, we would modify and narrow *Row*." As handed down, the Rehnquist *Webster* opinion concluded not, as the earlier drafts had done, that it narrowed *Roe* (or, as the Blackmun draft dissent had asserted, that it overruled *Roe*), but that the plurality would do so if a later case gave it the opportunity.

HODGSON'S CHOICE

Before Justice O'Connor refused to go along, Chief Justice Rehnquist's *Webster* draft was the low point for *Roe v. Wade* in Supreme Court jurisprudence. Indeed, had the Rehnquist draft retained a majority, it is difficult to disagree with the Blackmun assertion that *Roe* would no longer have survived. In particular, under the Rehnquist draft's new test for an abortion restriction — whether it "reasonably furthers the state's interest in protecting potential human life" — the *Roe* decision would have been virtually eviscerated.

Since the Rehnquist rebuff in *Webster*, *Roe* has not only survived but been strongly confirmed, despite the strong efforts of Chief Justice Rehnquist the other way. But it was, as the Duke of Wellington once said of Waterloo, a close-run thing. Had Justice O'Connor joined the Rehnquist draft opinion of the Court in *Webster*, *Roe* would have been relegated to the limbo of repudiated decisions.

The abortion issue came before the Court again the following term in the 1990 case of *Hodgson v. Minnesota*. A Minnesota law provided that no abortion should be performed on a woman under eighteen years of age until at least forty-eight hours after both of her parents had been notified. It further provided that the notice requirement should be effective unless the pregnant minor obtained a court order permitting the abortion to proceed — what the Justices were to term a "judicial bypass procedure."

The case confronted Chief Justice Rehnquist with a virtual Hobson's choice. This time he realized that he definitely did not have the votes for another *Webster*-like attempt. The only alternative was to forgo repeating his *Webster* effort, but that meant leaving the leadership role in *Hodgson* to others — notably Justices Stevens, O'Connor, and Kennedy. Unpalatable though the choice might be to a Chief Justice who felt as he did about *Roe v. Wade*, it was the only practical course open to Rehnquist.

The postargument *Hodgson* conference took place on December 1, 1989. A bare majority voted to uphold both provisions of the challenged law (Justices Brennan, Marshall, Blackmun, and Stevens voting the other way). Once again, Justice O'Connor was to be the key Justice in the case; her votes made it possible for the final decision to come down as it did.

After the conference, there was an interchange between Justices Stevens and O'Connor. The latter had urged, in a memo, that (as explained in a Stevens letter of December 7, 1989) "an otherwise unconstitutional parental consent requirement can be saved by a satisfactory judicial bypass procedure [and that] leads inexorably to the conclusion that a bypass will also save an invalid two-parent notification requirement." Justice Stevens wrote, "I am persuaded that the conclusion does not follow."

The Court had previously upheld a *one*-parent consent requirement if the state provided an "alternate procedure," such as a judicial bypass option. The Stevens letter expressed agreement with such a result. "In my judgment," the letter stated, "a single parent consent requirement for any surgical procedure performed on a minor is perfectly reasonable as a general rule, but it consti-tutes an undue burden if it does not contain an escape hatch for the exceptional case — *e.g.,* a Christian Scientist who will not permit a ruptured appendix to be removed to save a child's life. The absolute veto cannot stand without some form of state authorized bypass."

This was not the case, according to Justice Stevens, with the two-parent notification requirement at issue in *Hodgson*. "It seems to me . . . ," Stevens stated in his letter, "that a two-parent notification requirement for any surgical procedure would not survive a rational basis test because it is counterproduc-tive in broken family cases and is wholly unnecessary in the ideal family in which, as a practical matter, notice to either parent would constitute notice to both. A child who has one parent's consent to any form of surgery should not be compelled to go to court to obtain relief from a statute that is unconstitutional because it is irrational as applied in most cases."

After she had read the Stevens letter, Justice O'Connor spoke to its author and was apparently convinced by him. The next day, O'Connor wrote to the Chief Justice about "John's views." "[I]f I understand his approach correctly," O'Connor stated, "I think I can agree with it. This leads me to change my vote to reverse in 88-1125 and still to affirm in 88-1309." This meant that O'Connor was now voting to strike down both provisions of the Minnesota law.

Before the O'Connor switch, Justices Brennan, Marshall, Blackmun, and Stevens had been in dissent and Justice Brennan, the senior among them, had written, "Would you, Harry [Blackmun], take on the dissent?" With O'Con-nor's changed vote, there was a bare majority to invalidate both of the statute's challenged provisions. Presumably because he had been the catalyst in the construction of the new majority, the opinion was now assigned to Justice Stevens.

On February 7, 1990, Justice Stevens circulated a thirty-six-printed-page draft opinion of the Court holding invalid both the notice and judicial bypass provisions of the Minnesota law. As in his December 7 letter, Stevens drew a distinction between a one-parent consent requirement and a statute requiring notice to *both* parents. "We now conclude," the Stevens draft declared, "that the requirement of notice to both of the pregnant minor's parents is not reasonably related to legitimate state interests and that both parts of the statute are unconstitutional."

In the Stevens view, the constitutional objection to the two-parent notice requirement was not removed by the judicial bypass option. As the draft put it, "A judicial bypass that is designed to handle exceptions from a reasonable general rule, and thereby preserve the constitutionality of that rule, is quite different from a requirement that a minor—or a minor and one of her parents—must apply to a court for permission to avoid the application of a rule that is not reasonably related to legitimate state goals." The requirement that the bypass procedure must be invoked to avoid the two-parent notice requirement "represents no less of an unjustified governmental intrusion into the family's decisional process" than the notice requirement itself.

Once again, however, the majority did not hold. Justice Stevens circulated redrafts of his opinion, including a draft circulated on June 7, still headed "JUSTICE STEVENS delivered the opinion of the Court." [In the copy I have, someone had crossed out "delivered the opinion" and penned in "announced the judgment."] The change was made official, when a sixth draft was circulated on June 16, with its printed heading, "JUSTICE STEVENS announced the judgment of the Court."

The change occurred because, on June 11, Justice O'Connor sent around an opinion concurring in part and dissenting in part. As explained in her covering memo, "At the end of the day, I am back where I started. I agree with John [Stevens] that subdivision 2, the 2-parent notification, is invalid. But I agree with Tony [Kennedy] that subdivision 6, the 2-parent notification plus judicial bypass, passes constitutional muster."

The Court was now fragmented. Four Justices (the Chief Justice and Justices White, Scalia, and Kennedy) held that two-parent notification was constitutional, with or without bypass; four Justices (Justices Brennan, Marshall, Blackmun, and Stevens) held that two-parent notification was unconstitutional, with or without bypass; one Justice (Justice O'Connor) held that two-parent notification was unconstitutional without judicial bypass, but constitutional with bypass.

With the Court thus split, Justice Kennedy sent around a June 13 *Memorandum to the Conference* that informed the Justices that, because of the division, "John and I propose issuing a *per curiam* opinion along the lines of the one attached. The separate opinions would then be opinions concurring and dissenting from the judgement announced in the *per curiam*." The attached one-paragraph per curiam stated, "For reasons stated in separate opinions that follow, the judgment of the Court of Appeals in its entirety is affirmed." (The lower court had invalidated the two-parent notice requirement and upheld the judicial-bypass alternative.)

At the conference on June 14, opposition was expressed to the issuance of a per curiam. The next day, Justice Stevens, who had joined with Justice Kennedy on the per curiam suggestion, sent a *Memorandum to the Conference* negativing the idea. "After giving further consideration to the proposed use of a per curiam in this case . . . ," the memo began, "I have now concluded that I will not be able to join such a disposition."

If a per curiam were used, Justice Stevens pointed out, it "would constitute the only opinion for the Court and therefore what I regard as two unfortunate consequences would ensue. First, what would otherwise be my opinion for the Court in No. 88-1309, (drafted pursuant to Bill Brennan's assignment) would be converted into an opinion concurring in part and dissenting in part from the PC. secondly, the headnote for the PC would be meaningless and there would be no syllabus in the U.S. Reports." In particular, use of a per curiam would deprive any other opinion that was issued of the status of a Court opinion.

As it turned out, when *Hodgson* came down, Justice Stevens announced the judgment of the Court and his opinion striking down the two-parent notification provision (a holding agreed to by five Justices) and Justice Kennedy issued an opinion upholding the judicial bypass provision (a holding also agreed to by five Justices). The bare majority for both holdings was supplied by Justice O'Connor's vote.

While the Court appeared hopelessly fragmented on *Hodgson*, Justice Brennan sent a June 13, 1990, letter to Justice Marshall urging him to join as much of the Stevens opinion as possible. "I think," Brennan wrote, "it is important for John to get as much support as possible, now that Sandra has for the first time joined us in holding invalid a law regulating abortion."

The final O'Connor posture was the crucial element of the *Hodgson* decision. It meant that there was no real possibility of overruling *Roe v. Wade*. Hence, Justice Stevens could conclude, in a June 18 letter on *Hodgson*'s effect, "that whatever else may have happened, it is still the law that a woman's decision in favor of an abortion is a part of her liberty that is protected by the Due Process Clause, and as long as that is true the fact that a State may disapprove of abortion is not a sufficient reason for interfering with that basic liberty."

ROE REAFFIRMED

In a 1987 comment on Chief Justice Rehnquist, Justice Marshall said, "He has no problems, wishy-washy, back and forth. He knows exactly what he wants to do, and that's very important as a chief justice."

There is no doubt that William H. Rehnquist has been a stronger Court head than his predecessor. However, this chapter shows that he, too, has not always been able to impose his will upon the often primadonnaish individuals who make up the Court. There were few things on which Rehnquist felt more deeply than the need to overrule *Roe v. Wade*. Yet he was unable to accomplish his goal of casting *Roe* into limbo in the *Webster* case and did not really try again the next term in *Hodgson v. Minnesota*. *Hodgson*, indeed, with Justice O'Connor's first vote to strike down a law regulating abortion, has proved the Thermidor for the would-be Rehnquist "revolution" (to use the term in Justice Blackmun's draft *Webster* dissent) in abortion law.

Since *Hodgson*, the Court has strongly reaffirmed *Roe*. In the 1992 case of *Planned Parenthood v. Casey*, Chief Justice Rehnquist renewed his *Webster* effort to inter *Roe*, but he was again able to secure only four votes. Justice O'Connor, once more the key vote, not only remained true to her *Webster-Hodgson* posture but joined in writing an opinion that specifically rejected the invitation to overrule *Roe v. Wade*. On the contrary, the joint opinion of Justices O'Connor, Kennedy, and David H. Souter declared, "the essential holding of *Roe v. Wade* should be retained and once again reaffirmed. . . . the woman's right to terminate her pregnancy before viability is the most central principal of *Roe v. Wade*. It is a rule of law and a component of liberty we cannot renounce."

Justice Blackmun delivered a poignant separate *Casey* opinion in which he stressed that *Roe* still survived by only one vote and how "I fear for the darkness as four Justices anxiously await the single vote necessary to extinguish the light." However, with the replacement in 1993 of Justice White (always a consistent supporter of the Chief Justice's effort to overrule *Roe v. Wade*) by Justice Ruth Bader Ginsburg, *Roe* appears as secure for the foreseeable future as so controversial a decision can be.

2

Webster and
the Decision Process

Webster v. Reproductive Health Services is, to be sure, not typical of the Supreme Court's decision process. It is rare for a Chief Justice to be so rebuffed by his colleagues. (Though there are other examples as well, as we shall see in Chapters 5 and 6.) On the other hand, the case does tell us a great deal about the Supreme Court's decision process.

THE BRETHREN AND THEIR SISTER

In the first place, *Webster* shows that, if the Court can be led, it cannot be dominated by the Chief Justice. While it may be the custom to designate the high court by the name of its Chief, one who looks only to the powers of the Chief Justice will find it hard to understand this underscoring of his preeminence. In Justice Tom C. Clark's words in a 1956 article, "The Chief Justice has no more authority than other members of the court."

Understandably, the Justices themselves have always been sensitive to claims that the Chief Justice has greater power than the others. "It is vitally important," asserted Justice Felix Frankfurter in a 1956 letter to Justice Harold H. Burton, "to remember what Holmes said about the office: 'Of course, the position of the Chief Justice differs from that of the other Justices only on the administrative side.'" Two years later Frankfurter wrote to Justice Brennan, "any encouragement in a Chief Justice that he is the boss . . . must be rigorously resisted. . . . I, for my part, will discharge what I regard as a post of trusteeship, not least in keeping the Chief Justice in his place, as long as I am around."

Even a strong Chief Justice, such as Earl Warren, soon realized that he could not deal with the Justices in the way he had directed matters when he had been Governor of California. "I think," Justice Potter Stewart once said, "he came to realize very early, certainly long before I came here [1958], that this group of nine rather prima donnaish people could not be led, could not be told, in the way the Governor of California can tell a subordinate, do this or do that."

The *Webster* decision process also shows that the Supreme Court is an institution whose collegiate nature is underscored by the custom the Justices have had of calling each other "Brethren." But the Brethren can only be guided, not directed. As Justice Frankfurter stated in a letter to Chief Justice Fred M. Vinson, "good feeling in the Court, as in a family, is produced by accommodation, not by authority—whether the authority of a parent or a vote."

The Court "family" is composed of nine individuals, who constantly bear out what Justice Frankfurter once wrote to Justice Stanley Reed: "To be sure, the Court is an institution, but individuals, with all their diversities of endowment, experience and outlook determine its actions. The history of the Supreme Court is not the history of an abstraction, but the analysis of individuals acting as a Court who make decisions and lay down doctrines."

Professor Alexander Bickel of Yale, a leading constitutional scholar, used to portray the Supreme Court to his students as nine scorpions trapped in a bottle. That is, of course, an exaggeration. But the individual Justices do operate, as some of them have said, like nine separate law firms. Yet *Webster* demonstrates how the separate firms must cooperate in order to reach a decision. Even students of the Supreme Court do not fully realize that its decisions are basically collaborative efforts in which nine supreme individualists must cooperate to bring about the desired result.

Of course, the Brethren sobriquet became inappropriate as soon as Justice Sandra Day O'Connor was chosen in 1981 as what *Time* called "the Brethren's first sister." Over the years, in fact, the way in which Supreme Court Justices are designated has undergone an evolution.

When the Court was first established, the author of an opinion was designated "Cushing, Justice." In 1820 the form was replaced by "Mr. Justice Johnson" as opinion author. This style lasted more than a century and a half. Then, at a conference in June 1980, Justice Byron R. White suggested to the conference that, since a woman Justice was bound to be appointed soon, they should avoid the embarrassment of changing the style again at that time. All the others agreed, and the manner of designating the author of an opinion became simply "Justice Brennan."

The Court, however, tends to be a conservative institution, and some of the Justices opposed the change proposed by Justice White. A November 17, 1980, "Dear Chief" letter from Justice Harry A. Blackmun began, "If you are maintaining a permanent record on the vote to eliminate the use of 'Mr.,' please record me as in opposition."

"It seems to me," the Blackmun letter asserted, "that of late we tend to panic and to get terribly excited about some rather inconsequential things. I regard this as one of them. . . . So far as I am concerned, I think it would have been far better to let the present system, in force for many decades, continue until a woman is on the Court and her particular desires are made known. We seem to be eliminating, step by step, all aspects of diverseness, and we give impetus to the trend toward a colorless society."

Justice Powell also sent a November 17 letter to Chief Justice Burger. The letter was headed "Confidential" and stated, "I must say that I agree with Harry as to the change at this time in the traditional reference to a sitting member of this Court."

The Powell letter noted, "It is as certain as anything in this life can be that one of us will be replaced by a woman. In my view, this not only will be desirable; the choice of a woman may well be overdue, given the glacial changes in our society over the past two decades."

His view in this respect did not, however, lead Justice Powell to support the nomenclature change. Instead, his letter concluded, "it does seem more dignified, and perhaps less anticipatory of a political judgment, to defer making a change at this time. It certainly will be appropriate when a 'Sister' joins us."

A "sister" did, of course, join the Court: Justice O'Connor was appointed in 1981. Before then the Justices used to jest among themselves about the effect a woman Justice would have. Tradition says that the junior Justice answers the conference room door (one of them used to quip that he was the highest-paid doorman in the world). This led Justice Thurgood Marshall, the first black Justice, to describe his first year on the Court, "Here I am, born in the ghetto, worked my way up to be special counsel for the NAACP, a judge on the 2nd Circuit, solicitor general, and now, what do I hear? 'You boy, open that door!' "

As rumors of a female appointment gained ground, the Justices joked, first to Justice Rehnquist and then to the new junior Justice, John Paul Stevens, that when a woman came to the Court, he should be a gentleman and continue to answer the door. In the event, when O'Connor became the newest Justice, she assumed the doorkeeper's task without question. And the Justices continued to be called the Brethren even though a woman had joined their ranks.

INDEPENDENCE AND DISQUALIFICATION

Despite their awesome reputations, the Justices are nine very human individuals, each with a personal manner of doing things. Former Justice Arthur J. Goldberg recalled for me how, when he first came to the Court, the conference took a formal vote on whether the Justices should go to Capitol Hill for the State of the Union message. The motion to attend carried by only a bare majority and, despite the vote, Hugo Black and another Justice never did attend.

But Justice Black was always an individualist, who would persist in doing things his own way. The ritual intonation that opens each Court session ends with "God save the United States and this Honorable Court." One year a new member of the Court began bowing his head when those words were reached. The Justice beside him soon followed suit. It spread down the line until everyone bowed his head — except Justice Black, who continued to look straight out at the audience.

More recently, the Justices have expressed reservations about swearing-in ceremonies for new Justices at the White House. When such a ceremony was arranged in 1990 for Justice David H. Souter, Justice Stevens sent around a memo recalling his doubts about attending a similar function for Justice Anthony M. Kennedy in 1988. "I know," Stevens wrote, "that on that occasion I had serious misgivings about the possible separation of powers implications of the President's use of the occasion in a somewhat political way."

In 1991, when Justice Clarence Thomas was appointed, Justice Blackmun expressed the same sentiment: "The practice of having an oath administered in the White House lends further weight to the politicization of the appointment process. . . . I refused to attend the White House ceremony the last time, and I shall not attend this time, if there is one."

Chief Justice Rehnquist took a different view. He circulated a memo: "I am quite confident that the White House regards the oath-taking ceremony as a very important photo-opportunity and platform for the President, which it pursues without a great deal of regard for the consequences elsewhere."

Justice Antonin Scalia suggested a compromise in another memo. If the White House would forgo its ceremony, Scalia wrote, the Court could invite the President to a swearing-in at the Court and even allow cameras so that the President would have a "photo-op." Justice Scalia wrote that he was willing to allow cameras inside the Court only if "there is some offsetting benefit. I would consider the elimination of the White House ceremony to be such a bene-fit. . . . In order to make the arrangement attractive to President Bush (and later Presidents) I think we should allow minimally intrusive on-floor cameras and even lights. The President's men are going to want good theatre and attractive close-ups."

The only difficulty with his proposal, Scalia noted, was, "I believe in the camel's nose." On the other side, Chief Justice Rehnquist pointed out in his memo, "It is somewhat awkward to invite someone to your house on the condition that he not invite you to his house."

In the end, the camel did not get his nose inside the tent. All the other Justices sent memos to the Chief Justice opposing the televising of Justice Thomas's Court swearing-in; the ceremony was held without the cameras.

The complete independence of the Justices, vis-à-vis each other, is shown by their practice with regard to disqualifications. Whether and why a Justice will refuse to sit in a case is entirely up to the Justice concerned and no reasons are given for disqualifications or refusals to disqualify. Thus, in recent years, Justice O'Connor sent around memos disqualifying herself because counsel was a firm in which her husband had been a partner, her sister's husband had been a judge in the lower court, and her family's ranching corporation had an interest in the case. On the other hand, she refused to recuse herself when she had been told that a news program had stated that one of the parties "made a threat to me some years ago." Similarly, in a 1991 case challenging the merger of First American Bank and another bank, Justice Stevens circulated a memo which stated, "I concluded that the fact that Maryan and I maintain bank accounts at the First American Bank of Virginia was not a disqualifying circumstance. Since neither the issues nor the possible outcome of this case would seem to have any bearing on our status as depositors, I am still of that view."

In 1972, a formal motion was made by a party to disqualify Justice Rehnquist from participating in a case in which the Army's surveillance of civilians was at issue. It was entirely up to Rehnquist himself to decide whether to disqualify himself. He told the March 31, 1972, conference on the case (according to Justice William O. Douglas's notes) that "he will stay in the case tho he took part in the hearings before Ervin" (Assistant Attorney General Rehnquist had testified in support of the surveillance program before a Senate subcommittee headed by Senator Sam Ervin). Justice Rehnquist did sit in the case and, as it turned out, his vote was necessary for the bare majority decision of the Court.

There are times when the disqualification of a Justice may directly change the result in a case. In the 1985 case of *Eastern Airlines v. Mahfoud,* Justice Brennan managed to secure a majority for the result that he favored despite a conference vote the other way. Then, only a week before the decision was to be announced, he discovered that he had to disqualify himself because of his son's connection to Eastern. The judgment then was affirmed without opinion by an equally divided Court.

Not long ago, the Justices decided on a new disqualification policy. In a January 31, 1990, Memorandum to the Conference, Chief Justice Rehnquist stated that he had been informed that his nephew was an associate in a law firm representing one of the parties in a pending case, though he had not worked on the petition for certiorari and had not previously participated in the case. The memo noted, "I and other members of the Court have in the past disqualified ourselves when a person included in § 455(b)(5) was an associate in the law firm representing one of the parties before this Court, even though the person had not participated in the case before the Court or at previous stages of the litigation." Section 455(b)(5) applies when "a person within the third degree of relationship" to a judge "is acting as a lawyer in the proceeding." "The members of the Court," the Rehnquist memo went on, "have discussed this question among themselves, and have decided that § 455 does not require disqualification under these circumstances. Therefore, I shall participate in the consideration and disposition of this matter."

In February 1990, the Court formally announced that the Justices would no longer disqualify themselves in such a case, where a law firm appearing before the Court employs an associate who is a relative covered by § 455 but who did not participate in the case. On November 1, 1993, the Court issued a further statement that would have allowed Chief Justice Rehnquist to remain in the case, absent some special factor, even if his nephew had worked on it below. Such special factors would include a case where the relative had been lead counsel before the case reached the Court or when a relative's "compensation would be substantially affected by the outcome here."

Two members of the Court, Justices Blackmun and Souter, did not sign the 1993 announcement. If they or some other Justice were to refuse to follow the new disqualification practice, they could not be compelled to do so. The internal independence of each Justice means that the final word on disqualification is entirely up to the Justice concerned.

CONFERENCES WITH LITTLE CONFERENCING

How do the nine "separate firms" cooperate to reach the desired decision? In the first place, there is the conference, in which the Justices as a group discuss the cases argued before them. "When I first went on the Court," wrote Chief Justice Rehnquist in his book on the Supreme Court, "I was both surprised and dismayed at how little interplay there was between the various justices." In part, the lack of conference interplay has been a result of the proliferation of modern communications equipment in the Court.

Before Chief Justice Burger's tenure, all Supreme Court documents were typed with as many carbon copies as needed. Thus, copies of the memoranda on in forma pauperis, or Miscellaneous Docket, petitions (petitions for review filed by people too poor to pay the filing fee) were sent to each Justice. Because it was necessary to use very thin paper, these memoranda were called "flimsies." The junior Justices, who received the last copies, often had difficulty reading them.

This was changed when Chief Justice Burger sent around an August 7, 1969, memorandum: "The necessary steps are now being taken toward acquiring a Xerox machine in the building." The new copiers "will be utilized primarily in preparation and distribution of the Miscellaneous Docket memoranda ('flimsies' as they are commonly called.)" Since that time, ample copiers have been provided for the Justices and Court staff, and word processors and a computer have been introduced. Conservative as they are, however, some of the Justices were not entirely happy with the new technology. "You are quite right," wrote Justice White to Justice Blackmun on October 1, 1986. "These word processors just aren't reliable."

The availability of copiers and the other communications devices has had a baneful, though unintended, effect upon the operation of the Court. One privy to the working of the Warren Court quickly notes the crucial importance of personal exchanges among the Justices—both in conference discussions and, even more so, in the postargument decision process. Such exchanges became less significant in the Burger and Rehnquist Courts. This has been noted by the Justices themselves. Conference notes in recent years show less an interchange of views than flat statements of each Justice's position in the case. "Not much conferencing goes on" at the conference, Justice Scalia has confirmed. "In fact, to call our discussion of a case a conference is really something of a misnomer, it's much more a statement of the views of each of the nine Justices, after which the totals are added and the case is assigned."

Justice Scalia was referring to the conference, but his remark is equally applicable to the entire decision process. The constant personal exchanges in the Warren Court (much of it one-on-one lobbying by the Chief Justice and his allies or by opponents intended to influence votes) have given way to mostly written contacts through notes and memoranda. It is after all so much easier, now that each Justice has a personal computer, to make copies and send them around than to engage in protracted personal efforts to persuade others to change their positions. In the Court now, said former assistant attorney general Stuart M. Gerson in a 1993 speech, "there is a complete absence of decisional collegiality. . . . The culprit in this lack of collegiality . . . is the computer." In the Court, as in other institutions, technology intended to facilitate communication has made for less personal interchange.

The result may have changed the form, but not the necessity for collaboration among the nine individuals who make up the Court. The conference may involve less interplay among the Justices than it used to. Certainly, the discussion is less free than it was in the Court's early days when conferences were held in the Washington boardinghouses in which the Justices lived—often over their dinner tables, with suitable liquid refreshment.

The propensity of the Brethren then for that type of refreshment is shown by a famous story about the Marshall Court's conferences. This is how it was told by Albert J. Beveridge, Chief Justice Marshall's biographer: " 'We are great ascetics, and even deny ourselves wine except in wet weather,' [Justice Joseph] Story dutifully informed his wife. 'What I say about the wine gives you our rule; but it does sometimes happen that the Chief Justice will say to me, when the cloth is removed, 'Brother Story, step to the window and see if it does not look like rain.' And if I tell him that the sun is shining brightly, Justice Marshall will sometimes reply, 'All the better, for our jurisdiction extends over so large a territory that the doctrine of chances makes it certain that it must be raining somewhere.' " So far as is known, no such practice is followed in the Court today, though, as previously noted, the Justices still have individual pewter julep cups—at present, alas, filled only with drinking water.

The conference, as Justice Scalia says, now may be less an interchange than a statement of the views of the Justices. Still, it is the first formal statement of position by each Justice to the other members of the Court. Sketchy though it may be under the pressure of the present-day calendar, it does indicate both how the Justice would decide the case and, even if only briefly, the reasons why such a decision should be made.

The Chief Justice who begins the discussion of each case necessarily takes more time than any associate in the typical case, because, as Chief Justice Rehnquist's book describes it, "the Chief Justice begins by reviewing the facts and the decision of the lower court, outlining his understanding of the applicable case law, and indicating either that he votes to affirm the decision of the lower court or to reverse it." Inevitably, the Chief Justice "takes more time . . . because he feels called upon to go into greater detail as to the facts and the lower-court holding than do those who come after him."

The same may be true of Justices who take a different view than the Chief Justice. This was the case with Justice Brennan during his years on the Burger and Rehnquist Courts. As told by Chief Justice Rehnquist, Justice "Brennan, who frequently disagrees with me (and also disagreed with Chief Justice Burger) in important constitutional cases, and is therefore the first to state the view of the law with which he agrees, also frequently takes more time than the other associates."

It is not, however, the lengthy conference presentation that necessarily sways the Justices. At Court conferences, Justice Potter Stewart once told me, "Felix [Frankfurter], if he was really interested in a case, would speak for fifty minutes, no more or less, because that was the length of the lecture at the Harvard Law School."

Of course, Justice Stewart exaggerated—but not by that much. One thing the Justices who served with Frankfurter recall is his tendency to treat the conference as another Harvard seminar, in which he would lecture at great length to demonstrate his professorial erudition. "We all know," reads a 1954 Memorandum to Mr. Justice Frankfurter, signed "Wm. O. Douglas," "what a great burden your long discourses are. So I am not complaining. But I do register a protest at your degradation of the Conference and its deliberations."

At the other extreme, Justice Thurgood Marshall had a gift for a succinct phrase that sometimes cut to the heart of a case. When the Court in 1978 was asked to apply an endangered species law to save a few obscure fish, even though it meant destruction of a dam costing hundreds of millions, Marshall told the conference on the case, "Congress has the right to make a jackass of itself."

Which Justice—Frankfurter or Marshall—do you think had the greater influence on the conference decision process?

VOTING AND OPINION ASSIGNMENT

The quality of the *Webster* conference interchange may have borne out the Rehnquist-Scalia complaint that the conference now sees less of an interplay between the Justices than a mere statement of each of their views. But it was clear from their *Webster* statements just what almost all their positions were in the case. Five of the Justices voted to uphold the challenged Missouri abortion law.

Before we discuss *Webster* as an illustration of the Court's postconference process, a word should be said about the manner in which the Justices vote on cases. Commentators on the Court usually describe the voting process as one that takes place at the end of the conference discussion of a case. It is said that, while the conference discussion proceeds from the Chief Justice down, the vote at its end goes the other way, with the junior Justice voting first and then, in reverse order of seniority, back to the Chief Justice. The reason, we are told, is to make it less likely that the juniors will be influenced by how their seniors have voted.

It does not, in actual practice, work in this traditionally described manner. "I can testify," writes Chief Justice Rehnquist in his book on the Court, "that, at least during my fifteen years on the Court, this tale is very much of a myth; I don't believe I have ever seen it happen at any of the conferences that I have attended." By the time the discussion on a case has concluded, it is clear how the Justices would vote on it. Hence, a formal vote is not necessary and none has been taken for some years. To avoid errors on the matter, at the end of the conference discussion, the Chief Justice announces how he is recording the vote in the case, so that the others have the opportunity to make corrections if they disagree with the count.

On October 1, 1986, soon after Chief Justice Rehnquist took office, Justice Stevens circulated a Memorandum to the Conference, in which he pointed out "that there was once a time when the voting order on argued cases began with the junior justice and ended with the Chief Justice."

Perhaps tongue in cheek, the Stevens memo raised the question of whether the old practice should be revived for the benefit of the junior Justices: "Since we now have a Chief Justice who experienced the disadvantage of speaking only after most of his colleagues had already voted, I wonder if he might be sympathetic to considering a return to the Court's old practice of having the discussion of argued cases proceed down the ladder but have the voting then go up the ladder?"

The next step after the conference concludes its discussion of a case is for the opinion explaining the decision to be assigned to a particular Justice. Since Chief Justice Marshall placed his imprint upon the Court, its opinions have been authored by individual Justices, though issued as opinions of the Court when concurred in by a majority. Yet the decision on which Justice shall write the Court's opinion remains of crucial importance.

In *Webster,* the opinion was assigned by Chief Justice Rehnquist to himself. The assignment illustrates one of the most important powers of the Chief Justice — that of deciding who writes opinions. In exercising it, the Chief Justice determines what use will be made of the Court's personnel; the particular decisions he assigns to each Justice in distributing the workload will influence both the growth of the law and his own relations with his colleagues.

Since Chief Justice Roger B. Taney in the pre–Civil War period, it has been the settled practice for the Chief Justice to assign each opinion in cases where he is a member of the conference majority. If he is with the minority, the senior majority Justice assigns the opinion. Thus, in the 1989 case of *Texas v. Johnson* — the flag-burning case that Justice Blackmun called in a letter of June 19, 1989, "this difficult and distasteful little (big?) case" — Chief Justice Rehnquist was in the conference minority. Justice Brennan, senior in the majority, then assigned the case, notifying the Chief Justice, "I'll do an opinion for the Court in the above."

Sometimes the senior in the majority waives the right to assign a case. In the 1991 case of *Lankford v. Idaho,* a death sentence appeal, Justice Marshall's vote switch converted a bare majority to affirm into one to reverse. Chief Justice Rehnquist therefore wrote to Marshall, now senior in the new majority, "you should then assign the case." The Justice, however, wrote back: "Since Harry [previously the senior among the dissenters] had already assigned the dissent in this case, I am content to let him assign the majority opinion."

The senior Justice among those dissenting also assigns the dissenting opinion. Thus, in the important affirmative-action case of *Richmond v. Croson Company,* Justice Brennan wrote to Justices Marshall and Blackmun on October 11, 1988, "We three are in dissent in the above. Would you, Thurgood, take it on?"

Here, too, however, the right to assign may be waived. In the landmark "right-to-life" *Cruzan* case, Justice Brennan sent a December 11, 1989, "Dear Thurgood, Harry, and John" letter: "We four are in dissent in the above. I suggest that, because of the significance of this case, perhaps each of us might want to write his own."

Chief Justice Burger was severely criticized because he did not always follow the spirit of the established assignment practice. According to a comment in the British periodical the *Economist,* "Chief Justice Burger would sometimes vote against his instincts in order to preserve his prerogative of assigning the majority opinion." In other words, Burger would vote with the majority in order to control the assignment of opinions.

The one Justice who was willing to talk frankly about the Burger assignment practice spoke of it in a most denigratory fashion: "The great thing about Earl Warren was that he was so considerate of all his colleagues. He was so meticulous on assignments." Now, the Justice went on, "all too damned often the Chief Justice [Burger] will vote with the majority so as to assign the opinion, and then he ends up in dissent." Voting with the majority in this way certainly appears contrary to the spirit, if not the letter, of the Court's assignment practice.

Those privy to the Burger Court's decision process have alleged that the Chief Justice also went beyond the letter of the assignment tradition. A striking illustration is contained in the *Swann* school busing case, to be discussed in Chapter 6. Chief Justice Burger assigned the opinion there to himself, even though he had supported the minority view at the conference.

"He does it all the time," one of the Justices said about the Burger assignment practice. This was doubtless an exaggeration, but there were other cases as well where Chief Justice Burger assigned cases though he was not in the majority. The outstanding example perhaps occurred in *Roe v. Wade*. The Chief Justice assigned the opinion in that case to Justice Blackmun, though Burger was not then part of the majority.

In *Roe*, Justice Douglas circulated a strong memorandum that declared that the Burger assignment of the case was "an action no Chief Justice in my time would ever have taken. For the tradition is a longstanding one that the senior Justice in the majority makes the assignment." Hence, Douglas asserted, he, as senior member of the majority, should have assigned the case. "When, however, the minority seeks to control the assignment, there is a destructive force at work in the Court. When a Chief Justice tries to bend the Court to his will by manipulating assignments, the integrity of the institution is imperilled."

Not long before, Justice Douglas had written a memorandum to the Chief Justice complaining about the Burger assignment practice: "If the conference wants to authorize you to assign all opinions, that will be a new procedure. Though opposed to it, I will acquiesce. But unless we make a frank reversal in our policy, any group in the majority should and must make the assignment."

The Douglas *Roe* memo was leaked to the press and the *Washington Post* carried a story about it on July 4, 1972. By then, Justice Douglas was on vacation at his summer home in Goose Prairie, Washington. He sent Chief Justice Burger a written note saying his wife had told him "over the phone that the Washington Post today carries a nasty story about the Abortion Cases, my memo to the Conference, etc etc." Douglas wrote, "I am upset and appalled. I have never leaked a word concerning the cases, or my memo to anyone outside the Court."

"We have our differences," the Douglas note concluded, "but so far as I am concerned they are wholly internal; and if revealed, they are [illegible word] in opinions filed, never in 'leaks' to the press."

Chief Justice Burger replied in a July 27 letter headed "Personal Confidential." It stated that Douglas "seems to imply bad faith" on Burger's part and asserted, "The record . . . shows that I have never undertaken to assign from a minority position. Thus there is not the slightest basis for your statement."

Justice Douglas replied with an August 7 MEMORANDUM TO THE CHIEF JUSTICE, in which he repeated, "I wrote the memo for internal consumption only. I showed it to no one not on our staff. I did not 'leak' it to the press." Also, "I did not write the memo for posterity. It would be the least interesting of anything to those who follow." The Douglas letter assured the Chief Justice that, as far as he was concerned, "That chapter in the Abortion Cases is for me gone and forgotten."

Perhaps so; but there is no doubt that Chief Justice Burger's handling of *Roe v. Wade* did cause bitterness among the Justices. Thus, in June 1972, Justice Brennan penned a short memo to Justice Douglas, "I will be God damned! At lunch today, Potter [Stewart] expressed his outrage at the high handed way things are going, particularly the assumption that a single Justice if CJ can order things his own way. . . . Potter wants to make an issue of these things — maybe fur will fly this afternoon."

Of course, Chief Justice Burger also made use of more traditional assignment techniques, particularly the practice illustrated by *Webster* of assigning an important case to himself, since the Court in such cases should speak through its head. Perhaps the best example of this practice in the Burger Court occurred in the *Nixon* case, to be dealt with in Chapter 6. The decision there led directly to the forced resignation of President Richard M. Nixon, and there was discussion at the conference on whether the importance of the case should not lead to modification of the assignment practice. Justice Brennan said that the Court should emphasize its decision by issuing the strongest opinion possible and this could be done if the Court delivered a joint opinion — in the name of each of the participating Justices. The Court had done so only once before — in the 1958 Little Rock school desegregation case, where a joint opinion of the Justices dramatically underlined their unanimity. Interestingly, according to an October 8, 1958, memo by Justice Douglas, when the joint opinion was proposed in the Little Rock case, "The new format seemed silly to some of us, particularly Brennan and myself."

Now Justice Brennan proposed following the Little Rock precedent. But Chief Justice Burger refused to go along. "The responsibility is on my shoulders," he said. He would prepare the opinion and assigned it to himself in accordance with the traditional practice.

Chief Justice Burger also followed the practice of most Court heads by assigning the more significant cases to his allies, such as Justice Harry A. Blackmun in his earlier years and Justice Rehnquist in the later years of the Burger Court. He left lesser cases to his opponents on the Court, notably Justice Brennan.

Another technique that Chief Justice Burger employed was that of assigning a case to the most lukewarm member of the majority. An illustration can be found in a November 14, 1978, Burger letter to Justice Brennan: "Apropos your opinion (I believe at lunch Monday) whether Bill Rehnquist was an appropriate assignee of the above case, I had discussed this with Bill. He prefers his first choice disposition, i.e., no judicial review, but he was willing to write the holding to reflect the majority view otherwise. There were 8 to affirm and he fits the old English rule-of-thumb as the 'least persuaded,' hence likely to write narrowly."

Unfortunately there are risks in assigning an opinion to the "least persuaded" Justice. The hope is that the shaky vote will become increasingly firm as the Justice goes through the process of fashioning a reasoned opinion. But the opposite may well be the result. Thus, in a December 3, 1990, Memorandum to the Conference, Justice Scalia informed the others, "I was as firm as any of you in my opinion that the judgment in this case had to be an affirmance. I have found it impossible, however, to write it that way."

SORCERER'S APPRENTICE?

In a 1993 *New York Times* book review of a biography of Justice Oliver Wendell Holmes, a Washington lawyer who had been a Supreme Court law clerk stressed that, in Holmes's day, the judges "considered it their personal duty to explain in writing . . . why they reached a particular result." That is no longer true. "Not so today. Even highly respected Federal judges routinely assign opinion writing to . . . law clerks." In the Supreme Court, the "clerks spend their time drafting the lengthy decisions that are issued in the Justices' names."

A few weeks later, the *Times* published a letter from another lawyer, who had been a fellow law clerk, challenging the reviewer's statement as "the hyperbole of an advocate [that] inflates the perceived importance of law clerks." Referring to his own experience clerking for a Justice, the attorney asserted that, "Even if the Justice did not write every 'and' and 'the,' or turn phrases with Holmes's facility, it was the Justice who voted on the cases, the Justice who determined the legal theory for his vote and for his opinion, and the Justice who took the entire responsibility for the final opinion he signed." This was also said to have been the case with regard to the other Justices.

The dispute between the two former law clerks brings to mind a congratulatory letter that Justice Douglas wrote to Justice Rehnquist upon Rehnquist's 1971 appointment as a Justice. "I realize that you were here before as a member of the so-called Junior Supreme Court." Douglas was referring to Rehnquist's service as a law clerk to Justice Robert H. Jackson.

Once upon a time, the Douglas characterization of the clerk corps might have been taken as one made in jest. The exchange between the two former clerks shows that this is no longer the case. When we talk today about the drafting of Supreme Court opinions, we are dealing with a subject in which there is a sharp difference between appearance and reality and one which brings us to the controversial question of the role of the law clerks in the Court's decision process. Indeed, the use the Justices now make of their law clerks means, as the *Times* reviewer put it, that "no one knows what, if anything, the Justices themselves have written."

Justice Louis D. Brandeis was once asked why people respected the Supreme Court. His short answer was, "Because the Justices are almost the only people in Washington who do their own work." The legend that this remains true is still prevalent, and in his book on the Court, Chief Justice Rehnquist tells us that "the individual justices still continue to do a great deal more of their 'own work' than do their counterparts in other branches of the federal government."

The Rehnquist view account has been accepted both by the press and the public. "Alone among Government agencies," Anthony Lewis has written in the *New York Times,* "the court seems to have escaped Parkinson's Law. The work is still done by nine men, assisted by eighteen young law clerks. Nothing is delegated to committees or ghostwriters or task forces."

Before the Court moved into its present Marble Palace in 1935, what Justice Brandeis said was entirely true. The Justices then had no office facilities in their old Capitol Court space. They did their work at home, helped only by a messenger or a secretary or law clerk. Dean Acheson, who clerked for Justice Brandeis, later nostalgically recalled, "Poindexter, the messenger and I constituted the whole office staff; and Poindexter, half the household staff as well."

The practice of having law clerks started with Justice Horace Gray, who, starting in 1875, hired (at first at his own expense) a Harvard Law graduate each year to assist him in his work. In 1886, Congress provided each Justice with funds to pay for a secretary or clerk, with provision for law clerks in addition to secretarial assistance in 1919. Under Chief Justice Fred M. Vinson, the number increased to two. In the Burger Court, the number grew to three and then to four, with the Chief Justice having a fifth senior clerk.

According to Justice Brennan, "Tradition has it that Jeremy Bentham once remarked that law is not made by judge alone but by Judge and Company." If he were writing about the Supreme Court today, he would surely include law clerks in the company. The problem is that the company may, all too frequently, come to dominate the Judge.

It may be doubted that Justices such as Holmes and Brandeis used their clerks as more than research assistants. Charles Evans Hughes later recalled that, when he was an Associate Justice early in the century, "I kept them busy with dictation, hating to write in longhand," and, referring to research, "whatever was necessary in that line I did myself." Dean Acheson put it more succinctly, in describing his work as a Brandeis clerk, "He wrote the opinion; I wrote the footnotes."

Footnotes, to be sure, may be important parts of the opinions. The outstanding example, of course, is footnote 11 of the 1954 *Brown* school segregation opinion, which listed seven works by social scientists on the baneful psychological effect of segregation. Critics attacked the Court for relying not on law but on "psychological knowledge." As restrained a commentator as James Reston analyzed *Brown* the day after the decision in a *New York Times* column headed "A Sociological Decision."

The controversial footnote, which became a red flag to *Brown* opponents, was entirely the work of a Warren law clerk. In fact, the only change made by the Justices in the clerk's product was a minor one suggested by Justice Clark. In the draft of the *Brown* opinion originally delivered to the Justices, the footnote began with the citation: "Clark, Effect of Prejudice and Discrimination on Personality Development (Midcentury White House Conference on Children and Youth, 1950)." Justice Clark objected that this did not sufficiently identify the Clark who had written the article cited. He did not want people, particularly in his own South, to think that the Court was citing an antisegregation article that he — Tom Clark — had written. He therefore asked that the citation be changed to "K. B. Clark," so that no one would confuse the Justice with the author. In the final opinion, the name of the first author cited appears with initials, as Justice Clark had suggested — the only author in the footnote not identified solely by last name.

The law clerks' role is, however, no longer limited to the writing of footnotes. When he wrote about the use he made of his law clerks, former Justice Hughes worried that, if the clerks were used too much, "it might be thought that they were writing our opinions." That, indeed, is what has happened. In recent years the Justices have given their clerks an ever larger share of responsibility, including even the writing of opinions.

Complaints against the clerks' role have been common, including a noted 1957 article in *U.S. News & World Report* by William H. Rehnquist himself. Rehnquist stated that the Justices were delegating substantial responsibility to their clerks, who "unconsciously" slanted materials to accord with their own views. The result, Rehnquist complained, was that the liberal point of view of the vast majority of the clerks had become the philosophy espoused by the Warren Court.

The situation has, if anything, gotten worse in recent years. "In the United States," notes a 1986 *London Times* article, "judges have 'clerks', i.e., assistants who prepare and frequently write judgments which their masters often merely adopt and which a qualified observer can easily recognize as the work of a beginner."

An even harsher view of the clerk system was expressed by Philip B. Kurland, a leading constitutional scholar, a year after Chief Justice Rehnquist was appointed. As he noted, the law clerks now exercise a major role in the two most important functions of the Justices: (1) the screening of cases to determine which the Court will hear and decide; and (2) the drafting of opinions. "I think," Kurland asserted, "Brandeis would be aghast."

In a public lecture, Justice Stevens conceded that he did not read 80 percent of the certiorari petitions presented to the Court. Instead his clerks prepare memoranda summarizing those cases and issues and recommending whether or not certiorari should be granted. The Justice reads only those where the granting of certiorari is recommended. The only member of the Burger and Rehnquist Courts who personally went over petitions for review was Justice Brennan, who customarily shared the work with his law clerks. In a letter to Brennan, who was temporarily away from the Court, his clerks stated, "We are all fascinated by the certs and shudder to think that when you get back you may take some of them away from us. But if you're very nice we won't fight too hard."

In the 1972 Term, Justice Powell urged that the Justices combine their efforts in the screening process by having their clerks work together in one "cert pool." The certiorari petitions would be divided equally among all the clerks in the pool, and the cert memos prepared by them would be circulated to each of the Justices participating. The Chief Justice and Justices White, Blackmun, Powell, and Rehnquist agreed to join in the cert pool. Justices Douglas, Brennan, Stewart, and Marshall declined to participate. In the present Court, only Justice Stevens is not a member of the pool.

While the Justices make the final decision on what certiorari petitions to grant, *the* work on the petitions is done by the law clerks. In the vast majority of cases, the Justices' knowledge of the petitions and the issues they present is based on the clerks' cert memos, and they normally follow the recommendations in the memos. Sheer volume, if nothing else, has made this the prevailing practice.

The Justices themselves have expressed qualms about this delegation of the screening task. In declining to join the cert pool, Justice Douglas wrote to the Chief Justice: "The law clerks are fine. Most of them are sharp and able. But after all, they have never been confirmed by the Senate."

Some years earlier, Justice Frankfurter wrote to Justice Stewart, "The appraisal and appreciation of a record as a basis for exercising our discretionary jurisdiction is, I do not have to tell you, so dependent on a seasoned and disciplined professional judgment that I do not believe that lads — most of them fresh out of law school and with their present tendentiousness — should have any routine share in the process of disemboweling a record, however acute and stimulating their power of reasoning may be and however tentative and advisory their memos on what is reported in the record and what is relevant to our taking a case may be." Referring to a recent case, he told Stewart, "it is a striking illustration of which I have found many over the years, Term after Term, of the slanted way in which, through compassionate feelings and inexperienced predispositions, these . . . cases are reported to us on the strength of which, so predominantly, action is taken by the court."

An even more important delegation to the clerks involves the opinion-writing process itself. "As the years passed," said Justice Douglas in his *Autobiography*, "it became more evident that the law clerks were drafting opinions." Even the better Justices have made more extensive use of their clerks in the drafting process than outside observers have realized. Justice Frankfurter can be taken as an example. Some of Frankfurter's best-known opinions, notably his now famous dissent in the 1962 case of *Baker v. Carr*, were drafted almost entirely by his clerks. In the 1960 case of *Elkins v. United States*, Frankfurter dissented in an opinion based almost verbatim on a draft by one of his clerks. He then circulated a satiric dialogue criticizing the Court's decision, entitled "Doctor and Student" (in apparent imitation of the classic sixteenth-century work by Christopher St. Germain). A Frankfurter letter indicates that "both . . . the form and substance of Doctor and Student" were the product of another law clerk. The clerk in question, Anthony G. Amsterdam, was exceptionally able and the Justice relied on him extensively. Once he sent back an Amsterdam-prepared draft, with minor corrections in his own hand, with the comment, "If you approve of my revisions send to printer and duly circulate." To an outside observer, this may seem an egregious reversal of the proper roles of Justice and clerk — almost as though the law clerk system was being turned bottom-side up.

Justice Frankfurter himself characteristically expressed doubts about the working of the law clerk system. "I wonder," he wrote to Justice John Marshall Harlan in 1957, "how many who are reversing out of hand in these cases have read the record and not relied merely on the memoranda of their law clerks. And, since my curiosity is very alert this morning, I wonder how many of the law clerks have read the whole record in these cases." In a written note to Harlan a few years later, Frankfurter referred to those who "have mind all made up on basis of law clerk's bench memos, as I see the C.J. reading those bench memos."

Federal appeals Judge Richard A. Posner was even more blunt in a 1985 book "What are these able, intelligent, mostly young people doing? Surely not merely running citations in *Shepard's* and shelving the judge's law books. They are, in many situations, 'para-judges.' In some instances, it is to be feared, they are indeed invisible judges, for there are appellate judges whose literary style appears to change annually."

Chief Justice Rehnquist has candidly described the opinion-writing process. "In my case," Rehnquist said, "the clerks do the first draft of almost all cases to which I have been assigned to write the Court's opinion." Only "when the caseload is heavy" does Rehnquist sometimes "help by doing the first draft of a case myself." Rehnquist concedes that the "practice . . . may undoubtedly . . . cause raised eyebrows." Still, the Chief Justice asserts, "I think the practice is entirely proper: The Justice must retain for himself control not merely of the outcome of the case, but of the explanation of the outcome, and I do not believe this practice sacrifices either."

It is, of course, true that the decisions are made by the Justices — though, even with regard to them, the weaker Justices have abdicated much of their authority to their clerks. In most chambers, the clerks are not, to use a favorite expression of Chief Justice Warren, "unguided missiles." The Justices normally outline the way they want opinions drafted. But the drafting clerk is left with a great deal of discretion. The Justices may, in Rehnquist's phrase, "convey the broad outlines," but they "do not invariably settle exactly how the opinion will be reasoned through." The details of the opinions are left to the clerk, in particular the specific reasoning and research supporting the decision. The technical minutiae and footnotes, which are so dear to the law professor, are left almost completely to the clerks.

To be sure, the Justices themselves go over the drafts, and, said Chief Justice Rehnquist, "I may revise it in toto." But, he also admits, "I may leave it relatively unchanged." Too many of the Justices circulate drafts that are almost wholly the work of their clerks. Some, indeed, do little more than lend their names to their clerks' product. "These days," a recent book sums up the situation, "a Court opinion is probably put together by a clerk, relying mostly on language from earlier opinions. . . . The clerks draft most of the majority and dissenting opinions for most of the justices."

During one Court term, Justice Frank Murphy's law clerks were known in the Court as "Mr. Justice Huddleson" and "Mr. Justice Gressman." "Did you hear," Justice Douglas wrote to Black about a 1946 Murphy dissent, "Frank say Sat[urday] that he did not write the dissent in Mabee but was impressed when he saw it[?]" At about the same time, it used to be said in the Court that Chief Justice Fred M. Vinson did "all his 'writing' with his hands in his pockets."

More recently, a May 1991 memorandum from a Marshall law clerk complained that he was writing several dissents and did not have time for another. The memo suggested that the dissent in the case be given to Justice Blackmun.

There are, it is true, Justices who have the greatest difficulty in writing opinions. "Wouldn't it be nice if we could write the way we think?" lamented Justice Reed in 1941 to his colleague Justice Frankfurter. To which Frankfurter is said to have remarked, "The problem with Stanley is that he doesn't let his law clerks do enough of the work. The trouble with Murphy is that he lets them do too much of the work."

Sometimes, to be sure, Justices have an undeserved reputation of simply rubberstamping their law clerks' work. Thus, Fred Rodell's book on the Court points to Justice Tom C. Clark as a Justice who, "more than any of his brethren, . . . depends on his young fresh-from-law-school assistants to outline and even write his opinions for him." President Harry S. Truman once referred to Clark as "such a dumb son of a bitch. 'He's about the dumbest man I think I've ever run across.' "

To one familiar with Justice Clark's work, the Truman comment is almost ludicrous. Clark may not have been the intellectual equal of his more brilliant Brethren, but he developed into a more competent judge than most people realize. In fact, Clark has been one of the most underrated Justices in recent Supreme Court history. An examination of his Court files at the University of Texas reveals him as anything but dumb. The many drafts of opinions in his own handwriting belie the picture painted by Truman and Rodell.

Even more underrated as an opinion writer was Chief Justice Warren. Now, it is true that Chief Justice Warren's normal practice was to leave the actual drafting of opinions to his law clerks. He would usually outline verbally (though in important cases he would dictate the outline to Mrs. Margaret McHugh, his executive assistant) the way he wanted the opinion drafted. The outline would summarize the facts and how the main issues should be decided. The Chief Justice would rarely go into particulars on the details involved in the case. That was for the clerk drafting the opinion, who was left with a great deal of discretion, particularly on the reasoning and research supporting the decision.

Yet, in important cases, Chief Justice Warren would draft the opinion himself. This was notably true in the landmark *Brown* school segregation case.

It has always been assumed that Warren followed his normal procedure in the *Brown* drafting process. Indeed, the law clerk assigned to *Brown* said that he (the clerk) had prepared the *Brown* draft and described how, after he had been given the assignment, he worked on the draft for about twenty-four hours straight through without sleep.

The original draft of the *Brown* opinion is revealing. Headed simply "Memorandum" and undated, the draft is in Warren's handwriting, in pencil on nine yellow legal-size pages. It is basically similar to the final *Brown* opinion and shows us that the Chief Justice was primarily responsible not only for the unanimous decision, but also for the opinion in the case. The opinion delivered was essentially the opinion produced when Warren himself sat down and put pencil to paper.

In most cases, nevertheless, the drafting process is that recalled by one of Justice Reed's clerks: "The clerk had the first word, and he had the last word." The law clerks' "first word" has had a most unfortunate effect upon the Supreme Court product. Most obviously, it has led to an increase in the length, though plainly not the quality, of opinions. What Justice Douglas once wrote about Court opinions has become increasingly true: "We have tended more and more to write a law-review-type of opinion. They plague the Bar and the Bench. They are so long they are meaningless. They are filled with trivia and nonessentials."

As Justice Ruth Bader Ginsburg noted in a 1994 *New York Times* interview, the law clerks may be "highly intelligent. . . . But most of them are young and in need of the seasoning that experiences in life and in law practice afford." Law clerks have similar academic backgrounds with little other experience. For three years they have had drummed into them that the acme of literary style is the law review article. It is scarcely surprising that the standard opinion style has become that of the student-run reviews: bland and bloodless, prolix, platitudinous, always erring on the side of inclusion, full of lengthy citations and footnotes — and above all dull.

The individual flair that makes the opinions of a Holmes or a Cardozo literary as well as legal gems has become a thing of the past: "these days," states a book on the Rehnquist Court, "no one confuses Court opinions with literature." There is all the difference in the world between writing one's own opinions and reviewing opinions written by someone else. It is hard to see how an editor can be a great judge. Can we really visualize a Holmes or a Cardozo coordinating a team of law clerks and editing their drafts?

According to a federal appellate judge, "We need to reduce our dependence on the system of judicial apprenticeships and on a mass production model that will soon swallow us up." In the Supreme Court, as in most institutions, the balance of power has shifted increasingly to the bureaucrats and away from the nominal heads. The Justices have become the managers of a growing corps of law clerks, who increasingly write the opinions even in the most important cases. The swelling system of judicial apprenticeships threatens to repeat the story of the Sorcerer's Apprentice — though not necessarily with its happy ending.

DRAFTS AND MEMORANDA

After he had assigned the *Webster* opinion to himself, Chief Justice Rehnquist prepared a draft opinion of the Court, which was then printed and circulated to the other Justices. This is the normal procedure in the Court's opinion-writing process. Opinions are drafted in the chambers of the Justices to whom they were assigned and then printed before being sent around to the others for their comments and (hopefully) approvals. The opinions used to be sent to the print shop in the Court's basement, where they were set on hot-lead typesetters, in the type that is so familiar to Supreme Court aficionados. Modern printing technology has, however, now superseded the traditional printing process. In 1980, fifty-five word processors were installed in the Court. First used only for drafting opinions in the Justices' chambers, they soon took over the opinion-writing process. As described in *Congressional Quarterly's Guide to the U.S. Supreme Court,* "hot lead was dead and the draft opinions were circulated, revised, and printed on the computerized typesetting system."

Supreme Court decisions are, of course, determined by a majority of the Justices participating in a case. The Justices, as previously seen, indicate their votes during their conference discussions and the Chief Justice states his tally, as he has recorded it, at the end of the discussion. But conference votes are by no means etched in gold. They are tentative until the Court's decision and the opinion explaining it are announced. "It frequently happens," stated Justice Jackson during oral argument in the famous 1952 Steel Seizure case, "I myself have changed my opinion after reading opinions of the other members of this Court. And I am as stubborn as most. But I sometimes wind up not voting the way I voted in conference because the reasons of the majority didn't satisfy me."

The Justice assigned the opinion sends a draft to the other Justices for their comments and suggestions. The circulation of draft opinions dates from the beginning of this century. Such circulation, originally in carbon copies and now in computer printer copies, plays a crucial part in the decision process. It enables the other Justices to participate directly in the opinion-writing process, through their suggestions to the opinion writer or, if need be, by circulating their own opinions concurring in or dissenting from the draft Court opinion. At this stage, Justices are still free to switch their votes and often do so or threaten to do so in order to induce the opinion writer to follow their views.

Justice Brennan has told how the postdraft process works — though not always to secure the decision he favored: "I converted more than one proposed majority into a dissent before the final decision was announced. I have also, however, had the more satisfying experience of rewriting a dissent as a majority opinion for the Court."

Outside observers do not appreciate the importance of the Court's postdraft process. In a significant number of cases, the circulation of drafts leads to a change in votes or modification of the drafts to meet criticisms. Thus, in a May 22, 1989, letter to Justice Blackmun, Justice Stevens wrote, "Although I voted the other way at Conference and was asked by Bill Brennan to prepare a dissent, your opinion sent me back to the brief and I am now persuaded that you have the better of the argument. I therefore expect to join you."

Similarly, on June 13, 1988, Justice Scalia wrote to Justice White, who had circulated a draft opinion of the Court, "After struggling with this case, and drafting a heckofa dissent, I have concluded that you are right."

On the other hand, the joining Justice may be less certain. A January 12, 1988, "Dear Nino" letter from Chief Justice Rehnquist states, "Your opinion in this case may not have me convinced, but it assuredly has me 'snowed.' Please join me."

At other times, the pressure of the caseload may prevent a Justice from expressing his true views publicly. On May 26, 1988, Justice Blackmun wrote to Justice Brennan about the latter's draft opinion of the Court, "At conference I voted the other way. Although I remain somewhat uneasy and see problems down the road, I shall not write in dissent. Therefore, please join me. This, I suppose, is what Charlie Whittaker used to call his 'graveyard dissent.' " No one but the Justices knew that Blackmun did not agree with the opinion which he had joined.

Sometimes, the give-and-take between the Justices results in what a Justice has termed a "deluge of memoranda," which in turn may lead to a deluge of drafts, as the opinion writer tries to meet the suggestions in the Justices' responses to his draft. In the *Swann* school busing case to be discussed in Chapter 6, Chief Justice Burger had to circulate seven drafts before he could secure a majority to join his opinion. Justice Stevens had to write a similar number of drafts in the 1990 *Hodgson* case discussed in Chapter 1.

Webster illustrates the postdraft decision process in operation. The Rehnquist draft would have effectively overruled *Roe v. Wade,* even if it did not do so expressly. The Justices responded by bombarding Chief Justice Rehnquist with letters and memoranda objecting to the draft opinion. In the end, the Chief Justice lost his majority and had to speak only for a plurality which could not cast *Roe* into limbo.

In the *Swann* case, rejection of Chief Justice Burger's draft opinion of the Court had proceeded to the point of a substitute opinion being drafted in a memorandum by Justice Stewart to reflect the majority consensus which the Burger draft had refused to follow. That consensus was in favor of affirming the broad desegregation order issued by the district court, including its provision for school busing. Chief Justice Burger had, however, written a draft which upheld the limitations that the court of appeals had imposed upon the district court's busing order. Despite objections from the other Justices, the Chief Justice had persisted in his view in a second draft opinion.

At this point, the Justices who strongly supported affirmance of the busing order—notably Justices Douglas and Brennan—persuaded Justice Stewart to prepare a draft dissent which ended, "I would therefore affirm the District Court." This set the stage for a confrontation between the Chief Justice and those who favored a clear affirmance of the district court. In the Stewart draft the latter had an opinion that could easily be converted from a draft dissent into the opinion of the Court. If he persisted in the restricted approach taken in his two drafts, Chief Justice Burger risked losing his Court and having his effort to author the *Swann* opinion completely frustrated. That eventuality did not take place because, as a law clerk put it, "the C.J. evidently got wind of the developments, mainly that there was rapidly developing a solid Court for affirming [the district court]."

To understand what happened here, one must distinguish between the Supreme Court as it appears to the outside world and to those who participate in its decision process. The Court has always had a deserved reputation for preserving the confidentiality of its nonpublic proceedings. As far as the press and the public are concerned, the postargument stage in the Court is completely closed. The sole knowledge those outside the Court have about a case after oral argument is obtained from the announcement of the decision and the opinions filed by the Justices. Only those privy to the Court's internal workings are aware that the published opinions may not give anything like a true picture of the Court's decision process.

Internally, however, the Court building is a hotbed of gossip and rumor. Among the law clerks particularly, there is constant scuttlebutt that keeps the clerks and their Justices abreast of the latest developments in the give-and-take between the Justices. The Court's rumor mills may not grind slowly, but they do grind faithfully. Through them, Chief Justice Burger was soon made aware of the Stewart memorandum and the threat it posed to his own leadership in the *Swann* case.

When the Chief Justice learned that a majority was starting to form behind the Stewart draft, he realized that he would have to change his own draft substantially or lose hope of being the *Swann* opinion writer. The first thing to do, of course, was to head off the Stewart draft and prevent it from becoming the opinion of the Court. To accomplish this, Chief Justice Burger himself went to the Stewart chambers. He told the Justice that he had independently concluded that the district court had to be affirmed. He also said that he would use more of Stewart's language in his next draft of the opinion of the Court.

Justice Stewart's reaction was described by the same law clerk: "P.S. now felt that he had been completely boxed in and that if the C.J. circulated a draft affirming he would have to join." That is, indeed, what happened. The Chief Justice circulated a new draft affirming the district court and it eventually was joined by a unanimous Court, since it gave the Justices what they wanted most—an express affirmance of the district court.

Webster and *Swann* are of course unusual cases, since, as previously stated, it is rare for a Chief Justice to be so rebuffed by his colleagues. But the cases do illustrate the working of the postargument decision process and the crucial role played by draft opinions and the Justices' response to them. It is in the give-and-take of views following circulation of the draft opinion that the language of the final opinion is developed. The Justices respond to the draft with objections and suggestions which the opinion writer must meet if he is to secure a majority.

In *Webster* and *Swann,* the objections voiced by the Justices had to do with basic issues of constitutional law on which the majority was unwilling to give way. In other cases, suggestions may have to do with matters of style. Sometimes they may involve nothing more important than the vanity of the Justice concerned. In *Shapiro v. Thompson* (1969), the Brennan opinion of the Court struck down a one-year residence requirement for welfare assistance because it infringed upon the constitutionally guaranteed right to travel. Justice Stewart told Justice Brennan that he would join the opinion if he would delete the draft's analysis of the sources of the right to travel. Stewart said that he thought it sufficed to quote from his own opinion in the 1966 case of *United States v. Guest* on the issue. Brennan readily agreed to the Stewart changes.

At times a Justice may ask for semantic changes. In May 1963, Justice Harlan wrote to Justice Arthur J. Goldberg that he would join a Goldberg opinion if the word "desegregation" was substituted for "integration" in the opinion. " 'Integration,' " Harlan pointed out, "brings blood to Southerners' eyes for they think that 'desegregation' means just that—'integration.' I do not think that we ought to use the word in our opinions." A few years later, Justice Stewart objected to language in Justice Abe Fortas's draft opinion in *Tinker v. Des Moines School District* (1969), where the Court upheld the right of students to wear black armbands to protest the Vietnam conflict. "At the risk of appearing eccentric," Stewart wrote, "I shall not join any opinion that speaks of what is going on in Vietnam as a 'war.' " Fortas made the necessary changes so that the opinion referred to "the hostilities in Vietnam."

Similarly, in a November 19, 1990, letter to Justice Kennedy, the author of a draft opinion, Chief Justice Rehnquist made a suggestion which, he stated, was "probably a matter of style, rather than of substance." Rehnquist wrote, "I am somewhat put off by the first part of the second sentence of part IV on page 26, where you say 'we act as a front line of defense against state taxes which. . . .' If you insist on a metaphor, it seems to me that the proper figure of speech would be 'back stop' rather than 'front line of defense.' We are, after all, a Court of 'last' resort!"

Sometimes a draft may encounter objections because of its tone. Thus, in the 1991 case of *McCleskey v. Zant,* Justice Marshall circulated a draft dissent that began: "Today's decision departs so drastically from the norms that inform the proper judicial function that it can be characterized only as lawless." At this Justice Stevens wrote, on April 3, 1991, "Even though I agree that the majority's holding is outrageous, I wonder if the word 'lawless' is not too strong in the first sentence of your opinion." Stevens went on, "I am with you even if you do not make the change, but I think in the long run it might be prudent to do so." Justice Marshall replied the same day: "I took out the word 'lawless' within a minute after I received your note."

In the recent Court, Justice Blackmun was perhaps the most meticulous in his insistence upon proper draft phraseology. "I might as well take this opportunity," he wrote to Justice Scalia on August 27, 1991, "to make my annual tirade against the abuse of the kindly word 'parameter.' I have stated before that I shall join no opinion in which that mathematical term is employed. I feel much the same about 'viable,' but I have lost that battle here. The medical profession must suffer silently. But I shall fight the good fight of the mathematician about 'parameter.' "

Another time Justice Blackmun sent a November 24, 1989, letter after he had read a Marshall draft: "I am inclined to join your dissent, but I wonder about the continuous use of the female adjective and pronoun. . . . The defendant, after all, is a male. . . . I realize I am old-fashioned, but I suspect I have not joined the ultra-feminist movement to that extent."

An interesting Blackmun request for a change is contained in a June 6, 1988, letter on a Marshall draft opinion of the Court: "I must confess that I would feel easier if on page 6 the reference to the possibility of a suit for legal malpractice were eliminated. We really do not know whether the lawyer was possibly guilty of malpractice. Also — although I may be a little soft in the head — the lawyer was blind and has that to contend with."

The draft author, to be sure, will not always agree with suggested changes. The result then may have to be a compromise if the draft is to be accepted. The give-and-take here is illustrated by a December 21, 1988, letter from Justice Scalia to Justice White, to whom Scalia had suggested modifications in a draft that White had written: "Though I would much prefer the precise changes I suggested, four votes are even more clearly better than one than they are better than three, so I will join with the alterations you propose."

Of course, the draft writer may take offense at suggested alterations, particularly where they are more than stylistic. After he had received a draft criticizing his own draft from Justice Blackmun, Justice Stevens wrote back on June 27, 1989, "your [draft] is rather misleading. . . . You are usually more careful about the use of words of art." Justice Blackmun replied the same day, "I seem to have ruffled your feathers. One always regrets that, and I certainly do this time."

Sometimes the criticism of an opinion may be harsh. A striking example is contained in a 1964 Frankfurter-Harlan letter on the White opinion of the Court in *McLaughlin v. Florida,* which struck down a statute making it a crime for "any white man and negro woman, who are not married to each other [to] habitually live in and occupy in the nighttime the same room." This law was part of a chapter entitled "Adultery and Fornication," but, according to Justice White, "it is the only one [in the chapter] which does not require proof of intercourse along with the other elements of the crime."

At this Justice Frankfurter wrote, asking whether Justice White was "such a man of the world that he does not know that when a couple cohabit, I don't know for how long they did so in the Florida case they certainly fornicated. Indeed the only definition the Oxford Dictionary gives for cohabit is to live together as husband and wife in short being married and has he never heard of Taft C.J.'s famous sentence that what everybody knows judges are also supposed to know."

In a footnote, Frankfurter asked, "or did the whizzer assume they [cohabited] to read Plato's Dialogue to one another ????? in the original."

Even more biting was Justice Thurgood Marshall's comment on Justice Rehnquist's dissent in *Wallace v. Jaffree* (1985), which purported to show that all of the Court's decisions on the Establishment Clause of the First Amendment were based upon what Rehnquist termed "a mistaken understanding of constitutional history." More specifically, the Rehnquist dissent concluded that the settled Supreme Court jurisprudence on the clause was wholly contrary to the original intention of the framers of the First Amendment.

It is fair to say that virtually all historians have concluded that the Rehnquist constitutional history in *Jaffree* is completely wrong. Justice Marshall's comment on the matter was typically pithy and even more pointed. In the margin of his copy of the draft Rehnquist dissent circulated on January 30, 1985, Marshall wrote in red pencil: "Unadulterated B.S.!"

The Justices at times attempt to soften their criticism of a circulated draft with an attempt at humor. On June 18, 1991, Justice Stevens wrote to Justice Scalia after he had read the latter's draft dissent in a voting-rights case, "Sherlock Holmes, accompanied by a large, menacingly silent dog, has just paid me a visit. He wanted me to tell him how you found out that the 1982 Amendments to the Voting Rights Act were adopted in response to our decision in City of Mobile. Despite his inherently coercive interrogation, I refused to bark. The legislative history is still safely hidden in a locked cabinet."

In a June 19, 1991, letter, Justice Blackmun playfully replied to a Scalia draft criticizing a Blackmun opinion: "Questa scalata non è degna di un Scalia. Scendi e vedrai piu chiaro." (Such a climb is not worthy of a Scalia. Come down and see more clearly.) Justice Scalia is, of course, the first Justice of Italian ancestry.

DECISIONS AND OPINIONS

When Justices agree to a draft opinion, they send notes containing phrases such as "Join me" or "I agree." Justice Clark, whose flamboyant bow tie (worn even under the judicial robe) gave him a perpetual sophomoric appearance, always continued to flaunt his Texas background — his normal way of signifying agreement to an opinion was to write "Okey." On the other hand, Justice O'Connor simply wrote to Justice Scalia, author of the 1991 bus search opinion, "Me too."

If the draft opinion is joined by a majority of the Justices, it is ready to come down as the opinion of the Court — as soon as all other opinions in the case are finished. The tradition is that the Justices have as much time as they need to make up their minds finally and to write any concurring or dissenting opinions. Some Justices are noted in the Court for their slowness in deciding and writing opinions. In the Burger and Rehnquist Courts this was particularly true of Justice Blackmun, whom the others often compared to Justice Charles E. Whittaker, whose indecisiveness had been legend on the Warren Court.

There are times, of course, when the others desire a speedy decision and seek to prod the dilatory Justice. In the 1978 *Bakke* case on the constitutionality of affirmative-action programs, Justice Blackmun's failure to vote and write his separate opinion held up the decision for months. The Chief Justice went to see Blackmun, but the latter simply told him that he was not yet ready to vote. There was nothing further that Burger could do to speed up the tardy Justice. When he finally made up his mind and circulated his draft opinion, Blackmun included a May 1, 1978, memo expressing appreciation for "the patience of each and all of you." The case, the Justice wrote, "is of such importance that I refused to be drawn to a precipitate conclusion. I wanted the time to think about it and to study the pertinent material. . . . I do not apologize; I merely explain."

The attempt to pressure a Justice often leads to resentment among the Justices. In *Baker v. Carr,* the Warren Court's famous 1962 legislative-apportionment case, the decision was held up for weeks while the Court waited for an expected Clark dissent. Finally, on March 2, 1962, Justice Douglas sent around a memorandum: "I hope we can get No. 6 — *Baker v. Carr* down March 19th. This is an election year. If the lower court is to have an opportunity to act, the case should be disposed of soon." Douglas said that otherwise the case would be decided so late "that we [would be] powerless to act. I am sure there is no one here who wants to produce that result. But we should not drift into that situation."

The Douglas memo upset the others. Though no one was happy at Justice Clark's delay, they thought he had the right not to be pressed while he made up his mind. More important, the delay enabled Clark to think through his posture on the case. In the end, he switched his vote, changed his dissent to a concurrence, and converted a split decision into a six-Justice majority.

In view of his memo attempting to speed up the *Baker v. Carr* decision process, it is ironic that Justice Douglas himself was the object of a similar attempt by Justice Black in an earlier dispute over justice allegedly too long delayed. The case was *Fortson v. Morris* (1966), where election of the Georgia governor by the State Assembly, since no candidate had received a majority of the popular vote, was at issue. After the case was argued on December 5, Justice Black circulated a memo urging a decision on the next decision day, December 12 (the next scheduled decision day after that would be January 9). That was necessary, Black wrote, "to avoid keeping Georgia in this state of uncertainty." In a scrawled note to Justice Brennan the same day, Black wrote, "I feel that the Court will be negligent in its duty if the case does not go down. A STATE is entitled to know what it can do and not left suspended in mid air."

On December 7, Justice Douglas sent around a Memorandum to the Conference, strongly objecting to "Brother Black's memorandum urging that we get the opinions in this case down at the earliest possible moment." Douglas wrote that, if Black's proposal for decision by December 12 was adopted, there would not be enough time to write adequate opinions.

"There is one possible advantage," the Douglas memo asserted, "in getting the opinions down quickly in cases like this—that is, it forecloses any possibility of any member of the Court changing his mind. But the issue is a close one in the minds of the Court, a five to four vote indicating the narrowest of margins by which we make the decision. And I think that in itself argues for a more deliberate slow speed rather than a deliberate fast one."

The Douglas memo evoked a waspish response from Black, who answered with his own December 7 Memorandum for the Conference. It asserted, "It is impossible for me to believe that it would take any member of this Court a whole month to write out his dissenting views, whether he does so at a 'deliberate slow speed' or at a 'deliberate fast one.' " Justice Black referred to the difficulties that delay would present to the state. "To keep the State in doubt as to whether the Assembly will elect or whether provision must be made for one or more new elections means that the whole government of the State of Georgia must be at a standstill. The old Governor will not know when he goes out or under what circumstances a new Governor can come in."

Justice Black asserted, "Georgia should not be put in this unhappy predicament on the unsupported and, I believe, unsupportable assumption that it may take some member of this Court a month to write his views." Then Black took a sly dig at his quondam ally. "Brother Douglas says he 'would like time to work further on it [his opinion] beyond this week.' But he does not say that he wants or needs an extra month, and it is inconceivable that he does, in view of his well-known speed in writing all his opinions." The Black memo ended with unusually cutting language:

Finally, Brother Douglas' reason for saying we should wait a month is that some member of the present majority might change his mind and vote Brother Douglas' way—that is, to affirm. How long should Georgia be kept in ignorance of its constitutional power and have its machinery paralyzed on the hope that one of the present majority of five could be persuaded in some manner to reverse his vote? Members of this Court certainly are sufficiently mature to decide for themselves whether they need more time to announce their votes. Five have already indicated they need no more time by voting to reverse this case *now*. Whatever questionable reason there may be for waiting a few more days to announce this decision, Brother Douglas advances none whatsoever for keeping Georgia in doubt for an entire month.

As it turned out, the decision did come down on December 12 — as Justice Black had urged. But it did so, not because of Black's pressure, but because the others were ready by that date. As the Blackmun reaction to the *Bakke* pressure shows, it is ultimately up to the individual Justice to decide when finally to decide a case and issue any opinions explaining his vote. Justice Douglas put it succinctly in an October 23, 1961, Memorandum to the Conference, "When opinions have jelled, the case is handed down. When jelling is not finished, the case is held."

When the Justices' "opinions have jelled" and the decision in a case is ready to come down, it is formally announced in the ornate courtroom. The tradition of public announcement of decisions antedates the Constitution and has been followed since the first decision of the Supreme Court in 1792. As already stated, for over a century decisions were announced on Mondays. Decision Mondays ended in June 1958, when Chief Justice Warren began the present practice of delivering opinions when they are ready, rather than only on Mondays. Even outside the Court, not all considered the alteration a sign of progress. The *New York Times* believed that newspaper reporters had always admired the Court precisely because of its refusal to arrange its work for the convenience of the press.

When the decision is announced by the Court, the opinions are also made public. The Chief Justice asks the Justice who wrote the Court's opinion to announce the decision. Thus, on the morning of June 27, 1978, Chief Justice Burger leaned forward and stated to the hushed courtroom that Justice Powell would deliver the judgment of the Court in No. 76-811, *Regents of the University of California v. Bakke.*

The Justice who wrote the Court opinion announces the Court's decision, and the Justices who wrote concurring or dissenting opinions may state their views as well. It is up to the individual opinion writer whether to read the opinion, or summarize it, or simply to announce the result and state that a written opinion has been filed.

Decision days are among the most dramatic events in Supreme Court history. Few occasions have been more momentous than decision day in *Brown v. Board of Education.* Chief Justice Warren read the unanimous opinion striking down school segregation to a courtroom permeated with tension. The Warren tone may have been colorless, but his voice sounded a clarion for the civil-rights movement that was to transform the American society.

Similarly, in the *Swann* school busing case, Chief Justice Burger made what *Newsweek* termed "by far the most momentous Court pronouncement on school segregation since the landmark Brown decision of 1954." Much of the drama was, however, lacking, because Burger did not follow the practice of his predecessor in reading opinions. Instead, the standard Burger procedure was simply to announce the judgment with no elaboration or summary. At the time of *Swann,* Burger had not departed so fully from the prior practice. The Chief Justice announced *Swann* by briefly summarizing the opinion and stating the judgment.

As the Justice who wrote the Court opinion announces the decision and reads or summarizes the opinion, the impression is that of a virtuoso performance. But the opinion writer is, as Justice Frankfurter once put it, "not singing a solo." Our analysis of the *Webster* decision process shows that the final opinion is the result of a cooperative process. In the given case, in fact, the "orchestra" may contribute as much as, if not more than, the solo performer. All this, to be sure, remains hidden behind the red velour curtain. As far as those in the crowded courtroom were concerned, the *Webster* opinions delivered were the only Court products in the case. The reality, we saw, was different. The Chief Justice had written a far-reaching draft but could not lead a majority to agree to an opinion of the Court stating his view of the case. A strong Chief Justice can, however, often do what Chief Justice Rehnquist failed to accomplish in *Webster.* The next two chapters present ample materials to illustrate this point.

3

The Chief Leads the Court

After Earl Warren received a phone call on September 30, 1953, telling him that he was being appointed Chief Justice, he immediately wired his appreciation to President Dwight D. Eisenhower for "your designation of me to be Chief Justice of the Supreme Court." Warren made a common error here in referring to his new office. By October 3, when he sent in his letter of resignation as California Governor, Warren had the title straight. He was to become "Chief Justice of the United States." He would not only preside over the Supreme Court but would also be the head of the federal judicial system. For his additional duties, he would be paid five hundred dollars more than the eight Associate Justices.

In the Supreme Court's decision process, the Chief Justice can be a leader, but not a dictator. As administrative chief of the Court, and, even more so, of the federal judicial system, his power is greater than that over the Court's decision process — though, as will be seen, it, too, is not unlimited.

ADMINISTRATIVE CHIEF

As executive officer of the Court, the Chief Justice is primarily responsible for the internal functioning of that tribunal. The administrative details connected with the working of the Court are within the Chief Justice's control. At times, that control extends to petty details that some might think are beneath the attention of the highest judicial officer. Chief Justice Burger, for example, personally undertook the redecoration of the Supreme Court cafeteria and personally helped choose the glassware and china. He also redesigned the Court bench, changing it from a traditional straight bench to a "winged," or half-hexagon shape.

When he assumed his position, Chief Justice Burger was dismayed to find that his Supreme Court office was smaller than the one he had had as a judge on the federal court of appeals. Next door was the elegant conference room, which could serve admirably as a ceremonial office for the Court head. Burger did not go so far as to take over the conference room; instead, he placed an old desk in the room and moved the conference table to one side. Thus the conference room also became the Chief Justice's reception room.

The Burger use of the conference room irritated the others. Justice Hugo Black's wife noted in her diary that she was told "that C.J. Burger had decided to take the *Conference* Room for *his office!* Funny thing. Isn't that a kick! Hugo says he will not quarrel with him about such an insignificant matter but John Harlan called from Connecticut and was red-hot about it." In the end, however, Chief Justice Burger had his way; neither Justice Harlan nor any of the others saw fit to challenge the conference room takeover.

There are times, to be sure, when seemingly minor administrative details may have great symbolic significance. Chief Justice Warren used to recall that, when he first arrived in 1953, the Court had separate washrooms for Negroes. One of the first things he did was to eliminate the discrimination that was taking place right in the Court building itself.

It is hard for us today to realize the extent to which Jim Crow pervaded the highest Court less than half a century ago. At that time, the Justices and Court staff, except for menial employees, had always been white. In 1947, the law clerks wanted to give a Christmas party, inviting black employees. When Chief Justice Vinson discovered this, he brought the matter up before the conference. At least one of the Justices, Stanley Reed, said that he would not attend if the blacks were invited. When he was told, according to Justice Frankfurter's diary, that that would place the Court in a "terrible position . . . after all the noble utterances of the Court publicly against racial discrimination," Justice Reed said, "This is purely a private matter and I can do what I please in regard to private parties." Frankfurter interjected, "the very fact that we have been sitting here for nearly an hour discussing the right to hold the party makes it difficult to regard it as purely private. The Court is entangled no matter what way you look at it." The proposed Christmas party was quietly shelved.

But even the most conservative institution must adapt to changing conditions. After the ringing affirmation of racial equality in its *Brown* decision, the Court could no more continue the color line than it could maintain its separate white and black washrooms. In July 1954, the Court secured its first black page. A month later, Justice Frankfurter wrote to Chief Justice Warren, "It will interest you as much as it did me that the significance of the appointment of a Negro page should be noted abroad," and he enclosed a clipping on the matter from a London periodical. During the Warren tenure, the Court color line was further breached with the hiring of a number of black secretaries and law clerks (the first of the latter had been named by Justice Frankfurter in the 1948 Term).

Then, with Thurgood Marshall's appointment as a Justice in 1967, the Court itself became integrated.

Eight years earlier, the Court had given way on the annual party. At the end of 1959, the *New York Times* reported that "one of the last institutions holding out against the Christmas party succumbed last week," as the Court held its first such affair. This time, there was no question of whether the entire staff should be invited. Five of the Justices (Black, Frankfurter, Douglas, Brennan, and Stewart) were there. The others were not in Washington during the holiday recess. Then, in the 1963 Term, Chief Justice Warren ended a tradition of almost two centuries when he had the pages don long trousers and single-breasted jackets.

A more important Warren innovation was aimed at the one great defect of the Supreme Court's ornate courtroom. The chamber is a particularly handsome room, whose overpowering dignity befits the highest bench in the land. The room itself is as big as a basketball court, but there was no acoustical system in the place. Early in 1954, the *New York Times* reported, "Chief Justice Warren has come up with an astonishing idea. He thinks the members of the Court should be able to hear each other and be heard by lawyers . . . [so] the new Chief Justice has had the place wired for sound." Microphones were placed before each Justice, and a tape recorder installed to take down oral arguments.

Justice Frankfurter characteristically opposed the new sound system, insisting it would make the Justices too conscious of the audience. Frankfurter could, however, be contentious whenever alterations in the Court's procedure were proposed. In 1947, Chief Justice Vinson had proposed a change in the order of procedure on opinion day, so that admissions to the Supreme Court Bar, which allows lawyers to practice before the Court, would be the first order of business, with reading of opinions to follow. Vinson had acted as a courtesy to Senators and Congressmen, who had complained of having to wait for the completion of the opinions before presenting their constituents for admission. According to Justice Frankfurter's diary, "When it came to my turn I spoke somewhat at length on the importance of not breaking with a tradition that is as old as the Court, that tradition, particularly in this disordered world, which is a fragile fabric, should be adhered to as one of the greatest social forces of justice unless change is called for in the interest of the administration of justice. . . . I asked the Conference to think twice and thrice before disobeying the injunction, 'Remove not the ancient landmarks of thy Fathers.' "

To Justice Frankfurter, the prominence given to the admission of attorneys by the Vinson procedure change may have seemed misplaced. Others, too, have considered the personal admissions a waste of time. Under Chief Justice Warren's lead, the Court did not share these sentiments. Warren always stressed the importance of the admission ceremony. He used to say that the average lawyer would never have any opportunity to argue a case before the Supreme Court. The only experience he would ever have with the Court would be his admission to the Court Bar and he would consider that the pinnacle of his career. As Chief Justice, Warren said, he had the obligation to make that person feel accepted by the Court. That was why he would take the time personally to greet every applicant. "Every newly admitted attorney," reported *Newsweek* in 1955, "gets a smile" from the Chief Justice. Warren always thought that the admission ceremony was one of the most important means by which he could help humanize the Court's operation.

Warren's successor may have been miscast in the role of leader of the Court. In fact, Chief Justice Burger was more effective as a court administrator and as a representative of the federal courts before Congress than as a molder of Supreme Court jurisprudence. Looking back at the Warren years, Justice Byron R. White said to me that, as far as relations with Congress were concerned, "Things have changed . . . for the better as far as I can see. . . . Chief Justice Warren did have such a problem with the civil rights thing, and with prayers and reapportionment. Congress was in such a terrible stew that his name was mud [there], which rubbed off on all of us." Under Chief Justice Burger the situation was different. Few Chief Justices had better relations with Capitol Hill.

As for court administration, Chief Justice Burger played a more active role than any Court head since Chief Justice William Howard Taft. His administrative efforts ranged from efforts at fundamental changes, such as his active support of the creation of a new court of appeals to screen cases that the Supreme Court would consider, to attention to such petty details as the shape of the bench.

In addition, Chief Justice Burger was more effective than his predecessors as administrative head of the federal judiciary. The Chief Justice is not only the executive head of the Supreme Court. As David O'Brien points out in his book on the Court, "Over fifty statutes confer additional administrative duties, ranging from serving as chairman of the Judicial Conference and of the Board of the Federal Judicial Center to supervising the Administrative Office of the U.S. Courts and serving as chancellor of the Smithsonian Institute."

One Chief Justice, Harlan F. Stone, was virtually overwhelmed by the increase in administrative duties. Shortly before his death in 1946, Stone replied to a request by President Truman to assume an additional administrative responsibility. "Few are aware," Stone wrote, "that neither my predecessor, nor I . . . , have been able to meet the daily demands upon us without working nights and holidays and Sundays. The administrative duties of the Chief Justice have increased, and many other duties have been imposed on him by acts of Congress which my predecessors were not called on to perform."

The same year Justice Black reconciled himself for not being appointed to succeed Stone by pointing out, in a letter to Justice Sherman Minton, "The administrative work of the Chief Justice is a very heavy burden, and while I could perform it if I were compelled to do so, it is not the kind of task which adds glamour to the position."

The consolation, if there is one, is that, as administrative chief of the federal judicial system, the Chief Justice is not acting as head of the highest court. As Merlo J. Pusey stated in his biography of Chief Justice Hughes, "The Supreme Court could be left entirely out of the picture."

This does not mean, to be sure, that the Chief Justice will always get his own way in running the federal judiciary. In 1969, Justice Abe Fortas was forced to resign because of the disclosure that he had received a substantial fee from the family foundation of a financier later convicted of securities fraud. The Fortas imbroglio, as well as a milder controversy over the receipt by Justice Douglas of a $12,000-a-year fee from a foundation financed in large part by income from gambling, led Chief Justice Warren to urge restrictions on the outside activities of federal judges. Largely under the Chief Justice's pressure, the Judicial Conference (the governing body for the federal courts, headed by the Chief Justice) adopted strict rules of judicial conduct, including a code of ethics, rules requiring broad financial disclosure, and restraints on income from off-the-bench activities. The new rules did not apply to the Supreme Court, which alone has the power to prescribe rules for its members. Warren had told the Conference that the severe curbs on the lower federal judges would help him persuade the Supreme Court to go along with similar restrictions.

It was reported in the press that the new rules were resented by many federal judges, who felt that the Chief Justice had rammed them through the Judicial Conference. But even a strong Chief Justice such as Warren could not accomplish the same in the Supreme Court, where the Chief Justice is only the first among equals. At the June 13, 1969, conference, Warren moved that the Court formally adopt rules of conduct similar to those that now applied to the lower federal courts. The majority rejected the Warren proposal and the conference decided to defer further consideration until the new 1969 Term—that is, after Warren's retirement had finally taken effect. Under the new Chief Justice, the Justices did nothing about the matter. Indeed, without Warren there, the Judicial Conference itself felt free, at the beginning of November, to suspend the new rules for lower-court judges as too strict.

COURT CARS, TELEVISION, AND ADMINISTRATIVE DETAILS

Before Earl Warren became Chief Justice, neither he nor any of the Justices had an official car at his disposal. One night, he had his secretary call for a limousine to attend a White House dinner. Mrs. Warren protested that it was a needless extravagance, but he insisted that it would not be appropriate for the Chief Justice to call on the President in a taxicab. When they were told the car had arrived, they were shocked to find that it was a station wagon, with large lettering: WASHINGTON NATIONAL AIRPORT. The driver said they had thought the rental was for the airport, and this car had been used in order to take care of the baggage. It was too late to make other arrangements (and, besides, they would have had to pay in any case), so they went to the White House in it.

The arrival of the Chief Justice in the airport wagon created quite a stir in official Washington. Soon thereafter, the Chairman of the Senate Appropriations Committee added to an appropriations bill an amendment to provide the Chief Justice with an official car. It passed without discussion. Except for the White House incident, Warren later wrote, "I doubt that I would ever have had a government vehicle."

Though the Chief Justice has thus had an official car since Warren's day, the same has not been true of the Associate Justices. They have had to use their own vehicles for transportation. The practice developed for "home-to-office" transportation by Court car, to be provided where the Justice was without private transportation. In 1986, just after Chief Justice Rehnquist took office, Congress passed a law that, in the words of a November 20, 1986, memo prepared for the new Chief Justice, "undercuts the Court's authority to provide home to work transportation."

It is almost ludicrous that the Justices of our highest court, with their ever increasing workload, should have to spend time on such a matter. Nevertheless, the Chief Justice scheduled discussion of "the question of 'home to office' transportation" at the November 26 conference and a committee of Justices White, Marshall, and Scalia was appointed to investigate and report. Their report, sent to the conference December 4 for discussion the next day, recommended "that the Court seek to obtain corrective legislation expressly authorizing home-work transportation." The report also stated, "The Committee recommends *against* seeking the views of the Attorney General or the Comptroller General. Such recourse seems beneath the dignity of this Court."

Instead of seeking the recommended legislation, Chief Justice Rehnquist tried to resolve the matter himself. On January 9, 1987, the Chief Justice wrote to the Court Marshal, "It has been called to my attention that there may be occasions on which a member of the Court is without regular transportation by private automobile from home to office and may require the furnishing of transportation by Court car in order to attend Court business." Rehnquist gave the example of a Justice whose car was out of commission. "On such occasions," the Rehnquist letter stated, "I believe the statute discussed in my earlier memorandum allows Court cars to be used for this purpose, and I authorize you to make them available."

The Chief Justice's resolution proved acceptable. A September 17, 1987, Rehnquist memo informed the Justices, "After some rather lengthy negotiations I have received a copy of a memorandum from Senator Proxmire, directed to the Chairmen of the appropriate Senate and House committees, concluding that it would be proper for me to allow the resumption of our practice in providing home-to-office transportation for Justices that existed prior to the enactment of H. R. 3614 last October." The Chief Justice gave his opinion that "this is the best we can do for now. Therefore, effective Monday, September 21st, I authorize the use of Court vehicles to transport Bill, Thurgood, and Harry from home to office and return."

A few years later, in a July 26, 1991, letter to Justice Marshall, Chief Justice Rehnquist summarized what he called "the brouhaha we had about use of Court cars shortly after I became Chief Justice five years ago." As the Chief Justice put it, "the key to Congressional authorization for that use is the concept of 'official business.' At that time, the dispute was whether home-to-office transportation constituted 'official business.' . . . because of an arrangement I made with Senator Proxmire . . . we were allowed to designate home-to-office transportation as official business where there was good reason for a Justice not to drive himself."

In the Court's actual operation, the Justices do have to deal with many other matters not directly connected with the decision process. Thus, they have had to concern themselves with security problems. A January 25, 1991, memorandum from the Court Marshal states, "In view of the present Mid-East situation and world-wide threats of terrorism, I have been requested to re-emphasize our previous reminders concerning one's personal security." The memo emphasized the problems of letter and package bombs and outlined precautions for the Justices to take. An earlier memo, on March 17, 1988, noted 122 personal threats against Justices during the previous year and urged security measures "on out of town trips."

Among the most important administrative decisions made by recent Chief Justices have been those refusing to allow broadcasters in the Courtroom. Chief Justice Warren's posture on the matter is shown by an anecdote related by Fred W. Friendly. After Friendly had been appointed president of CBS News, he met Warren at a 1964 cocktail party. The Chief Justice wished Friendly well in his new job. In thanking the Chief Justice, Friendly said he hoped that he would still head CBS News when they had television cameras on the moon and on the floor of the Supreme Court. Warren responded with a smile, "Good luck! You will have more luck with the former than the latter."

Later that year, the Chief Justice turned down a CBS request to televise the Supreme Court arguments in cases on the constitutionality of the 1964 Civil Rights Act. Warren wrote that "the Court has had an inflexible rule to the effect that it will not permit photographs or broadcasting from the courtroom when it is in session." The Chief Justice was sure that the Court "has no intention of changing that rule."

Chief Justice Burger adopted a similar attitude. When a network asked permission to carry live coverage of the arguments in what promised to be a landmark case, the Chief Justice replied with a one-sentence letter: "It is not possible to arrange for any broadcast of any Supreme Court proceeding." Handwritten at the bottom was a postscript: "When you get the Cabinet meetings on the air, call me!"

The issue of broadcasting in the courtroom has also concerned the Rehnquist Court. In the last chapter, we saw how the Justices negatived the request to televise Justice Thomas's Court swearing-in. A similar request was refused by Chief Justice Rehnquist, with the approval of the conference, for the televising of his own investiture. Since then, the Court has refused requests to photograph the robing room and the conference room, as well as the handshaking ceremony among the Justices before they go on the bench, by *Life* magazine and a TV station; network requests to broadcast and televise the swearings-in of Justices Kennedy and Souter; a radio station's request to broadcast the argument in the 1988 case of *Morrison v. Olson;* and even a request to demonstrate TV equipment in the courtroom.

Particularly in recent years, the Court has had something of an adversarial relationship with the press. This has been particularly true since publication of the derogatory accounts, especially of Chief Justice Burger, by two reporters in their 1979 best-seller *The Brethren.* The Chief Justice was deeply hurt by these accounts about his performance, and was gleeful when he told me that copies of the book were remaindered at ninety-eight cents in a Washington bookstore. But all the Justices were sensitive to the effect of *The Brethren* on the public perception of the Court. In a 1979 memorandum to the others soon after the book was published, Justice Rehnquist urged that it would be unwise for the Court to take certain action, "especially . . . in light of the microscopic scrutiny which our actions are apt to receive for a while."

At times, the Justices' hostile attitude toward the press has been justified. On June 12, 1987, Chief Justice Rehnquist sent around a Memorandum to the Conference that began, "It is with considerable unhappiness that I transmit to you the enclosed memorandum from Sheryl Farmer, Secretary to Toni House [the Court's Public Information Officer], giving a narrative summary of an event which occurred yesterday afternoon in the Conference Room." The Justices had agreed to allow Tim O'Brien, of ABC News, to film the conference room. According to the Farmer memo referred to by the Chief Justice, "About fifteen minutes into the filming, I noticed O'Brien was looking in the fireplace, leaned over to pick up sheets of paper and began looking through them. I immediately asked him to put them back, making him aware that he was there as a guest. A few minutes later I noticed that he was thumbing through a list of some kind that I didn't remember him bringing into the Conference Room. I noticed he was making notes but I couldn't determine if they were from the list or from the filming. When I asked him, he said they were notes on the filming."

The Rehnquist memo stated, "The 'list' which Tim O'Brien had apparently pulled out of the fireplace was the eight-page summary of circulating opinions which I distribute each week—this one for May 20, 1987." The Chief Justice concluded, "I think Tim O'Brien, if he did what he appears to have done, has committed a rather gross breach at least of courtesy if not of ethics, and that something should be done about it." Rehnquist asked the Justices to let him know how they felt about this.

Each of the Justices replied criticizing what O'Brien had done—some in strong language. The Scalia letter was typical: "I am formally appalled—which means not really surprised but for the record wish to be noted as surprised—by the incident you describe." Justice O'Connor wrote that the incident "simply illustrates again that journalists will get their news wherever they can find it."

Justice Marshall caustically noted, "This incident enforces my original vote to keep the press out of the conference room (period)."

However, there was the feeling among the Justices, as the Scalia letter put it, "that 'boys will be boys.' " In addition, there was the question of what to do about it. In the words of Justice Brennan's reply to the Chief Justice, "I don't think we should overlook the incident but beyond having him in to discuss it I'm at a loss what to suggest." After O'Brien wrote a letter of apology to the Chief Justice ("I was wrong to do it. . . . I deeply regret it"), the matter was dropped.

In his memo on the O'Brien incident, Chief Justice Rehnquist noted, "I am confident that I have the authority to take . . . steps on my own." Similarly, there is no doubt that the Chief Justice could have responded as Court head to the broadcast requests. But Rehnquist did not act on his own. On all these matters, he sought the opinion of the other Justices.

That has been the general practice in the Court, where, as the *Washington Post* described it, "This kind of one-person, one-vote democracy prevails in just about everything the justices do. . . . They take few actions without consulting each other." Often they spend time on petty details that, one would think, should be the concern of others — whether an Assistant Clerk should be given the new title of Deputy Clerk ("I am in favor of this alteration," Chief Justice Rehnquist wrote in a memo, "and seek your approval of it"), whether the Court police should prohibit note-taking and placing of arms on the backs of chairs in the Courtroom (Justice Blackmun raised this matter at a September 1988 conference), and even the heating in chambers.

In their internal democracy, the Justices often function through committees. Thus, we saw that a three-Justice committee investigated and reported on the question of transportation to Court. There are also standing committees. A September 27, 1988, Rehnquist Memorandum to the Conference informed the others, "Sandra and Nino have agreed to continue to serve on the Court Standing Committee for the Budget, and Sandra has agreed to continue to serve on the Cafeteria Committee."

In many ways, the Court resembles a club in its internal functioning. That is true, for example, with regard to the Justices' birthdays. A typical March 7, 1991, memo by Chief Justice Rehnquist notes, "Nino will celebrate his birthday on March 11th; let us have our usual wine in the Justice's Dining Room on Friday, March 15th after Conference."

Like other "clubs," the Justices have their "social secretary," who arranges functions such as the invitations to the annual Gridiron Club dinner. On January 9, 1987, Chief Justice Rehnquist wrote to Justice Powell, "I see that the annual Gridiron Club invitations have come out, and following our usual procedure I am taking this opportunity to advise you, as social secretary, that I do plan to accept this year." Interestingly, Rehnquist went on, "I daresay that my confirmation hearings last summer will be the subject of some reference, and I might as well be there to see it myself rather than just read about it in the paper."

Since Justice Powell's retirement, Justice Scalia has been the Court's "social secretary." As such, he has inherited duties such as that noted in a memo by him of "My duties in connection with the Court Christmas Party [which] include reporting to you with regard to the cost. As in the past, the cafeteria fund will cover much of the expense, and the Marshal has informed me that a contribution of $25 from each Justice will take care of the balance."

PRIMUS INTER PARES — BUT PRIMUS

Chief Justice Warren could, as seen, pressure the Judicial Conference to follow his views on federal court administration (though it did change its mind after he had retired). But even as strong a Chief Justice as Warren could not get the Supreme Court to do his bidding in the matter. As far as the Court is concerned, the Chief Justice's position is not at all legally superior to that of his colleagues. The Chief Justice, as Justice Frankfurter once wrote to Justice Brennan, is emphatically not "the boss" of the Court.

The Chief Justiceship should not, however, be approached only in a formalistic sense. Starting with John Marshall, the greatest of the Chief Justices have known how to make the most of the extralegal potential inherent in their position. The Chief Justice may be only primus inter pares; but he is *primus*. Somebody has to preside over a body of nine, and it is the Chief Justice who does preside, both in open court and in the even more important work of deciding cases in the conference chamber. It is the Chief Justice who directs the business of the Court. He controls the discussion in conference; his is the prerogative to call and discuss cases before the other Justices speak.

In addition, we saw that it has become the settled practice for the Chief Justice to assign the writing of Court opinions. This function has been called the most important that pertains to the office. In discharging it, a great Chief Justice is similar to a general deploying his army. It is he who determines what use will be made of the Court's personnel; his employment of the assigning power will influence both the growth of the law and his own relations with his colleagues.

A great Chief Justice such as Earl Warren speedily discovers the potential in the office. In doing so, he uses to the full the attributes that had made him a success in his pre-judicial career — in Warren's case that of California Governor. The primary assets of a successful governor are after all that he must be a leader, able to guide others toward attainment of his program, and must be capable of working effectively with people whom he cannot coerce, such as members of the legislature, whose cooperation is essential. He must be an effective conciliator of diverse viewpoints, never letting intraparty strife destroy the essential unity of purpose needed for political success. He must be able to administer, capable of controlling all the different facets of the modern executive branch. Above all, he is more likely to be a success if he projects a reputation for fairness and integrity and has an aura of competence and prestige.

All these attributes were possessed by Governor Warren, and they gave him his outstanding political successes in California. Those became the same attributes that enabled him to make the transition successfully from the executive mansion to the high Court.

Justice Frankfurter once compared a great Chief Justice's manner of presiding over the Court to Arturo Toscanini leading an orchestra. Warren brought more authority, more bravura, to the Chief Justiceship than had been the case for years. The Justices who sat with him have all stressed that Warren may not have been an intellectual like Frankfurter, but then, as Justice Potter Stewart once stated, "he never pretended to be one." More important, said Stewart, he possessed "instinctive qualities of leadership." When Stewart was asked about claims that Justice Black was the intellectual leader of the Court, he replied, "If Black was the intellectual leader, Warren was the *leader* leader." According to Justice Stewart, Warren "didn't lead by his intellect and he didn't greatly appeal to others' intellects; that wasn't his style. But he was an instinctive leader whom you respected and for whom you had affection, and . . . , as the presiding member of our conference, he was just ideal."

LEADERSHIP IN EARLIER COURTS

Describing her 1835 visit to the Supreme Court, the British writer Harriet Martineau told how she heard Chief Justice John Marshall deliver an opinion in his "mild voice" and gave her impression of his colleagues on the bench: "the three Judges on either hand gazing at him more like learners than associates." Virtually every estimate of the Marshall Court agrees with the Martineau characterization. Though the Justices on his bench were men of intellectual stature, they were overshadowed by the Chief Justice, who dominated his Court as few judges have ever done.

To be sure, during his first years on the bench, the Court was composed of Federalists who were to be expected to share Marshall's nationalistic views. However, in 1811, after Gabriel Duval and Joseph Story replaced Justices Samuel Chase and William Cushing, the Court had a Republican majority. Yet, as his leading biographer tells us, "Marshall continued to dominate it as fully as when its members were of his own political faith and views of government. In the whole history of courts there is no parallel to such supremacy."

What gave Marshall his commanding influence? Certainly it was not his intellect and learning. Justice Story was his equal in the first and by far his superior in the second, and Justice William Johnson had both a strong intellect and a far better education. Justice Bushrod Washington would also have been a prominent judge on any other Court. All three Justices, however, stood in Chief Justice Marshall's shadow throughout their tenure.

In the end, Marshall's dominance over his associates rested upon the elusive quality we call leadership — about which we can paraphrase Justice Stewart's celebrated aphorism on pornography: "I could never succeed in [defining it].

But I know it when I see it." Whatever the qualities of judicial leadership may be, Marshall plainly possessed them to the ultimate degree.

Unfortunately, the decision process of the Marshall Court remains a closed book. We know that the Justices used to meet in conference to discuss the cases before them. But we do not know what went on during those conferences or during other stages of the decision process. Everyone assumes that Chief Justice Marshall himself was the catalyst behind the leading decisions of his Court— that he led the Justices to the results that he strongly favored and that he personally wrote the opinions in all the important cases disposed of by his Court.

Indeed, it is even assumed that Chief Justice Marshall played the same dominant role in cases where the formal opinion was delivered by others. When the Court upheld the Supreme Court's appellate power over state court decisions in *Martin v. Hunter's Lessee* (1816), Marshall did not deliver the opinion because a personal interest in the case led him to decline to participate. According to Albert J. Beveridge's classic biography of the great Chief Justice, however, "it has been commonly supposed that Marshall practically dictated" Justice Story's opinion of the Court in the case.

We know a little more about the decision process of the Court presided over by Marshall's successor, Chief Justice Roger B. Taney. Taney, too, is considered to have been a strong Chief Justice who led his Court in modifying Marshall's nationalist doctrines by his Jacksonian focus on state power. Paradoxically perhaps, in the few cases in which we have some idea of what went on behind the scenes in the Taney Court, the leadership role was not performed by the Chief Justice. This was particularly true in *Dred Scott* (1857) — the Taney Court's most famous case — where the Justices had originally voted to dispose of the case on a narrow technical ground. That the Justices changed their mind and decided to deal with the crucial issues of Negro citizenship and congressional power to prohibit slavery in the territories was due not to the Chief Justice, but to a motion of Justice James M. Wayne of Georgia, who later told a Southern Senator that he had "gained a triumph for the Southern section of the country, by persuading the chief-justice that the court could put an end to all further agitation on the subject of slavery in the territories."

A leading case where we do know that the Chief Justice led the Court was decided later in the century under Chief Justice Morrison R. Waite. Waite himself was a little-known Ohio lawyer who was chosen only after President Ulysses S. Grant failed in his efforts to reward several cronies with the position. On the bench, Waite had nothing of the grand manner — the spark that made Marshall and the other great Chief Justices what they were. A humdrum, pedestrian lawyer, he remains a dim figure in our constitutional history. "I can't make a silk purse out of a sow's ear," wrote Justice Samuel F. Miller a year after Waite's 1874 appointment. "I can't make a great Chief Justice out of a small man."

Yet, if Waite was not a great Chief Justice, he was able to lead the Court to one of its most important decisions — that in the 1877 Granger Cases. "Judged by any standards of ultimate importance," Justice Frankfurter tells us in his book on the Commerce Clause, Waite's ruling in the Granger Cases "places it among the dozen most important decisions in our constitutional law." It upheld the power of the states to regulate the rates of railroads and other businesses — a holding, never since departed from, that has served as the basis upon which government regulation in this country has essentially rested.

So far as we know, it was Chief Justice Waite himself who both led the Court to its *Granger* decision and wrote the opinion which has since served as the foundation for governmental regulation of business. Interestingly, the Granger Cases illustrate not only the Chief Justice's leadership role but also the cooperative nature of the decision process even in a case where that role prevails. Chief Justice Waite's *Granger* opinion was greatly influenced by an outline prepared by the Court's leading legal scholar, Justice Joseph P. Bradley. Bradley called Waite's attention to the common law on the subject, especially Lord Chief Justice Hale's seventeenth-century statement that when private property is "affected with a publick interest, it ceases to be juris privati [of private right] only." But the *Granger* opinion was more than a rehash of the Bradley outline. Waite articulated his opinion in language broad enough to transform the whole course of the law of business regulation. In the words of a contemporary, "Suffice it, that the decision itself in its general breadth and purpose has no precedent."

At a time when governmental regulatory power was beginning to be judicially restricted, Chief Justice Waite was able to persuade his Court that the Constitution permitted regulation of businesses such as railroads. Waite was only following the time-honored judicial technique of pouring new wine into old bottles. He read and expounded Lord Hale in the spirit of the industrial era. He tore a fragment from the annals of the law, stripped away its limited frame of reference, and re-created it in the image of the modern police power. Waite himself was clear from the beginning of the case on the decision that should be reached. "The position taken," he wrote in a letter a few weeks after the decision, "seemed to me to be the only safe one. Necessarily the power is a dangerous one, but that may be said of all and any other in the hands of dishonest legislators." When Justice Miller congratulated him on his role in the case, Chief Justice Waite wrote back, "I confess that I am weak enough to feel pleasure when my friends are satisfied with what I have tried to do well."

WHITE AND RULE OF REASON

During this century, there have been many examples of how a Chief Justice can lead the Court to the decision which he favors. An early illustration occurred soon after President Taft promoted Justice Edward Douglass White to the Court's center chair in 1910. White had been a competent Justice for sixteen years, but few would rate him as a superior Chief Justice — though he did improve the atmosphere within the Court by what Chief Justice Hughes was to recall as his attempt "to create an atmosphere of friendliness and to promote agreement in the disposition of cases."

Yet it was Chief Justice White who led the Court to the decision of what a contemporary commentator called "the main question of the day" — "the regulation by law of corporate activity in its relation to the country at large." *Harper's* at the time noted that a number of Supreme Court decisions had "been awaited with country-wide suspense and attention." Nevertheless, none of them had "caused the market and the whole industrial and commercial world to pause more perceptibly than have the cases of the Government against the Standard Oil Company and the American Tobacco Company. They came to be known simply as the Trust Cases. For months the financial markets have virtually stood still awaiting their settlement."

The key decision in the Trust Cases (1911) arose out of the government's prosecution of the Standard Oil Company under the Sherman Anti-Trust Act. The lower court had found the great oil monopoly in violation of the Act and had ordered its dissolution. A unanimous Supreme Court upheld the dissolution ruling. Yet, ironically, though the government won the case, it had to accept an interpretation of the Sherman Act which greatly reduced that law's effectiveness. The Court ruled that Standard Oil's practices constituted "unreasonable" restraint, which the Act prohibited. Thus was born the so-called *rule of reason* in antitrust cases. As it was put in Chief Justice White's opinion, "in every case where it is claimed that an act or acts are in violation of the statute the rule of reason . . . must be applied."

The rule of reason was almost entirely the handiwork of the Chief Justice; Justice Holmes called White's "invention of the rule of reason . . . [t]he Chief Justice's greatest dialectical coup." Certainly it was the principal legal legacy of White's Court tenure, devised entirely by the Chief Justice and adopted at his urging.

The Court took unusual security precautions in the Trust Cases. The normal practice was for the writer of a draft opinion to circulate printed copies. In the Trust Cases, we are informed by a letter of Justice Willis Van Devanter to a federal judge, the Court voted not to send the White opinion to the printer, but to circulate typewritten copies by hand. After that was done, the Justices voted on the Chief Justice's opinion in a Saturday, May 13, 1911, conference. All were in favor of the dissolution, but the first Justice Harlan dissented on the rule of reason. The Van Devanter letter states that six Justices agreed to join White's opinion, while one (his name is not given) was in doubt and would probably concur. Over the weekend, however, the doubt was resolved, and, when the Chief Justice announced the decision to a crowded courtroom on Monday, May 15, all except Justice Harlan had joined the opinion of the Court.

Justice Harlan delivered a strong dissent, which Chief Justice Hughes later recalled as "a passionate outburst seldom if ever equaled in the annals of the Court." Harlan pointed out what the Chief Justice had done. The deci-

sion, Harlan asserted, was an example of "the tendency to judicial legislation . . . [t]he most alarming tendency of this day, in my judgment, so far as the
safety and integrity of our institutions are concerned." Chief Justice White had
led the Court "to so construe the Constitution or the statutes as to mean what
they want it to mean." The result was "that the courts may by mere judicial
construction amend the Constitution . . . or an Act of Congress."

All the same, it was difficult to disagree with a decision that asserted that it
was only interpreting a law "by the light of reason." Justice Holmes pointed this
out in his comment to a law clerk about the White *Standard Oil* opinion: "The
moment I saw that in the circulated draft, I knew he had us. How could you be
against that without being for a rule of unreason?"

HUGHES AND "CONSTITUTIONAL REVOLUTION, LTD."

Charles Evans Hughes was sixty-eight when he was appointed Chief Justice in
1930 — the oldest man till then chosen to head the Court. However, he
undertook his new duties with the vigor of a much younger person. In addition,
his more than distinguished career endowed him with prestige that few in the
highest judicial office have had. "He took his seat at the center of the Court,"
Justice Frankfurter was to write, "with a mastery, I suspect, unparalleled in the
history of the court."

As a leader of the Court, indeed, Hughes must be ranked with the greatest
Chief Justices. Whatever the test of leadership, in Frankfurter's words, "Chief
Justice Hughes possessed it to a conspicuous degree. In open court he exerted
this authority by the mastery and distinction with which he presided. He
radiated this authority in the conference room."

The new Chief Justice's leadership abilities were precisely what the Court
needed to enable it to confront its most serious crisis in almost a century. Under
Hughes's predecessor, Chief Justice Taft, the Court's conservative core had
carried their laissez-faire interpretation of the Constitution to the point where
there was, in the famous Holmes phrase, "hardly any limit but the sky to the
invalidating of [laws] if they happen to strike a majority of the Court as for any
reason undesirable." In *Planned Parenthood v. Casey,* the 1992 abortion case, the
Court itself stated that the pre-Hughes decisions were "exemplified by" the 1923
decision in "*Adkins v. Children's Hospital* . . . in which this Court held it to be an
infringement of constitutionally protected liberty of contract to require the
employers of adult women to satisfy minimum wage standards."

By the time of the Hughes Court, the *Planned Parenthood* opinion tells us, "the
Depression had come and, with it, the lesson that seemed unmistakable to most
people in 1937, that the interpretation of contractual freedom protected in
Adkins rested on fundamentally false factual assumptions about the capacity of
a relatively unregulated market to satisfy minimal levels of human welfare."
When Chief Justice Hughes ascended the bench early in 1930, the country was
already deep in the most serious economic crisis in our history. The crisis only

became worse as the Hughes term went on — putting the entire leadership of the country, and not least the Court itself, to perhaps its most severe test.

The new Chief Justice had to meet the test with a Court composed almost entirely of Justices who had served under his predecessor. Four of the five Justices who had made up the *Adkins* majority (Van Devanter, McReynolds, Sutherland, and Butler) were still on the bench, serving as the nucleus for decisions extending the Taft Court's jurisprudence. Despite this the new Chief Justice was able to persuade a bare majority that the Constitution should no longer be treated as a legal sanction for laissez-faire. Writing in 1941, Justice Jackson asserted, "The older world of *laissez-faire* was recognized everywhere outside the Court to be dead." It was Chief Justice Hughes who ensured that the same recognition penetrated the Marble Palace.

It is true that Chief Justice Hughes, like other Court heads who ultimately led important changes in Court jurisprudence (Chief Justice Warren, in particular, comes to mind) proceeded slowly during his first years in the Court's center chair. In 1937, however, he was able to lead the Court to what amounted to a veritable revolution in the Court's jurisprudence, which one commentator characterized as "Constitutional Revolution, Ltd."

It is too facile to state that the 1937 change was merely a protective response to President Franklin D. Roosevelt's Court-packing plan adding Justices to change the anti–New Deal decisions — to assert, as did so many contemporary wags, that "a switch in time saved Nine." The furor over the President's proposal obviously had repercussions within the Court's marble halls. As FDR himself expressed it, "it would be a little naive to refuse to recognize some connection between these decisions and the Supreme Court fight." At the same time, it misconceives the nature of the Supreme Court and its manner of operation as a judicial tribunal to assume that the 1937 change in jurisprudence was solely the result of the Court-packing plan. The 1937 reversal reflected changes in legal ideology common to the entire legal profession. The extreme individualistic philosophy upon which the Justices had been nurtured had been shaken to its foundations. If laissez-faire jurisprudence gave way to judicial pragmatism, it simply reflected a similar movement that had taken place in the country as a whole.

In an unpublished 1934 draft opinion, Justice Benjamin N. Cardozo had asserted, "A gospel of laissez faire . . . may be inadequate in the great society that we live in to point the way to salvation, at least for economic life." The conception of the proper role of government upon which the pre-1937 decisions were based was utterly inconsistent with an era which demanded ever expanding governmental authority. "Leviathan hath two swords: war and justice," stated Thomas Hobbes in a famous passage. The need to deal effectively with the great economic crisis of the 1930s had, nevertheless, made it plain that the armory of the State had to include much more than these two elementary weapons. Before the New Deal, government was chiefly negative; its main task, apart from defense, was to support the status quo and maintain some semblance of fair play while private interests asserted themselves freely. Under the Roosevelt Administration, government became positive in a new sense.

For the Supreme Court, Canute-like, to attempt to hold back indefinitely the waves of ever increasing governmental authority was to set itself an impossible task. "Looking back," declared Justice Owen J. Roberts in 1951, "it is difficult to see how the court could have resisted the popular urge for uniform standards throughout the country — for what in effect was a unified economy." The laissez-faire doctrine, upon which the operation of American government had been essentially based since the founding of the Republic, had by then proved inadequate to meet pressing economic problems.

The national economy could be resuscitated only by extended federal intervention. For the government in Washington to be able to exercise regulatory authority upon the necessary national scale, it was essential that the Supreme Court liberalize its construction of the Constitution. To quote Justice Roberts again, "An insistence by the court on holding federal power to what seemed its appropriate orbit when the Constitution was adopted might have resulted in even more radical changes in our dual structure than those which have been gradually accomplished through the extension of the limited jurisdiction conferred on the federal government." In the 1992 *Planned Parenthood* case, the Court itself referred to "the terrible price that would have been paid if the Court had not overruled as it did."

Writing to Felix Frankfurter in 1936, Justice Harlan F. Stone complained about the lack of Hughes leadership in repudiating the still-prevalent laissez-faire jurisprudence. The problem in the Court, Stone asserted, "can be summed up in two phrases which you have doubtless heard me repeat before: lack of vision and the unwillingness of certain gentlemen to trust their own intellectual processes. . . . The worst of it is that the one [Hughes] that you find it most difficult to understand is the one chiefly responsible."

If Hughes was "responsible" for the fact that the Court went too slowly before 1937, he was also responsible for the reversal in jurisprudence that occurred that year — a reversal so great that its effects do justify the "constitutional revolution" characterization. And it is usually overlooked that the decision first signaling the reversal was reached before the President introduced his Court-packing plan. On March 29, 1937, Chief Justice Hughes announced a decision upholding a minimum-wage law, basically similar to the one the *Adkins* Court had held to be beyond governmental power. The Court's confession of error was announced a month after the President's proposal, but the case itself was decided in conference among the Justices about a month before the publication of the Court-packing plan. The circumstantial evidence strongly bears out the statement made some years later by Chief Justice Hughes: "The President's proposal had not the slightest effect on our decision."

There is no doubt that it was the Chief Justice himself who led the Court to repudiate cases such as *Adkins*. The Court to which Hughes came contained, we saw, four of the conservative Justices who had made up the *Adkins* majority. It also contained three liberal Justices (Brandeis, Stone, and Cardozo), who were strongly in favor of overruling the *Adkins* line of cases. The remaining members were the Chief Justice and Justice Owen J. Roberts, who had taken his seat at the same time as Hughes. Roberts himself was far from an outstanding Justice. "Who am I," he wrote after leaving the bench, "to revile the good God that he did not make me a Marshall, a Taney, a Bradley, a Holmes, a Brandeis or a Cardozo."

Justice Roberts was nevertheless to play a crucial role as the swing vote in the Hughes Court. It had been his key vote that enabled the conservative bloc to prevail in decisions striking down important New Deal measures during the first part of Chief Justice Hughes's tenure. It was Justice Roberts's vote as well that enabled the Chief Justice to bring about the great jurisprudential reversal that took place in 1937.

It was Chief Justice Hughes who persuaded Justice Roberts to vote with the new majority in the minimum-wage case. The success of his efforts was, of course, crucial to the Court's acceptance of increased governmental power as the foundation of the new constitutional jurisprudence. Hughes himself fully realized the crucial importance of the Roberts vote. He later told how, when the Justice told him that he would vote to sustain the minimum-wage law, he almost hugged him—which, coming from one with so great a reputation for icy demeanor, says a great deal.

BACK TO MARSHALL

It was because of the Hughes lead and his successful persuasion of Justice Roberts that the Chief Justice was able to announce the decision upholding the minimum-wage law and overruling *Adkins.* According to Justice Jackson, who sat at the government counsel table when the opinion was read, "the spectacle of the Court that day frankly and completely reversing itself . . . was a moment never to be forgotten."

On the same day, the Court dealt squarely with federal statutes similar to several it had annulled in the 1934–36 period. This time the Court upheld laws providing for farm debtors' relief, collective bargaining in the nation's railroads, and a penalizing tax on firearms analogous to one that it had struck down earlier. Well could Justice Jackson, then a leading New Dealer, chortle, "What a day! To labor, minimum-wage laws and collective bargaining; to farmers, relief in bankruptcy; to law enforcement, the firearms control. The Court was on the march!"

These cases, in Volume 300 of the *Supreme Court Reports,* were to prove but the prelude to an even more drastic change in constitutional jurisprudence. To demonstrate the extent of the change, one has, to use the method stated by Edward S. Corwin, only to "turn to Volume 301 of the *United States Supreme Court Reports,* a volume which has a single counterpart in the Court's annals. I mean

Volume 11 of *Peters's Reports,* wherein is recorded the somewhat lesser revolution in our constitutional law precisely 100 years earlier, which followed upon Taney's succession to Marshall."

On page 1 of 301 U.S., there is printed the April 12, 1937, decision of the Court in *National Labor Relations Board v. Jones & Laughlin Steel Corp.* In it, the constitutionality of the National Labor Relations Act of 1935 was upheld. Justice Jackson was to term the decision there the most far-reaching victory ever won on behalf of labor in the Supreme Court. This was no overstatement, for the 1935 Act was the Magna Carta of the American labor movement. It guaranteed the right of employees to organize collectively in unions and made it an unfair labor practice prohibited by law for employers to interfere with that right or to refuse to bargain collectively with the representatives chosen by their employees.

The Labor Act was intended to apply to industries throughout the Nation, to those engaged in production and manufacture as well as to those engaged in commerce, literally speaking. But this appeared to bring it directly in conflict with prior decisions drastically limiting the scope of the Federal Government's authority over interstate commerce, including some of the decisions of the 1934–36 period on which the ink was scarcely dry. In the *Jones & Laughlin* case, these precedents were not followed. "These cases," laconically stated Chief Justice Hughes for the Court, "are not controlling here." Instead the Hughes opinion gave the federal power over interstate commerce its maximum sweep. Mines, mills and factories, whose activities had formerly been decided to be "local," and hence immune from federal regulation, were now held to affect interstate commerce directly enough to justify congressional control.

Once again, there is no doubt that the Chief Justice himself was primarily responsible for the *Jones & Laughlin* decision. In his Hughes biography, Merlo J. Pusey emphasized the vigor and thoroughness with which the Chief Justice presented *Jones & Laughlin* at the conference. He also stated that Hughes told him that he had not "pleaded with Roberts to save the NLRB." The Hughes disclaimer should be taken with a grain of salt. Strong Chief Justices, such as Hughes and Earl Warren, are noted for their success in persuading their colleagues to follow their views. Hughes never denied publicly that he had influenced Justice Roberts's vote. All he stated in his *Autobiographical Notes* was, "I am able to say with definiteness that [Roberts's] view in favor of *{Jones & Laughlin}* would have been the same if the President's bill had never been proposed." Of course, it would have, since it was the Chief Justice's persuasion, not the President's threat, that led to the Roberts vote.

Justice Jackson was later to say that, in *Jones & Laughlin,* "Hughes' vigorous championship of federal power under the commerce clause is reminiscent of Marshall." For the first time since the days of Chief Justice John Marshall, federal regulatory authority was given the broad sweep intended by the Framers.

The *Jones & Laughlin* decision was not, however, the end of the 301 U.S. constitutional revolution. It was followed six weeks later by three equally significant decisions, also printed in 301 U.S., upholding the constitutionality of one of the most important of the New Deal innovations, the Social Security Act of 1935. That law, which for the first time brought the Federal Government extensively into the field of social insurance, had been held unconstitutional by the lower court. The Supreme Court, however, in a precedent-making opinion by Justice Cardozo, reversed, holding that the scheme of old-age benefits provided for by the federal law did not contravene any constitutional prohibition. In so doing, the Court gave the broadest possible scope to the congressional power to tax and spend for the general welfare, even though its reasoning on this point was inconsistent with its 1936 decision invalidating the Agricultural Adjustment Act.

In addition, the Court upheld the unemployment compensation schemes established under the Social Security Act. The decisions sustaining that law put an end to fears that unemployment insurance and old-age benefit laws might prove beyond the power of either states or nation, as minimum-wage regulations had been held to be under the pre-1937 Court. Henceforth the United States was not to be the one great nation powerless to adopt such measures.

Though the Social Security decisions were not announced by him, it cannot be doubted that Chief Justice Hughes led the Court in reaching them. The decisions rested upon an expansive view of the federal spending power, and Hughes had won the Court's approval of just so broad a view in an earlier case.

The decisions in 301 U.S. formed the heart of the constitutional revolution of 1937. Breaking with its previous jurisprudence, the Supreme Court upheld the authority of the Federal Government to regulate the entire economy under its commerce power and to use its power to tax and spend to set up comprehensive schemes of social insurance. The catalyst behind the new decisions was the leadership furnished by Chief Justice Hughes. Because of it, Supreme Court jurisprudence was finally able to move with the society into the twentieth century.

MASTERS OF THE CONFERENCE AND OTHERS

All students of the Court assume that John Marshall, above all, must have been a conference virtuoso, but that is based largely upon his reputation as the Chief Justice who dominated his Court as no other Court head has ever done. How Marshall, Taney, or the other early Chief Justices actually conducted their conferences is something that remains within the realm of speculation, since there is no historical evidence on the matter.

During the present century, we have come to know more about what has gone on in the Court's conference room. In particular, we have learned that the two greatest modern Chief Justices, Hughes and Warren, both were masterful in their leadership of the conference. The next chapter will be devoted to Chief Justice Warren as a leader of the Court. In terms of efficiency, however, even he must yield to Chief Justice Hughes, who was specifically characterized by Justice Louis D. Brandeis as "a very efficient Chief Justice."

Again, we may say that, however the attributes of leadership may be defined, Chief Justice Hughes possessed them in full measure. In Justice Frankfurter's previously quoted phrase, Hughes "radiated . . . authority in the conference room." The Hughes manner of conducting the Court's business has been described by Frankfurter, who had served as a Justice under him: "In Court and in conference he struck the pitch, as it were, for the orchestra. He guided discussion by opening up the lines for it to travel, focusing on essentials, evoking candid exchange on subtle and complex issues, and avoiding redundant talk. He never checked free debate, but the atmosphere which he created, the moral authority which he exerted, inhibited irrelevance, repetition, and fruitless discussion."

In another passage Frankfurter wrote that the "word which for me best expresses the atmosphere that Hughes generated . . . was taut. Everything was taut. . . . Everybody was better because of Hughes, the leader of the orchestra."

The Hughes conferences were military-like models of efficiency. According to Justice Brandeis, these "lasted six hours and the Chief Justice did virtually all the speaking." This was an exaggeration, but Hughes is still noted for his tight control over the conference discussion. Rarely did any Justice speak out of turn, and Hughes made sure that the discussion did not stray from the issues he had stated in his incisive presentation. For him, Justice Frankfurter later told an interviewer, "the conference was not a debating society." When differences began to produce more heat than analysis, the Chief Justice would blow his whiskers out and say, "Brethren, the only way to settle this is to vote."

The leading biography of Chief Justice Harlan Fiske Stone, Hughes's successor, tells how, at a 1932 conference, then-Justice Stone asked permission to read an opinion that he had not had time to print and circulate. It asserted that the majority opinion in a case was wrong and explained why. "Stone naturally expected full discussion, followed by the Chief's recommendation that the case go over a week to consider his views. Not so; when Stone finished reading, Hughes said: 'Very powerful memorandum. Case goes down on Monday.' "

Shortly after this incident, Justice Stone wrote to John Bassett Moore, a leading international lawyer, "I have no hesitation in saying that I think discussion of our cases should be much fuller and freer, and that in many instances an adjournment over for a week after preliminary discussion might produce more satisfactory results." When he succeeded Hughes as Chief Justice, Stone put this idea into practice.

Stone on Olympus, however, shows that the qualities that make for an outstanding Justice are not necessarily the qualities that make for a good Chief Justice. There is no doubt that, since his appointment to the Court in 1925, Stone had made his mark as a superior Justice. He had been a leader in the fight against equating the Constitution with laissez faire, as well as in the movement to conform the Court's jurisprudence to the "felt necessities" of the changing times. By the time of Chief Justice Hughes's retirement in June 1941, Stone was recognized as the intellectual leader of the Court. He was, therefore, the natural choice to succeed to the Chief Justiceship—acknowledged as such by both his colleagues and the country. Hughes himself told President Roosevelt that Stone's record gave him first claim upon the honor.

Time wrote that "it liked the idea of a solid man as Chief Justice to follow Charles Evans Hughes. And solid is the word for Chief Justice Stone—200 lb., with heavy, good-natured features and a benign judicial air." Yet, impressive though the new Chief Justice may have been as a figure of justice, he proved anything but a leader in the Hughes mold. Indeed, Stone at the head of the Court was the very antithesis of the Hughes model of dynamism and efficiency.

Justice Frankfurter recalled that while the Hughes passion for efficiency made everything in his Court "taut . . . Stone was an 'easy boss.' " After he had attended the new Chief Justice's first conference, Frankfurter wrote to Stone about "the relaxed atmosphere and your evident desire to have our conferences an exchange of . . . views of nine men."

Chief Justice Hughes had conducted the conference in the manner of a strict teacher in the classroom: discussion was brief and to the point and woe to the Justice who spoke out of turn. On the other hand, Justice Douglas recalled in his *Autobiography,* "When Stone became Chief Justice, our Conference was never finished by four-thirty or five. We moved the starting time back, first to eleven and then to ten o'clock, but we still could not finish by six on Saturday. We would come back . . . on Monday and . . . again go into Conference at four and sit until five or six. Sometimes we still would be unfinished by the end of the day and have to go back into Conference at ten on Tuesday morning, and again at four in the afternoon on Tuesday. Once we even had Conference on Wednesday from ten to noon and from four to six—to finish up the previous Saturday's Conference List. Under Stone we were, in other words, almost in a continuous Conference."

Like the law professor that he once was, Chief Justice Stone was slow to cut off debate in his anxiety to have all issues thoroughly explored. The result was a freewheeling discussion in which the Chief Justice was more a participant than a leader. "The Chief Justice," commented Justice Reed, "delighted to take on all comers around the conference table and . . . to battle, . . . for his views." Stone, says Justice Frankfurter, had "the habit . . . of carrying on a running debate with any justice who expresses views different from his."

Justice Potter Stewart once told me that he heard that "Stone's problem was that, at a conference, he himself always insisted upon having the last word, and that's not the way you preside—always arguing with the person that had spoken." Discussion became wrangling, and the Justices emerged from these interminable meetings irritated and exhausted, their differences inflamed from excessive argument. The Stone method only exacerbated the personal and professional differences in what soon became one of the most divided Courts in our history.

Even worse, however, than Chief Justice Stone as a leader of the Court was his successor. In fact, Fred M. Vinson may have been the least effective Court head in the Supreme Court's history. His appointment was due primarily to his close friendship with President Truman, who hoped that his skill at getting along with people would enable him to restore peace to a Court that had become splintered under Chief Justice Stone.

The new Chief Justice was (as his predecessor had been) a large man — in the Frankfurter phrase, "tall and broad and [with] a little bit of a bay window." Throughout his career, Vinson had been known for his skill at smoothing ruffled feathers. But his hearty bonhomie was not enough to enable him to lead the Court effectively. The Justices looked down on the new Chief Justice as the possessor of a second-class mind. Even Justice Reed, the least intellectually gifted of the Roosevelt appointees, could dismiss the dour-faced Chief, in a letter to Justice Frankfurter, as "just like me, except that he is less well-educated." Frankfurter himself could characterize Vinson in his diary as "confident and easy-going and sure and shallow. . . . he seems to me to have the confident air of a man who does not see the complexities of problems and blithely hits the obvious points."

Phillip Elman, who had clerked for Frankfurter and was one of the most knowledgeable Court watchers, wrote to the Justice about "the C.J." from the Solicitor General's Office: "What a mean little despot he is. Has there ever been a member of the Court who was deficient in so many respects as a man and as a judge. Even that s.o.b. McReynolds, despite his defects of character, stands by comparison as a towering figure and powerful intellect. . . . this man is a pygmy, morally and mentally. And so uncouth."

Chief Justice Vinson was even more inept than his predecessor in leading the conference. According to Frankfurter's diary, Vinson presented cases in a shallow way. He "blithely hits the obvious points . . . disposing of each case rather briefly, by choosing, as it were, to float merely on the surface of the problems raised by the cases."

When Chief Justice Vinson supported Justice Tom Clark's appointment, Washington wags said it was because he wanted someone on his Court who knew less law than he did. Throughout his tenure, the Justices were openly to display their contempt for their Chief. As a law clerk recalled it, several of Vinson's colleagues "would discuss in his presence the view that the Chief's job should rotate annually and . . . made no bones about regarding him — correctly — as their intellectual inferior."

Vinson was, however, to be succeeded by the most effective of modern Chief Justices, who was to illustrate clearly the leadership potential in the Court's center chair. His tenure was to be a striking demonstration of how a strong Chief Justice can lead even the strongest of Supreme Courts.

4

Super Chief in Action

To those who served with him, Earl Warren will always be the Super Chief," Justice William J. Brennan used to say. Brennan had been Chief Justice Warren's closest associate on the Court and, more than any of the Justices, Brennan missed Warren after the latter retired.

Earl Warren was proud of his reputation as a great Chief Justice. Once, after he had delivered a talk to hundreds of students in the basement lounge of Notre Dame Law School, he was responding to questions. A student in the back of the packed lounge began a question, "Some people have suggested that you'll go down in history with Marshall as one of the two greatest Chief Justices." Warren smiled broadly and interrupted, "Could you say that again—a little louder please? I'm having a little trouble hearing."

ARRIVAL OF THE SUPER CHIEF

In most respects Earl Warren could have been a character out of Sinclair Lewis or Sherwood Anderson. Justice Potter Stewart once said, "Warren's great strength was his simple belief in the things we now laugh at: motherhood, marriage, family, flag, and the like." These, according to Stewart, were the "eternal, rather bromidic, platitudes in which he sincerely believed." These were the foundation of Warren's jurisprudence, as they were of his way of life.

When we add to this Warren's bluff masculine bonhomie, his love of sports and the outdoors, and his lack of intellectual interests or pretensions, we end up with a typical representative of the Middle America of his day. Except for one thing—Warren's leadership abilities. When he arrived at the Court, those abilities soon became apparent.

All the Justices who served with Chief Justice Warren recognized his leader-ship role. In his *Autobiography,* Justice Douglas ranked Warren with Marshall and Hughes as "our three greatest Chief Justices." Justice Brennan told me that it was the Chief Justice who was personally responsible for the key decisions during his tenure. The Justices who sat with him all stressed that Chief Justice Warren may not have been an intellectual like Justice Frankfurter, but then, as Justice Stewart said to me, "he never pretended to be one." More important, Stewart told me, "he had instinctive qualities of leadership."

Chief Justice Warren himself brought more authority to the Chief Justiceship than had been the case for years. The most important work of the Supreme Court, of course, occurs behind the scenes, particularly at the conferences where the Justices discuss and vote on cases. As Justice Brennan recalled it, the Justices soon developed the practice of gathering in the conference room before Chief Justice Warren arrived and rising to their feet as he entered. Then after they went through their formal ritual of exchanging handshakes, Warren would take his seat at the head of the table and call out, in his cheerful tone, "Hey-ho, let's get going." He would then go down the cases on the conference agenda. His job was essentially that of presenting the issues involved before opening the floor to discussion by the others.

In an interview, Justice Fortas summarized the Warren conference forte: "It was Warren's great gift that, in presenting the case and discussing the case, he proceeded immediately and very calmly and graciously to the ultimate values involved — the ultimate constitutional values, the ultimate human values." In the face of such an approach, traditional legal arguments seemed inappropri-ate, almost pettifoggery. To quote Fortas again, "opposition based on the hemstitching and embroidery of the law appeared petty in terms of Warren's basic value approach." We shall see the Warren technique in operation — particularly in the *Brown* school segregation case.

In a discussion of the Warren conference technique, Justice Stewart once remarked, "always, after stating the case, [Warren] would very clearly and unambiguously state his position." Then, hesitating, Stewart modified his statement: "I said always, but there would be an exception every now and then. About one in a hundred cases, there would be some tax case in which there would be some conflict in the circuits, and . . . he would say, 'Look, our duty is to resolve this conflict. I'm not a tax lawyer. I'll go whichever way you want to go on this, just go with the majority and get this conflict resolved. . . . I just have no view on this one.' "

Even in those cases, says Stewart, "I often thought to myself he only does that when he can't see something involving these eternal, rather bromidic, plati-tudes in which he sincerely believed." It should be noted, as Stewart recognized, that "they were not platitudes for him: the family or the underprivileged or the widows or the orphans. . . . With him it wasn't cant and you very soon realized that it wasn't."

Describing Warren's role at the conference, Justice Byron White said in an interview that "he would state his position and he . . . was quite willing to listen to people at length . . . but, when he made up his mind, it was like the sun went down, and he was very firm, very firm about it."

Justice Brennan, talking to a reporter after Warren had retired, said, "It is incredible how efficiently the Chief would conduct the Friday conferences, leading the discussion of every case on the agenda, with a knowledge of each case at his fingertips." All the Justices who served with him lay stress on Warren's ability to lead the conference.

Warren's conduct of the conference was entirely different from that of his predecessors, Chief Justices Stone and Vinson. He would rarely contradict the Justices at the conference, and he would make sure that each of them had his full say — even Justice Frankfurter, whose tendency to treat the session as a Harvard seminar would grate on the Chief Justice just as much as it did on the others. Warren, Justice White said, "never felt he had to get the last word in." As Justice Stewart summarized it, "he was an instinctive leader whom you respected and . . . , as the presiding member of our conference, he was just ideal."

A reading of the conference notes of Justices on the Warren Court reveals that the Stewart estimate was accurate and that, after an initial period of feeling his way, the Chief Justice was as strong a leader as the Court has ever had. In almost all the important cases, the Chief Justice himself led the discussion toward the decision he favored. If any Court can properly be identified by the name of one of its members, his Court was emphatically the *Warren* Court and, without arrogance, he, as well as the country, knew it. When we consider the work of the Warren Court, we are considering a constitutional corpus that was directly a product of the Chief Justice's leadership.

CONFERENCE LEADERSHIP

Chief Justice Warren's leadership of the conference and the Court is shown most spectacularly in the soon-to-be discussed *Brown* segregation case. A Chief Justice is, however, known not only by the legal landmarks that he influences. His leadership is also reflected in the more ordinary decisions. Chief Justice Warren's ability to lead the conference as soon as he took over the presiding role may be seen from Justice Tom Clark's conference notes in five cases from 1953 and 1954 during Warren's first term as Chief Justice. None of the cases was of any great importance. Instead, they enable us to see how Warren conducted the conference in comparatively run-of-the-mill cases, free of the pressures under which, according to the Holmes aphorism, "Great cases like hard cases make bad law."

In *Howell Chevrolet Company v. National Labor Relations Board,* the Board had acted against a large Chevrolet dealer in California, which claimed as a defense that its business did not "affect commerce," as required by the National Labor Relations Act. At the November 14 conference on the case, Chief Justice

Warren's statement was incisive and to the point: "This is not a corner grocery case, as was argued. The method of operation puts them in the stream of commerce. I'd sustain the Board." And all agreed except Justice Douglas, who subsequently dissented, without opinion.

The other cases saw the same type of Warren presentation. *Wilko v. Swan* involved the issue of whether an agreement to arbitrate a future controversy was a waiver of the right to sue under the Securities Act. Chief Justice Warren's conference statement on October 24 said, "As I see it, we have to reconcile the arbitration statute with the Securities Act. I'd say they could not waive their statutory rights [under the Securities Act] and I'd reverse."

United States v. New Britain presented the question of the relative priority of federal and municipal liens on the proceeds of a mortgage foreclosure sale of property to which the liens attached. At the October 24 conference, Chief Justice Warren stated, "If this were an insolvency case, the United States would have priority, but this is not such a case. If Congress wanted it to have priority, then it would have said so. The prior in time, prior in right theory should govern." All agreed except Justice Douglas. And when Justice Minton delivered the Court's opinion based on the Chief Justice's statement, there was no dissent.

In *United States v. Binghamton Construction Company,* the issue was whether the schedule of minimum-wage rates in a government construction contract was a "representation" or "warranty" that the contractor would not have to pay more, even if the prevailing wage rates in the area were higher. Chief Justice Warren started the December 5 conference discussion by saying, "The only point in it is that the Government is a guarantor according to respondent. The Government disclaimed responsibility on its announcement of the minimum scale. Respondent had no right to rely on it." All agreed and the Chief Justice himself delivered a unanimous opinion on March 8, 1954, in favor of the government. The winning counsel in the case, incidentally, was Warren E. Burger. This was the first case argued by Assistant Attorney General Burger in the Supreme Court.

Of the 1953 Term cases under discussion for which we have Justice Clark's notes, the most interesting was *Public Utilities Commission of California v. United Air Lines.* The case was argued on November 12 and 13, a month after Chief Justice Warren arrived at the Court. United had argued that it was not subject to the California commission's jurisdiction on rates charged for transportation between the California mainland and Catalina Island. United contended that the federal Civil Aeronautics Board had exclusive authority over these rates. At the November 14 conference, Warren urged, "the state should be permitted to proceed. There's nothing to show the state is going to do all the horribles pictured by United. They should proceed through the administrative process." Except for Justices Reed and Douglas, the others agreed. Douglas thought the case was peculiarly appropriate for declaratory judgment, and wrote a dissent, joined by Reed, to that effect.

The case was decided on November 30 by a short per curiam, on the authority of a decision requiring exhaustion of administrative remedies. The

Chief Justice apparently thought better of participating in a case involving a California agency whose members he had appointed as Governor. The report of the case states (not entirely accurately in view of his conference participation), "The CHIEF JUSTICE took no part in the consideration or decision of this case."

OTHER LEADERSHIP ILLUSTRATIONS

A Chief Justice's leadership may be shown in his ability to persuade his colleagues to adopt or not adopt a certain position. Chief Justice Warren's ability in this respect is strikingly shown in his success in inducing the Justices to follow his lead in the *Brown* segregation case, as well as in *Reynolds v. Sims* and the other leading cases discussed later in this chapter. Just as significant, we shall see, Warren stressed the importance of a unanimous *Brown* opinion and he continued to emphasize that point in the other segregation cases decided by his Court.

In 1958, Chief Justice Warren called a special term of the Court so that the Justices could hear arguments during their summer recess in August and grant speedy relief against the Arkansas refusal to allow blacks to attend Central High School in Little Rock. Following the Warren urging at the conference, the Justices quickly agreed to a decision resoundingly reaffirming the duty of state officials to obey the law as laid down by the Supreme Court. But the desired unanimity was soon threatened by Justice Clark.

The Justice from Texas was troubled by the way in which the Court had handled the case. He prepared a draft dissent that objected to the action the Chief Justice had taken to decide the case so quickly in the August Special Term. "The case," the Clark draft declared, "should be considered in its regular course, not by forced action. Of all tribunals this is one that should stick strictly to the rules. To do otherwise is to create the very situation that the Constitution prohibits, the existence of a preferred class."

For a Southern Justice to have broken the *Brown* tradition of the Court speaking with one voice in segregation cases could have had unfortunate consequences. Happily, however, Justice Clark did not go beyond venting his emotions in his draft. This was a situation where Chief Justice Warren was at his best in one-on-one sessions. When Clark talked over the matter with Warren, there is no doubt that the Chief Justice used all his persuasive powers to induce the Texan not to break the Court's unanimity in the face of what Warren called in his *Memoirs* "the great notoriety given Governor Faubus' obstructive conduct in the case."

There were other cases as well where the Warren persuasion led Justice Clark to change his mind and adopt the position that Warren favored. A good illustration is contained in the decision process in *Estes v. Texas* (1965), where the television-in-the-courtroom issue came before the Warren Court. Billie Sol Estes, the defendant in a notorious trial that received national attention, claimed that the televising of his trial deprived him of due process. The conference was sharply divided on the case, voting by a bare majority that the televising of the Estes trial did not involve any constitutional violation.

But the bare majority did not hold. Justice Clark, who had voted for affirmance at the conference, sent around a Memorandum to the Conference stating that he had changed his mind and now concluded "that the perils to a fair trial far outweigh the benefits that might accrue in the televising of the proceedings." Clark switched his vote and ultimately wrote the opinion of the Court reversing Estes's conviction.

Chief Justice Warren felt strongly about television in the courtroom. In the Warren papers in the Library of Congress, there is a copy of the remarks the Chief Justice made to his law clerk about the *Estes* case. As taken down by the clerk, Warren said that, with televised trials, "it is proposed that we turn back the clock and make everyone in the courtroom an actor before untold millions of people. We are asked again to make the determination of guilt or innocence a public spectacle and a source of entertainment for the idle and curious." Television, Warren told his clerk, "deprives the courtroom of the dignity and objectivity that is so essential for determining the guilt or innocence of persons whose life and liberty hinge on the outcome of the trial."

Feeling as strongly as he did, the Chief Justice did what he could to persuade the members of the tentative *Estes* majority to switch to the Warren posture on television. Nor can it be doubted that Warren played a key part in the switched Clark vote. Since the Chief Justice had his categorical opinion on the baneful effect of television in the courtroom, this was just the sort of thing he would talk over with Justice Clark on their morning walks part of the way to the Court building.

The Warren leadership may be seen in two 1955 Term cases, now of interest only to Supreme Court specialists, in which the Chief Justice induced the Court to go beyond the literal language of the statute to reach what he considered the just decision. In *Mastro Plastics Corp. v. National Labor Relations Board,* the Taft-Hartley Act provided that no collective-bargaining agreement could be terminated or modified unless sixty days' notice was given before the agreement's expiration date. Any employees who engaged in a strike during the sixty-day period would lose their status as employees, which meant that they would also lose their protection under the Act. Did this bar apply where the strike during the period was intended as a protest against unfair labor practices of the employer?

A literal reading of the Taft-Hartley provision would require an affirmative answer. But that was not the way Chief Justice Warren proposed to read the statute in his presentation at the conference on the case. "I wouldn't hold the strike against the union," he stated at the outset of his discussion. "The purpose of Congress was to have them bargain freely. . . . The union can't bargain at the table if the employer can go out and destroy the union. That wouldn't bring peace." In the Warren view, it was not realistic to say that the union's only remedy against unfair labor practices was to complain to the National Labor Relations Board. "The right to go before the Board," said Warren, "is an empty gesture" because it would involve "too long a delay."

The Warren refusal to follow the literal language of the statute set the tone for the others. Justices Reed, Douglas, Burton, and Clark agreed with the Chief Justice, with Justices Frankfurter, Minton, and Harlan indicating they would vote the other way. The importance of the Warren lead may be seen from the reaction of Justice Black, normally as pro-labor as any of the Justices. When Warren finished his conference presentation, Black declared, "I wish I could come out that way. But the language is so clear I couldn't read into it such an interpretation." Black conceded, "I might change, but, as of now, I can't get around the clear language. It's an outrageous situation to put the union in such a position, but it does."

As it turned out, Justice Black ultimately followed the Warren lead and joined the opinion of the Court, written by Justice Burton, which followed Warren's conference approach. Justice Frankfurter wrote a strong dissent, joined by Justices Minton and Harlan. He was bitter over what he felt was the Court's rewriting of the statute. On February 14, 1956, he wrote to Justice Reed, who had strongly supported Warren at the conference, "If I did not have . . . a cast-iron stomach, your attitude toward congressional legislation would give me ulcers." What the Court was doing was "nullifying a provision of Congress. Your compassionate heart says, 'The hell with it! We are not going to allow an employer who is guilty of [unfair] labor practices to get away with it.' It is not to be assumed that Congress intended this." Yet the Chief Justice persuaded the Court to hold that that was exactly what Congress had intended.

Chief Justice Warren's willingness to lead the Court in construing a statute liberally to reach what he considered the fair result may also be seen in *Indian Towing Co. v. United States.* The statute was the Federal Tort Claims Act. It imposes liability in tort upon the United States "in the same manner and to the same extent as a private individual in like circumstances." Plaintiffs sued the United States when a barge towed by them was damaged. They claimed the accident occurred because of the negligence of the Coast Guard, which had failed to keep a lighthouse in proper operation. The government relied on an exemption in the Tort Claims Act for damages caused by performance of discretionary functions by U.S. officials.

Even before the oral argument on October 13, 1955, Justice Frankfurter prepared a memorandum, circulated October 7, that stated, "the real question in the case before us is whether the negligent failure of the Coast Guard in its duty to maintain a lighthouse is within or without the Tort Claims Act." But how could the failure be within the Act if it was within the Coast Guard's discretion to decide whether and where it would operate lighthouses?

At the October 15 conference, the Chief Justice indicated a simple way out of the dilemma. As he saw it, "The discretionary act is putting the lighthouse where it is. After it was put there, liability attaches." In other words, there is a difference between the discretion to undertake a function such as providing lighthouse service and, once the discretion is exercised in the affirmative, the negligent operation of a particular lighthouse. The government may possess discretionary authority to perform or not to perform certain functions; but that should not immunize it from liability where the functions are performed negligently in circumstances where a private person could be liable.

"Is there anything so distinctive about lighthouses," Chief Justice Warren asked at the conference, "that lifts it from [this rule of] liability?" He answered that there was "nothing unique" about them. "There were no private persons to carry on such service and so the Government took it over." He gave as an example of a comparable private service the operation of lights on a railroad bridge, where the railroad would be liable in similar circumstances. He noted that the Tort Claims Act contained an exemption from liability for damages caused by carriage of the mail. Yet, "if a mail sack was thrown through a store window, the U.S. would be liable."

"The question," the Chief Justice concluded his conference presentation, "is: shall we take the plain purpose of the Act or shall we limit it? Congress has made it very broad and it can narrow it if that is desirable."

Chief Justice Warren's statement pointed the way to the *Indian Towing* decision. A Frankfurter opinion for a bare majority of the Court held the U.S. liable on the theory outlined by the Chief Justice. As soon as he received Justice Frankfurter's draft, Warren sent back a handwritten note on November 10, "I like your opinion in *Indian Towing* Company but out of courtesy to the other side will withhold formal agreement until the dissent is circulated."

SUPER CHIEF AND *BROWN I*

In an oft-quoted 1966 statement, Vice President Hubert Humphrey declared that if President Eisenhower "had done nothing else other than appoint Earl Warren Chief Justice, he would have earned a very important place in the history of the United States." If Earl Warren himself had done nothing else other than lead the Court to its unanimous *Brown* decision, he would have earned an important place in the judicial pantheon.

We need not, in Justice Frankfurter's phrase, "subscribe to the hero theory of history" to recognize that outstanding judges make a great difference in the law. It made a great difference that Earl Warren, rather than his predecessor, Fred M. Vinson, presided over the Court that handed down the *Brown* decision. *Brown* itself was the watershed constitutional case of this century. Justice Reed, who participated in the *Brown* decision, told one of his clerks that "if it was not the most important decision in the history of the Court, it was very close." When *Brown* struck down school segregation, it signaled the beginning of effective enforcement of civil rights in American law.

In *Brown,* black plaintiffs challenged the constitutionality of segregated schools in four states and the District of Columbia. Before *Brown,* the Court had followed the rule laid down in *Plessy v. Ferguson* (1896), that segregation was not unconstitutional, provided that there were "equal but separate accommodations for the white and colored races." The subsequent structure of racial discrimination in much of the country was built on this "separate but equal" doctrine.

Brown first came before the Court when Chief Justice Vinson sat in its center chair. When the Justices discussed the case on December 13, 1952, Vinson stated that he was not ready to overrule *Plessy v. Ferguson.* A May 17, 1954 Memorandum for the File *In re Segregation* Cases by Justice Douglas states, "Vinson was of the opinion that the *Plessy* case was right and that segregation was constitutional." Vinson stressed the cases following *Plessy.* There was, he declared, a whole "body of law back of us on separate but equal" and the Court should not overrule this substantial jurisprudence. What was needed, according to Vinson, was time to deal with the racial problem. "We can't," he said, "close our eyes to the seriousness [of the problem] in various parts of the U.S. We face the complete abolition of the public school system in the South."

With the Chief Justice indicating that he was in favor of upholding segregation, the Vinson Court was far from ready to issue a ringing pronouncement in favor of racial equality. Indeed, had Vinson presided over the Court that decided *Brown,* the result would have been a sharply divided decision. According to the Douglas Memorandum for the File, "In the original conference there were only four who voted that segregation in the public schools was unconstitutional. Those four were Black, Burton, Minton and myself. . . . So as a result of the informal vote at the 1952 conference, . . . if the cases were to be then decided the vote would be five to four in favor of the constitutionality of segregation in the public schools."

Justice Frankfurter's count was for a bare majority the other way. In a May 20, 1954, letter to a colleague three days after the unanimous *Brown* decision was announced, Frankfurter wrote, "I have no doubt that if the *Segregation* cases had reached decision last Term there would have been four dissenters — Vinson, Reed, Jackson and Clark — and certainly several opinions for the majority view. That would have been catastrophic."

The "catastrophe" was avoided when *Brown* was set for reargument in the next Court term and, in the interim, Chief Justice Vinson suddenly died. "This is the first indication that I have ever had that there is a God," Frankfurter caustically remarked to two former law clerks when he heard of Vinson's death. The Justice must have felt confirmed in his comment when Earl Warren was appointed as Vinson's successor. For, under the new Chief Justice, the Court was able to issue its landmark ruling striking down segregation and to do so unanimously, without a single concurring or dissenting voice to detract from the forthrightness of the decision.

Both the decision and the unanimity were attributable directly to Chief Justice Warren's leadership. A few days before the *Brown* decision was announced, Justice Harold H. Burton wrote in his diary, "It looks like a un-animous opinion—a major accomplishment for his [Warren's] leadership." And, just after the *Brown* opinion was read, Burton wrote to Warren, "To you goes the credit for the character of the opinions which produced the all important unanimity."

The new Chief Justice led the Court to its unanimous decision by first setting a completely different conference tone than his predecessor. Warren began his first *Brown* conference on December 12, 1953, with a strong statement on the unconstitutionality of segregation: "I don't see how in this day and age we can set any group apart from the rest and say that they are not entitled to exactly the same treatment as all others. To do so would be contrary to the Thirteenth, Fourteenth, and Fifteenth Amendments. They were intended to make the slaves equal with all others. Personally, I can't see how today we can justify segregation based solely on race."

As far as *Plessy v. Ferguson* was concerned, said Warren, "the more I've read and heard and thought, the more I've come to conclude that the basis of segregation and 'separate but equal' rests upon a concept of the inherent inferiority of the colored race. I don't see how *Plessy* and the cases following it can be sustained on any other theory. If we are to sustain segregation, we also must do it upon that basis." Warren then asserted that "if the argument proved anything, it proved that that basis was not justified."

The Chief Justice's conference presentation was a masterly illustration of the Warren method of leading the conference. It put the proponents of *Plessy* in the awkward position of appearing to subscribe to racist doctrine. Justice Reed, who spoke most strongly in favor of *Plessy*, felt compelled to assert that he was not making "the argument that the Negro is an inferior race. Of course there is no inferior race, though they may be handicapped by lack of opportunity." Reed did not, however, suggest any other ground on which the Court might rely to justify segregation now.

When the conference was finished, it appeared that Chief Justice Warren had six firm votes for his view that segregation should be ruled invalid. Two Justices, Jackson and Clark, indicated that they would vote the same way if an opinion could be written to satisfy them. Only Justice Reed still supported the *Plessy* doctrine.

The Chief Justice now devoted all his efforts to eliminating the danger of dissenting and concurring opinions. During the months that followed, he met constantly with his colleagues on the case, most often talking to them informally in their chambers. That was the way he had been able to accomplish things back in California. The result in *Brown* showed that he had not lost any of his persuasive powers in the Marble Palace.

Despite the Chief Justice's efforts, there are indications that Justice Reed persisted in voting to uphold segregation until the end of April 1954. By then, however, the Justice stood alone and Warren continued to work on him to change his vote, both at luncheon meetings and in private sessions. Then, toward the end, the Chief Justice put it to Reed directly: "Stan, you're all by yourself in this now. You've got to decide whether it's really the best thing for the country." As described by Reed's law clerk, who was present at the meeting, Warren was typically restrained in his approach. "Throughout the Chief Justice was quite low-key and very sensitive to the problems that the decision would present to the South. He empathized with Justice Reed's concern. But he was quite firm on the Court's need for unanimity on a matter of this sensitivity."

Ultimately, Justice Reed agreed to the unanimous decision. He still thought, as he wrote to Justice Frankfurter, that "there were many considerations that pointed to a dissent." But, he went on, "they did not add up to a balance against the Court's opinion. . . . the factors looking toward a fair treatment for Negroes are more important than the weight of history."

At the conference that took the vote to strike down segregation, it was agreed that the opinion should be written by the Chief Justice. The writing of the *Brown* opinion was done under conditions of even greater secrecy than usual. The extreme secrecy was extended to the entire deliberative process in the segregation case. Thus, the covering note to a Frankfurter memorandum on the fashioning of a decree in the case stated at the end: "I need hardly add that the typewriting was done under conditions of strictest security."

The Justices also took steps to ensure that the way they voted would not leak out. No record of actions taken in *Brown* was written in the docket book that was kept by each Justice and was available to his clerks. In his *Memoirs,* Chief Justice Warren tells us that at the conference at which the opinion was assigned, "the importance of secrecy was discussed. We agreed that only my law clerks should be involved, and that any writing between my office and those of the other Justices would be delivered to the Justices personally. This practice was followed throughout and this was the only time it was required in my years on the Court."

Toward the end of April, after he had secured Justice Reed's vote, the Chief Justice was ready to begin the drafting process. On April 20, Justice Burton wrote in his diary, "After lunch the Chief Justice and [I] took a walk around the Capitol then went to his chambers where he uttered his preliminary thoughts as to author segregation cases." Soon thereafter Warren went to work on the *Brown* draft opinion.

As stated previously, Chief Justice Warren's normal practice was to leave the actual drafting of opinions to his law clerks. He would only outline the way he wanted the opinion drafted and would rarely go into particulars on the details involved in the case. That was for the clerk drafting the opinion, who was left with a great deal of discretion, particularly on the reasoning and research supporting the decision.

It has been assumed that this procedure was also followed in the *Brown* drafting process. However, the draft opinion that I found in Warren's papers in the Library of Congress shows that it was the Chief Justice himself who wrote the first *Brown* draft. Headed simply "Memorandum" and undated, it is in Warren's handwriting, in pencil on nine yellow legal-size pages.

Chief Justice Warren's *Brown* draft definitely set the tone for the final opinion. It was written in the typical Warren style: short, nontechnical, well within the grasp of the average reader. The language is direct and straightforward, illustrating the point once made by one of his law clerks: "He had a penchant for Anglo-Saxon words over Latin words and he didn't like foreign phrases thrown in if there was a good American word that would do."

The Warren *Brown* draft was based on the two things he later stressed to Earl Pollock, the clerk primarily responsible for helping on the *Brown* opinion: the opinion should be as brief as possible, and it was to be written in understandable English, avoiding legalisms. The Chief Justice told Pollock he wanted an opinion that could be understood by the layman. This was repeated in the Warren May 7 memorandum transmitting the draft opinion to the Justices. The draft, wrote the Chief Justice, was "prepared on the theory that the opinions should be short, readable by the lay public, non-rhetorical, unemotional and, above all, non-accusatory."

The Warren draft contains the most famous passages in the *Brown* opinion. First, after referring to the decision facing the Court, the draft states, "In approaching it, we cannot turn the clock of education back to 1868, when the Amendment was adopted, or even to 1895 {sic} when *Plessy v. Ferguson* was decided."

The Warren draft also contains *Brown*'s striking passage on the baneful effect of segregation on black children: "To separate them from others of their age in school solely because of their color puts the mark of inferiority not only upon their status in the community but also upon their little hearts and minds in a form that is unlikely ever to be erased."

Concern with the impact of segregation on the "hearts and minds" of black children was typical of the Warren approach. In the case of segregation, this view had roots in Warren's contact with Edgar Patterson, his black driver while he was Governor of California. Patterson later recalled how he used to talk to the Governor about his early years. Warren would ask, "Tell me about how you felt when you were a little kid, going to school. And then I used to tell him about some of the things that happened in New Orleans, the way black kids felt." Patterson thought that the *Brown* opinion "almost quoted the ideas that he and I used to talk about on feelings . . . things that he picked up as he was asking questions about how the black man felt, how the black kid felt." Just before Warren's death, Patterson visited him in Georgetown University Hospital and told him his *Brown* decision "seemed to be based on our discussion of my early school life in New Orleans." Warren laughed and indicated that many other factors had entered into the decision.

In addition, it was the Warren draft that stressed the changed role of education in the contemporary society, as contrasted with the situation when the Fourteenth Amendment was adopted ("No child can reasonably be expected to succeed in life today if he is deprived of the opportunity of an education") and also posed the crucial question presented to the Court: "Does segregation of school children solely on the basis of color, even though the physical facilities may be equal, deprive the minority group of equal opportunities in the educational system?" — as well as its answer: "We believe that it does."

An early draft of the memorandum transmitting the *Brown* draft to the Justices declared, "On the question of segregation in education, this should be the end of the line." If that was true, it was mainly the Chief Justice's doing — even more than commentators on *Brown* have realized. The Warren *Brown* draft shows us that the Chief Justice was primarily responsible not only for the unanimous decision, but also for the opinion in the case. This was one case where the drafting was not delegated. The opinion delivered was basically the same as that originally written by Warren himself.

The final *Brown* draft was circulated on May 13, 1954, in printed form. The next day, Saturday, May 15, was a conference day. At lunch — a large salmon provided by Secretary of the Interior Douglas McKay — the Justices were entertained by Justice Burton. Just before, Burton wrote in his diary, the "conference finally approved Segregation opinions and instructions for delivery Monday — no previous notice being given to office staffs etc so as to avoid leaks. Most of us — including me — handed back the circulated print to C.J. to avoid possible leaks."

When the *Brown* opinion was delivered, the Justices were well aware that they had participated in what Justice Frankfurter termed "a day that will live in glory." A few days earlier, in a note to Warren joining the opinion, Frankfurter wrote: "When — I no longer say 'if — you bring this cargo of unanimity safely to port it will be a memorable day no less in the history of the Nation than in that of the Court. You have, if I may say so, been wisely at the helm throughout this year's journey of this litigation. *Finis coronat omnia.*"

BROWN ENFORCEMENT

The *Brown* case presented two principal questions: (1) Was school segregation constitutional? (2) If it was not, what remedy should the Court decree? The Court's decision on May 17, 1954, answered the first of these questions in the negative. The Warren opinion of the Court, based upon the Chief Justice's draft, ruled that school segregation violated the rights of plaintiff black children. It did not, however, make any provision for enforcement.

There is an undated note, written on a Supreme Court memo pad in Justice Frankfurter's handwriting, that reads, "It is not fair to say that the South has always denied Negroes 'this constitutional right.' It was NOT a constitutional right till May 17/54."

The change in Justice Frankfurter's posture on segregation was explained by him during a 1960 conference. "During the Conference," states a January 25, 1960, handwritten note by Justice Douglas, "Frankfurter . . . said if the cases had been brought up [before *Brown*] he would have voted that segregation in the schools was constitutional because 'public opinion had not then crystallized against it.' He said the arrival of the Eisenhower Court heralded a change in public opinion on this subject and therefore enabled him to vote against segregation. Bill Brennan's response was 'God Almighty.' "

The May 17, 1954, *Brown* opinion declared the right against segregation, but it made no provision for vindication of the new right. Instead, Chief Justice Warren's opinion concluded by announcing that the Court was scheduling further argument on the question of appropriate relief. The situation was summarized in the *New York Times* account of the *Brown* decision: "when it returns in October for the 1954–1955 term [the Court] will hear rearguments then on the question of how and when the practice it outlawed today may finally be ended."

The theme for the second *Brown* decision and opinion was set by Chief Justice Warren himself at the conference that met on Saturday, April 16, 1955, following the oral reargument on the terms of the decree earlier in the week. Warren's presentation opening the conference stated the main lines of what became the Court's enforcement decision. First, the Chief Justice rejected various proposals that had been discussed in the Court: appointment of a master (a lawyer chosen to work out the terms of an enforcement decree), fixing of a date for completion of desegregation, requiring specific desegregation plans from defendant school districts, and imposing of procedural requirements — all of which were also rejected by the Court's decision. Then he emphasized that the Court should furnish guidance to the lower courts. "the opinion ought to give them some guidance. It would make it much easier and would be rather cruel to shift it back to them and let them flounder." As Warren summed it up, "I think there should be an opinion with factors for the courts below to take into account rather than a formal decree." The opinion-not-decree approach had the advantage of less formal precision and hence greater flexibility. Flexibility in enforcement was also the keynote of the ground rules Chief Justice Warren suggested to guide the enforcement process.

Once again, the Warren presentation set the theme both for the conference and the decision. And once again the conference agreed that the unanimous opinion should be written by the Chief Justice. Warren stressed to his clerks that the opinion should be as short as possible and cover the main points he had made at the conference: that enforcement be flexible, under accepted equity principles, and that it take into account various factors to be briefly listed to serve as ground rules for the lower courts.

As was true in *Brown I,* the drafting of the *Brown II* opinion was primarily by the Chief Justice himself. In May 1955, Warren once more put pencil to paper and produced a draft opinion. The original is again in pencil in the Chief Justice's handwriting on six yellow legal-size pages and headed *"Memo."* As was true of Warren's *Brown I* draft, the *Brown II* draft is similar to the final *Brown II* opinion and contains most of the latter's language.

The most noted change in Warren's *Brown II* opinion was made at Justice Frankfurter's urging. The Chief Justice had closed his original draft: "The judgments of the Courts of Appeal are accordingly reversed (except Delaware) and the causes are remanded to the District Courts to take such proceedings and enter such orders and decrees consistent with this opinion as are necessary and proper to admit plaintiffs and those similarly situated in their respective school districts to the public school system on a non-discriminatory basis at the *earliest practicable date.*"

In the final *Brown II* opinion, this was changed to: "The judgments below, except that in the Delaware case, are accordingly reversed and the cases are remanded to the District Courts to take such proceedings and enter such orders and decrees consistent with this opinion as are necessary and proper to admit to public schools on a racially nondiscriminatory basis *with all deliberate speed* the parties to these cases" (italics added).

When the *Brown II* opinion declared that the lower courts were to ensure that blacks were admitted to schools on a nondiscriminatory basis "with all deliberate speed," it led to learned controversy on the origins of the oxymoronic phrase — itself so untypical of the normal Warren mode of expression. The phrase itself comes from Justice Oliver Wendell Holmes. But it was used before him by the British poet Francis Thompson in an 1892 poem, "The Hound of Heaven." After a newspaper account credited Justice Frankfurter with suggesting the term in *Brown II,* several correspondents wrote asking whether he had gotten it from Thompson. The Justice replied, in a letter to one reporter, that "the phrase has a legal lineage older than Thompson's use of it. In . . . 1909, Mr. Justice Holmes wrote to his friend, Sir Frederick Pollock, 'in your chancery's delightful phrase, with all deliberate speed.' . . . Again, in his opinion in *Virginia v. West Virginia,* 222 U.S. 17, 20, he stated 'in the language of the English Chancery, with all deliberate speed.' "

Justice Frankfurter wrote to other correspondents, "I have made the most assiduous search to find Holmes's authority for saying this was a Chancery phrase" — but "all to no avail." Nor has anyone else succeeded in tracing it to its alleged English legal derivation. "Yet," as Frankfurter insisted, "it cannot be that Holmes pulled it out of the air."

But, if we remain uncertain where Justice Holmes obtained the phrase, what is certain is that Justice Frankfurter got it from Holmes and the *Brown II* opinion got it from Frankfurter. It is true that commentators on *Brown II* have all assumed that this was the case; but they have had to support the assumption by largely circumstantial evidence. However, two letters by Justice Frankfurter to the Chief Justice enable us to confirm definitely that the Justice was responsible for the "all deliberate speed" language.

These letters show that Chief Justice Warren had discussed the opinion with Justice Frankfurter even before his draft opinion was circulated, and the

Justice had then suggested the Holmes phrase. On May 24, 1955, Frankfurter wrote that he had read the draft "and I am ready to sign on the undotted line." But Frankfurter went on, "I still think that *'with all deliberate speed,'* *Virginia v. West Virginia,* 222 U.S. 17, 22, is preferable to 'at the earliest practicable date.'"

Chief Justice Warren did not make the change in his circulated draft. So Justice Frankfurter sent him a May 27 letter repeating the suggestion: "I still strongly believe that 'with all deliberate speed' conveys more effectively the process of time for the effectuation of our decision. . . . I think it is highly desirable to educate public opinion — the parties themselves and the general public — to an understanding that we are at the beginning of a process of enforcement and not concluding it. In short, I think it is far better to habituate the public's mind to the realization of this, as . . . the phrase 'with all deliberate speed' . . . [is] calculated to do."

Chief Justice Warren did, of course, finally accept the Frankfurter suggestion and the "all deliberate speed" phrase remains the most striking one in the *Brown II* opinion. More important was the two-edged nature of the phrase. It ensured flexibility by providing time for enforcement; but it also countenanced delay in vindicating constitutional rights. "All deliberate speed" may never have been intended to mean indefinite delay. Yet that is just what it did mean in much of the South.

Some of the Justices, including the Chief Justice, later indicated that it had been a mistake to qualify desegregation enforcement by the "all deliberate speed" language. Justice Black's son quotes him as saying, "It tells the enemies of the decision that for the present the status quo will do and gives them time to contrive devices to stall off segregation." This Black statement is inconsistent with what he said at the April 16, 1955, conference on the *Brown* enforcement question. The Justice then had indicated that the Court should not try to settle the segregation issue too rapidly. If it attempted to do so, Black told the conference, its decree "would be like Prohibition." Black, in fact, was the one Justice who predicted at the conference that the movement toward desegregation in the South would at best be only "glacial."

The Chief Justice, too, came to believe that it had been a mistake to accept the "all deliberate speed" language. In his later years Warren concluded that he had been sold a bill of goods when Justice Frankfurter induced him to use the phrase. It would have been better, he later said, to have ordered desegregation forthwith. By then, however, Justice Black's prediction of the "glacial" pace of desegregation had proved, if anything, overoptimistic. The Justices had, to be sure, not expected enthusiastic compliance by the South. But the extent of opposition was something that had not been foreseen. Looking back, Warren, at least, felt that much of the defiance could have been avoided if the South had not been led to believe that "deliberate speed" would countenance indefinite delay. When a comparable problem arose in 1964 in connection with enforcement of the "one-person–one-vote" principle in legislative apportionments,

Chief Justice Warren did not hesitate to urge immediate enforcement, regardless of the problems in individual states in adapting to the new rule.

Except in the *Brown* case, in fact, Chief Justice Warren never let the question of enforcement affect his decisions. He always felt that the Justices' duty was only to decide the cases before them as they thought the Constitution required. Warren's Court career was the living example of the old maxim: *Fiat justitia et ruant coeli* (Let justice be done though the heavens should fall).

But he did not expect the heavens to fall. Once, after the Court had ordered the release of an army prisoner, one of his law clerks had asked him how they were going to make the army do that. Chief Justice Warren just laughed and said, "Don't worry about it. They will do it." The clerk persisted and referred to the Andrew Jackson statement about John Marshall having to enforce his own decision.

"Look," Warren said in reply, "you don't have to worry. If they don't do this, they've destroyed the whole republic, and they aren't going to do that. So you don't even have to worry about whether they are going to do it or not—*they're going to do it!*"

LEADERSHIP AND REAPPORTIONMENT

The 1964 case referred to above in which the one-person–one-vote principle was laid down as the constitutional rule was *Reynolds v. Sims*. It arose out of challenges to the apportionment of both houses of the Alabama legislature. The apportionment issue had arisen two years earlier in *Baker v. Carr,* which had decided that the Court had jurisdiction over cases challenging legislative apportionments, though they had until then been held to involve only "political questions" beyond judicial competence. Several of the Justices, including Chief Justice Warren, had also wanted to decide the merits in *Baker v. Carr* and apply a standard of equality of population to legislative apportionments. They were not, however, willing to apply it to more than one house.

Chief Justice Warren, in particular, was influenced by his experience in California, where only the Assembly was apportioned by population. Each California county was represented by one state senator, regardless of population. In his *Memoirs,* Warren called this the "Federal System of Representation" because of its resemblance to that in the United States Constitution. Warren had believed that the system worked fairly and he thought that the equal-population requirement should not extend to similar state senates.

The same belief was expressed during the conference discussions that followed the arguments in November 1963 of *Reynolds v. Sims.* Led by the Chief Justice, most of the Justices quickly decided that the lower-house apportionments, which were not based on equality of population, were invalid. But neither Warren nor the others were willing to apply the population standard to both houses of the state legislature.

That a majority of Justices changed their minds was a direct result of Chief Justice Warren's lead. The Chief Justice had assigned the *Reynolds* opinion to himself at the November 22 conference — the conference at which the Justices received word of President John F. Kennedy's assassination. As Warren started to work out his reasoning, he came to realize that his California experience should not be determinative.

Justice Brennan related for me how the Chief Justice burst without ceremony into Brennan's chambers after he had begun work on the reapportionment opinion. "It can't be! It can't be!" declared the Chief Justice. Warren proceeded to tell the Justice that the equal-population standard must apply to both Houses of a state legislature. Warren persuaded Brennan, and later Justices Black, Douglas, and Goldberg, of the correctness of his new position.

That Chief Justice Warren should have been the catalyst for the across-the-board adoption of the equal-population standard was ironic in view of his opposition to that standard when he was Governor of California. After his opinion in *Reynolds v. Sims* was announced, *U.S. News & World Report* quoted from a 1948 speech by Governor Warren that had effectively killed a reapportionment effort in California. "I believe we should keep . . . our present system of legislative representation," Governor Warren had declared. He rejected the idea "of restricting the representation in the [state] senate to a strictly population basis" for "the same reason that the Founding Fathers of our country gave balanced representation to the states of the union — equal representation in one house and proportionate representation based on population in the other."

After Chief Justice Warren had concluded that *Reynolds v. Sims* had to be decided by an equal-population standard applicable to both houses, he was talking to Francis X. Beytagh, the law clerk working on the case. He began to laugh and remarked, "You know I gave a speech some years ago in California supporting our reapportionment system there." He said it was based on the federal principle that the Court was rejecting. "You know," he went on, "I never really thought very much about it then. As a political matter it seemed to me to be a sensible arrangement. But now, as a constitutional matter, with the point of view of the responsibilities of a Justice, I kind of got to look at it differently." Beytagh recalls that the Chief Justice was not at all troubled by the fact that he had taken an entirely different position as Governor. "I was just wrong as Governor," Warren later told another law clerk.

Chief Justice Warren prepared a memorandum for Beytagh that outlined what he wanted to say in the *Reynolds* opinion. He stressed the equal population standard as the rule for both houses and the rejection of the federal analogy. Beytagh then went to work on the draft. At first, he tried to write as narrowly as possible. But he soon concluded that the Chief Justice wanted the kind of broad-brush opinion that was ultimately issued.

Perhaps the most noted passage in the *Reynolds* opinion is the statement "Legislators represent people, not trees or acres. Legislators are elected by voters, not farms or cities or economic interests." Beytagh told me that when

Warren saw that language, "he got a kick out of it. He kind of laughed and said that's not a bad way of expressing the whole notion."

The approach embodied in this famous *Reynolds v. Sims* passage had been indicated in a question asked by the Chief Justice at the March 31, 1964, argument on a companion case to *Reynolds* (weeks after he had concluded that the equal-population rule had to govern in both houses of a state legislature): "Isn't the basic issue whether these appellants and all other people in the State . . . have proper representation, whether they are city people or farmers, liberals or conservatives, or whatever?"

One of the things that Warren emphasized to Beytagh was the question of remedies. The Chief Justice referred to the "all deliberate speed" language of the second *Brown* case and made it plain that he did not want any such language in the *Reynolds* opinion. Aside from a suggestion at the end of the opinion that where an election was actually in progress it might be appropriate for a court temporarily to stay its hand, there was a clear indication that no remedial delay would be allowed.

Even though the Warren *Reynolds v. Sims* opinion was more far-reaching than the conference discussion, it was quickly accepted by a majority. As a Justice who participated in the case remembered it, "The opinions issuing from the chambers of the Chief Justice in those cases were joined without the slightest apparent hesitation or reservation by Justices Black, Douglas, Brennan, and Goldberg, and eventually secured the vote of Justice White as well." That that result was accomplished was due entirely to the Warren leadership. It was Warren alone who decided that the conference consensus was wrong and that the equal population standard had to govern all state legislative apportionments. The Chief Justice also personally persuaded Justice Brennan and the others who joined his opinion that the federal analogy should not be followed. Had Warren not changed his mind and convinced the others that his new position was correct, the law on the subject would be entirely different. Because Chief Justice Warren led the Court to the *Reynolds* decision, Anthony Lewis could sum up the 1963 Term in the *New York Times* as "one of extraordinary importance for Court and country. Not since 1954 [when *Brown* was decided] . . . have any Term's decisions so deeply affected American institutions."

The far-reaching nature of the *Reynolds* decision is shown by a letter written just after the oral argument to retired Justice Frankfurter by Justice Harlan, who dissented. Harlan wrote telling of his "despondency that I no longer have you as an active colleague—this being particularly accented today by the constitutional convention into which the Court convened itself at the Conference today on the first reapportionment cases."

On the other hand, Anthony Lewis, in the *New York Times,* characterized decision day in the *Reynolds* case as "one of the great days in the Supreme Court's history" and asked, "Where would we be today if the Supreme Court had not been willing ten years ago to tackle the great moral issue of racial discrimination that Congress had so long avoided?"

Chief Justice Warren never had doubts about the reapportionment decisions. He maintained that if the one-person–one-vote principle had been laid down years earlier, many of the nation's legal sores would never have festered. "If [the principle] had been in existence fifty years ago," he later insisted, "we would have saved ourselves acute racial troubles. Many of our problems would have been solved a long time ago if everyone had the right to vote, and his vote counted the same as everybody else's. Most of these problems could have been solved through the political process rather than through the courts. But as it was, the Court had to decide."

The Chief Justice was well aware that *Reynolds v. Sims* was the political death warrant for undetermined numbers of rural legislators whose seats would now be reapportioned out of existence. Soon after the decision, Warren flew to his home state of California to hunt with his sons and some old friends. One of them was asked to invite the Chief Justice to go with some state senators on a trip to hunt quail. When Warren was asked if he wanted to drive down and join them, he looked incredulous. "All those *senators?*" he inquired in mock horror. "With *guns?*"

MIRANDA V. ARIZONA

Justice Douglas tells us in his *Autobiography* that when Warren Burger succeeded Earl Warren as Chief Justice, he told the conference that the Court should overrule a number of Warren Court decisions — particularly those in the *Gideon* and *Miranda* cases. These were two of the famous trilogy of criminal-law cases decided by the Warren Court: *Mapp v. Ohio* (1961), *Gideon v. Wainwright* (1963), and *Miranda v. Arizona* (1966). They will be dealt with in reverse order in our discussion of the leadership role of Chief Justice Warren in those decisions.

Writing in the *New York Times* in 1965, Anthony Lewis pointed out that the difficulty of the Court's work was insufficiently appreciated by either the Court's critics or its admirers. When the Court reversed a conviction, the decision was judged only in terms of the "poor downtrodden defendant" or the "vicious criminal threatening our peace."

Yet the criminal cases that come to the Court can rarely be dealt with in light of the individual attitude toward the particular defendant. Lewis illustrated the point by referring to "a typical criminal case that comes before the Court these days. A suspect has been arrested and brought to a local police station; he asks to see a lawyer, and the police say no; after questioning by a relay of officers he confesses. Should the confession be admissible as evidence — or excluded because it resulted from the denial of counsel?"

The Sixth Amendment guarantees the right to counsel in "all criminal prosecutions." But, as Lewis noted, "the Constitution does not answer the critical question: When does the right to counsel begin?" Though Lewis published his article almost a year before *Miranda v. Arizona* came to the Court, his illustrative case presented the very question posed in *Miranda*. The answer given in *Miranda* made that case one of the most controversial before the Warren Court.

Ernesto A. Miranda had been convicted in Arizona of kidnapping and rape. He had been arrested and taken to an interrogation room, where he was questioned without being advised that he had a right to have an attorney present. After two hours, the police secured a confession that was admitted into evidence over Miranda's objection. The state supreme court affirmed the conviction.

Miranda was argued early in 1966. The Chief Justice's questions and comments during the argument foreshadowed the decision. One of the points for the Court to decide was when the police "focused" on the defendant so as to trigger his Fifth and Sixth Amendment rights — whether at the stage of police interrogation or only when an accusation was made. To Warren, the accusatory stage was reached with Miranda's arrest. "I didn't know," the Chief Justice commented during the argument, "that we could arrest people in this country for investigation. Wouldn't you say it was accusatory when a man was locked in jail?"

The Chief Justice also indicated that Miranda's right to consult counsel was not affected by whether or not he could pay for a lawyer. "When does the right to counsel attach?" Warren asked, "Does inability to hire mean less generous treatment by the law?"

Last of all, the Chief Justice stressed the failure to advise Miranda of his rights — a focal point of the *Miranda* opinion. When counsel argued that the test was one of voluntariness of the confession, Warren came back with, "Wouldn't the best test be simply that the authorities must warn him?" Then the defendant could intelligently decide if he wanted to talk without counsel. "Do you agree," Warren asked, "that if a man says I would like to talk to a lawyer, the police should not interrogate?"

Justice Fortas, who had been on the *Miranda* Court, told me that the *Miranda* decision "was entirely his" — that is, Warren's. The Chief Justice's leadership led the Justices both to their decision in the case and the setting out of what the opinion called "concrete constitutional guidelines" for police interrogation.

At the March 4, 1966, conference, Chief Justice Warren left no doubt where he stood. As at the argument, the Chief Justice stressed that no warning had been given by the police. In such a case, the police must warn someone like Miranda of his right to silence, that anything he said could be used against him, that he could have a lawyer, and that he could have counsel appointed if he could not afford one.

The Chief Justice told the conference that such warnings had been given by his staff when he had been a district attorney. He placed particular emphasis upon the practice followed by the Federal Bureau of Investigation and explained how it worked. The "standard" FBI warning covered the essential requirements Warren had posited. The Chief Justice told the conference that the FBI's record of effective law enforcement showed that requiring similar warnings in all police interrogations would not impose too great a burden.

Another Justice who was present said to me, "the statement that the FBI did it . . . was a swing factor. I believe that was a tremendously important factor, perhaps the critical factor in the *Miranda* vote."

The conference was closely divided. Justices Black, Douglas, Brennan, and Fortas supported Chief Justice Warren, though they were not united on the grounds for reversal. Justice Douglas felt that the reversal should be based on the right to counsel and the interrogation by the police "without providing one." Justice Black, on the other hand, said, "I think the focus is on the privilege against being a witness against himself. From the time government begins to move against a man, when they take him into custody, his rights attach. This . . . was inherently coercive and [they] can't make him be a witness against himself."

Justice Brennan also urged that the decision should turn on the Fifth Amendment privilege. His view, as he summarized it in a May 11 memorandum, was "that the extension of the privilege against the states . . . inevitably required that we consider whether police interrogation should be hedged about with procedural safeguards effective to secure the privilege . . . namely, 'The right of a person to remain silent unless he chooses to speak in the unfettered exercise of his own will.' "

The *Miranda* majority agreed on the Warren approach to the case after the Chief Justice explained his reasoning in his draft opinion. Above all, he persuaded the others to accept what amounted to a code of police procedure governing interrogation of suspects. Even the *New York Times* thought that the Warren opinion went too far in this respect, saying that the listing of procedures was an "over-hasty trespass into the legislative area." Chief Justice Warren himself had no doubts in the matter and, relying on his years as a criminal prosecutor as well as the FBI experience, persuaded a majority to agree to his far-reaching opinion. The opinion of the Court that the Chief Justice delivered in *Miranda* was essentially the same as the draft that he had originally circulated.

The *Miranda* dissents were notable for their sharp tone, charging, in the words of the Harlan dissent, that the decision was "heavy-handed . . . and entails harmful consequences for the country at large." When he had read Justice Harlan's draft dissent, Justice Brennan prepared a short concurrence that began, "I join the Court's opinion in these cases and write merely to emphasize that the Court has not [been as extreme] as the dissents suggest."

Justice Brennan showed his draft concurrence to the Chief Justice. Warren expressed concern at the prospect of a separate opinion by a member of the majority. Though Brennan explained that the concurrence was being written solely for emphasis, Warren was not mollified. Justice Brennan finally agreed to neither circulate nor issue the concurrence. Here, too, was an example of the Warren leadership. He did not want an opinion as important as *Miranda* to be diluted by any concurrence, even though it was intended to stress its author's support for the opinion of the Court. No less than Chief Justice Marshall, who had instituted the opinion-of-the-Court practice in place of seriatim separate opinions by each Justice, Earl Warren understood the crucial importance of having the Court speak with one voice.

In his May 11 memorandum, Justice Brennan declared that the *Miranda* opinion "will be one of the most important opinions of our time." *Miranda* also turned out to be the most controversial of the Warren Court's criminal-law decisions, and it gave rise to anguished complaints from law enforcement officers throughout the country. They denounced *Miranda* for putting, as Mayor Sam W. Yorty of Los Angeles said, "another set of handcuffs on the police department." *Miranda* was condemned on Capitol Hill and became a major issue in Richard M. Nixon's presidential campaign.

On the other hand, *Miranda,* as much as anything, exemplified Chief Justice Warren's basic approach. Every so often in criminal cases, when counsel defending convictions would cite legal precedents, Warren would bend his bulk over the bench to ask, "Yes, yes — but were you fair?" The fairness to which the Chief Justice referred was no jurisprudential abstraction. It related to methods of arrest, questioning of suspects, police conduct, and the like — matters that Warren still understood as intimately as when he himself was doing the prosecuting years earlier as district attorney in Alameda County, California. The *Miranda* decision was the ultimate embodiment of the Warren fairness approach.

GIDEON V. WAINWRIGHT

During the *Miranda* argument, Chief Justice Warren stated that "this [case] is not much different from *Gideon.*" He was referring to *Gideon v. Wainwright* (1963) — the Warren Court's landmark case on the right to counsel. The book by Anthony Lewis, *Gideon's Trumpet,* and the movie based upon it have made Clarence Gideon and his case a part of American folklore. But few people realize that the *Gideon* decision resulted directly from Warren's leadership. Not long before Gideon's petition was filed, the Chief Justice's law clerks had been instructed by one of the prior term's clerks, "Keep your eyes peeled for a right to counsel case. The Chief feels strongly that the Constitution requires a lawyer."

Gideon had been convicted in a Florida court of breaking and entering a poolroom with intent to commit a crime — a felony under Florida law. The trial judge refused Gideon's request for counsel, and he had to conduct his own defense. The highest Florida court affirmed. Gideon then sent a petition to the Supreme Court for certiorari. The petition was laboriously scrawled in pencil in schoolboy-type printing on lined sheets furnished by the Florida prison. Gideon's papers arrived at the Court on January 8, 1962 — one of nine in forma pauperis petitions in that morning's mail.

Gideon's petition claimed that he had been denied due process because, "When at the time of the petitioners trial he ask the lower court for the aid of counsel, the court refused this aid. Petitioner told the court that this Court made decision to the effect that all citizens tried for a felony crime should have aid of counsel. The lower court ignored this plea." At the trial, when the court had denied his request for appointed counsel, Gideon had asserted, "The United States Supreme Court says I am entitled to be represented by counsel."

Gideon was, to be sure, wrong in his assertion. The leading case then was *Betts v. Brady,* where the Court had held in 1942 that an indigent defendant did not have a due-process right to appointed counsel in a noncapital case unless he could show that, under the special circumstances of his case, he could not obtain a "fair trial" without a lawyer. Gideon's petition did not claim any such "special circumstances," and, as Lewis put it in his book, the petition was not the type that evoked the rare comment in the Clerk's Office, where the petitions were sorted, "Here's one that I'll bet will be granted." On the contrary, says Lewis, "In the Clerk's Office it had no ring of history to it."

But Lewis and other Court watchers were unaware of two crucial facts. One was that, as we saw, the Warren law clerks had been instructed to find in the mass of I.F.P. petitions just such a right-to-counsel case. The second was that, in their discussions on *Carnley v. Cochran,* a case then pending, the Justices had come close to overruling *Betts v. Brady.* In fact, the Court had been sharply divided on *Betts v. Brady* at the February 25, 1962, *Carnley* conference. However, before *Carnley* was decided, Justice Whittaker resigned and Justice Frankfurter became incapacitated by a stroke. This gave the Chief Justice, who was in favor of discarding the *Betts v. Brady* rule, the votes for a four-to-three decision overruling *Betts.* Warren decided, nevertheless, that it would be unwise to overrule an important precedent by a bare majority of only a seven-man Court. The case was assigned to Justice Brennan, who drafted an opinion of the Court reversing Carnley's conviction within the *Betts v. Brady* rule. It was after this that Chief Justice Warren told his clerks to look for a right to counsel case that would give the Court an opportunity to overrule *Betts v. Brady.*

Carnley and the Warren instructions made the *Gideon* case the proverbial needle in the in forma pauperis haystack. The Chief Justice's law clerks had the special duty of scrutinizing the I.F.P. applications and preparing a memorandum (then called a "flimsy," from the thin paper carbon copy sent to each Justice). When the Warren clerk who prepared the flimsy considered the case worthy of consideration, he attached the red envelope containing the original petition to his memo. This was done in Gideon's case and served as a red flag that this was a right-to-counsel case that might serve as a vehicle for overruling *Betts v. Brady.*

The *Gideon* certiorari conference took place June 1, 1962. At Chief Justice Warren's urging, the Court voted to grant cert, with only Justice Clark for denial. Even the normally conservative Justice Harlan had written at the end of his clerk's cert memo, "YES, I think the time has come we should meet the Betts question head-on." The order granting cert stated that counsel were requested to discuss the question, "Should this Court's holding in Betts v. Brady . . . be reconsidered?"

On June 18, Gideon sent another penciled petition: "I do desire the Court to appoint a competent attorney to represent me in this Court." At the conference on June 22 (the last of the 1961 Term) Chief Justice Warren suggested that Abe Fortas, soon to be appointed to the Court himself, should be assigned to represent Gideon. The Justices all concurred. The Court Clerk put in a call to Fortas, locating him in Dallas, and Fortas said he would be happy to serve.

"If an obscure convict named Clarence Earl Gideon," declared Attorney General Robert F. Kennedy in a speech after the Supreme Court decision, "had not sat down in his prison cell with a pencil and paper to write a letter to the Supreme Court . . . , the vast machinery of American law would have gone on functioning undisturbed. But Gideon *did* write that letter . . . and the whole course of American legal history has been changed."

Yet it was Chief Justice Warren more than anyone who was responsible for the *Gideon* decision. It was the Chief Justice who wanted his clerks to find a case like *Gideon,* led the Justices in granting cert in the case, and suggested that Fortas be assigned to argue it. Those were the crucial steps that made the *Gideon* decision inevitable. The rest was anticlimax — though none but the Justices were privy to that reality.

Gideon was argued on January 15, 1963. In his *Autobiography,* Douglas called the Fortas argument the best he had heard. But the Fortas eloquence was only the battering of an open door. The Justices, including Justices Clark and Harlan, who had not been willing to go that far the previous year in *Carnley,* had reached a consensus on overruling *Betts v. Brady.* Led by Chief Justice Warren, the January 18 conference quickly agreed that *Betts v. Brady*'s time had come.

The conference voted unanimously to reverse Gideon's conviction and to overrule *Betts v. Brady.* They followed Warren's suggestion to limit the opinion to the case at hand, without addressing the question of how far the new right to assigned counsel extended. The Chief Justice assigned the opinion to Justice Black — a gesture particularly appreciated by the others because Black had delivered the dissent in *Betts v. Brady.* When Justice Black wrote the opinion, he simply based it on his previous dissent, and he was able to circulate a draft within two weeks. The decision was announced for a unanimous Court on March 18.

To one interested in how an effective Chief Justice operates, the *Gideon* case is a good illustration of the Warren fairness in assigning opinions. He did not take the "big" cases for himself, except where, as in the *Brown* segregation case, he thought it was important that the Court speak through the Chief Justice, or, as in *Reynolds v. Sims* or *Miranda v. Arizona,* he wanted to bear the brunt of the expected criticism. The Justices all received their share of the important opinions, though he naturally gave more of them to those who were his supporters and would express themselves in the manner closest to his own views.

There is nothing inconsistent in this with the proper assignment of opinions. "I think it is very fair," Justice White, himself never one of the Warren inner circle, conceded to me, "for a Chief Justice to assign opinions to the people who (a) are on his side; (b) will do the job the way the Chief Justice would best like it done, and I think that's part of the prerogatives of the Chief Justice." The Chief Justice, as White said, might rightly assign an opinion to one Justice rather than another because "he felt that [the Justice] would more accurately or better reflect the sentiment that he would like to see reflected."

It is also erroneous to judge the fairness of opinion assignments by focusing only on the stars of the Court calendar. "Every year on this Court we get 'dogs' of cases," Justice Stewart once explained to me. "These are the cases where you knew, right from the moment you started to work on it, it would add nothing to the jurisprudence of the United States at all. You had to do the best you could, but it was a 'nothing' case, except extremely hard and arduous. Every term there are cases like that."

Justice Stewart recalled Warren's fairness in assigning the dogs as well as the stars. "I remember," he says, "the Chief Justice typically and invariably would take more than his share of those, you know. So that if you got assigned one, you wouldn't resent it. He got more than his share; you wouldn't feel you were just getting this stuff."

MAPP V. OHIO

The one decision in the *Mapp-Gideon-Miranda* trilogy that was not the result of Chief Justice Warren's leadership was *Mapp v. Ohio* (1961). Instead, the key Justice in the *Mapp* decision process was Justice Clark. It may, however, be doubted that *Mapp* would have been decided as it was without the Chief Justice's strong support. That and the importance of the decision justify the discussion of *Mapp* that follows.

According to a *New York Times* survey of the 1960 Term, the decision in *Mapp v. Ohio* was the "most far-reaching constitutional step of the term." Justice Fortas went even further when I asked him about the case. "To me," he said, "the most radical decision in recent times was Mapp against Ohio." *Mapp* deserves this characterization because it overruled the 1949 decision in *Wolf v. Colorado* — until then one of the cornerstones of our criminal law. *Wolf* held that the exclusionary rule was not required by the U.S. Constitution in state criminal cases. The result was, in the words of the *Wolf* opinion, "that in a prosecution in a State court for a State crime the Fourteenth Amendment does not forbid the admission of evidence obtained by an unreasonable search and seizure."

Dollree Mapp was the catalyst. She had been convicted of having obscene books and pictures. Mapp had refused to admit the police without a search warrant, but they forcibly opened her door, physically subdued her, searched the house, and discovered what they claimed were obscene materials. For her part Mapp maintained that her conviction was invalid because the Ohio statute prohibiting possession of obscene books and pictures violated the First Amendment.

The memorandum by his law clerk to Justice Clark recommending that he vote to take the appeal, confirmed that the "main point" presented to the Supreme Court was the constitutionality of the Ohio statute barring possession of obscene material. "I think," the clerk wrote, "it should fall under Smith v. California" — a 1960 case holding that for an obscenity conviction, the statute must require that defendant have knowledge of the material's obscene character. The memo from Justice Harlan's clerk similarly stated, though more categorically, "This is an obscenity case."

The briefs and arguments in the Supreme Court were devoted also to the First Amendment issue. Only the brief of the American Civil Liberties Union, appearing as amicus curiae, briefly referred to *Wolf* and asked the Court to reexamine and overrule it, though without any argumentation to support the request.

At the March 31, 1961, conference after the argument, the discussion continued to be devoted almost entirely to the constitutionality of the Ohio obscenity statute. Chief Justice Warren set the theme by declaring that the law "cuts across First Amendment rights. It's too broad a statute to accomplish its purpose, and on that basis I'd reverse." All the others agreed that the conviction should be reversed on the First Amendment ground. As Justice Stewart put it, "if this stuff isn't covered by the First and Fourteenth" Amendments, it was hard to see what would be.

The conference discussion and vote was summed up by Justice Stewart in a 1983 lecture on the *Mapp* case: "At the conference following the argument, a majority of the Justices agreed that the Ohio statute violated the *first* and fourteenth amendments."

In his conference discussion, Justice Douglas had agreed with the reversal on the First Amendment. But significantly he also gave *Wolf* as an alternate ground for reversal and said that he was prepared to vote to overrule that case. The Chief Justice and Justice Brennan indicated that they would vote with Justice Douglas on *Wolf,* but when there was no support on this from the others, the three agreed to go along with the reversal on First Amendment grounds. The case was assigned to Justice Clark, who wrote the final opinion overruling *Wolf* and applying the exclusionary rule to the states.

Years after *Mapp* was decided Justice Stewart told me, "I remember how amazed I was when the Justice Clark circulation in *Mapp v. Ohio* hit my desk." Stewart never learned from the others how the *Mapp* majority had agreed to decide as it did. However, as he said in his lecture, "I have always suspected that the members of the soon-to-be *Mapp* majority had met in what I affectionately call a 'rump caucus' to discuss a different basis for their decision." His suspicion was confirmed, he told his audience, when he learned for the first time from my biography of Chief Justice Warren "that an impromptu caucus of the *Mapp* majority took place in an elevator at the Court immediately after the conference at which the case was discussed."

What happened, as I learned from one of the participants in the "rump caucus," was that Justice Clark changed his mind just after the conference discussion of *Mapp*. On the elevator after leaving the conference room, the Texan turned to Justices Black and Brennan and asked, "wouldn't this be a good case to apply the exclusionary rule and do what *Wolf* didn't do?"

Under questioning by the others, Justice Clark confirmed that he was serious and that he had, indeed, shifted his ground to the anti-*Wolf* position. The Clark switch made four Justices in favor of the *Wolf* overruling. The key was now Justice Black, who, if persuaded, would become the fifth vote. Black tended to a restrained approach in Fourth Amendment cases. In his discussion with Justices Brennan and Clark, however, the Alabaman showed willingness to agree to a decision overruling the *Wolf* holding that the states were not required to apply the exclusionary rule, though he indicated that he still had difficulty in doing it on Fourth Amendment grounds alone.

Justice Clark then circulated a draft *Mapp* opinion on April 22. The Clark draft was substantially similar to the opinion of the Court that he ultimately delivered. It held categorically that, under the Fourth and Fourteenth Amendments, all evidence obtained by illegal searches and seizures is inadmissible in a state court.

After he had read the draft, Justice Brennan wrote to Justice Clark, "Of course you know I think this is just magnificent and wonderful. I have not joined anything since I came with greater pleasure." Justice Black sent a penciled note, after receiving a revised draft, telling Clark that none of the statements made "raise insuperable barriers for me." Though Black agreed to the *Mapp* opinion, he felt that he had to explain his vote in a separate concurrence. It stated that though, in his view, the Fourth Amendment alone did not bar illegally seized evidence, the Fourth, taken together with the Fifth Amendment's ban against self-incrimination, required the exclusionary rule.

Chief Justice Warren, and Justices Douglas, Brennan, and even Black agreed without difficulty to Clark's changed approach in *Mapp*. To the others, however, the draft opinion of the Court reversing on the *Wolf* ground came as a complete surprise. "I was shocked," said Justice Stewart in his 1983 lecture on *Mapp*, "when Justice Clark's proposed Court opinion reached my desk. I immediately wrote him a note expressing my surprise and questioning the wisdom of overruling an important doctrine in a case in which the issue was not briefed, argued, or discussed by the state courts, by the parties' counsel, or at our conference following the oral argument." Justice Stewart wrote a short memorandum stating that he expressed no view on the constitutional issue which the Court decided. Justice Harlan delivered a strong dissent disagreeing with the overruling of *Wolf* and asserting that the majority opinion was "notably unconvincing."

As previously stated, *Mapp* was the one case in the Warren Court's criminal-law trilogy where the Chief Justice did not lead the Court to its decision. Warren had presented the case to the conference as a First Amendment case and had recommended reversal because the Ohio statute "cuts across First Amendment rights." But he had supported Justice Douglas when he stated that the Court should vote to overrule *Wolf.* And when Justice Clark shifted his ground to the anti-*Wolf* position and wrote his opinion applying the exclusionary rule to the states, Warren immediately agreed to join the changed approach articulated in the Clark draft. Presumably, the Chief Justice indicated his support for the draft in his discussions on the case and urged the new majority to stand firm in ensuring that it came down as the opinion of the Court. Without Warren's support, indeed, it may be doubted that the tentative majority behind the Clark opinion would have held, bearing in mind Justice Black's indecisiveness in the matter.

GAULT AND *TOTH* CASES

The cases discussed in this chapter show Earl Warren as a strong Chief Justice who was usually able to lead his Court to the decisions he favored. If we look at the Warren Court landmarks — *Brown, Reynolds, Miranda, Gideon,* and *Mapp* — we find that in all but *Mapp,* it was the Chief Justice who was the catalyst for the decisions rendered. And, in *Mapp,* we just saw, Warren's support was essential for the forming consensus to overrule *Wolf* and hold that the states were bound by the exclusionary rule.

In *Gideon v. Wainwright,* Chief Justice Warren was the Court member most responsible for the decision, even though, to the public, the key men behind the Court's ruling were Abe Fortas, who argued the case, and Justice Black, who delivered the opinion. In *In re Gault* (1967), Justice Fortas, who wrote the opinion, apparently was the leading force behind what became a leading case in juvenile law. But it was actually Warren's conference statement that pointed the way to the *Gault* decision.

The *Gault* case arose when Paul L. Gault, a fifteen-year-old, had been committed as a juvenile delinquent to a state institution by an Arizona juvenile court for making indecent telephone calls. He sought habeas corpus, alleging that he had been denied the basic rights of criminal defendants. The state court rejected his claim, holding that due process requirements in juvenile proceedings were not the same as in criminal trials. Justice Fortas, who wrote the opinion, said to me that he had spent much of the summer between the 1965 and 1966 Terms working on what became the most important opinion he wrote while he was on the Court.

Within the Court, however, it was the Warren conference presentation that led the Court to its *Gault* decision. "Even if non-criminal," Warren had declared at the *Gault* conference, "the same due process must be provided." Minimally, said the Chief Justice, there must be a lawyer, proper notice of the proceedings to the family, a fair warning of the charges, and confrontation. Following the Warren lead, the majority agreed that "the same due process" should be applied to juvenile as to criminal proceedings. The Fortas *Gault* opinion followed the approach Warren had outlined, holding that full due-process rights applied in juvenile proceedings.

The Warren ability to lead the Court may also be seen in *Toth v. Quarles* (1955), where the Court followed the Chief Justice to reach a tentative decision and then reversed itself when Warren announced that he had changed his mind. Flying to Winston Churchill's funeral in 1965, former President Eisenhower criticized the Warren Court's decisions in cases involving Communists. Chief Justice Warren, on the same plane, asked what he would do with Communists and the former President said, "I would kill the s.o.b.s." Warren replied, "Perhaps that could be done in the Army, but it could not be done through civilian courts."

The line between civil and military power, upon which the Chief Justice's reply rested, was drawn, in large part, by decisions of the Warren Court starting with *Toth v. Quarles*. Toth had served with the Air Force in Korea. He had been honorably discharged and was working in a steel plant in Pittsburgh when he was arrested and charged with killing a Korean civilian. The former airman was flown to Korea to be judged by a court-martial. The Uniform Code of Military Justice authorized courts-martial of civilians if they had committed serious crimes while in service.

Chief Justice Warren, at the conference, saw no difficulty in affirming court martial power. "Congress," he said, "made the reasonable choice of making the soldier subject to court-martial jurisdiction." Warren viewed the case as "just an extension of the old fraud statute of 1863," which subjected former servicemen to military jurisdiction for frauds against the United States, committed while in service. Indeed, Warren urged, "it is less objectionable than the old fraud statute. It has a better test — serious offenses." All agreed with the Chief Justice except for Justices Frankfurter, Black, and Douglas. (Justice Jackson had died in the meantime, and Justice Harlan had not yet been confirmed as his replacement.)

Justice Reed circulated a draft opinion of the Court. After Justice Frankfurter looked at Reed's draft, he prepared a dissent, which began, "This case has nothing to do with the War Powers, nor do the legal questions it raises bring into relevance General Sherman's assessment of war. Considering his compassionate nature, even his experience might not have prepared him for the iron aspect of peace furthered by the Court's attitude toward the Bill of Rights." Justices Black and Douglas also dissented.

Because of Justice Harlan's pending confirmation, the dissenters persuaded the majority to wait until there was a full Court before deciding such a significant case. The case was, therefore, reargued and discussed at a conference in the following term. Chief Justice Warren began by announcing that he had changed his position. "At the heart of the Constitution," he said, "is that courts-martial were for discipline and that is all. . . . The Constitution's 'necessary and proper' clause does not apply to it after service. . . . The case is of greatest importance for civil liberties. I don't believe [the provision] is consistent with jury trial of civilians."

The Warren change of position led the Court to reverse its stand. This time only Justices Reed, Burton, and Minton voted to affirm. The others all agreed with the Chief Justice, whose leadership was the key factor in the *Toth* decision. Had Warren not changed his mind, the draft prepared by Justice Reed would have come down as the opinion of the Court. When Warren explained why the decision should be in favor of the former serviceman, the Reed opinion became a dissent. The *Toth* opinion of the Court became that by Justice Black, who expanded on the theory stated by the Chief Justice at the second conference.

In his draft opinion, Justice Black had quoted a statement by Thomas Jefferson that referred to "trial by jury as the only anchor ever yet imagined by man by which a government can be held to the principles of its Constitution." Justice Frankfurter persuaded Black to remove the quote because it "strikes me as a bit of humorless hyperbole. I cannot regard the jury, any more than any other political device, as the final word of wisdom or as indispensable to the free human spirit. . . . I cannot for the life of me believe that the Constitution is less regnant in Baltimore, where, as a matter of long tradition, trial by jury is waived in all but two or three percent of the criminal cases (including capital), than it is here in Washington, or in Alabama, or in Massachusetts."

As noted, Justice Black took out the Jefferson quote from his opinion. But he refused to take out a reference to Macaulay, even though Justice Frankfurter had asserted in his letter to Black, "Macaulay was a great historian, but not the most accurate."

MIRROR OF THE MAN

In a commemorative article in the *American Bar Association Journal* on Chief Justice Warren's death in 1974, Justice Douglas wrote that, while Warren would be remembered most for the major cases such as the *Brown* school segregation case, "in many ways the lesser cases mirrored . . . the man." Warren the man, as well as the leader of the Court, was well shown in the 1967 case of *Brooks v. Florida.* Tyrone Brown, the law clerk who worked on the case has said that the case "will never be significant . . . but I think, for me at least, it revealed volumes about the character of the man."

The *Brooks* case arose out of a food riot by blacks in a Florida prison. Brooks and the others involved were stripped naked and placed in bare punishment cells which the Supreme Court described as "the windowless sweatbox . . . a barren cage with a hole in one corner into which he and his cell mates could defecate." For two weeks, they were kept in these cells on a daily diet of twelve ounces of thin soup and eight ounces of water. Within minutes after Brooks was brought from the cell, he signed a confession. The confession was used to convict him of participating in the riot. The highest state court affirmed. Brooks filed an in forma pauperis petition for certiorari.

At the certiorari conference, the Justices voted eight-to-one, with Chief Justice Warren dissenting, not to take the case. The consensus was that it involved a matter of internal prison discipline in which the Court should not become involved. Warren was indignant at the decision to deny cert. He told

Brown to work up a draft dissent. Brown prepared a number of drafts, but the Chief Justice kept saying that they were not strong enough.

At a 1994 conference on the twenty-fifth anniversary of Chief Justice Warren's retirement, Brown described what happened next:

> So he called me to his office a third time. Rising from his chair, he said, "Let's tell them what really happened. Tell them that the authorities placed these men in threes in tiny sweat boxes for two weeks, naked and on a starvation diet with just a hole in the floor to defecate in! Tell them that they brought these men out, still naked, and forced written confessions from them! Tell them that these confessions were used to convict these men of new crimes, that many years were added to the terms they already were serving. Tell them what really happened," said the Chief, "in plain language. Put it in those books," said he, pointing to the bound volumes of *United States Reports* on the shelves in his office, "and let *posterity* decide who was right!" So, that was what we did."

Warren circulated an extremely sharp draft dissent on November 9, 1967, and, as Brown describes it, "just kind of sat in his office and waited."

Soon thereafter, the Justices came in one by one and joined the dissent. By the next conference on the case, the Chief Justice had the votes of all, not only for the granting of cert, but for summary reversal. Warren had Brown draft a short per curiam to that effect, which was issued December 18, 1967.

Cases like *Brooks* and the others discussed in this and the previous chapter demonstrate the Warren leadership in both the landmark and lesser cases. Well could Warren reply, when, on his retirement, a reporter asked him to describe the major frustration of his Court years, that he could not think of any. Breaking into a wide smile, the retired Chief Justice declared, "It has not been a frustrating experience."

5

Burger Rebuffed

He looked, a reporter wrote, "as though he had been cast by Hollywood for the part of Chief Justice." With his snow white hair and broad shoulders, Warren E. Burger was an almost too perfect symbol of the law's dignity as he delivered his last Supreme Court opinion on July 7, 1986. What no one in the crowded courtroom realized was that the opinion announced by the Chief Justice was not the one that he had wanted to deliver. That opinion had been rejected by the Justices, and the manner in which they did so and induced Burger to rewrite his opinion to meet their views strikingly illustrates how the Court, rather than the Chief Justice, may control the decision process.

BURGER ON OLYMPUS

The great Chief Justices have all known how to make the most of the potential inherent in their position in the Court's center chair. We have just seen that this was notably true of Earl Warren. He brought more authority to the position of Chief Justice than had been the case for years, and the Warren Court bore the image of its Chief Justice as unmistakably as had the earlier Courts of John Marshall and Charles Evans Hughes. The high bench was emphatically the *Warren* Court.

This was not the case under Warren E. Burger. To be sure, Chief Justice Warren was a tough act to follow. But, even on its own terms, the Burger tenure was not marked by strong leadership in molding Supreme Court jurisprudence. Burger may in appearance have been the casting director's ideal, but he was miscast when it came to leading the Court in the Marshall-Warren manner.

Burger himself was formed from a different mold than Warren. Although, as a reporter once pointed out, his "white maned, broad-shouldered presence on the bench is very reminiscent of his predecessor's," the men beneath the dignified exteriors were completely dissimilar. Burger's background was mostly in a law firm in St. Paul. He had nothing like the spectacular career and broad experience in politics of Warren, although he had been active in the Republican party in Minnesota. He worked in Harold E. Stassen's successful campaign for governor, and in 1952 he was Stassen's floor manager at the Republican convention, when Minnesota's switch supplied the necessary votes for Dwight D. Eisenhower's nomination.

After the election, Burger was appointed assistant attorney general in charge of the Claims Division of the Department of Justice. This experience led directly to one of his most noted opinions as an appellate judge. Issued in 1964, it held that a government contractor might not be debarred from further government contracts without notice and hearing. Burger told me that the ruling was directly influenced by the many debarment orders that had come across his desk in the Justice Department — "issued in the name of the Secretary of the Navy; but the actual decision was made by some Lieutenant, J.G., way down the line."

In 1956, Burger was named to the U.S. Court of Appeals in Washington, D.C., where he developed a reputation as a conservative, particularly in criminal cases. Then, in 1969, came what Justice Harlan, in a letter to Burger, called his "ascendancy to the Jupitership of Mount Olympus." Burger was sworn in as Chief Justice in June 1969 and headed the Court until his 1986 retirement.

Chief Justice Burger's critics contend that he stood too much on the dignity of his office and was aloof and unfeeling. Intimates stress his courtesy and kindness and assert that the office, not the man, may have made for a different impression. "The Chief," Justice Blackmun, who grew up with him, told a *New York Times* interviewer, "has a great heart in him, and he's a very fine human being when you get to know him, when the tensions are off. One has to remember, too, that he's under strain almost constantly."

In Chapter 4 we saw how the Justices who served with him stressed Chief Justice Warren's fairness in assigning opinions. His successor, on the other hand, was criticized for his treatment of those who disagreed with him. Justice Lewis Powell at one time cast a critical fifth vote in an emotional criminal case. Chief Justice Burger tried hard to get Powell to change his vote, and, after resisting weeks of pressure, Powell told another Justice: "I'm resigned to writing nothing but Indian affairs cases for the rest of my life." Or as Justice Blackmun said in another *New York Times* interview, "If one's in the doghouse with the Chief, he gets the crud."

Chief Justice Burger was always sensitive to what he perceived to be slights to his office and to himself; throughout his tenure he had an almost adversarial relationship with the press. According to one reporter, "He fostered an atmosphere of secrecy around the court that left some employees terrified of being caught chatting with us."

Chief Justice Burger was particularly concerned about leaks to the press. He once circulated a memorandum to the conference headed "CONFIDENTIAL" because a reporter had attempted to interview law clerks. "I have categorically directed," Burger declared, "that none of my staff have any conversation on any subject with any reporter. . . . I know of no one who is skilled enough to expose himself to any conversation with a reporter without getting into 'forbidden territory.' The reporter will inevitably extract information on the internal mechanisms of the Court, one way or another, to our embarrassment."

It cannot be denied that, from his "Middle Temple" cheddar, made according to his own recipe, to the finest clarets, Burger is somewhat of an epicure. One of the social high points of a 1969 British-American conference at Ditchley, Oxfordshire, that I attended was the learned discussion about vintage Bordeaux between Burger and Sir George Coldstream, head of the Lord Chancellor's office and overseer of the wine cellar at his Inn of Court. The Chief Justice was particularly proud of his coup in snaring some cases of a rare Lafite in an obscure Washington wine shop.

The effectiveness of a Chief Justice is, of course, not shown by his epicurean tastes. Indeed, the one Justice who was willing to talk frankly about Burger's professional performance was most uncomplimentary. Burger, according to this Justice, "will assign to someone without letting the rest know, and he has five [votes] before the rest of us see it." The Justice also complained about the Burger conduct of conferences in criminal law cases. "If it's a case in which a warden is the petitioner, the Chief Justice goes on and on until the rest are driven to distraction."

The Chief Justice's votes were based upon his own scale of values, which were different from those that had motivated members of the Warren Court. When he considered a fundamental value to be at stake, Burger could be as stubborn as his predecessor. "Someone," he insisted to a law clerk, "must draw the line in favor of basic values and, even if the vote is eight-to-one, I will do it." As Justice Douglas once put it, in a case on which Burger had strong views, "The CJ would rather die than affirm."

Among the things the Chief Justice felt strongly about was the dignity of the legal profession. Despite the Court's acceptance of lawyer advertising, Burger constantly railed against it. He also was quick to condemn poor professional performance. In a 1974 case, he wrote to the others, "The petitioner's counsel was somewhat above mediocre but the State's case was *miserably* presented." Because of this, the Court should "at least appoint amicus curiae for California and begin our drive to force the States to abandon their on-the-job training of their lawyers in this Court." In a 1975 case involving a doctor, he circulated a memorandum urging that the opinion should contain "a few well chosen (?) comments about the gross fraud perpetrated by this 'quack.'"

The Chief Justice also complained about undue use of the courts. At a conference on a 1972 case, Burger asserted that the case was "much ado about nothing by a do-gooder lawyer attacking what is really a social problem for the legislature."

But the Chief Justice also had his doubts about legislative attempts to cure social evils through massive regulatory schemes. A 1977 Burger letter speaks deprecatingly of the Occupational Safety and Health Act. "It may well be another one of those 'monsters' passed by Congress as an assumed response to some need. The response probably goes beyond need, but that is not our business." Then, with the wry humor that was too rarely displayed in public, he asserted: "I would be willing to give $1.00 to every one of the 535 who would certify under oath to having read this legislation before voting on it. It wouldn't cost me much."

Burger was greatly offended when the Court in 1971 reversed the conviction of a young man for wearing a jacket emblazoned with the words "Fuck the Draft" in a courthouse. The Chief Justice was particularly upset by the opinion's quoting the offensive four-letter word. He prepared a two-paragraph dissent, ultimately withdrawn, which, according to the covering memo, "is the most restrained utterance I can manage." In the draft dissent, Burger wrote, "I, too, join a word of protest that this Court's limited resources of time should be devoted to such a case as this. It is a measure of a lack of a sense of priorities and with all deference I submit that Mr. Justice Harlan's 'first blush' was the correct reaction. It is nothing short of absurd nonsense that juvenile delinquents and their emotionally unstable outbursts should command the attention of this Court."

Even though the Chief Justice may have felt strongly about them, these were relatively minor matters. On more important concerns Burger came to the Court with an agenda that included a dismantling of the jurisprudential edifice erected by the Warren Court, particularly in the field of criminal justice. In large part, Burger owed his elevation to the highest judicial office to his reputation as a tough "law and order" judge. He had commented disparagingly on the Warren Court decisions on the rights of criminal defendants. As Chief Justice, he believed that he now had the opportunity to transform his more restrictive views into positive public law.

Chief Justice Burger expressed opposition during most of his tenure to the landmark criminal procedure decisions of the Warren Court, but he was never able to persuade a majority to cast those cases into constitutional limbo. The same was true of other aspects of Burger's anti-Warren agenda. No important Warren Court decision was overturned by the Burger Court. If Chief Justice Burger had hoped that he would be able to undo much of the Warren "constitutional revolution," he was clearly to be disappointed.

In retrospect, Chief Justice Burger was more effective as a court administrator and as a representative of the federal courts before Congress than as a leader and molder of Supreme Court jurisprudence. However reluctantly, one must conclude that Warren Burger was miscast in the role of leader of the Court—a fair but harsh description of a man who devoted so much of his life to the bench and worked as hard as he could to improve the judicial system and one who also could be warm and charming in his personal relationships. Yet his personality was, in many ways, contradictory—in the words of one reporter, "at once gracious and petty, unselfish and self-serving, arrogant and insecure, politically shrewd yet stupid and heavy-handed at dealing with people."

Of course it was more than these personality contradictions that damaged Chief Justice Burger's effectiveness as a leader of the Court. A major part of his failure may be attributed to the manner in which he presided at conferences and assigned opinions. But an important factor was his inadequacy as a judge. One who examines the decision process in important cases must reluctantly conclude that Burger was out of his depth. Although the picture in some accounts of his intellectual inadequacy is certainly overdrawn, most of his colleagues could run intellectual rings around the Chief Justice.

GRAMM-RUDMAN IN THE DOCK

The opinion referred to at the beginning of this chapter, the last announced by Burger as Chief Justice, disposed of the case of *Bowsher v. Synar.* That case— more popularly known as the Gramm-Rudman case because it struck down the budget control law of that name—was the Burger Court's most significant separation-of-powers decision. But its consequences are broader than the immediate issue presented. During the *Bowsher* oral argument, Solicitor General Charles Fried told the Justices that the proponents of constitutionality of the challenged statute were trying to "scare" them with the argument that upholding the lower-court ruling that the law was unconstitutional would endanger independent agencies such as the Federal Trade Commission and the Federal Reserve Board.

At this, Justice Sandra Day O'Connor interposed, "They scared me with it."

Court observers stressed the significance of *Bowsher* because of its potential impact on the independent agencies that play so important a role in federal law. The years before *Bowsher* had seen a revival of the claim that the independent agencies were unconstitutional because, though they exercised "executive power," they were not subject to presidential control. The argument against the agencies received the support of the Reagan Department of Justice. Attorney General Meese went out of his way to question the constitutionality of the independent agencies in a widely reported 1985 speech. According to Meese, "[w]e should abandon the idea that there are such things as 'quasi-legislative' or 'quasi-judicial' functions that can be properly delegated to independent agencies." Instead, all "federal agencies performing executive functions are themselves properly agents of the executive."

The argument against the independent agencies has far-reaching implications. Its scope was pointed out by a federal court in a 1986 case challenging the constitutionality of the Federal Trade Commission: "[Plaintiff] is asking us to adopt a principle that would make every independent federal administrative agency unconstitutional; for the logic of its argument is not limited to the Federal Trade Commission but extends to . . . the other well-known, long-established federal agencies whose members the President selects but cannot remove (before their terms expire) without cause. [Plaintiff] thus is asking us to decree a fundamental change in the structure of American government."

Soon after Mr. Meese made his speech, Senator William Proxmire commented on it in the Senate: "Suppose the view of Attorney General Meese prevails. Then what? Then Mr. Meese and his Department of Justice will have the power, and the only power, to enforce the law in this vast, rambling, complex Federal Government. Would anyone except the administration really want that? Mr. President, if the opinion of Mr. Meese . . . prevail[s], there could be swift and sudden social and economic revolution in this country."

In the *Bowsher* case itself the Supreme Court dealt with the functions assigned to the Comptroller General under the 1985 Gramm-Rudman Act. The Comptroller General is appointed by the President but may be removed by a Congressional joint resolution. Gramm-Rudman was a drastic attempt by Congress to eliminate the now endemic federal deficit. The Act set a maximum deficit amount for federal spending for each of the fiscal years 1986 through 1991. If, in any fiscal year, the budget deficit exceeded the prescribed maximum by more than a specific sum, the Act required across-the-board cuts in federal spending to reach the targeted deficit level. These reductions were to be accomplished under the Act's "reporting provisions," which required the Directors of the Office of Management and Budget and the Congressional Budget Office to submit their deficit estimates and program-by-program reduction calculations to the Comptroller General, who, after reviewing the Directors' joint report, then was to report his conclusions to the President. The President then had to issue a "sequestration" order mandating the spending reductions specified by the Comptroller General, and the sequestration order became effective unless, within a specified time, Congress legislated reductions to remove the need for the sequestration order.

Twelve congressmen, led by Representative Mike Synar, brought an action challenging the validity of the Gramm-Rudman Act. The lower court held that the statute violated the Constitution. The case was then appealed to the Supreme Court.

BOWSHER CONFERENCE

The postargument *Bowsher* conference began with the usual handshakes exchanged by the Justices — a custom begun at the end of the last century by Chief Justice Melville W. Fuller, who inaugurated the practice, in his biographer's words, "to prevent rifts from forming." But at the *Bowsher* conference, the formal greetings could not mask the underlying tension due to both the public controversy surrounding the case and the Justices' knowledge that the decision would signal the end of the Burger era.

The *Bowsher* conference discussion showed that all except Justices Byron White and Harry A. Blackmun were for invalidating the Gramm-Rudman Act. The Chief Justice stated, "Comptrollers have always thought they were Congressional aides and not independent." Burger then stressed the powers vested in the Comptroller General. "The 1985 Act," he said, "pointedly refused to give the President the powers vested here in the Comptroller General. He's required to decide and issue reports to the President that binds the latter. The implementing responsibility is in the Comptroller General."

Burger referred to *Myers v. United States* (1929), where the Supreme Court held that the President has unlimited removal power over officers appointed by him and *Humphrey's Executor v. United States* (1935), which held that Congress could limit the President's removal power over members of independent agencies, such as the Federal Trade Commission, to removal only for cause. *"Myers,"* the Chief Justice told the others, "said the power of removal was crucial to the Presidency. But that power as to the Comptroller General rests with Congress without any meaningful review anywhere." Burger concluded by asserting, *"Humphrey* did not overrule *Myers."*

The implication in Chief Justice Burger's conference statement was that presidential removal power is a constitutional sine qua non for all officers executing laws. The further implication was that the rule is also true for the FTC-type independent agency—which casts doubt on those agencies' constitutionality, as well as on the *Humphrey* case, which had upheld their validity.

Justice Brennan, who spoke next, rejected the Burger implications. As Brennan saw it in his conference statement, "this case raises only the concern with keeping basic governmental powers distinctly separate. That is, what is problematic about Gramm-Rudman is that it involves a blending of legislative and executive functions."

Brennan continued,

> I do not believe that there is any such thing as "inherently executive" activity. Rather, the executive function is only that which Congress leaves to be done in order to carry out the enforcement of laws it passes. But once executive power is delegated, Congressional power must cease: having made its choice in drafting legislation, Congress' participation must end. Having chosen to leave tasks for administrators, Congress cannot also control the administration and execution of its enactment. . . . Congress cannot itself maintain charge of the tasks it leaves to be performed upon the enactment of a bill into law. For this reason, then, Congress cannot keep the power directly to supervise the officer it leaves with the task of administering and executing a law. If Congress controls that officer, it controls executive as well as legislative power. And such a blending of those powers violates the fundamental principle of separation of powers in the most literal sense.

To Justice Brennan the significance of removal power was that it was "the power to *control.* Therefore, to the extent that Congress asserts power to remove an executive officer, Congress asserts a power to control that officer's execution. The Constitution does not permit Congress to do that."

Justice Brennan urged the Court specifically to reject the anti-*Humphrey* implications of Chief Justice Burger's remarks. "I would," the Justice declared, "make very clear that *Humphrey's* is still good law. The notion that Congress can limit the President's power to remove as long as Congress does not itself participate in the removal process is no longer open to question." It was important, Brennan stressed, that *Humphrey* be confirmed because the opinion of Judge Scalia (as he then was) in the lower court had cast doubt on *Humphrey* as a precedent. "It [is] important," Brennan told the conference, "to reaffirm *Humphrey's* . . . because the District Court opinion includes a lot of dictum which questions the continuing validity of *Humphrey's*. This dictum is wrong and unwarranted, and we should make this very clear."

The other majority Justices agreed that, as Justice O'Connor put it at the conference, "The Act violates basic separation of powers concerns." The reason, she said, was that "executive branch powers are given to the legislative and you can't do that—the Comptroller General is a legislative person." Justice Stevens stated the same view. "The Comptroller-General," he asserted, "is an agent or arm of Congress. The decision by a legislative person is the flaw for me." To Justice Powell, the statute's defect was that "the delegation was to execute a substantial portion of law and Congress reserved the power to remove."

Justice Rehnquist took a somewhat different approach. The question, as he saw it, was, "Can the Comptroller General participate in execution?" To Rehnquist, the key was not the removal provision. "Removal," he told the conference, "doesn't seem too important to me. It's lack of presidential control rather than the congressional power of removal that's the flaw."

Justice Rehnquist's conference statement was consistent with the Burger implication that Presidential power over officers vested with executive functions was crucial to constitutionality. But the inference here, too, was that "lack of presidential control" might invalidate agencies like the FTC, which were also not subject to presidential control.

In a June 2, 1986, "Dear Chief" letter, Justice O'Connor summarized the conference accord on the matter: "My review of the conference notes indicates that, with the possible exception of Bill Rehnquist, those who voted to affirm hoped to make sure that the opinion not cast doubt on the constitutionality of independent agencies."

BURGER DRAFT

Despite the fact that his conference statement was inconsistent with the above conference consensus, Chief Justice Burger assigned the opinion to himself. When the Chief Justice circulated his May 31, 1986, draft *Bowsher* opinion, it became apparent that he had not felt bound by the conference rationale. Instead, the Burger draft expressed an expansive view of presidential power that did bring into question the constitutionality of the independent agencies.

The draft's key section started with the truism: "The Constitution does not contemplate that the President alone will 'faithfully execute' the laws." The President is given the power to appoint officers to carry out executive functions and "the draftsmen of the Constitution recognized that a President could not fulfill his Constitutional duties without the power to remove any of his officers who failed to execute his policies faithfully. The commissions issued to many of the major executive officers have recited that the holder serves 'during the pleasure of the President.' "

As Chief Justice Burger summarized the *Myers* case, it emphasized that the Constitution "grants to the President the executive power of the Government, i.e., the general administrative control of those executing the laws, including the power of appointment and removal of executive officers — a conclusion confirmed by his obligation to take care that the laws be faithfully executed."

The Burger draft referred to the *Humphrey* case only to assert that the holding there "is wholly consistent with the Court's holding in *Myers,* and the *Humphrey's Executors* Court took pains to distinguish the *Myers* decision." The draft did not mention the *Humphrey* holding limiting presidential removal power or the Court's emphasis there on the independence of the FTC-type agency. Instead, Burger quoted *Humphrey* on the need to maintain the independence of the three branches, including the *Humphrey* Court's assertion, "The sound application of a principle that makes one master in his own house precludes him from imposing his control in the house of another who is master there."

The Burger draft also noted that a 1982 case had "reaffirmed the teaching of *Myers* that the President has 'supervisory and policy responsibilities of the utmost discretion and sensitivity . . . and management of the Executive Branch — a task for which "imperative" reasons requir[e] an unrestricted [Presidential] power to remove the most important of his subordinates. . . .' "

The Chief Justice concluded that, "from 1789 to the present, it has been recognized that the President's authority to direct his subordinates is enforced through the power of removal." That power, the draft asserted, "is . . . even more crucial to the management of the government and execution of the law than it was . . . in 1789."

Next in the Burger draft came a paean to presidential removal power: "A modern President must depend upon literally thousands of subordinates to give effect to the President's policies with fidelity. A subordinate of the Executive Branch . . . must be subject to replacement promptly if a President's policies are to be given effect. . . . [B]ecause the power of removal over Executive Branch officers resides in the President, Congress may not retain the sole power of removal of an officer charged with the execution of the laws." To permit Congress to retain that power would be "precisely the type of aggrandizement by one branch of Government that our Constitutional scheme was designed to prevent."

The rest of the Burger draft found that the Comptroller General was entrusted with executive powers by the challenged statute and that "these functions of the Comptroller General constitute the performance of duties explicitly conferred by the Constitution on the President to execute laws enacted by Congress." The ultimate conclusion was that "the powers vested in the Comptroller General under § 261 violate the command of the Constitution that the President 'shall take Care that the Laws be faithfully executed.' "

POSTDRAFT CONFLICT

All of the members of the conference majority except Justice Rehnquist objected to the Burger draft. The first to do so was Justice Stevens. In a June 2, 1986, letter to the Chief Justice, Stevens wrote, "I think your opinion casts substantial doubt on the legal status of independent agencies and that it would be a serious mistake for the Court to adopt this approach."

Justice Stevens asserted "that the rationale of the decision was that the function performed by the Comptroller General could not be performed by an arm of the Legislature unless Congress itself performed that function by the normal process of legislating." This, Stevens urged, should be "the central rationale . . . rather than *Myers*." Stevens was to state this view more fully in his *Bowsher* concurrence. Stevens issued his separate opinion (concurred in by Justice Marshall) although, as the Chief Justice's May 31 Memorandum to the Conference transmitting his draft stated, "There was some expression by those voting as to the importance of a single opinion."

Justice Thurgood Marshall sent a June 2 "Dear Chief" letter seconding the Stevens letter. Marshall declared, "Your current draft's focus on the need for the President to be 'master of his own house' raises a host of important issues — including the propriety of independent agencies — that we do not have to consider at this time."

Reference has already been made to Justice O'Connor's June 2 letter and its statement that the majority had hoped to make it clear that the decision should not bring the constitutionality of the independent agencies into question. "I fear," O'Connor wrote in the same letter, "that the opinion as now written . . . does just that. For example, the draft discusses *Myers* extensively, and suggests that it stands for the general proposition that the power to appoint carries with it the general power to remove. Yet, with the exception of quoting some general language about separation of powers, the draft disregards *Humphrey's Executor* almost entirely. As I read *Humphrey's*, it limits *Myers* considerably by suggesting that Congress can impose significant limitations on the President's removal power over executive officers *even if* they perform 'executive functions.' "

In Justice O'Connor's view, the draft was wrong in suggesting "that the constitutional infirmity of the Act lies in the fact that the President does not have the power to remove the Comptroller General. In my view, precisely the obverse is the problem: The infirmity lies in the fact the *Congress* does have the power to remove, not in the fact that the *President* does not."

To Justice O'Connor, the basic principle was "that Congress may not both create laws and implement them." In her view, Gramm-Rudman was invalid because it violated this principle. "By giving itself the sole power to remove the Comptroller General, Congress has retained so much control over the office that it is, in effect, participating in the execution of the law it created. . . . This kind of aggrandizement, our case makes clear, is impermissible."

The next day, June 3, Justice Powell wrote to the Chief Justice: "I share generally the views expressed by other Justices who have written you. . . . I could not join an opinion that casts substantial doubt on the constitutionality of the independent agencies, and do not think the vote at the Conference supports such a view."

The Chief Justice also received a longer June 3 letter from Justice Brennan. "I agree," Brennan's letter began, "with what has been said by Sandra, John and Thurgood that the reasoning of the opinion in this case must be that Congress cannot retain the power to remove an officer charged with executing the law, and that the opinion should not rely on the rationale that the President must have power to remove such officers. Moreover, I think it very important that the opinion explain the basis and importance of this distinction, since it is only by doing so that we shall make clear that we are not questioning the viability of independent agencies."

The Brennan letter then discussed the separation of powers and its application to the case.

> Whether this separation has been observed does not depend upon the formal designation of an officer as being within one or another branch of Government. Rather, it depends upon which branch holds the power actually to *control* that officer. Congress cannot retain the power directly to control an officer to whom it has delegated the task of executing a law whether that officer is formally designated an officer of the legislature or of the executive branch. . . . [T]he power to control is conferred by the power to remove. Thus, to the extent that Congress retains the power to remove a particular officer, it possesses the power to control that officer's performance. It is for this reason, and not because the power to remove is somehow "inherently executive" that the power to remove is entangled in separation of powers questions.

Justice Brennan wrote that there was a difference between "qualifying the President's power to remove" and retention of the removal power itself by Congress.

> *Myers* and *Humphrey's Executors* can be understood in light of this distinction. In *Myers* Congress retained power to participate in the removal of an officer performing executive functions. This gave Congress direct control over an officer executing the law and thus violated the fundamental precept that Congress not

control execution in addition to legislation. In *Humphrey's Executors,* on the other hand, Congress did not itself participate in the removal process, but simply limited the President's power to remove at will. In upholding the provisions for removal of FTC Commissioners, *Humphrey's Executors* made clear that the dictum in *Myers* suggesting that the President's removal power must remain unfettered was incorrect.

Justice Brennan then pointed out his difficulty with the Burger draft's treatment of the *Myers* and *Humphrey* cases. "My concern is that by not making the distinction between *Myers* and *Humphrey's Executors* express, the opinion will give credence to the view—strongly suggested by the District Court—that *Humphrey's Executors* was wrong and that the *Myers* dictum was correct. I think that the opinion in this case must expressly draw the distinction between Congress having the power to remove and the President not having that power, and must clearly explain that our decision is based solely on the fact that Congress has removal power (and thus control over) the officer charged with executing the Budget Deficit Act."

The Brennan letter concluded with reaffirmation of the point the Justice had emphasized at the conference—the need to "make very clear that *Humphrey's* is still good law." To make this point explicit, Brennan wrote,

> [T]he opinion also should reaffirm the holding in *Humphrey's Executors* that Congress can create independent agencies (*i.e.,* agencies staffed by officers not removable at the President's pleasure). The District Court opinion includes a lot of dictum that questions the continuing validity of *Humphrey's Executors.* This dictum is simply wrong. The notion that Congress can to some extent limit the President's power to remove as long as Congress does not itself participate in the removal process is no longer open to question. Indeed, the First Congress limited the President's power to remove the Comptroller two weeks after the so-called "Decision of 1789." In addition, the ICC, the United States Shipping Board (now the Federal Maritime Commission), the FTC, and perhaps other independent agencies, were created by the Congress long before our decision in *Humphrey's Executors.* Finally, even were there some reason to doubt the strength of the conclusion in *Humphrey's Executors,* a very large part of Government has been developed in reliance on that decision, and so the force of *stare decisis* is very powerful.

On June 4, the Chief Justice sent around a Memorandum to the Conference that indicated that he did not think the objections to his draft opinion were really important: "After reviewing carefully the various comments and memos, I conclude the essence of the problem is whether we skin the tiger from the neck to the tail or vice versa. Either way suits me, and the printer is now turning the tiger around. The hide, however, will look the same—at least as I see it." With an attempt at bonhomie, which, coming from him, too often struck a false note, the Chief Justice wrote at the bottom of the memo: "I'll try to have it around before your second martini!"

REVISED DRAFT AND DECISION

Despite the memo, Chief Justice Burger did substantially change the passages to which the Justices had objected in a second draft circulated on June 5. In it, as in the final *Bowsher* opinion, the *Myers* case was stated only for the proposition that Congress might not directly participate in the removal power. As in the final opinion, too, more emphasis was placed on the *Humphrey* case. The new draft stated specifically, "*Humphrey's Executors* involved an issue not presented either in the *Myers* case or in this case—i.e., the power of Congress to limit the President's power to remove an officer 'wholly disconnected from the executive department.' . . . At the same time, the Court cast no doubt on the specific holding of *Myers* dealing with an executive officer that a direct Congressional role in the removal of such an officer is improper." The revised draft supported this statement by a footnote (also contained in the final opinion) which indicates that *Bowsher* does not involve "casting doubt on the status of 'independent' agencies because no issues involving such agencies are presented here."

The revised draft was essentially similar to the final *Bowsher* opinion. But it did contain a statement that the *Humphrey* "Court characterized the Federal Trade Commissioner as an officer who 'occupies no place in the executive power vested by the Constitution in the President,' but acts only 'in the discharge and effectuation of . . . quasi-legislative or quasi-judicial powers, or as an [officer of an] agency of the legislative or judicial departments of the government.' "

This statement led to a June 6 letter from Justice Brennan, which informed the Chief Justice, "Your second draft does indeed accommodate many of my concerns. However, I still have problems with sections of the opinion that, I am afraid, still may cast doubt upon the continuing viability of many—if not all—independent administrative agencies. I refer in particular to . . . the description of agency functions as 'quasi-legislative' or 'quasi-judicial' in contradistinction to 'executive' functions that only the President or officers removable at his pleasure may perform."

"My concern," Justice Brennan wrote, "is that reintroducing such notions as whether some function is 'quasi-legislative' or 'quasi-judicial' will encourage claims that all sorts of independent agency activity is neither, and that it must therefore be under the President's control. In other words, I am afraid that reintroducing this analysis will cast doubt upon the legality of much of the work of independent administrative agencies despite disclaimers that the question is presented. This problem can easily be avoided simply by not using this terminology in the discussion."

Justice Brennan further suggested that "rather than quoting the language from *Humphrey's Executors,* I would simply describe the result in that case." In place of the *Humphrey* quote to which he objected, Brennan proposed the following description of *Humphrey*: "The Court upheld the statute, holding that 'illimitable power of removal is not possessed by the President' with respect to certain kinds of administrative bodies that, like the FTC, were 'created by Congress to carry into effect legislative policies' embodied in statutory enactments. 295 U.S., at 628–629. The court distinguished *Myers,* reaffirming its holding that congressional participation in the removal process of executive officers is unconstitutional, but 'disapprov[ing]' expressions in that opinion 'beyond the point involved.' *Id.* at 626." Chief Justice Burger included most of this suggested passage in his final opinion.

With the terminology changes suggested by Brennan, the Burger opinion was acceptable to the majority Justices (except for Justices Stevens and Marshall, who concurred only in the judgment). The consensus was that stated by Justice Powell, in his June 12 letter joining Burger's opinion, "I certainly do not want to undercut the type of independence the great administrative agencies have enjoyed, and I do not think your opinion — as now drafted — does this."

Chief Justice Burger took the same view. In a June 6, 1986, letter to Justice Brennan, he referred to the *Bowsher* footnote that distinguished the FTC-type agencies from the Comptroller General and stated, "I think I've made it clear we are casting no doubt on the SEC, FTC, EPA, etc."

There is also a June 10 letter to Justice Stevens in which the Chief Justice stated "the basic rationale of the opinion." First, Burger wrote, the "central point" of the final opinion was not that " 'the Comptroller General is not removable by the President, and therefore may not be entrusted with executive powers.' On the contrary, the central point is that the Comptroller General is removable by Congress, and therefore may not be entrusted with executive powers."

Justice Stevens had written a June 9 "Dear Chief" letter in which he had argued that the opinion's rationale would "invalidate . . . a statute which authorized the functions to be performed by an independent agency such as the Federal Reserve Board." Chief Justice Burger answered this point in his June 10 letter, writing, "The ability of the Federal Reserve Board to undertake the functions assigned to the Comptroller General under the Act is, of course, not before us."

The Chief Justice defended the language of his second draft opinion, stating in his letter, "Even if it were, I confess that I do not understand your suggestion that the second draft would cast doubt on that ability, since, unlike the Comptroller General, the members of the Federal Reserve Board are removable by Congress only by way of impeachment. Moreover, the opinion specifically distinguishes questions relating to the status of independent agencies. See Op. at 9–10 & n.4. Because of this distinguishing language, the opinion would not, as you suggest, invalidate 'a newly created executive agency whose officers have civil service status,' if such an agency were ever created."

Thus, his *Bowsher* opinion was rewritten by Chief Justice Burger to meet the objections raised by his first draft's implication that agencies exercising executive powers — that is, charged with carrying out the laws — had to be subjected to the President's unlimited removal power. Instead, as his letter to Justice Stevens states, the key to the final *Bowsher* opinion "is that the Comptroller General is removable by Congress, and therefore may not be entrusted with executive powers."

Consequently, the *Bowsher* decision may be summed up as follows: Congress may determine the nature of the executive duty imposed by the statute which it enacts. But once Congress makes its choice in passing a law, its role ends. Congress can thereafter control the execution of its law only by passing new legislation. In this case, by placing the responsibility for execution of the statute in an officer subject only to its removal power, *Bowsher* concludes, "Congress in effect has retained control over the execution of the Act and has intruded into the executive function. The Constitution does not permit such intrusion."

On the other hand, had the Burger draft come down as the final *Bowsher* opinion, it would have completely unsettled our administrative law jurisprudence. The other Justices were quite correct in their assumption that, under the draft, considerable doubt would have been cast upon the constitutionality of the independent agency. The draft's thesis was that "the sole power of removal of an officer charged with the execution of the laws . . . resides in the President." Since the independent agencies are "charged with the execution of the laws," the implication is that their members must be subject to removal at will by the President—which would, of course, completely destroy their independence.

Instead of a decision repudiating the doctrine of the unconstitutionality of the independent agencies, *Bowsher* might have been interpreted, in the federal court's already quoted words, as a "decree [of] a fundamental change in the structure of American government"—"a seismic constitutional change . . . that would make every independent federal administrative agency unconstitutional."

6

The Court Leads the Chief

He crossed the bridge with this," a Justice who had participated in the *Swann* school busing case said. "He tried to take over the Court. He didn't succeed and never tried this blatantly again."

The Justice was referring to Chief Justice Warren E. Burger's efforts to mold the decision and opinion in the *Swann* case to reflect his own more restricted view of desegregation power, even though that view was opposed by a majority of the Justices. In this sense, the *Swann* decision process, like that in the just-discussed *Boswher* case, involved a power struggle between the Chief Justice and the Justices who refused to accept the Burger lead in the case. As the Justice quoted above put it, "The Chief Justice was determined to carry the day, and we were equally determined he wouldn't — and we had the votes."

SWANN AND DESEGREGATION ENFORCEMENT

Swann v. Charlotte-Mecklenburg Board of Education (1971) was the Burger Court's most important desegregation case. The starting point of the Court's desegregation jurisprudence is, of course, the *Brown* case discussed in Chapter 4. But the Warren Court really had it relatively easy in *Brown* and its progeny. The blatant discrimination involved in segregation in education and other public programs made it a simple matter for the Warren Justices to decide the cases that came before them. As a book on the Burger Court puts it, "Civil rights in the [Warren Court] was a good guys/bad guys issue . . . and there was no doubt on which side the Court was on."

The basic problem for the federal courts, once *Brown* had ruled in 1954 that school segregation was unconstitutional, was how to enforce the *Brown* principle. Resolution of that problem, too, was relatively straightforward. Once the

Justices saw that the *Brown* "all deliberate speed" formula was interpreted to countenance indefinite delay, they replaced it with the requirement of what *Green v. County School Board* (1968) called a desegregation "plan that promises realistically to work, and promises realistically to work *now*."

Yet even *Green* (the Warren Court's last desegregation case) was a relatively simple case. The school district involved in *Green* was a rural one with relatively little residential segregation; half of its population was black. It contained two schools, one on the east side of the county (almost entirely white) the other on the west side (entirely black). The dual school system could thus be eliminated by the simple remedy of geographic zoning. The *Green* Court pointed out that this "could be readily achieved . . . simply by assigning students living in the eastern half of the county to the New Kent School and those living in the western half of the county to the Watkins School."

This remedial suggestion provided for attendance under a modified "neighborhood school" concept. The same remedy would prove inadequate in urban areas with entirely different residential patterns. In those areas, would neighborhood schools be sufficient to meet the constitutional standard? Or would more drastic remedies be appropriate — for example, busing between white and black areas to ensure meaningful integration?

These questions were soon answered by the Burger Court, which had to deal with the segregation problem in urban school districts — first of all in the urban South and then in northern cities containing large black ghettos. The *Swann* case, decided in the second Burger term, was the Burger Court's first major school case. It gave rise to a serious conflict between the new Chief Justice and the majority. The latter was ultimately able to frustrate the Burger effort to weaken the remedial power of the federal courts in desegregation cases.

The *Swann* decision upheld the far-reaching desegregation order issued by the district court, which included efforts to reach a seventy-one to twenty-nine white-black ratio in the schools and provisions for extensive busing to help attain that goal. About 10,000 students were involved — one-fourth of the schoolchildren in the district.

At the conference, Chief Justice Burger began his discussion on the merits of *Swann* by querying "whether any particular demands are either required or forbidden. *Brown I* said the right is a right to be free from discrimination — separation solely because of race was outlawed." This was the theme the Chief Justice was to repeat in the first drafts of his *Swann* opinion. Burger told the conference that the Court had "to look at the facts to see if there is evidence of discrimination. The rigidity of 71-29 by [District Judge] McMillan disturbs me. There must be some play in the joints — perhaps a 15 percent leeway?"

The Chief Justice was supported at the conference only by Justice Black. "I have always had the idea," Black told the conference, "that people arrange themselves often to be close to schools. I never thought it was for the courts to change the habits of the people in choosing where to live."

The other Justices expressed support for the district court. Justice Harlan, the moderate conservative who might normally have been expected to vote with the Chief Justice, indicated his strong agreement with the district court. "The neighborhood school is not a constitutional requirement if departure from it is necessary to disestablish a segregated system. . . . Busing is not an impermissible tool."

The same view was expressed by the other Justices. Justice Douglas repeated the position he had taken in a strong June 27, 1970, memorandum, where he had urged that "bussing is a permissible tool for ending desegregation" and "the question of the precise need for bussing in a particular community is singularly appropriate for determination by the District Court." Justice Brennan, too, stressed the district court's discretion to select the appropriate method in each case. "But there can be no doubt that where busing is the only way to achieve the required amount of integration, the district judge has the power and duty to order it."

Justice Marshall, as the only black on the Court, spoke briefly and in a restrained manner that masked the intense feelings he must have had during the discussion. At one point, Marshall referred to the so-called "freedom-of-choice" plans that had been stricken down by the Warren Court. "There is no such thing," he declared, "as freedom of choice for the Negro child in the South."

The majority also disagreed with Burger on the requirements imposed by *Brown*. Their view was stated by Justice Stewart, whom the Chief Justice might also normally have hoped to rely upon. "Not only desegregation," Stewart asserted, "but affirmative integration is required." That was necessary to "convert to a unitary school system."

The conference discussion indicated a clear majority to affirm. Chief Justice Burger and Justice Black were alone. Despite this, the Chief Justice himself prepared the draft *Swann* opinion — another violation of the established Court practice of having the Chief Justice assign the opinion only when he is a member of the majority. In his *Autobiography,* Justice Douglas complained of the Burger assignment of the *Swann* opinion to himself, saying that the Chief Justice "kept the opinion for himself, though he was in the minority. As a result months passed without any progress being made to obtain a consensus in the Court, and the opinion finally filed was not his but a compound."

The reason it took so long for *Swann* to come down was that the Chief Justice wrote draft after draft in which he stuck to the restricted view of desegregation power that he had stated to the conference, as well as his narrow interpretation of the requirements imposed by *Brown*. It took six Burger drafts before the *Swann* opinion was acceptable to the Justices and then only because the Chief Justice had adopted the majority view on the key issues in the case.

The crucial issue in *Swann* was that of the remedial power of the courts in desegregation cases. As Justice Douglas had stated at the conference: "The problem is what is the power of the court without the help of Congress to correct a violation of the Constitution." He then pointed to the broad remedial powers of the courts in other areas. "If there is an antitrust violation, we give a broad discretion." The same should be true here.

Even though the Douglas view on remedial power was supported by the conference majority, the Chief Justice circulated a draft *Swann* opinion that stated a most restricted view of remedial power in such a desegregation case, which the draft contrasted with what it termed "a classical equity case" — for example, removal of an illegal dam or divestiture of an illegal corporate acquisition. "Here, however, we are not confronted with a simple classical equity case, and the simplistic, hornbook remedies are not necessarily relevant. Populations, pupils or misplaced schools cannot be moved as simply as earth by a bulldozer, or property by corporations."

According to the Burger draft, "the ultimate remedy commanded by *Brown II*, restated and reinforced in numerous intervening cases . . . was to discontinue the dual *system*." The judicial power was limited to measures aimed at "[d]iscontinuing separate schools for two racial groups." The consequence of such measures "would be a single integrated system functioning on the same basis as school systems in which no discrimination had ever been enforced." The implication was that federal courts could act to bring about only the situation that would have existed had there never been state-enforced segregation. This was virtually to give the Supreme Court imprimatur to the view stated years earlier by a lower federal court that "the Constitution . . . does not require integration. It merely forbids discrimination" — a view repudiated by the *Swann* conference majority.

Chief Justice Burger's efforts to limit the remedial power of the district courts were frustrated by the other Justices. Their pressure led the Chief Justice to modify his restricted approach, and the final *Swann* opinion adopted a very broad conception of remedial power. Burger was virtually forced to this result by a draft opinion prepared by Justice Stewart after the Chief Justice had refused to modify his position in the drafts circulated by him. The Stewart draft could easily be converted into the opinion of the Court desired by the conference consensus. When he learned that a majority was forming behind the Stewart opinion, the Chief Justice knew that, if he persisted in his restricted approach, he risked losing his Court and the authorship of the *Swann* opinion. To avoid this result, the Chief Justice circulated a new draft accepting the majority view on the *Brown* requirements and the scope of the judicial desegregation power.

Hence, the final *Swann* opinion specifically rejected the view stated in the Burger draft that the remedial power in this type of case was somehow less than that in the classical equity case: "a school desegregation case does not differ fundamentally from other cases involving the framing of equitable remedies to repair the denial of a constitutional right. The task is to correct, by a balancing of the individual and collective interests, the condition that offends the Constitution. . . . Once a right and a violation have been shown, the scope of a district court's equitable powers to remedy past wrongs is broad, for breadth and flexibility are inherent in equitable remedies." Remedial discretion includes the power to attempt to reach a goal of racial distribution in schools comparable to that in the community and to order extensive busing if that is deemed appropriate to "produce an effective dismantling of the dual system."

The most important thing about the *Swann* decision was its recognition of broadside remedial power in desegregation cases — secured over the Chief Justice's vigorous opposition. *Swann* goes far beyond the no-segregation principle laid down in *Brown*. Under *Swann* the federal courts do have the power to issue whatever orders may be necessary to bring about an integrated school system — the broad and flexible power traditionally exercised by courts of equity. This includes extensive busing if deemed appropriate to attain the goal of what the Court in 1969 had called "insuring the achievement of complete integration at the earliest practicable date."

There is no doubt that the *Swann* decision process involved a power struggle between the Chief Justice and a majority of the Court and that, as the Douglas *Autobiography* puts it, "Burger lost out." To quote again the Justice mentioned at the beginning of this chapter, "The Chief Justice was determined to carry the day, and we were equally determined he wouldn't — and we had the votes."

His lack of votes induced Burger to agree to rewrite and ultimately to issue a *Swann* opinion that the others were willing to accept. Describing the redrafting process, the same Justice said, "We tried to save as much as we could [from the Burger drafts] so that the Chief Justice wouldn't lose face — but if he had to lose face, so be it." As it turned out, it never came to the latter alternative.

At the same time, the majority Justices could feel that they had accomplished a great deal in ensuring that the original Burger view did not prevail. Had the original Burger draft come down as the final *Swann* opinion, it would have marked a serious setback for enforcement of civil rights. The negative tone taken by the Chief Justice to the district court's busing order would have sent a clear message that the Warren Court's expansive approach to desegregation would no longer be followed. In its place there was to be a restricted attitude toward the remedial powers of the federal courts that would render them powerless to achieve more than cosmetic changes in segregated school systems.

Instead, the signal sent by *Swann* was one of solid support for judges who took vigorous measures to end dual school systems. The discretion which the Chief Justice had originally sought to deny them was now confirmed in strong language by the Supreme Court. They were told that they had broadside authority to order any remedies, including busing, to root out "all vestiges of state imposed segregation." With *Swann,* the federal courts were, more firmly than ever engaged in the business of actively ensuring the achievement of desegregation.

DE JURE VERSUS DE FACTO SEGREGATION

Swann marked the culmination of the Burger Court decisions on de jure segregation. If such segregation by law has been shown, in the words of the *Swann*
opinion, the scope of a district court's equitable powers to remedy past wrongs
"is broad, for breadth and flexibility are inherent in equitable remedies."

Cases involving de jure segregation — segregation required by law — must,
however, be distinguished from cases involving de facto segregation where,
as *Swann* put it, "racial imbalance exists in the schools but with no showing
that this was brought about by discriminatory action of state authorities." In
the de facto case, the Burger Court held that the courts might not act to remedy
the situation; the segregation was caused, not by law, but by such factors as
housing patterns.

In practice, the de jure–de facto distinction means that using *Swann* to
eliminate dual school systems is possible only in the South. *Brown, Green,* and
Swann did lead to substantial progress in integration in southern states. "No
comparable progress," Justice Powell pointed out in the soon-to-be discussed
Keyes case, "has been made in many nonsouthern cities with large minority
populations primarily because of the de facto–de jure distinction nurtured by
the courts."

Chief Justice Burger had tried to include the de jure–de facto issue in his
Swann opinion. In his early *Swann* drafts, he stressed that the Court's target was
school segregation only: "it does not and cannot embrace all the problems of
racial prejudice in residential patterns, employment practices, location of
public housing, or other factors beyond the jurisdiction of school authorities,
even when those patterns contribute to disproportionate racial concentrations
in some schools."

The Burger attempt to take the lead on the de jure–de facto issue was
resisted by the others. "I feel," Justice Brennan wrote to the Chief Justice on
December 30, 1970, "that an attempt to decide the *de facto* situation is
unwarranted by the facts of this case." Justice Douglas was even blunter. In a
March 6, 1971, letter to the Chief Justice, referring to the Burger draft language
quoted in the previous paragraph, Douglas objected that this "paragraph
excludes from *de jure* segregation relevant to school problems both restrictive
social covenants and racial public housing." Douglas asserted that "such state-
sanctioned practices are included in *de jure* segregation for purposes of the
public school problem." The Justice asked the Chief Justice "not [to] decide the
scope of *de jure* segregation . . . and restrict *Swann* to the case where there has
been a dual school system." If that were done, Douglas concluded, "Then I
could join *Swann*." To secure the Douglas vote, the Chief Justice omitted the
offending passage from the *Swann* opinion.

The fullest discussion of the de jure–de facto distinction came during
the decision process in *Keyes v. Denver School District No. 1* (1973). The
Denver school system had never been operated under constitutional or statu-

tory provisions that either mandated or permitted racial segregation. However, schools in one area of the city were overwhelmingly black or Hispanic.
The district court had found that this was the result of intentional race-
conscious decisions by the school board in constructing schools and drawing
attendance zones.

Chief Justice Burger did not even attempt to play a leadership role in the
Keyes decision. At the postargument conference, he stated only, "This is not the
typical *Brown* case — 66% white, 14% Negro, 20% Chicano. . . . [No] one
was denied admission to school on racial grounds. . . . Plaintiffs have the
burden to show discrimination." In his view, that burden had not been met.

The majority, however, followed an entirely different approach. They expanded the concept of de jure segregation, holding that it could be shown not
only when segregation was required or permitted by law, but also when
segregated schools resulted from the intentional acts of the school board. Since
the Denver board had followed a deliberate segregation policy, there could exist
a predicate for a finding that the entire school system was segregated de jure.

The most interesting aspect of *Keyes,* however, was the Court's implicit
resolution of the de jure–de facto issue. There was intensive discussion of that
issue during the *Keyes* conference. Yet, so far as the conference notes made
available indicate, Chief Justice Burger did not contribute substantially to
the discussion.

It was primarily Justice Powell who made the de jure–de facto distinction
part of the *Keyes* agenda. At the *Keyes* conference, Powell stated strong disagreement with the distinction. "The distinction between de jure and de facto," the
Justice declared, "can't be defended constitutionally or logically. The Court has
worked itself into a position that ignores that population trends have been the
product of state action of all sorts."

Justice Powell urged the abandonment of the de jure–de facto distinction.
But the others, except for Justice Douglas, refused to take that step — though
Justice Brennan did state that the distinction troubled him also. The prevailing
view was stated by Justice Rehnquist: "It never occurred to me to reject the
distinction between de jure and de facto."

Justice Powell then wrote a separate *Keyes* opinion that expanded on his view
that the de jure–de facto distinction should not be perpetuated. In its place
there should be "a uniform national rule." If segregated schools exist, the courts
may order whatever steps may be necessary to secure an integrated system.
However, the Powell opinion also strongly questioned "any remedial requirement of extensive student transportation solely to further integration. . . .
There is nothing in the Constitution, its history, or — until recently — in the
jurisprudence of this Court that mandates the employment of forced transportation of young and teenage children to achieve a single interest, as important
as that interest may be."

On April 3, 1973, soon after he had read the Powell *Keyes* draft, Brennan
sent around a Memorandum to the Conference. "At our original conference

discussion of this case, Lewis first expressed his view that the de jure–de facto distinction should be discarded. I told him then that I too was deeply troubled by the distinction." Nevertheless, the majority "was committed to the view that the distinction should be maintained, and I therefore drafted *Keyes* within the framework established in our earlier cases." While he was "still convinced that my proposed opinion for the Court is, assuming the continued vitality of the de jure–de facto distinction, a proper resolution of the case, I would be happy indeed to recast the opinion and jettison the distinction if a majority of the Court is prepared to do so."

But there was an internal inconsistency in the Powell approach that made it unacceptable. While it would have meant the end of the de jure–de facto division, it would also have meant the virtual end of busing as a desegregation remedy. Segregation would have been subjected to uniform treatment through the country; but the courts would have been divested of the power to order transportation to further integration — even in the *Swann*-type case where dismantling of a dual school system could not be accomplished without busing.

Justice Brennan made this point in his April 3 memo: "Although Lewis and I seem to share the view that de facto segregation and de jure segregation (as we have previously used those terms) should receive like constitutional treatment, we are in substantial disagreement, I think, on what the treatment should be. Unlike Lewis, I would retain the definition of the 'affirmative duty to desegregate' that we have set forth in our prior cases, in particular *Brown II, Green,* and *Swann.* Lewis's approach has the virtue of discarding an illogical and unworkable distinction, but only at the price of a substantial retreat from our commitment of the past twenty years to eliminate all vestiges of state-imposed segregation in the public schools." To go along with Justice Powell might lend weight to his view on busing. Thus it might be better to treat *Keyes* as a de jure case and avoid the de facto issue.

The Brennan view was accepted by the others and the *Keyes* opinion did not discuss the de jure–de facto distinction. In practice, nevertheless, since the Powell rejection of the distinction was spoken in dissent (supported only by Justice Douglas), *Keyes* confirmed the distinction as the basis of desegregation jurisprudence. Once again, however, Chief Justice Burger did not play a significant part in the Court's resolution of an important constitutional issue. From his *Swann* passage on the matter which the others had pressured him to omit, Burger was plainly opposed to the Powell rejection of the de jure–de facto distinction. Yet he did not even attempt to lead the Court in its refusal to follow the Powell view.

OPINION BY COMMITTEE

The importance of the Chief Justice's power to assign opinions has been stressed throughout this book. In exercising the assigning power, the Chief Justice has been compared to a general deploying an army. Certainly, the

superior Court heads have jealously guarded their opinion-assigning prerogative. It is hard to imagine a Marshall or a Warren agreeing to have
that prerogative taken away in any case—much less an important one. Yet
that is just what Chief Justice Burger did agree to in *Buckley v. Valeo* (1976),
where the Court decided important issues on presidential power and the
First Amendment.

Before the Court in *Buckley* was the Federal Election Campaign Act, as
amended in 1974, and its provisions for appointment of members of the
Federal Election Commission and those dealing with political contributions
and expenditures. As set up by the Act, the Commission was composed of six
voting members: two to be appointed by the President Pro Tempore of the
Senate, two by the Speaker of the House, and two by the President, subject to
confirmation by both houses of Congress. The lower court rejected the claim
that the statute's appointment provision violated the constitutional requirement for Presidential appointment of all federal officers.

Though their final decision on the appointment of FEC members was
unanimous, the Justices were closely divided at the postargument conference.
Chief Justice Burger began by pointing out, "Congress can delegate what it
itself may do. But some of the things the Commission can do, Congress can't."
Because the FEC had executive functions, Congress could not appoint its
members. "That goes too far," Burger asserted, "and I'd have to reverse."

The Chief Justice was supported by Justices Blackmun and Rehnquist.
However, Justices Brennan, White, Marshall, and Powell made statements for
affirmance. Since Justice Stewart passed on the issue, the conference vote was
four to three in favor of the appointment provision.

The opinion in *Buckley* was an "opinion by committee." Justice Stewart
urged that a committee of the Justices should draft a per curiam opinion. The
Chief Justice reluctantly agreed and gave up his function of leading the Court in
the case to a committee composed of Justices Stewart, Brennan, and Powell.
The committee divided the work among the various members of the Court. The
final draft was reviewed by a committee of law clerks from the different
chambers; as Justice Powell put it in a January 19, 1976, letter, it was the job of
"the 'Clerks Committee' to harmonize stylistic and verbiage differences between the several Parts subject, of course, to review by each of us."

The section on the appointment of FEC members was written by Justice
Rehnquist. It held that the FEC appointment provision violated the constitutional provision for appointment of "Officers of the United States" by the
President, subject to senatorial confirmation. The Rehnquist draft striking
down the appointment provision was joined by the other Justices, including
those who had voted the other way at the conference.

The other issues in *Buckley,* involving the Election Act provisions dealing
with political contributions and expenditures, gave the Justices more difficulty,
and the conference was divided. The Chief Justice expressed doubts on the
contribution limits set by the statute. Ultimately, however, all but the Chief

Justice went along with the decision to uphold the limits, agreeing with the conference statement by Justice Stewart — it was "for Congress to fix the limits and not for us to second guess."

With regard to the expenditure provisions, Chief Justice Burger set the conference theme when he said, "This is pure speech." Justice Stewart, who was to write the portion striking down the expenditure restrictions, stated that they were "wholly unconstitutional under the First Amendment." And for Justice Powell the provisions were "the most drastic abridgements of political speech since the Alien and Sedition Acts." Justices Brennan, White, and Marshall dissented from the conference consensus on the expenditure provisions (though Brennan ultimately agreed).

Though the Chief Justice had voted with the majority on expenditures, he did not play a part in the opinion drafting. Here, too, the Burger abdication of responsibility to the "opinion by committee" process prevailed. The portion of the *Buckley* opinion dealing with expenditures was written by Justice Stewart, who treated expenditures as a form of political speech. The Stewart portion held that the statute infringed upon the First Amendment freedom to speak without legislative limits on candidacies for public office.

Can we imagine either Chief Justice Hughes or Chief Justice Warren transferring his assigning power to a committee of the Justices and then playing no significant part in the decision or drafting process in such an important case? Yet that is precisely what Chief Justice Burger did in *Buckley*. In a 1969 case where a Burger draft had been substantially changed by the other Justices, the Chief Justice sent around a covering October 29 Memorandum for the Conference with his final draft, which stated that the draft "resembles the proverbial 'horse put together by a committee' with a camel as the end result. But then even the camel has proven to be useful." Perhaps so, but it may be doubted that a strong Chief Justice would have been so flippant about having his core function as Court head taken away from him.

Finally, a footnote to *Buckley* because it indicates why *Time* called Justice Rehnquist the Burger Court's "most self-consciously literate opinion writer" — even though my example is not from a Rehnquist opinion. The *Buckley* opinion had rejected the argument, accepted by the court of appeals, that the governmental interest in equalizing the relative ability of individuals and groups to influence elections justified the contribution limitations. In a November 10, 1977, Memorandum to the Conference in a later case, Justice Rehnquist stated his impression of the court of appeals' acceptance of this argument in *Buckley*: "The Court of Appeals there, it seemed to me, appeared to say that in order to achieve the 'compelling state interest' of allowing everybody to be heard to some extent, Congress did not abridge the First Amendment by preventing some people from talking as much as they wanted. This seemed to me like something out of George Orwell, or like Rousseau's idea that people would be forced to be free."

WATERGATE TAPES CASE

In many ways, the most spectacular case decided by the Burger Court was *United States v. Nixon* (1974) — the Watergate tapes case — for it led directly to the forced resignation of the President. The case itself arose from a motion filed by the Watergate Special Prosecutor for a subpoena directing President Nixon to produce certain tape recordings of his conversations with aides and advisers. Following the return of an indictment against top White House aides and others for crimes arising out of the scandal, the Special Prosecutor determined that the tapes were relevant evidence and a subpoena was issued. The President moved to quash the subpoena, asserting that conversations between a President and his close advisers were privileged and that the doctrine of separation of powers precluded judicial review of his privilege claim. This view would have meant unqualified presidential immunity from judicial process.

The President's claim was characterized by the Court in a 1977 case as "a claim of absolute Presidential privilege against inquiry by the coordinate Judicial Branch." The claim was rejected by the eight Justices (Justice Rehnquist having disqualified himself) who met in conference on July 9, 1974 — the day after the oral argument. The Justices were united in holding that the President must turn over the subpoenaed tapes, although none disputed the existence of some executive privilege. The conference discussion in this respect was summarized in a July 12 "Dear Chief" letter circulated by Justice Powell: "we are all in accord that there is a privilege of confidentiality with respect to presidential conversations and papers. We also agreed that it is a qualified privilege and not absolute or unreviewable; and, in this case, that the Special Prosecutor has made a showing which overcomes the privilege and justifies *in camera* review."

However, according to the Powell letter, "We were not entirely in agreement as to the standard to be met in overcoming the privilege. . . . [S]ome of us emphasized that a President of the United States (and it must be remembered that we are speaking not just of the present incumbent) must be entitled to a higher level of protection against disclosure than a citizen possessing no privilege who is charged with crime or who may be a witness in a criminal case." The opposing view was stated by Justice White, who was to write the draft on the matter that formed the basis for the *Nixon* opinion.

Another matter on which there was some difference at the conference was that of the authorship of the opinion. Justice Brennan said that the Court should emphasize its decision by issuing the strongest opinion possible and this could be done if the Court delivered a joint opinion — in the name of each of the participating Justices. The Court had done so only once before — in the 1958 Little Rock school desegregation case, where the joint opinion of the Justices dramatically underlined their unanimity.

Chief Justice Burger refused to go along. "The responsibility is on my shoulders," he said. He would prepare the opinion and would circulate its different parts as he finished them. But the drafts he sent around took a more expansive view of presidential power than the others were willing to accept. The Justices refused to go along and virtually wrested the opinion-drafting process from the Chief Justice in order to secure an opinion that they could join.

The Chief Justice circulated his draft *Nixon* opinion in five separate sections. The heart of the Burger draft, as of the final *Nixon* opinion, was its section on "The Claim of Executive Privilege." The draft was far more favorable to the presidential claims than the final opinion.

Though the Burger draft, like the final opinion, rejected the presidential claim of absolute privilege, the draft went on to say, "Since we conclude that the legitimate needs of the judicial process may outweigh presidential privilege when the privilege is based solely on the generalized need for confidentiality, it is necessary, in a given case to resolve these competing interests in a manner that preserves the essential functions of each branch."

The implication is that, where an "essential" function of the President is involved, the privilege claim may prevail even over the needs of the judicial process. This implication is strengthened by the draft's later development of the notion of presidential "core functions," which would also prevail in any privilege case. According to the draft, "Under Article II a President, for example, exercising certain of his enumerated war powers, as in repelling a hostile attack, or exercising the veto power, or conducting foreign relations is exercising powers at the very core of his constitutional role. The courts have shown the utmost deference to presidential actions in performance of these core functions."

The difficulty with the "core function" approach is indicated by the following queries written by a Justice on his draft copy: "What does this mean? May St. Clair [Nixon's counsel] argue other core functions at stake? What is a core function?"

The Burger draft recognized foreign relations and military secrets as involving "core functions" of the President, but it also recognized that the core-function concept is not limited to these matters. Instead, it stated that "by referring to the deference due to all discussions of military and foreign policy secrets, we intend to intimate no view that discussion of highly sensitive domestic policies, for example, devaluation of the currency, imposition or lifting of wage and price controls, would not be entitled to a very high order of privilege, since the economic consequences of disclosure of such discussions could well be as pervasive and momentous as the disclosure of military secrets."

If that was true of "highly sensitive domestic policies," the same might be true of other domestic acts involving presidential duties "lying at the core of Article II authority." The core-function concept has what Justice Black once termed "accordion-like qualities." It is capable of expansion or contraction in each individual case, since it is without any defined limits to ensure that it will be kept within proper bounds; thus counsel for the President could argue in *Nixon* that "core functions [are] at stake." As the draft put it, "The courts have shown the utmost deference to presidential actions in the performance of . . . core functions." If a court finds that a "core function" is involved, under the Burger approach, the President's prerogative in the matter must remain untouched.

OPINION BY COMMITTEE AGAIN

In discussing the final *Nixon* opinion, a Justice who took part in the case characterized it to me as "opinion by committee." His characterization is supported by a paper in his file on the case. Typed on one page and without any identification, it reads simply:

Opinion Outline

    I.   Facts [HAB]
    II.   Appealability [WOD]
   III. Intra-branch dispute [WJB or beefed-up WEB version]
   IV. Rule 17(c) [BRW]
    V. [Merits of executive privilege: WEB: LFP as revised by PS]
   VI. Standards to be met before in camera inspection is ordered [LFP as revised by WJB]
  VII. The Court's judgment and order [WJB]

When the Justices saw how weak the Burger draft was, especially the crucial section on executive privilege, they concluded that substantial revisions were necessary. Rather than wait for new drafts by the Chief Justice, they decided to send him their own drafts of the different sections for him to use in his redrafts. These sections were to be drafted primarily by the Justices whose initials appear next to them.

An important consequence of the *Nixon* drafting process was the absence of that primary ingredient of superior Supreme Court opinions—one strong hand. Instead, there was the opinion by committee, and the committee had to use as its foundation the unsatisfactory Burger draft. Once again, to soften the rebuff to the Chief Justice, the other Justices used his draft language as much as possible. The result was that much of the final opinion reads as though it was the work of at least two authors.

The other Justices were particularly unwilling to accept the Burger draft on executive privilege with its doctrine of core functions, which they felt tilted the balance unduly in favor of the presidential claim. The executive-privilege section was primarily redrafted by Justice Stewart, who had prepared a draft on the subject even before the Chief Justice had sent around his draft. As far as possible, Stewart also used the Chief Justice's language in his redraft; but he eliminated the core-function analysis.

By this point, it had been made clear to Chief Justice Burger that he could not secure a majority (indeed, he would remain virtually alone) if he did not abandon his core-function analysis, and he gave way. On July 23 he circulated a new draft of the executive-privilege section. It was a modified version of the Stewart redraft. The core-function concept was now completely eliminated.

The Burger redraft and the opinion as a whole was approved at a conference which met at 1:30 P.M. on July 23. The final printed draft was sent around later that day and met no objection. The next day the decision was announced and the opinion summarized by the Chief Justice to a packed courtroom. Seventeen days later President Nixon resigned.

But the *Nixon* decision did more than cast the President into political limbo. It marked a rejection by the Court of the "Imperial Presidency" concept — a concept that Chief Justice Burger tried so hard to support in his draft opinion. What the case has meant to our constitutional system was dramatically shown by former Chief Justice Warren's reaction when he was told how the Court was going to decide. That happened just after the July 9, 1974, conference on the case. When the conference ended, Justice Brennan left his chambers and climbed into his red VW square-back sedan. Driving from the Court, he turned west on Constitution Avenue and headed to Georgetown University Hospital, where his old comrade-in-the-law Earl Warren was being treated for a heart attack that had felled him a week earlier.

Justice Brennan found Warren, then eighty-three, surprisingly alert and in good spirits. The man Brennan fondly called "Super Chief" had avidly followed politics and the law since his retirement as Chief Justice five years before. He was eager to hear the latest on the *Nixon* case, then before the Court.

Justice Brennan had a lot to confide. He told Warren about the conference on the case and indicated that the eight Justices participating had decided unanimously that Nixon must turn over the crucial tapes to the court. The case had provoked a "lively discussion," Brennan said. "It was very quickly apparent," he told Warren, "that the President would be treated like any other person."

When the Justice told Warren the news, the old Chief Justice lifted himself from the pillows. "Thank God, thank God, thank God!" Warren declared fervently. "If you don't do it this way, Bill, it's the end of the country as we have known it."

Soon after Brennan left, Warren suffered a cardiac arrest. He died that evening, knowing that the Imperial Presidency had been categorically repudiated by the Supreme Court.

DONALDSON AND RIGHT TO TREATMENT

As previously stated, Chief Justice Burger had strongly held views where he believed a fundamental value to be at stake. An effective Chief Justice does not, however, act as Burger did, in Justice Douglas's previously quoted characterization: "The CJ would rather die than affirm." In this respect, there is an important difference between an Associate Justice and the Chief Justice. Talking about Justice Douglas, a law clerk once commented, "Douglas was just as happy signing a one-man dissent as picking up four more votes." A Chief Justice who acted similarly would soon find that he did not have a Court to lead.

Even the strongest Chief Justice finds that he may have to compromise his views in order to secure a palatable, if not (in his view) the optimum decision. Thus, Chief Justice Hughes went along with the 1936 *Carter Coal* decision interpreting federal regulatory power most restrictively to avoid a decision striking down a New Deal statute by a bare majority. In his *Jones & Laughlin* opinion the next year, the Chief Justice was able to follow the expansive approach discussed in Chapter 3. But that was true only because he then had the votes to make it the opinion of the Court.

A more recent example is the position of Chief Justice Rehnquist in *Pennell v. San Jose* (1988), where a rent control ordinance required "the hardship to a tenant" to be taken into account in determining whether a proposed rent increase would be reasonable. Justice Scalia wrote an opinion holding that this resulted in an unconstitutional forced subsidy for poor tenants. There is little doubt that Chief Justice Rehnquist, as ideologically conservative as any Justice—he had, after all, been dubbed "the [Burger] Court's Mr. Right" by *Newsweek*—agreed with Scalia on the merits. But, realizing that the votes were lacking to strike down the ordinance, he wrote an opinion of the Court avoiding the merits, holding instead that the constitutional claim was premature, since the hardship provision had not been used to reduce the rent in an actual case.

This chapter has shown that, too frequently, Chief Justice Burger would persist in his views rather than compromise. The result, all too often, was a decision opposed to the Burger view—even when, as in *Swann* and *Nixon,* the opinion came down in the Chief Justice's name. A not so well-known example of the Burger posture occurred in *O'Connor v. Donaldson* (1975). Donaldson, who had been confined in an institution as mentally ill, sued, claiming he had been improperly detained and denied treatment in violation of his constitutional rights. The court of appeals affirmed a jury verdict in his favor, ruling that "a person involuntarily civilly committed to a state mental hospital has a constitutional right to receive such individual treatment as will give him a reasonable opportunity to be cured or to improve his mental condition."

The appeals court had relied on a 1966 decision where the Court of Appeals for the District of Columbia had first held that committed mental patients had a right to treatment. This holding was reaffirmed by the D.C. court on numerous occasions, but it had been vigorously contested by Judge Warren E. Burger (then a member of that court). Now that he was Chief Justice, Burger saw the *Donaldson* case as an opportunity to repudiate the right-to-treatment holding that he had opposed while on the court of appeals.

At the conference after the January 15, 1975, oral argument, the Chief Justice stated his view on what he saw as the main issue. He began by categorically summarizing the holding below on the matter: "Treatment was held to be the quid pro quo for confinement as a constitutional matter." Burger rejected this holding in strong language, declaring, "The instruction that he is entitled to treatment giving him a realistic opportunity to be cured or improved is nonsense."

Justices Powell and Rehnquist agreed that there was no constitutional right-to-treatment. But only Powell followed Burger's view that the decision should turn on that issue. The other Justices kept away from the right to treatment issue. Justice Stewart, who was to play a crucial role in the case, said that the constitutional right involved here was the "right to release from unconstitutional state custody." As Stewart put the key question, "Is the fellow not dangerous to anyone and not getting treated?" If so, said the Justice, he is "constitutionally entitled not to be confined. I'd go further and say he can get out whether or not he's getting treatment if he's not a danger to himself or others."

(I should state parenthetically that this reconstruction of the conference and vote differs from the version in *The Brethren* — the 1979 book that caused such a sensation because it purported to reveal what went on behind the Court's red velour curtain. I have found, however, that all too much of *The Brethren*'s account of the Court's decision process is similarly incomplete and inaccurate.)

My own version of the *Donaldson* conference and vote is based on the conference notes and tally sheet of a Justice who was present. The tally sheet summarized the vote on the case as follows (with Justice Douglas, then undergoing treatment at the Rusk Institute in New York, not participating):

REVERSE:	White
AFFIRM:	Brennan, Marshall, Blackmun, Powell, Rehnquist
PASS:	Chief Justice, Stewart

Despite this vote and the fact that only Justice Powell had supported his view that the opinion should reject the holding that there was a right to treatment, Chief Justice Burger took the *Donaldson* opinion himself. Once again, the Chief Justice assigned a case although he had not voted with the majority. Here, too, the majority did not challenge the Burger action, inconsistent though it was with long-settled Court practice. Justice Douglas, who had protested the Chief Justice's assignment in other cases where Burger had not been in the majority, was seriously ill at the time and the others let the matter pass without objection.

The Chief Justice's draft opinion of the Court contained a complete rejection of the right-to-treatment approach which Burger had opposed on the D.C. Court of Appeals and which had been the basis of the lower court holding in *Donaldson* itself. The Burger draft minced no words on the subject. It began by making the point stressed by the Chief Justice at the conference — that this case was before the Court for it "to decide whether there is a constitutional right to treatment for persons involuntarily committed to state institutions by reason of mental abnormality."

The draft gave short shrift to the notion that there was any such constitutional right to treatment. The Burger conclusion on this was categorical: "In sum, we reject the reasoning of the Court of Appeals and can discern no other basis for equating the federal constitutional right not to be confined without due process of law with an absolute constitutional right for involuntarily committed mental patients to either receive adequate psychiatric treatment or be released."

But the Burger draft did not stop with the effort to inter what the Chief Justice's conference presentation had termed the right-to-treatment "nonsense." There was also language in the draft that might have even greater potential for the rights of those in involuntary confinement. "There can be little doubt," declared the draft, "that in the exercise of its police power a State may confine individuals solely to protect society from the dangers of significant antisocial acts or communicable disease." By indicating that people could be confined for "significant antisocial acts," the Chief Justice was opening the door to a drastic expansion of the substantive power of confinement itself.

From the extracts just quoted, it can be seen that the Burger *Donaldson* draft opinion of the Court went far beyond the conference consensus on the case. It is true that the draft concluded by affirming the verdict in Donaldson's favor. But the affirmance could not mask the fact that the Burger draft focused almost entirely on the right-to-treatment issue and that the Chief Justice's effort to render that right stillborn had not been approved by the conference majority.

Once again, the Justices would not accept the Burger draft. This time the lead was taken by Justice Stewart, who circulated a strong memo that declared, "I am opposed to plunging into these extraneous issues," such as the right to treatment. Stewart also prepared a draft dissent that ignored the right-to-treatment issue. It stressed that "the issue in this case [is] a narrow one." The treatment issue, to which the Burger draft had been devoted, was relegated to a footnote. There was no occasion here, the note said, to decide that issue. "In its present posture this case involves not involuntary treatment but involuntary custodial confinement." The draft dissent took particular aim at the Burger indication that people could be confined for "significant antisocial acts." "May the State," Stewart asked, "fence in the harmless mentally ill solely to save its citizens from exposure to those whose ways are different?" The answer was self-evident. "One might as well ask if the State, to avoid public unease, could incarcerate all who are physically handicapped or socially eccentric. Mere public intolerance or animosity cannot constitutionally justify the deprivation of a person's physical liberty."

This time, however, Chief Justice Burger did not give way. He circulated a Memorandum to the Conference that insisted on the correctness of his view: "In short, the question whether there is a constitutional right-to-treatment is fairly presented by this case and . . . we relieve ourselves of no difficult problems, and indeed will create serious problems, by brushing it under the rug."

By now, however, it was too late for the Chief Justice to control the disposition of the case. No one had joined his draft; instead a Court was forming behind Justice Stewart's draft dissent. At this point, the Chief Justice decided to yield to Stewart. He sent around a memo which noted, "Potter seems to have four and a fraction votes (with Bill Douglas not voting), and I am happy to have him try his hand at an opinion." Justice Douglas, now senior Justice in the majority, also wrote to Justice Stewart, "if, as I assume, it is my task formally to assign the opinion for the Court, I assign, of course, to you." Stewart then converted his draft dissent into an opinion of the Court, which (after five drafts) was announced as the *Donaldson* opinion.

The Justices' refusal to join the Chief Justice's draft *Donaldson* opinion has made a substantial difference for the rights of those confined for mental illness. Even apart from the broader implications in the Burger extension of commitment power to protection against "significant antisocial acts," his draft would have left the right to treatment developed by the lower federal courts stillborn as a constitutional right.

Justice Stewart's final *Donaldson* opinion did not deal with the right to treatment. This left it open to the lower federal courts to continue their development and enforcement of that right. Thus, the lower court in *Donaldson* later affirmed that a person involuntarily confined in a mental hospital "has a constitutional right to such individual treatment as will help him to be cured or to improve his mental condition." This means that there is a judicially enforceable right to treatment whenever an individual is involuntarily committed.

Thus the lower *Donaldson* court approach to the right to treatment issue is now established federal constitutional doctrine. The Supreme Court's *Donaldson* opinion has not affected this at all and the post-*Donaldson* cases have been able to refine and enforce the right. This would, of course, have been impossible had the Burger draft come down as the opinion of the Court.

THE LOST LEADER

One must conclude, however reluctantly, that Warren Burger was lost as the leader of his Court. Burger began his tenure with a definite program to overrule the principal Warren Court decisions. According to Justice Douglas's *Autobiography*, Chief Justice Burger "announced in Conference . . . from time to time the precedents we should overrule. *Miranda, Gideon, . . . Reynolds v. Sims* and many others were on the list." Though, as Douglas put it, "Burger worked hard on it," he was never able to secure the rollback in Warren Court jurisprudence that headed his agenda. In 1983 a book was published entitled *The Burger Court: The Counter-Revolution That Wasn't.* The subtitle is a succinct summary of the Burger Court in operation. It can, indeed, be said that no important Warren Court decision was overruled during the Burger tenure. Some of them were narrowed by Burger Court decisions; others were, however, not only fully applied but even expanded.

We can see this even in the field of criminal justice, where Chief Justice Burger was most eager to disown the Warren heritage. The transformation of constitutional law in the criminal justice field during the Warren years had culminated in the celebrated *Gideon, Mapp,* and *Miranda* trilogy. The latter two in particular were decisions for which the Warren Court was widely criticized—denounced for putting "another set of handcuffs on the police." Testifying before a Senate subcommittee just after *Miranda,* Truman Capote plaintively asked, "Why do they seem to totally ignore the rights of the victims and potential victims?"

Though the Warren criminal cases became a major issue of Richard Nixon's presidential campaign, the Justices appointed by Nixon did not tilt the Court to the point of repudiating them. In fact, one of the Warren criminal trilogy was substantially expanded by the Burger Court. In *Gideon,* Chief Justice Warren had told the conference that it was "better not to say [the right to counsel applies in] 'every criminal case,' if we don't have to here." Warren told the others, "maybe it's best just to decide this case." The Court followed Warren's suggestion to limit the *Gideon* decision to the case at hand and held only that there was a right to assigned counsel in the felony case at issue, without addressing the question of how far the new right extended.

The Burger Court not only followed *Gideon,* it expanded it to every case in which imprisonment is imposed as a penalty, regardless of whether the crime involved is classified as a felony, misdemeanor, or even petty offense. *Gideon* also only upheld the right to counsel at the criminal trial. The Burger Court extended the right to counsel to preliminary hearings—that is, before any formal accusation and trial—and gave practical effect to the right of the accused to represent himself if he so chose and knowingly and intelligently waived the right to counsel.

Chief Justice Burger was strongly opposed to *Mapp* and *Miranda;* but he was not able to secure the votes needed to overrule those cases. Early in the Burger tenure, indeed, a majority of the Justices indicated that they were dissatisfied with the *Mapp* exclusionary rule. Before a majority could act on the dissatisfaction, however, two of the *Mapp* opponents retired. Justice Powell, one of the replacements, was not prepared to overrule *Mapp,* though he was willing to narrow the exclusionary rule. *Mapp* was not overruled; but the later Burger years saw a narrowing of the exclusionary rule, culminating in a good-faith exception toward the end of Burger's tenure.

Miranda had a similar fate in the Burger Court. The Chief Justice himself was anything but a partisan of *Miranda.* In a 1977 case where the Court refused to act on the request of twenty-two states to overrule *Miranda's* procedural ruling, the Chief Justice circulated a December 29, 1976, memorandum stating, "I will probably write separately focusing on the utter irrationality of fulfilling Cardozo's half-century old prophecy—which he really made in jest—that some day some court would carry the Suppression Rule to the absurd extent of suppressing evidence of a murder victim's body."

Despite his disapproval of *Miranda,* the Chief Justice never succeeded in overruling that decision. The most the Burger Court did was to narrow *Miranda,* though that hardly affected the essentials of its doctrine. In the end, Burger himself realized that *Miranda* still remained as a pillar of defendants' rights.

The same was true in the other areas of Warren Court jurisprudence, including desegregation, the First Amendment, reapportionment, other aspects of equal protection, and judicial review in operation. In all these areas, the central premises of the Warren Court decisions were not really challenged by its successor. The core principles laid down in the Warren years remained as securely rooted in our constitutional law as they were when Chief Justice Burger first took his seat.

7

Individual Justices
Lead the Court

When Earl Warren became Chief Justice, he was so much the judicial novice that he did not even have a robe of his own for his swearing-in ceremony. He had to borrow a spare that was hurriedly found in the Court's robing room. Surprisingly, it was too long even for his tall frame, and he tripped over it as he stepped up to the raised bench to take his place in the Chief Justice's seat after he had taken the Judicial Oath. Because of this, he later wrote, "I suppose it could be said that I literally stumbled onto the bench."

There was, however, to be little stumbling as he took over his role as head of the Court. Warren, as we saw, was to lead the Court as effectively as any Chief Justice in our history.

Just as the most inspiriting general must have troops to follow his lead, even under a strong Chief Justice, the Associate Justices play a pivotal part. At times, indeed, it is the Associates, who lead the Court to its decisions. We have seen how the Justices as a unit can act to block attempts by the Chief Justice to dictate decisions and opinions opposed by the majority. But individual Justices may also lead the Court to particular decisions — performing the function in the decision process ostensibly discharged by the Chief Justice. That is true even where the Justice concerned does not appear to the public to have played a significant part in the decision. From the Court's earliest days, there have been Justices who have led the Court to important decisions — taking over, at least temporarily, the leadership role in the decision process.

COOLEY AND CURTIS

The Supreme Court decision process before Chief Justice Roger B. Taney's tenure remains a closed book. Taney himself was a strong Chief Justice —

"second only to Marshall in the constitutional history of our country," wrote Felix Frankfurter in 1937 — who undoubtedly led his Court to most of its significant decisions. In the Taney Court's two most consequential decisions, however, the leadership role was performed by individual Justices rather than the Chief Justice. The first was the Taney Court's most successful resolution of a crucial constitutional issue, the second its greatest failure. Yet neither the success nor the failure was a result of the Chief Justice's leadership.

The first case was *Cooley v. Board of Port Wardens* of the Port of Philadelphia (1852). It resolved an important issue that until then had remained undecided — that of the reach of the Commerce Clause and the proper scope of state power over interstate commerce. Before *Cooley,* the Justices had avoided direct resolution of the question of whether the power to regulate commerce was vested exclusively in the Federal Government. The question came before the Supreme Court with increasing frequency because of the growing resort by the states to regulatory legislation.

Chief Justice Taney and his colleagues vacillated on the commerce issue, confirming, in the 1847 License Cases, the power of the states to regulate the sale of liquor imported from abroad, and then, in the 1849 Passenger Cases, striking down state laws imposing a tax on foreign passengers arriving in state ports. The confusion in the Court was shown by the plethora of judicial pronouncements to which it gave rise. Nine opinions were written in the first case and eight in the second; in neither was there an opinion of the Court in which a majority was willing to concur.

That the commerce issue was resolved in *Cooley* was a result, not of Chief Justice Taney's leadership, but of the lead given by Justice Benjamin R. Curtis. It was Curtis who fashioned a workable compromise between the competing views on the commerce issue and one that best served the economic interests of the nation. Justice Curtis had taken his Court seat only two months before the *Cooley* case was argued and was thus an ideal judge to write a compromise opinion between the extremes of exclusive congressional power advocated by some of the Justices and the Taney view of coextensive concurrent state power over commerce.

Chief Justice Taney concurred silently in the Curtis *Cooley* opinion. Why he did so has always been a matter for speculation. As Chief Justice, he could, if he chose, make himself spokesman for the Court. That he did not do so shows that he could not carry a majority for his own approach. If he did not accept the *Cooley* compromise, it would have meant the same fragmented resolution of the commerce issue that had occurred in the prior cases. Taney's concurrence in the *Cooley* compromise made it possible for the law at least to be settled with some certainty on the matter (it was only after *Cooley,* asserted Charles Warren in his now classic history of the Court, "that a lawyer could advise a client with any degree of safety as to the validity of a State law having any connection with commerce between the States").

After the *Cooley* decision, Justice John Catron wrote to James Buchanan, "Curtis is a first rate lawyer — exceedingly fair-minded — and writes smoother than any man on the Bench." Justice Curtis worked out the theory behind the *Cooley* decision and induced the others to accept it. Just before the *Cooley* decision was announced, Curtis wrote to his uncle, "I expect my opinion will excite surprise. . . . But it rests on grounds perfectly satisfactory to myself, and it has received the assent of five judges out of eight, although for twenty years no majority has ever rested their decision on either view of this question, nor was it ever directly decided before."

The *Cooley* case itself arose out of a Pennsylvania law requiring vessels using the port of Philadelphia to engage local pilots or pay a fine. Since there was no federal statute on the subject, the question for the Court was that of the extent of state regulatory power over interstate commerce where Congress was silent on the matter. It was contended that the pilotage law violated the Constitution because the Commerce Clause had vested the authority to enact such a commercial regulation exclusively in Congress. To the question whether the power of Congress was exclusive, Justice Curtis answered, Yes and no — or, to put it more accurately, Sometimes yes and sometimes no. There remained the further inquiries: When and why yes? When and why no?

These questions were answered with a doctrine of what may be termed "selective exclusiveness." If the states are excluded from power over commerce, the Curtis opinion said, "it must be because the nature of the power, thus granted to Congress, requires that a similar authority should not exist in the States." If that is true, the states must be excluded only to the extent that the nature of the commerce power requires. When, Curtis asked, does the nature of the commerce power require that it be considered exclusively vested in Congress?

Justice Curtis answered that this depended on whether the particular subjects of regulation were ones "imperatively demanding a single uniform rule, operating equally on the commerce [throughout] the United States; [or] demanding that diversity which alone can meet the local necessities." Under *Cooley,* whether the states may regulate depends upon whether it is essential that the subjects of the regulation be governed by a uniform national system. Where national uniformity of regulation is not necessary, the subject concerned may be reached by state law. That is the case with a law for the regulation of pilots like that at issue in *Cooley.*

In his letter to Buchanan, Justice Catron referred to the issue presented in *Cooley* and concluded, "But the question is now settled." That this could be said was due almost entirely to Justice Curtis, who both fashioned the *Cooley* test and persuaded the majority to accept it. Yet Curtis did more in *Cooley* than resolve the commerce issue by compromise. He stated a balancing test which makes the validity of governmental action depend upon a weighing of the interests involved. Under *Cooley,* state regulation of commerce depends upon balancing the circumstances of the locality which may tilt in favor of local regulation, on the one hand, and the national need for uniformity, on the other. In *Cooley,* Justice Curtis led the Court to a new balancing approach to law that fore-shadowed modern constitutional jurisprudence.

DRED SCOTT

If the *Cooley* decision was the Taney Court's greatest success, the *Dred Scott* decision was its greatest failure. *Dred Scott* is undoubtedly the most discredited decision in Supreme Court history. For more than a century the case has stood as a monument of judicial indiscretion; as Justice Robert H. Jackson acidly commented in a 1941 book, "One such precedent is enough!"

In *Dred Scott,* the Court decided in the legal forum the most pressing political issue of the day — the power of Congress to exclude slavery from the territories. Dred Scott was a slave who had been taken by his owner to the Wisconsin Territory. He sued for his freedom in a federal court in Missouri, arguing that his service in territory from which slavery had been excluded by the Missouri Compromise passed by Congress in 1820 made him a free man. Scott's claim raised the issue of whether Congress possessed the constitutional authority to prohibit slavery in the territories. But there was more in the case than this. Defendant had filed a plea alleging that Scott was not a citizen and hence could not sue in a federal court because of diversity of citizenship, since "he is a Negro of African descent; his ancestors . . . were brought into this country and sold as slaves." This posed the even broader question of whether, under the Constitution, even a free Negro could be a citizen.

When the Court first considered *Dred Scott* in conference, however, a majority were of the opinion that the case should be decided without considera-tion of the two crucial issues. As Justice Curtis wrote to his uncle, "The Court will not decide the question of the Missouri Compromise line, — a majority of the judges being of opinion that it is not necessary to do so." The conference concluded both that the issue of citizenship was not properly before them and that they need not consider the Missouri Compromise because Scott's status was a matter for Missouri law and had already been determined against him by the state's highest court. Justice Samuel Nelson was selected to write an opinion disposing of the case in this manner.

Had the Nelson opinion (limiting itself to Scott's status under Missouri law after his return to that state) prevailed as the opinion of the Court, the *Dred Scott* case would scarcely be known today except to the curious student of high-bench miscellany. But the Justices soon departed from their initial resolve to decide the case without considering the issues of citizenship or slavery in the territories.

Justice Nelson circulated a five-thousand word draft. Yet, as Don Fehren-bacher puts it in what is now the leading book on the *Dred Scott* case, "The ink was scarcely dry on Nelson's draft . . . before the Court majority reversed itself and decided to take hold of the thornier problems that he had so carefully avoided." It did so not because Chief Justice Taney led the Justices to reverse their decision. On the contrary, the catalyst for the change was an individual Justice—James M. Wayne, a Georgian, who, while serving as a judge in Savannah, had sentenced an offender for "keeping a school for Negroes." Two years before *Dred Scott,* he had declared that there was no possibility that even free blacks "can be made partakers of political and civil institutions of the States, or those of the United States." "Here," Fehrenbacher tells us, "the conspicuous figure was Wayne. He made the key motion and later confirmed that the key initiative had been his alone." Justice Curtis also wrote to his brother that the change was brought about by Justice Wayne. As Curtis recalled it, "it was urged upon the court, by Judge Wayne, how very important it was to get rid of the question of slavery in the Territories, by a decision of the Supreme Court, and that this was a good opportunity of doing so."

Justice Wayne moved in conference that the decision deal with the two vital issues that Justice Nelson was omitting. "My own and decided opinion," he said, "is that the Chief Justice should prepare the opinion on behalf of the Court upon all of the questions in the record." The five who voted in favor of Wayne's motion were from slave states. Wayne himself later told a southern Senator that he had "gained a triumph for the Southern section of the country, by persuading the chief-justice that the court could put an end to all further agitation on the subject of slavery in the territories."

Chief Justice Taney himself did not play a major part in the conference that adopted Wayne's motion. On the other hand, according to Curtis's brother, the Justice "in the conferences of the court, explained in the strongest terms that such a result, instead of putting an end to the agitation in the North, would only increase it." In addition, Curtis stressed that it was "most unadvisable to have it understood that the decision of these very grave and serious constitutional questions had been influenced by considerations of expediency." The fact that the five votes for the new decision were by southerners would lead to anything but Wayne's conference prediction that "the settlement . . . by judicial decision" would result in "the peace and harmony of the country." Instead, as Horace Greeley put it in the *New York Tribune,* settlement of the slavery issue by the Court meant submitting it to five slaveholders and "I would rather trust a dog with my dinner."

After Justice Wayne's motion had been adopted, something happened that one hopes would be impossible today. Two of the Justices—Catron and Grier—had written President-elect Buchanan that, in Catron's words, "a majority of my brethren will be forced up to this point [that is, to rule on the constitutional issues of citizenship and slavery in the territories]." These letters to Buchanan were intended to inform the President-elect of the Court's plan to have the Court issue a broad majority opinion. Justice Catron urged Buchanan to write to Justice Grier (a fellow Pennsylvanian), who hesitated to join the new majority, telling him "how necessary it is—and how good the opportunity is to settle the agitation by an affirmative decision of the Supreme Court."

Buchanan did write to Grier, who showed the letter to Chief Justice Taney and Justice Wayne and then wrote to Buchanan that he fully concurred with the need for decision on "this troublesome question." He was afraid that the case would be decided on sectional lines; so "that it should not appear that the line of latitude should mark the line of division in the Court," he would concur with the Court's opinion. Both Justices wrote Buchanan that the Court's decision would not be announced until just after the inauguration because of the Chief Justice's poor health.

By present-day standards, the correspondence between Buchanan and two members of the Court was improper. Even more so was Buchanan's pressure on Justice Grier, at the invitation of another Justice, to join the majority. To say, as Charles Warren's history of the Supreme Court does, that it was not infrequent at the time for Justices to tell a friend or relative the probable outcome of a pending case scarcely excuses Buchanan and the Justices concerned. Buchanan was not just a friend; he was the new President and was hoping to use the information and his influence over Grier for political purposes. Even given the more permissive standards of an earlier day, the propriety of their conduct cannot be defended.

Yet this is not to say, as was widely charged at the time, that the *Dred Scott* decision itself was the result of a conspiracy between Buchanan and the southern members of the Court. Though Lincoln asserted, in his famous "House Divided" speech, that the decision was the product of an understanding between "Stephen, Franklin, Roger, and James" in which "all worked upon a common plan . . . drawn up before the first lick was struck," all we know about the case indicates that it did not happen that way.

What led to the *Dred Scott* decision was Justice Wayne's desire to, as he said in his previously quoted statement to a Southern Senator, gain a triumph for the South by a Court decision in its favor on the crucial issue of slavery in the territories. It was thus Wayne who led the Justices to their ill-fated decision, with Chief Justice Taney going along with the Wayne initiative. It was also on Wayne's motion that the Chief Justice was to write the opinion "upon all of the questions in the [case]."

When, on March 6, 1857, the aged Chief Justice read his *Dred Scott* opinion, his voice was so weak that, during much of the two hours in which he spoke, it sank almost to a whisper. "No wonder," declaimed Greeley's *Tribune,* soon after the decision was announced, "that the Chief Justice should have sunk his voice to a whisper . . . knowing that he was engaged in a pitiful attempt to impose upon the public." To Greeley and other abolitionist editors, the decision was a patent triumph for slavery — a view that was accepted by the South as well.

On the face of it, then, Justice Wayne had been correct when he looked upon his crucial role in the decision process as a southern triumph. Justice Curtis later confirmed to his brother that Wayne had told the conference that "the peace and harmony of the country required the settlement of the constitutional questions involved by judicial decision." Wayne, Curtis said, "regarded it as a matter of great good fortune to his own section of the country, that he had succeeded in producing a determination, on the part of a sufficient number of his brethren, to act upon the constitutional question which had so divided the people of the United States."

In his concurring *Dred Scott* opinion, Justice Wayne stated that the issues involved had become so controversial "that the peace and harmony of the country required the settlement of them by judicial decision." Seldom has wishful thinking been so spectacularly wrong. *Dred Scott* brought about anything but peace and harmony — either for the Court or for the country. Instead, the *Dred Scott* decision was a major factor in precipitating the political polarization of the nation. With it collapsed the practical possibility of resolving by political and legal means the issues which divided the nation. Thenceforth, extremists dominated the scene. Bloodshed alone could settle the issue of slavery and of the very nature of the Union, which that issue had placed in the balance.

LOCHNER AND HOLMES

Aside from *Dred Scott* itself, *Lochner v. New York* (1905) is now considered the most discredited decision in Supreme Court history. In his book on the Court, Chief Justice Rehnquist terms *Lochner* "one of the most ill-starred decisions that it ever rendered." When commentators discuss the case at all, they use it as a vehicle to illustrate the drastic change in jurisprudence during the twentieth century, which has seen the Holmes dissent in *Lochner* elevated to established doctrine.

The *Lochner* decision struck down a New York law that prohibited bakery employees from working more than ten hours a day, or sixty hours a week. The law was challenged as a violation of due process. "The Statute in Question is Not a Reasonable Exercise of Police Power," declared the brief attacking the law.

The case gave the Supreme Court great difficulty. The Justices originally voted by a bare majority to uphold the law. The first Justice Harlan confided to his son that the case was then assigned to him and that he wrote a draft opinion of the Court. Justice Rufus W. Peckham wrote a strong draft dissent. Before the case came down, however, there was a vote switch. The Peckham dissent became the opinion of the Court and the Harlan opinion a dissent. It is not known who changed his vote, though it is likely that it was Chief Justice Melville W. Fuller. Though Fuller had voted to uphold other maximum-hour laws, his biography by Willard L. King tells us that "the ten-hour law for bakers seemed to him to be 'featherbedding,' paternalistic, and depriving both the worker and employer of fundamental liberties."

What makes *Lochner* pertinent to our present discussion is the fact that, here too, the decision process in a key Supreme Court case was led, not by the Chief Justice, but by one of his colleagues. It is probable that it was Justice Joseph

McKenna who persuaded the majority not to follow earlier cases upholding maximum-hour laws. In those cases, the laws regulating hours of labor were upheld by the Court as health measures. In *Lochner*, Justice McKenna, whose father had been a bakery owner and who had grown up around bakeries in California, persuaded Chief Justice Fuller and others in the majority that bakery work was not dangerous and that the health rationale was a sham.

Incidentally, the *Dred Scott* and *Lochner* cases show that vote switches have been a factor in the Supreme Court's decision process throughout its history. *Lochner* also shows that five-to-four decisions are not at all a recent invention of the Justices. For our present purposes, however, both cases demonstrate how an individual Justice can lead the decision process even in landmark cases.

In both *Lochner* and *Dred Scott*, to be sure, the leadership of the individual Justices led to judicial disaster, resulting in the two most censured decisions of the Court. Yet *Lochner* is remembered today for more than the Court's unfortunate decision. Aside from its use as the horrible example of what we now consider the wrong kind of judicial activism, *Lochner* is known for its now classic dissent by Justice Oliver Wendell Holmes, celebrated for its oft-quoted aphorisms. Indeed, the Holmes *Lochner* opinion is probably the most famous dissent ever written. "There is a famous passage," Justice Benjamin N. Cardozo wrote, "where Matthew Arnold tells us how to separate the gold from the alloy in the coinage of the poets by the test of a few lines which we are to carry in our thoughts." The flashing epigrams in Holmes's *Lochner* dissent do the like for those who would apply the same test to law.

Justice Holmes is usually considered the most influential Associate Justice ever to sit on the Supreme Court. In a speech on Chief Justice John Marshall, Holmes once said that "if American law were to be represented by a single figure, skeptic and worshiper alike would agree without dispute that the figure could be one alone, and that one, John Marshall." If American law were to be represented by a second figure, most jurists would say that it should be Holmes himself. For it was Holmes, more than any other legal thinker, who set the agenda for modern Supreme Court jurisprudence. In doing so he became as much a part of American legend as law: the Yankee from Olympus — the patrician from Boston who made his mark on his own age and on ages still unborn as few men have done. To summarize Holmes's work is to trace the development from nineteenth-century law to that of the present day.

There is no doubt, indeed, that a major part of twentieth-century Supreme Court doctrine is a product of the Holmes handiwork. As summarized by Judge Richard A. Posner in *The Essential Holmes*, the Justice's contributions include: (1) judicial restraint in cases involving challenges to regulatory laws; (2) the Clear and Present Danger Test and the "marketplace of ideas" conception of free speech that has served as the foundation for the Court's current expansive conception of the First Amendment; (3) rejection of the rule that federal courts should be free to disregard state court decisions and to fashion federal rules to decide cases involving questions of state law; and (4) the principle that state prisoners can seek federal habeas corpus to claim that they have been convicted in violation of the Constitution.

Nevertheless, as Judge Posner pointed out, "the primary vehicles of Holmes's innovations were dissenting opinions that, often after his death, became and have remained the majority position." At the time they were delivered, the Holmes dissents spoke only for their author's conception of the proper legal doctrine. While Holmes was on the Court, its jurisprudence remained dominated by the concepts that he was ultimately to relegate to legal limbo. The Justice's dissents may have sounded the clarion of the coming constitutional era. But they did not really influence our law until after his death. However crucial may have been the role that Holmes played in American jurisprudence, it cannot be said that, as a Justice, he played a dominant part in the Supreme Court decision process.

JUSTICE AS LAWGIVER

In terms of his role in the decision process, Justice William J. Brennan was actually the most influential Associate Justice in Supreme Court history. Brennan served as the catalyst for some of the most significant decisions during his tenure. He was the leader of the Court's liberal wing under Chief Justices Warren, Burger, and Rehnquist. More important, the Brennan jurisprudence set the pattern for much of American legal thought as the century drew toward its end. So pervasive was the Brennan influence that the British periodical the *Economist* headed its story on his retirement, "A Lawgiver Goes."

Before his 1956 appointment by President Eisenhower, Brennan had been a judge in New Jersey for seven years, rising from the state trial court to its highest bench. "One of the things," Justice Felix Frankfurter once said, "that laymen, even lawyers, do not always understand is indicated by the question you hear so often: 'Does a man become any different when he puts on a gown?' I say, 'If he is any good, he does.' " Certainly Justice Brennan on the highest bench proved a complete surprise to those who saw him as a middle-of-the-road moderate. He quickly became a firm adherent of the activist philosophy and a principal architect of the Warren Court's jurisprudence. Brennan had been Frankfurter's student at Harvard Law School; yet if Frankfurter expected the new Justice to continue his pupilage, he was soon disillusioned.

In a 1958 letter to Justice Harlan, Frankfurter wrote about "Bill Brennan. 'Too much ego in his cosmos.' . . . 'Is . . . Bill as cocksure as his opinions indicate?' Cocksureness begets sensitiveness, and as his erstwhile teacher, I have to be particularly careful with Bill." At the 1994 Warren Court Conference at the University of Tulsa, Brennan told how Frankfurter had said "at a dinner one night . . . that while he had always encouraged his students to think for themselves, 'Brennan goes too far.' "

Justice Brennan soon became Chief Justice Warren's closest colleague. The two were completely dissimilar in appearance. Warren was a broad-shouldered six-footer; Brennan is small and feisty, almost leprechaun-like in appearance; yet he has a hearty bluffness and an ability to put people at ease. Brennan's unassuming appearance and manner mask a keen intelligence. He was perhaps the hardest worker on the Court. Unlike many Justices with strong views, Justice Brennan was always willing to mold his language to meet the objections of his colleagues, a talent that would become his hallmark on the Court. Thus, we shall see, it was he who suggested the compromise approach that characterized the decision in the landmark *Bakke* case, as well as the intermediate standard of review that has governed in sex discrimination cases.

On the Warren Court, Justice Brennan soon became a member of a group of four Justices (with the Chief Justice and Justices Black and Douglas—those whom Judge Learned Hand once referred to as "the Jesus Quartet") who favored activist solutions to constitutional issues. In 1962, with the retirement of Justices Felix Frankfurter and Charles E. Whittaker, and their ultimate replacement by Justices Arthur J. Goldberg, Abe Fortas, and Thurgood Marshall, a majority for the Four's position was secured. It was then that our law entered its most important period of development since its formative era—remaking much of the legal corpus in the process. Justice Brennan was a leader in this development.

After Chief Justice Warren's retirement, Justice Brennan was no longer the trusted insider. Instead, he became the leader of the Burger Court's liberal wing and the Justice who tried above all to keep the Warren flame burning. Even under Chief Justice Burger, Justice Brennan was able to secure the votes for his position in many important cases. In his last years, the Court, under Chief Justice William H. Rehnquist, moved more toward the right and Brennan spoke increasingly in dissent. However, in the Rehnquist Court also, Justice Brennan was able to gain notable victories, particularly in the areas of abortion, separation of church and state, freedom of expression, and affirmative action. He was primarily responsible for the decisions just before his retirement that flag burning was protected by the First Amendment and upholding broad Congressional authority in the field of affirmative action.

To appreciate the Brennan contribution, we should have some understanding of the conflict between activism and judicial restraint that has played such a significant part in Supreme Court jurisprudence. There is an antinomy inherent in every legal system: the law must be stable and yet it cannot stand still. It is the task of the judge to reconcile these two conflicting elements. In doing so, jurists tend to stress one principle or the other. Stability and change may be the twin sisters of the law, but few judges can keep an equipoise between the two.

Justice Brennan never pretended to try to maintain the balance. He was firmly on the side of change, leading the Supreme Court's effort to enable the law to cope with rapid societal change. Before Brennan's appointment, the Court had been divided between two antagonistic judicial philosophies that differed sharply over the proper role of the judge. In simplified terms, the division was between judicial activism and judicial self-restraint. The rule of restraint had been the doctrine that Justice Holmes had advocated so vigorously in dissent. By the time Justice Brennan came to the Court, the Holmes approach had become established doctrine. Under it, the Justices came to recognize governmental restrictions on property rights to an extent never before permitted in American law. At the same time, they saw that unless individual rights were correlatively expanded, the individual would virtually be shorn of constitutional protection: hence, this century's shift in American constitutional law to emphasis on the protection of personal rights. The growth of governmental authority disturbed the Justices. They tried to preserve a sphere for individuality even in a society in which individuals stood dwarfed by the power concentrations that confronted them.

In such a society, the issues confronting the courts have also begun to change. Judges like Brennan came to believe that even the Holmes canon could not suffice as the bedrock of judicial review. Justice Brennan was willing to follow the rule of restraint in the economic area. It was, indeed, the opinion that Brennan wrote (although it was labeled "per curiam") in *New Orleans v. Dukes* (1976), that confirmed the Burger Court's deferential approach in cases involving challenges to economic regulation.

Justice Brennan may have been willing to follow the canon of judicial restraint in the economic area, but he felt that the Bill of Rights provisions protecting personal liberties imposed on the judges more active enforcement obligations. When a law was alleged to infringe upon the personal rights the Bill of Rights guaranteed, challenged legislation had to be scrutinized with greater care. Justice Brennan rejected the philosophy of judicial restraint because he believed that it thwarted effective performance of the Court's constitutional role. Judicial abnegation, in the Brennan view, meant all too often judicial abdication of the duty to enforce constitutional guarantees.

On the Warren Court, Justice Brennan became the Chief Justice's principal lieutenant. So consequential was his role, in fact, that Dennis J. Hutchinson, an editor of the *Supreme Court Review,* declared that to call it the "Warren Court" is a misnomer: "it was 'the Brennan Court.' " As shown by my analysis of Chief Justice Warren in action, this assertion unduly denigrates Warren's leadership. Still, it is hard to argue with Hutchinson's conclusion that "Brennan emerges clearly as the most important justice of the period."

Brennan was the Justice to whom the Chief Justice turned to write the opinions in some of the most important cases during the Warren years — particularly where the tentative majority was unsure of the reasoning to support its decision. The outstanding example is *Baker v. Carr* (1962), which Warren himself termed in his *Memoirs* "the most important case of my tenure on the Court." It ruled the federal courts competent to entertain an action challenging legislative apportionments as contrary to equal protection. Before *Baker,* the Court had held that legislative apportionment presented a "political question" beyond judicial competence. In *Baker,* the Brennan opinion supplied the rationale for the decision overruling the earlier cases and holding that attacks on legislative apportionments may be heard and decided by the federal courts.

The *Baker* opinion was the foundation for the rule laid down in *Reynolds v. Sims* (discussed in Chapter 4) that the Constitution lays down an "equal population" principle for legislative apportionment. Under this principle, substantially equal representation is demanded for all citizens.

Just as important is the *Baker* illustration of the Brennan juristic approach. Justice Frankfurter, Brennan's old teacher, had warned in a 1946 opinion against courts entering "this political thicket." The *Baker v. Carr* opinion replied, "The mere fact that a suit seeks protection of a political right does not mean that it presents a political question." That, commented the *Economist*, was the Brennan watchword.

Even more striking was the Warren reliance upon Justice Brennan to write the opinion in the highly controversial case of *Cooper v. Aaron* (1958), where the Governor of Arkansas had defied a federal court order to desegregate Central High School in Little Rock. This was the unique case where the opinion of the Court was issued in the names of all the Justices, listed individually as authors of the opinion. What Hutchinson called "the anonymous dirtywork of crafting" the opinion was, however, actually performed by Justice Brennan, upon whom the Chief Justice again relied in what the Warren *Memoirs* said was "the one event that greatly disturbed us during my tenure and that was the . . . Little Rock case."

Justice Brennan was able to make another substantial contribution to the law on racial discrimination in *Green v. County School Board* (1968) — the Warren Court's most important post-*Brown* desegregation decision. The case was assigned to Brennan and he was determined to clear the doubts about *Brown* enforcement that had been created by *Brown II*'s use of the "all deliberate speed" formula. The Justice decided to write a *Green* opinion that would deal with the problem as forcefully as possible and, at the same time, be modeled on the *Brown I* opinion itself, which Chief Justice Warren had stated in a memo was to be "short, pungent, and to the point." As told by his law clerks, Brennan wanted "to sweep away much of the dogma that has grown up in *de jure* litigation to hinder desegregation efforts . . . [to stress] the duty of school boards to maximize integration where feasible." In sum, the clerks say, "what the Justice wanted to do was to arm the . . . 'right' courts of appeals and judges, with the ammunition to go after the recalcitrants."

The Brennan *Green* opinion was the strongest on the subject since *Brown* itself; as the *Swann* case discussed in the last chapter shows, it set the tone for future desegregation jurisprudence. Justice Brennan's opinion imposed the affirmative duty to immediately dismantle all dual school systems — a duty that required school authorities to "come forward with a plan that . . . promises realistically to work *now*." If they did not come forward with such a plan, the courts could do so. From the *Brown* invalidation of segregation, the Court had moved to the *Green* affirmative duty to provide a fully integrated school system.

Well could Warren write in a note to Brennan, when the Chief Justice joined the *Green* opinion, "When this opinion is handed down, the traffic light will have changed from *Brown* to *Green*. Amen!"

In *Green*, Justice Brennan had written an opinion that stated the new approach to be followed in desegregation cases. When the others joined his draft, it became Supreme Court doctrine, even though it was entirely the handiwork of one Justice, who was thus the leading force in the *Green* decision process. Brennan was also the leader in two other landmark Warren Court decisions. The first was *New York Times Co. v. Sullivan* (1964), where Justice Brennan gave a new perspective to freedom of expression by ruling that the governmental power to fix the bounds of libelous speech is confined by the Constitution. A public official had recovered substantial libel damages against a newspaper. The Brennan opinion reversed, holding that the newspaper publication was protected by the First Amendment, which required a "rule that prohibits a public official from recovering damages for a defamatory falsehood relating to his official conduct unless he proves that the statement was made with 'actual malice' — that is, with knowledge that it was false or reckless disregard of whether it was false or not."

Justice Brennan's opinion was based upon the "general proposition that freedom of expression upon public questions is secured by the First Amendment." It gave effect, Brennan wrote, to the "profound national commitment to the principle that debate on public issues should be uninhibited, robust, and wide-open, and that it may well include vehement, caustic, and sometimes unpleasantly sharp attacks on government and public officials."

The crucial point for our purposes about *New York Times v. Sullivan* is that the Brennan opinion was based upon a theory that had not even been discussed at the conference on the case, which had voted to decide on an entirely different narrow ground. Justice Brennan first announced his new approach to libel law when he circulated his draft opinion. The Chief Justice played practically no part in the decision process (though, in fairness to him, it should be pointed out that he was overburdened at the time by his work as chairman of the Warren Commission investigating President Kennedy's assassination). It was Justice Brennan who led the *New York Times* decision process: he propounded the novel theory that has since governed the law on the subject, and he persuaded the other Justices to adopt it — in the process warding off several threatened dissents.

Another case where Justice Brennan led the Court to its decision was *Shapiro v. Thompson* (1969). Though it is little known except to specialists, no Warren Court decision has had a more far-reaching legal impact. In *Shapiro,* the Justices had originally voted to uphold a state law requiring a year's residence for welfare assistance on the ground that it had a rational basis in the state's desire to use its resources for its own residents. Chief Justice Warren prepared a draft opinion of the Court following the original conference consensus. Vote switches, however, caused the case to be reargued and a majority then voted to strike down the residence law. The opinion was assigned to Justice Brennan, who now persuaded his colleagues to reject the rational-basis approach and strike down the residence requirement on a broader theory. Though a different standard of review had not been discussed at the conference, the Brennan draft greatly expanded the scope of review in equal protection cases. The draft ruled that since the requirement restricted the fundamental right to travel, it had to be supported by a *compelling* governmental interest and none was present here.

The expanded scope of judicial review in such a case was not only the Brennan handiwork. It was the Justice who marshaled a Court behind his new approach; he personally persuaded wavering Justices (notably Justice Stewart) to join his opinion. Since Chief Justice Warren adhered to his original opinion and dissented, it was Justice Brennan who performed the role of leading the Court to the *Shapiro* decision.

The result has been a substantial enlargement of the Court's review power. Under Brennan's *Shapiro* opinion, the test of mere rationality gives way, in cases involving fundamental rights, to one of strict scrutiny under which a challenged law will be ruled invalid unless justified by a "compelling" governmental interest. Since *Shapiro*, judicial review has taken place within a two-tier framework, with two principal modes of analysis: strict scrutiny and mere rationality. The tier in which legislation is placed all but determines the outcome of constitutional challenges. Legislation is virtually always upheld under the rationality test, since a law is almost never passed without any rational basis. The converse is true under the compelling-interest test: If a statute is subject to strict scrutiny, it is nearly always struck down.

Justice Brennan's *Shapiro* approach has become established doctrine. It has been applied to a wide range of rights deemed fundamental: the rights guaranteed by the First Amendment, the right to vote, the right to marry, and the right of women to control their own bodies, including the right to terminate pregnancies.

Roe v. Wade, which upheld the last of these rights, was based directly upon the Brennan *Shapiro* approach. In striking down state abortion laws, the Court applied the compelling-interest test. "Where certain 'fundamental rights' are involved . . . ," states the *Roe* opinion, "regulation limiting these rights may be justified only by a compelling state interest." The state's determination to recognize prenatal life was held not to constitute a compelling state interest, at least during the first trimester of pregnancy.

It may be doubted that *Roe v. Wade* would have been decided this way if Justice Brennan's *Shapiro* opinion had not laid the doctrinal foundation. Had *Shapiro* confirmed the rational-basis test as the review standard even in cases involving fundamental rights, *Roe v. Wade* would have been deprived of its juristic base. One of the most controversial Court decisions might never have been made.

It was, perhaps, to be expected that the Brennan role would be diminished when the Warren Court gave way to the Burger and Rehnquist Courts. But it did not turn out that way. Justice Brennan continued to play the role of judicial lawgiver until his 1990 retirement. Thus, it was the Justice who led the Burger Court in laying down the law governing sexual discrimination — a subject left untouched by the Warren Court. Following Chief Justice Burger's lead, the Court had, in 1971, reviewed a sexual classification under the rational-basis test. Had the Justices continued to follow that approach, it would have aborted the substantial development in sex discrimination law that has since occurred. That that did not happen was largely the result of two Brennan opinions.

In *Frontiero v. Richardson* (1973), Justice Brennan felt, as he indicated in a memorandum to the Justices, "that this case would provide an appropriate vehicle for us to recognize sex as a 'suspect criterion.' " Accordingly, he wrote an opinion that provided for strict scrutiny in sexual-classifications cases. The statute provided benefits for "dependents" of armed-services members. A serviceman could always claim his wife as a "dependent," but a servicewoman could claim her husband only if he actually depended upon her for over half of his support. The opinion agreed with the contention that "classifications based upon sex, like classifications based upon race, alienage, and national origin, are inherently suspect and must therefore be subjected to close judicial scrutiny." Brennan's opinion held the *Frontiero* statute invalid, not under the rational-basis test, but under the strict-scrutiny requirement of compelling interest.

Justice Brennan could, however, secure only three other votes for his *Frontiero* opinion. To obtain the majority, he compromised in the next sex discrimination case, *Craig v. Boren* (1976). *Craig* struck down an Oklahoma law prohibiting the sale of beer to males under the age of twenty-one and to females under the age of eighteen. Such a law was held a denial of equal protection to males eighteen to twenty-one years of age. Justice Brennan realized there that he could not secure a Court for a *Frontiero*-type opinion that treated sex as a suspect classification subject to the compelling-interest requirement. Instead, the *Craig* opinion enunciated an in-between standard, stricter than the rational-basis test, but not as strict as the compelling-interest requirement. "To withstand constitutional challenge, . . ." states the Brennan opinion, "classifications by gender must serve important governmental objectives and must be substantially related to attainment of those objectives." This test has enabled the Court to apply a stricter standard of review in sex discrimination cases than would have been permitted under the narrow rational-basis standard. Under the test, a number of sexual classifications have been ruled invalid that would have been upheld had the rational-basis test been the governing review standard.

We cannot, however, obtain a complete picture of the Brennan influence on the decision process if we limit ourselves to the cases in which he authored opinions of the Court. The Brennan impact on our constitutional corpus extends far beyond his own opinions. His forte was his ability to lead the Justices to the decisions he favored, even at the cost of compromising his own position, as in the adoption of the review standard that now governs in sex discrimination cases. More than any Justice in recent years, Brennan was the strategist behind Supreme Court jurisprudence — the most active lobbyist (in the nonpejorative sense) in the Court, always willing to take the lead in trying to mold a majority for the decisions that he favored.

His was the behind-the-scenes influence in first securing constitutional recognition for the right of privacy in *Griswold v. Connecticut* (1965). The Connecticut law at issue prohibited the use of contraceptives even by married couples. The conference agreed that the law was invalid, following the view expressed by Justice Douglas that it violated the First Amendment right of association. Only Justice Black had disagreed, asserting sarcastically, "The right of association is for me a right of assembly and the right of the husband and wife to assemble in bed is a new right of assembly for me."

Justice Douglas wrote a draft opinion of the Court basing the decision on the right of association. Before circulating, however, he sent Justice Brennan a copy. Brennan wrote to Douglas urging him to abandon his right-of-association approach. Instead, Brennan suggested the privacy rationale, urging that a right of privacy could be inferred from the Bill of Rights' specific guarantees and explaining how that could be done. Justice Douglas followed the Brennan suggestion, and the final *Griswold* opinion ruled that there is a constitutionally protected right of privacy that was violated by the Connecticut law.

It was also Justice Brennan who was responsible for the upholding of affirmative-action programs in *Regents of the University of California v. Bakke* (1978), the leading case on the subject. Justice Powell, whose vote provided the five-to-four majority, had decided to vote against affirmative-action programs. Justice Brennan persuaded him to rule in his crucial opinion that while the quota provisions in the medical school admissions program before the Court were invalid, race could be considered a factor in determining what students to admit. This has enabled almost all affirmative-action programs to continue in operation.

Griswold, Bakke, and the Brennan opinions discussed bear ample witness to his success as a judicial "lawgiver." The decisions and doctrines to which the Justice led the Court were all based upon his concept of a flexible constitutional law which is constantly being adapted to meet contemporary needs that the Framers could not have even dimly foreseen. The cases discussed show that he succeeded in elevating his view of the Constitution to the level of accepted doctrine.

Above all, the Brennan jurisprudence was based upon what he once termed "the constitutional ideal of human dignity." This is what led him to his constant battle against the death penalty, which he considered a violation of the Eighth Amendment ban against cruel and unusual punishment. The battle to outlaw capital punishment was a losing one for Justice Brennan, but it was the only major one he did lose in his efforts to ensure what he said was "the ceaseless pursuit of the constitutional ideal." The ultimate Brennan legacy was that, as stressed in the last chapter, no important Warren Court decision was overruled while the Justice sat on the Burger and Rehnquist Courts.

BRENNAN AND *BRANDENBURG*

The Brennan role in the cases in which he wrote the opinion of the Court, as well as in cases such as *Griswold* and *Bakke* where the key opinions were by others, has been adequately documented by myself and other writers. There is, however, another important case where the central part played by Justice Brennan is all but unknown. The case is *Brandenburg v. Ohio* (1969), which did away with the Clear and Present Danger Test, one of the great contributions by Justice Holmes to modern constitutional law. That *Brandenburg* accomplished this result was the consequence of Justice Brennan's redraft of the *Brandenburg* opinion, although the Justice's name does not appear in the public report of the case.

The Clear and Present Danger Test was developed by Justice Holmes to deal with speech that advocates unlawful action. Before then, such speech was not protected by the First Amendment. That was true because the law concentrated upon the words used alone and condemned those that, in Judge Learned Hand's words in a 1917 case, "counsel or advise others to violate the law."

The great Holmes contribution to the subject was to remove the constitutional focus from the words alone to their relation to the circumstances in which they were used. It is not enough that the words used advocate unlawful action. There must be a direct nexus between the words and the action; more specifically, there must be "a clear and present danger" that the words *will* trigger unlawful action. As Justice Holmes stated his test in 1919, "The question in every case is whether the words used are used in such circumstances and are of such a nature as to create a clear and present danger that they will bring about the substantive evils that Congress has a right to prevent."

Under the Holmes test, speech may be restricted only if there is a real threat—a danger, both clear and present, that the speech will lead to unlawful action. The stress is not, as in the prior law, on the words themselves, but on their relation to the circumstances in which they are used. If speech will result in action that government can prohibit, then the speech itself can constitutionally be reached by governmental power, but only where there is a clear and present danger that the action will result from the speech.

The Holmes test marked a sharp break with the earlier law on the subject. And it was a break that transformed First Amendment law. According to a commentator, "Supreme Court decisions . . . before World War One reflected a tradition of pervasive hostility to the value of free speech." In the decades following the war the situation changed drastically, as the Court came to consider the First Amendment freedom as what Justice Cardozo called "the matrix, the indispensable condition, of nearly every other form of freedom." The changing law in this area was, in large part, a consequence of the Supreme Court's adoption of the Clear and Present Danger Test. In 1943, the Court could declare, "It is now a commonplace that censorship or suppression of expression of opinion is tolerated by our Constitution only when the expression presents a clear and present danger of action of a kind the State is empowered to prevent and punish."

In 1951, however, the Court decided *Dennis v. United States,* which turned out to be what even a restrained observer calls "a debacle for the First Amendment." *Dennis* showed that the Holmes test could be used to restrict speech in a manner reminiscent of the earlier law. The *Dennis* Court upheld the conviction of leaders of the American Communist Party under the first federal sedition law enacted in peacetime since the Sedition Law of 1798. Looking back at the case, it is hard not to conclude that the *Dennis* defendants were convicted for advocacy which could not be considered any threat to government in this country. Historical hindsight has given added perspective to the caustic comment in Justice Douglas's *Dennis* dissent: "How it can be said that there is a clear and present danger that this advocacy will succeed is, therefore a mystery." Yet that is exactly what the *Dennis* Court did say while it professed to apply the Holmes Test.

Perhaps *Dennis* was yet another casualty of the Cold War, which exercised a kind of hydraulic pressure in the law as in other areas of American life, before which even settled principles of law would bend. It was not until eighteen years after *Dennis,* in *Brandenburg v. Ohio,* that the Court was able to decide a case involving advocacy of unlawful action that was not colored by the fact that the advocacy at issue was part of the Cold War climate. In *Brandenburg,* defendant was prosecuted not for advocacy connected with the Communist movement, but for the racist advocacy connected with the Ku Klux Klan.

Clarence Brandenburg was a Klan leader who had been convicted of violating an Ohio law that prohibited "advocat[ing] . . . the duty, necessity, or propriety of crime, sabotage, violence or unlawful methods of terrorism as a means of accomplishing industrial or political reform." The evidence was the film of a Klan meeting that showed twelve hooded figures, guns, and a burning cross. Words were heard about "burying the nigger" and "sending the Jews back to Israel." Defendant made a speech in which he said, "We're not a revengent organization, but if our President, our Congress, our Supreme Court, continues to suppress the white, Caucasian race, it's possible that there might have to be some revengeance taken." He also urged "Marching on Congress . . . four hundred thousand strong."

At the *Brandenburg* conference, all the Justices agreed that the conviction should be reversed. Chief Justice Warren assigned the opinion to Justice Fortas, who had begun to make a reputation because of his First Amendment opinions. Two months after the conference, on April 11, 1969, Justice Fortas circulated a draft opinion. The Fortas draft stated his version of the test to govern this type of case: Under it, advocacy of unlawful action might be proscribed only where it was "directed to inciting or producing imminent lawless action and is attended by present danger that such action may in fact be provoked."

The test thus stated would have virtually returned the law to the Clear and Present Danger Test as stated by Justice Holmes. The key to the Holmes test is the nexus between the speech and the lawless action advocated. The Fortas draft stated the nexus requirement in a manner closer to Holmes than *Dennis,* requiring that the advocacy "is attended by present danger that such [lawless] action may in fact be provoked." This is almost the Holmes standard.

As it turned out, however, *Brandenburg* did not come down as a Fortas opinion. Though the Justice had circulated his opinion in April 1969 and quickly secured the necessary votes, he followed Justice Harlan's suggestion to delay its announcement. Before then, the events occurred that led to Justice Fortas's forced resignation from the Court. The *Brandenburg* opinion was than redrafted by Justice Brennan, who eliminated all references to the Clear and Present Danger Test and substituted the present *Brandenburg* language: "where such advocacy is directed to inciting or producing imminent lawless action and is likely to incite or produce such action." The Brennan redraft was issued as a per curiam opinion.

The leading Fortas biography states that the *Brandenburg* per curiam was "only slightly altered by William Brennan from the final Fortas draft." This drastically understates Justice Brennan's *Brandenburg* role. It is true that his redraft changed only a small percentage of what Justice Fortas had written. But the changes completely altered the nature of the *Brandenburg* opinion, converting it from one that confirmed the Clear and Present Danger Test to one that did away with that test as the governing standard.

The test stated by Justice Fortas required "present danger that such [lawless] action may in fact be provoked" (essentially the Holmes test, since there appears to be little difference between the Holmes "clear and present danger" and the Fortas "present danger"). The Brennan redraft changed the test by substituting the requirement that the advocacy be directed to producing imminent lawless action and that it "is likely to incite or produce such action." Thus, for the Fortas requirement that there be a "present danger" that there will be lawless action (almost a restatement of the Holmes test), Justice Brennan substituted the requirement that the advocacy will produce unlawful action that is about to take place (which is an entirely different test).

The *Brandenburg* redraft was a vintage example of Justice Brennan in action. By changing a few words in the Fortas draft, Brennan completely altered the cast of the *Brandenburg* opinion. So far as is known, none of the other Justices had any comment on the Brennan changes. Perhaps they did not even realize what he had done in the seemingly slight alterations he made. What is clear is that the whole Court joined the *Brandenburg* per curiam.

Had the Fortas draft come down as the opinion of the Court, *Brandenburg* would have been a case virtually reaffirming the Holmes Clear and Present Danger Test. Instead, as redrafted by Justice Brennan, *Brandenburg* substituted its own test for that developed by Justice Holmes. Because of *Brandenburg,* Justice Brennan could assert in a later case, "This Court long ago departed from 'clear and present danger' as a test for limiting free expression."

In its final Brennan version, the *Brandenburg* test is even more protective of speech than the Clear and Present Danger Test. Indeed, as Anthony Lewis tells us, "*Brandenburg v. Ohio* gave the greatest protection to what could be called subversive speech that it has ever had in the United States, and almost certainly greater than such speech has in any other country." All this was the result of the Brennan redrafting of the Fortas *Brandenburg* draft.

As the Fortas biography has it, the final *Brandenburg* opinion was "only slightly altered" by Justice Brennan from the Fortas draft. Yet, though those changes may constitute only a small percentage of the opinion, they made for a quantum change in the law — substituting an entirely new test expanding First Amendment protection for speech advocating unlawful action for the Fortas return to a modified Holmes Clear and Present Danger Test. If, in the *Economist*'s phrase, Justice Brennan was, indeed, a lawgiver, *Brandenburg* is the paradigmatic illustration of this.

NIXON, BLACK, AND *TIME V. HILL*

One morning in January 1986, wrote Leonard Garment in the *New Yorker,* "I got a phone call from Richard Nixon. 'Did you see Tony Lewis's review of that book in Sunday's Times?' he asked. 'Why don't you check it out? Maybe we'll find out what really happened in that case.' "

"That case" was *Time, Inc. v. Hill,* a case that had been decided by the Supreme Court in 1967. "That book" was my new volume, *The Unpublished Opinions of the Warren Court.* It analyzed eleven important Warren Court cases, including *Time, Inc. v. Hill,* in the light of conference notes, draft opinions, and memoranda written by the Justices during their decision process. (These previously secret documents had been made available while I was doing research for a judicial biography of Chief Justice Warren.)

Nixon was interested in *Time, Inc. v. Hill* because it was the only case that he had argued in the Supreme Court. Moreover, it was a case that he had lost when he thought he had the better of the argument. He learned from *Unpublished Opinions* how the Court had originally decided in his favor. The draft opinion of the Court by Justice Fortas was converted into a dissent when several of the Justices switched their votes.

When he learned of the decision from the Clerk of the Court, Garment telephoned Nixon at his apartment. "He listened, asked one or two questions about the authorship of the opinions, and then said, 'I always knew I wouldn't be permitted to win a big appeal against the press.' " Nixon had not, however, lost the case because of the personal antagonism of the Justices. Indeed, the two members of the Court who personally detested Nixon the most — Chief Justice Warren and Justice Fortas — voted for his position throughout the decision process on the case.

Time, Inc. v. Hill is noteworthy, however, not only because of Nixon's connection with it. The case was another striking example of one in which the decision process was led by an individual Justice — this time by Justice Hugo L. Black. It was the Black influence, not anti-Nixon sentiment among the Justices, that led to Nixon's loss.

Time, Inc. v. Hill was based upon a New York law giving statutory protection to the right of privacy. The statute makes it an actionable tort to use the name, portrait, or picture of any person "for advertising purposes, or for the purposes of trade" without written consent. This action arose out of a story in *Life* magazine about a Broadway play, *The Desperate Hours,* which had been inspired by the experience of James J. Hill and his family, who had been held hostage in their home by escaped convicts. The play was fictionalized and had added scenes of violence for dramatic effect. The *Life* article portrayed the play as a reenactment of the Hills' experience, and it contained photographs of scenes acted in the house where the Hills had been held. Hill sued *Life's* publisher under the New York privacy statute. Hill alleged that the *Life* article falsely represented that the play mirrored the Hill family's experience. The New York courts awarded Hill $30,000.

To the press, of course, *Time, Inc. v. Hill* was newsworthy primarily because it marked Richard M. Nixon's debut before the Justices. The Justices differed in their estimate of Nixon's presentation. Former Justice Fortas told me that his performance was "mediocre." But others disagree. One Justice said to me that he was "first rate" during the original argument in April 1966. At lunch after the argument, the Justices expressed surprise at how good he was. On the other hand, according to the same Justice, Nixon did not really seem to have his mind on the case during the October 1966 reargument, when he had taken time off from stumping for congressional candidates to appear before the Court.

Although Warren made no secret of his antipathy toward Nixon (Warren's son once said that Nixon was one of only two men whom the Chief Justice termed an "evil man" — the other was a right-wing oil magnate), he consistently voted for Nixon's position in the *Hill* case. In the first conference on the case, the Chief Justice declared, "It's a fictionalization of these people's experience and false and, in that circumstance, there's no First Amendment problem. In this limited application, I see no threat to a free press." Justice Black took the opposite position, saying "newspapers have the right to report and criticize plays. This is nothing but a statute prohibiting the press from publishing certain things." The conference agreed with Chief Justice Warren and voted six-to-three to affirm the New York judgment, with Justices Black, Douglas, and White voting for reversal.

Chief Justice Warren assigned the case to Justice Fortas, who circulated a sixteen-page draft opinion of the Court. The Fortas draft contained what one of the Justices said was an "invective" against the press — Leonard Garment wrote that its "language . . . verged on excoriation." After summarizing the case, Fortas declared, "The facts of this case are unavoidably distressing. Needless, heedless, wanton injury of the sort inflicted by *Life's* picture story is not an essential instrument of responsible journalism."

The Fortas draft rejected the claim that the *Life* article was privileged as a newsworthy article because it was "a fictionalized version of the Hill incident, deliberately or heedlessly distorted beyond semblance of reality." Justice Fortas concluded that, as applied to such an article, the New York statute was not "in fatal collision with the freedom of the press. The deliberate, callous invasion of the Hills' right to be let alone—this appropriation of a family's right not to be molested or to have its name exploited and its quiet existence invaded—cannot be defended on the ground that it is within the purview of a constitutional guarantee designed to protect the free exchange of ideas and opinions. This is exploitation, undertaken to titillate and excite, for commercial purposes."

The Fortas draft did not, however, come down as the opinion of the Court because of a dispute between Justices Fortas and White over the interpretation by the New York courts of the state's privacy statute. This led to an order setting the case for reargument in which counsel were requested to clarify the New York law on the matter.

Before the Court reconsidered the case, Justice Black circulated a sixteen-page printed memorandum on which, according to his wife's diary, he had worked all summer. The memo stressed the baneful effect that the tentative majority decision would have on First Amendment rights. Under the Fortas draft opinion, Justice Black asserted, the First Amendment prohibition against abridging freedom of speech and the press "has added to it . . . the language 'unless a majority of the United States Supreme Court in its sole, unreviewable wisdom decides that it would or might serve the public interest to curtail or penalize publication of certain matters.' "

Justice Black was particularly biting in his comments on the language in Fortas's proposed *Times v. Hill* opinion. Its consequence would be a chilling effect that would frighten the press so much that publishers would hesitate to report news as long as there was "doubt as to the complete accuracy of the newsworthy facts." That result, Black concluded, would hardly be consistent with the intent of the Framers "to guarantee the press a favored spot in our free society." Indeed, the Black memo went so far as to assert, "After mature reflection I am unable to recall any prior case in this Court that offers a greater threat to freedom of speech and press than this one does, either in the tone and temper of the Court's opinion or in its resulting holding and judgment."

The scathing Black memorandum had the effect its author intended. At the postreargument conference, the Court changed its decision and voted seven to two for reversal. Only Chief Justice Warren and Justice Fortas still voted for affirmance. Justice Black, as senior majority Justice, assigned the case to Justice Brennan.

The new Brennan opinion of the Court held that in a case like *Time, Inc. v. Hill,* plaintiff must show not only "fictionalization," but also "knowledge of the falsity or that the article was prepared with reckless disregard of the truth." The case was remanded to give the New York courts an opportunity to apply the statute in the constitutionally prescribed manner.

The Black memorandum, in his wife's words in her diary, "got the Court on his *Time* Magazine Libel case." Indeed, it is not too much to say that it was Justice Black who led the Court to its *Time, Inc. v. Hill* decision. Had he not written his strong memorandum, it is probable that Richard Nixon would have won his case. The Fortas draft had been based upon what Fred Rodell called its author's "tremendous respect" for the right of privacy — a right which, to Justice Fortas, outweighed even the First Amendment in a case such as *Time, Inc. v. Hill*. Fortas himself, according to Bruce A. Murphy, his leading biographer, "had what can only be termed a hatred of the press." To Justice Fortas, as he told a friend, reporters were "mongers," who were both "dirty" and "crooked" and "destroy[ed] people." Garment tells us that Fortas always maintained that the *Life* article that forced his resignation had been Time, Inc.'s punishment of him for his stand in the *Hill* case.

Justice Black's position was, of course, entirely different. His First Amendment posture was not affected by any abuses the press might have committed. Black's fundamentalist approach to the Constitution led him to place freedom of the press, specifically guaranteed, above a right such as privacy, which did not have any express constitutional foundation.

At any rate, as Garment put it in his *New Yorker* article, one of the ironies of *Time, Inc. v. Hill* "is that after all the speculation about how the Court would respond to Richard Nixon, the [factor] that determined the course of the *Hill* case was not antagonism toward Nixon by any member of the Court." Instead, it was the differing views on the press animating Justices Fortas and Black that was crucial to the outcome. And it was the Black leadership that ultimately led to Nixon's loss of the case. Once again an individual Justice had been the catalyst in the Court's decision process.

8

Vote Switches

In 1993, four Los Angeles police officers were tried in a federal court for the now notorious beating of Rodney King, even though they had been acquitted the year before in a state court prosecution for the same beating. Their second trial could not have taken place because of the constitutional prohibition against double jeopardy if there had not been a vote switch in *Bartkus v. Illinois,* decided by the Warren Court in 1959.

VOTE SWITCHES OVER THE YEARS

Throughout this book, we have seen that the Justices' votes are anything but chiseled in stone. On the contrary, vote switches have been a prominent feature of the decision process throughout the Supreme Court's history.

From the earliest date that we know anything about the internal operations of the Court—when Roger B. Taney was Chief Justice (1837–64)—we can point to cases in which Justices changed their votes during the decision process. The *Dred Scott* case—the Taney Court's most spectacular decision—furnishes a striking example. The Justices there, we saw in the last chapter, originally voted to decide the case on a narrow ground that avoided the crucial constitutional issues. They then changed their minds and agreed that the Court should decide those issues so that they could be resolved for the country. The issues were resolved, but in a manner so offensive to public opinion outside the South that the decision only served as a catalyst for the conflict that had now become inevitable.

The last chapter also showed that a vote switch produced the unfortunate result in the *Lochner* case—the Court's second most discredited decision. A changed vote also led to the decision in *Pollock v. Farmers' Loan & Trust Co.*

(1895), popularly known as the Income Tax Case—arguably the third most criticized decision in the Court's history. The case is remembered today largely because both counsel and Court used it as a vehicle for attacking what they saw as the socialistic tendencies that were invading the law. The common legal view at the time was expressed during the oral argument by Joseph Choate, considered the leading advocate of the day, who declared that the challenged tax "is communistic in its purposes and tendencies, and is defended here upon principles as communistic, socialistic—what shall I call them—populistic as ever have been addressed to any political assembly in the world."

Addressing the Justices directly, Choate warned, "If you approve this law . . . and this communistic march goes on," the law would thenceforth be helpless. To uphold the income tax, Choate argued, would be "to enunciate . . . a doctrine worthy of a Jacobin Club . . . of a Czar of Russia" the "new doctrine of this army of 60,000,000—this triumphant and tyrannical majority—who want to punish men who are rich and confiscate their property."

For our purpose, the Income Tax Case is relevant because its five-to-four decision was produced by a switched vote by one of the Justices, who had been in favor of sustaining the tax, to the antitax side, which gave the latter its bare majority. At the time it was believed that it was Justice George Shiras who had changed his mind, and he was widely blamed for wrecking the income tax. More recent commentators have questioned whether it was really Justice Shiras who had switched, or whether it was some other Justice. At any rate, what has been termed "The Mystery of the Vacillating Jurist" remains to this day essentially unsolved.

In more recent Courts, the vote switch has remained an essential feature of the decision process—resulting in changed decisions even in leading cases. This chapter is primarily concerned with changed votes in the Warren and Burger Courts. There is, however, substantial evidence of vote fluidity in the Courts headed by Chief Justice Warren's two predecessors. A 1968 study of the Stone and Vinson Courts by J. Woodford Howard, Jr., stresses "how commonplace, rather than aberrational" vote switches were in those Courts. Indeed, statistics show that votes were changed in 61 percent of the cases decided under Chief Justices Stone and Vinson. The figure is little different for the Warren years–55 percent.

Vote switches affected the results in major decisions of the Stone and Vinson Courts. As important as any case to come before those Courts was *Everson v. Board of Education of Ewing Township* (1947), for it laid the foundation for the decisions during the past half century on the separation of church and state. At issue was a state law providing for bus transportation for all schoolchildren, including those attending Catholic parochial schools. Just as important as the decision upholding the law was the adoption in Justice Black's opinion of the Court of the wall-of-separation metaphor: "In the words of Jefferson, the clause against establishment of religion by law was intended to erect 'a wall of separation between Church and state.' " This statement has been the lodestar in subsequent Establishment Clause jurisprudence.

All the Justices accepted the notion of a wall of separation between church and state. There was, however, sharp disagreement during the decision process on application of the principle to the bus transportation law. At the postargument conference, only Justices Frankfurter and Wiley B. Rutledge would have invalidated the law and Frankfurter said that he had voted "with difficulty." Rutledge, on the other hand, expressed no doubts. "First," he declared, "it has been books, now buses, next churches and teachers. . . . Every religious institution in [the] country will be reaching into [the] hopper if you sustain this." To which Chief Justice Vinson lamely replied, "I try to think [only] of [the] case before me."

It has been assumed that there were vote switches in *Everson,* since Justice Robert H. Jackson began his dissent by stating that, "contrary to first impression," he could not join the decision. Papers of the Justices confirm that there were, indeed, crucial vote changes in the case. Justices Jackson and Harold H. Burton changed their votes from affirmance to reversal, making a four-to-four division. That left the decision up to Justice Frank Murphy, who had passed at the conference. After much hesitation, he voted to uphold the busing law.

What makes the key Murphy vote of special interest is that it was contrary to the Justice's normal posture in this type of case. Yet, though he wrote to Justice Rutledge expressing "my admiration of the superb [dissenting] opinion you wrote," the decisive factor for Justice Murphy was apparently his own Catholic religion. "If I err," he wrote to a federal judge just after *Everson* was announced, "I want to err on the side of religion." And a letter to the sister heading a Catholic school, which Murphy's biographer states was authored by him, says that *Everson* "is a great step forward for those in the faith who desire . . . education in Catholic schools." Had Justices Jackson and Burton not switched, it is possible that Justice Murphy would have joined the Rutledge dissent, since his vote then would not have been necessary to uphold the program so helpful to Catholic education.

Justice Black, whose *Everson* opinion has set the tone for Establishment Clause jurisprudence, had not been at all sure on his final vote in the case. Justice Douglas's *Everson* conference notes report statements by the other Justices, but none by Justice Black—only the word "affirms" next to Black's name. The first draft opinion prepared by Black pointed out that the Catholic Church derived a "benefit" from the busing law and that the law therefore came close to "the verge of state support to a religious sect." But this passage was not in the final opinion, which remained true to the Black conference vote to uphold the law.

Justice Black did, however, change his vote in *Martin v. City of Struthers* (1942), and the switch changed the outcome in an important First Amendment case decided by the Stone Court. *Martin* arose out of the conviction of a Jehovah's Witness for distributing literature in violation of an ordinance prohibiting the ringing of doorbells by persons distributing handbills, circulars, and the like. At the conference, Chief Justice Stone said that he could not vote for such a "complete prohibition." Justice Black, on the other hand, pointed out that Struthers was an industrial community in which many employees worked night shifts and slept during the day. Black said that he feared that if the Court upheld the Witnesses' invasion of the privacy of the home, there would be "the greatest growth of organizations that there ever has been for going to people's homes." The next case, he prophesied, might well involve Witnesses' invading a Catholic church, if no restraints were upheld. Echoing his conference statement, Justice Black soon circulated a memorandum opinion holding that a city such as Struthers could reasonably enact its ordinance to protect privacy.

Though he countered objections to his draft in a second circulation, Justice Black soon decided that his vote was wrong and reversed himself. This converted a five-to-four decision in favor of the ordinance to a bare majority the other way. A Frankfurter memo states that the Black switch was induced by his desire not to have the conference dissenters appear "greater champions of liberty" than he was. Frankfurter also noted that a Black law clerk had warned the Justice that "liberals" would criticize him if he let his original opinion stand. Whatever the reason, the Black switch meant a decision by a new majority invalidating the Struthers ordinance under the First Amendment.

Martin saw Justice Black, normally an absolutist in First Amendment cases, take a conference position that exalted privacy of the home over freedom of expression. *Terminiello v. Chicago* (1949) saw a similar restrictive conference approach to speech by Justice Douglas, usually Justice Black's closest ally in First Amendment cases. But Douglas, too, switched his vote—converting a bare majority for affirmance of a conviction for delivery of a racist speech that caused a riot into one the other way.

Terminiello, a defrocked Catholic priest, made a speech to a Chicago audience of about eight hundred, in which he denounced Catholics, Jews, and blacks in extreme language. Outside, what the Court called "a howling mob" of over a thousand gathered, threw rocks at the windows, forced open the doors, and tried to break into the building. Terminiello was convicted of violating a breach-of-the-peace ordinance. The trial judge had charged the jury that breach of peace includes any "misbehavior" that "stirs the public to anger, invites dispute, brings about a condition of unrest, or creates a disturbance."

The *Terminiello* case is remembered today largely because of the sardonic comment in Justice Jackson's dissent that the Constitution was never intended as "a suicide pact." In its day, however, *Terminiello* was, as Sidney Fine's biography of Justice Murphy characterizes it, "viewed as a free-speech classic." For our purposes, *Terminiello* was relevant because, as Justice Murphy's notes show, no one at the *Terminiello* conference was more certain than Justice Douglas that Terminiello's conviction was valid. It was "speech plus," he told the conference, "it was close to shouting 'fire' in [a] theater," it was "throwing a lighted match in an explosive situation." Justices Reed, Black, Murphy, and Rutledge disagreed and voted to reverse. But the other four voted with Justice Douglas (with Justice Frankfurter making the most forceful statement in support of Douglas — the "speech here," he said, "may have had the effect of striking someone in the face"), so that there was a bare conference majority to affirm.

Chief Justice Vinson assigned the opinion to Justice Douglas, who had been the strongest of the conference majority favoring affirmance. Douglas, however, soon decided to change his vote. Instead of the opinion of the Court indicated by his conference posture, the Justice sent around a draft reversing the conviction, but "written," as he wrote, "on a ground not argued" — namely, the trial judge's charge, which brought speech protected by the First Amendment within the breach-of-the-peace definition. Justice Douglas circulated the opinion initially only among the four Justices who had voted for reversal. His own switch made it the opinion of the Court.

The Douglas vote switch converted *Terminiello* from a case illustrating a permissible restriction upon speech into one that, as already noted, used to be considered a free-speech classic. The dissenters (the original conference majority) were unusually bitter about the decision and the vote change that had brought it about. Justice Jackson in particular delivered an unusually strong dissent. His feeling on the matter was pithily encapsulated in a Jackson doggerel quoted by Fine:

> *If a special size street riot puts you flat upon your back,*
> *Be philosophical with Douglas, Murphy, Rutledge, Reed and Black;*
> *As you lie there bashed and bleeding, with your muscles badly hurt'n*
> *Say a little prayer for Vinson, Jackson, Frankfurter and Burton.*

THE WARREN SWITCH TO ACTIVISM

During his first years on the Supreme Court, Chief Justice Warren moved slowly to find his jurisprudential roots. In his early terms, Warren, more often than not, was to be found with the conservative wing among the Justices. A student of the Court, Glendon Schubert, wrote that Warren then was "primarily a collectivist with strong authoritarian leanings" who showed "a trained incapacity to oppose the government in criminal cases."

In this period, the new Chief Justice was anything but the activist that he later became. Instead, Schubert declared, "Warren . . . had moved directly into former Chief Justice Vinson's position of moderate conservatism." While, as Warren put it, he was still "feeling [his] way," the Court's neophyte was largely under the influence of Justice Frankfurter and, more often than not, followed the latter's position of judicial restraint. Much of the early history of the Warren Court can, indeed, be presented in terms of the relationship between Chief Justice Warren and Justice Frankfurter.

When Warren came to the Court, he was assiduously courted by Justice Frankfurter, who sought to win the new Chief Justice to his own judicial philosophy. At first, the courtship appeared successful. Within a few years, however, the Chief Justice became a vigorous adherent of judicial activism, rejecting the Frankfurter posture. The altered Warren approach was accompanied by increasing personal recrimination between the Chief Justice and his rejected mentor, which culminated in unprecedented acrimonious exchanges in open court.

Justice Frankfurter, according to Justice Stewart, "was as fickle as a high school girl. I understand . . . that, when Earl Warren first came to the Court as Chief Justice, Felix was going around Washington saying, 'This is the greatest Chief Justice since John Marshall and maybe greater.' And by the time I got here [1958], Felix Frankfurter had very much been disenchanted by the Chief Justice."

Justice Stewart's account is not overdrawn. At the beginning, Justice Frankfurter's appraisal of the new Chief Justice was glowing. A few days after Chief Justice Vinson's death, Frankfurter wrote, "What is most needed in a Chief Justice is what the Germans call *ein Tonangeber* — a tone-giver: one who by his example generates in the others complete dedication to the work of the Court." Soon after Chief Justice Warren had been sworn in, Justice Frankfurter indicated that the Court had found its *Tonangeber*.

Oliver Gates, the son of an English friend, had inquired about the new Chief Justice. "You ask," Justice Frankfurter wrote back less than a month after Warren's appointment, "Whether I 'like' him. The short answer is I do and I am sure you would. But I shall detain you longer to answer your other question: What do I 'think of him?' "

Justice Frankfurter's answer conceded that the new Chief Justice "has not had an eminent legal career, but he might well have had had he not been deflected from the practice of the law into public life. He brings to his work that largeness of experience and breadth of outlook which may well make him a very good Chief Justice provided he has some other qualities which, from what I have seen, I believe he has."

The Frankfurter letter concluded with a warm estimate: "The upshot of it all is that I like him as a human being. He is agreeable without being a back-slapper; he is informal but has a native dignity. Perhaps I ought to add that his interest in baseball is as great but as sensible as yours. For the reasons that I have indicated I also think he will turn out to be a very good Chief Justice."

Justice Frankfurter's early attitude toward the new Chief Justice was summed up in an April 1954 letter written to Justice Jackson, on a problem before the Court: "E. W . . . showed the understanding that comes from caring for real responsibility that that problem implies. What a pleasure to do business with him."

In 1947, John Gunther had asserted that Earl Warren had "little intellectual background, little coherent philosophy." As soon as he took his place on the bench, however, the Chief Justice was faced with a choice that would have to be made between the antagonistic judicial philosophies of Justices Black and Frankfurter. In simplified terms, the Black-Frankfurter division was that discussed in the last chapter between judicial activism and judicial restraint. Justice Black had been the leading advocate of activism on the pre-Warren Court. He was willing to follow the rule of restraint only in the economic area. But he felt that the Bill of Rights provisions protecting personal liberties imposed on the Court more active enforcement obligations. To Justice Frankfurter, judicial restraint was the proper posture for a nonrepresentative judiciary, regardless of the nature of the asserted interests in individual cases.

To Justices Black and Frankfurter, Chief Justice Warren's accession presented an opportunity to acquire a crucial convert. As Fred Rodell put it, "both Frankfurter and Black badly wanted him on their side and recruited him, from conference sessions, to Court corridors, to chats in chambers." The situation was graphically described in *Time* after Warren retired: in his early years the new Chief Justice was "a large, powerful sphere of iron drawn between two magnetic poles." At first, he was drawn toward Justice Frankfurter. As time went on, however, Warren, more a man of action than reflection, found Justice Black's activist posture preferable.

The Chief Justice first signaled his movement toward judicial activism by dramatically announcing a vote switch to the conference. The conference was on two 1955 cases involving Communist membership. They resulted in the first Warren Court decisions dealing with alleged Communists — the decisions that at the time were sharply attacked by critics of the Court and led to the "Impeach Earl Warren" campaign.

During Warren's flight to attend Winston Churchill's funeral with Dwight Eisenhower, the former President expressed disappointment that the Chief Justice had not turned out to be the "moderate" he had expected. Warren asked Eisenhower what decisions had led to his disapproval. "Oh, those Communist cases." "What Communist cases?" asked Warren. "All of them," was the reply.

It was the Court's decisions on Communists that led the *American Mercury* to declare in 1958 that Warren was "Eisenhower's worst appointment." By then, the President agreed with this assessment. When an interviewer later asked Eisenhower what was his biggest mistake, he replied heatedly, "The appointment of that s.o.b. Earl Warren."

When the first Communist case came before the Court in the 1953 Term, however, Chief Justice Warren took the position that both the *American Mercury* and the President approved. The case — *Emspak v. United States* — arose out of refusals to answer questions concerning Communist membership before the House Committee on Un-American Activities. Emspak had based his refusals to answer on primarily "the first amendment, supplemented by the fifth." The lower courts had held that that was not enough to invoke the constitutional privilege against self-incrimination.

Chief Justice Warren began his conference presentation by saying, "It gets down to the question whether he actually claimed his privilege." The Chief Justice recognized that, "we should not indulge in technicalities." But here the defendant wanted "to eat this pie and have it. He did not want to testify and yet not look guilty. We should not condone that action." Warren said that he would vote to affirm.

The strongest conference statement the other way was made by Justice Black, who spoke after the Chief Justice. "We should not condone a committee," Black declared, "that indicates that claiming the privilege is wrong. We would be condoning the committee's actions if we affirm. The Fifth Amendment is not bad and to claim his privilege is not bad. I don't believe in being strict on this claim. Here it would be bad for this Court to erect technical barriers."

Except for Justices Frankfurter and Douglas (who passed), the others indicated that they would vote to affirm, though several expressed the wish, as Justice Jackson put it, that congressional committees "would manage their work better and not abuse their power." Chief Justice Warren assigned the majority opinion to Justice Reed. His draft opinion not only refused to accept the Fifth Amendment claim, but also contained a strong rejection of the claim that the refusal to answer questions about Communist membership was protected by the First Amendment. This was an issue that had not been discussed at the conference and one that the Court had until then been careful not to decide.

Justice Black, in particular, bristled at the Reed draft. He wrote to the Justices, "Except by outright repeal I cannot readily conceive of a way to give less effective meaning to the First Amendment than Justice Reed does in the opinion he has circulated in this case." Justice Black asked that the others "not go along with his opinion until its devastating effect on free speech and press can be pointed out in dissent."

The Black objection led Justice Jackson to suggest that Justice Black move to have the case reargued. Black wanted Justice Frankfurter to move the reargument motion, but he declined. At the bottom of the letter from Frankfurter to that effect, Justice Black penned in, "I made the motion Saturday May 15 — and it was carried, Reed & Minton voting against it."

Emspak was then set for reargument in the 1954 Term. The Court also fixed argument the same day for *Quinn v. United States*, which came to the Court toward the end of the 1953 Term and presented a similar fact pattern. *Emspak* and *Quinn* were argued and discussed together in conference, in April 1955.

The conference began with the Chief Justice's dramatic announcement: "I have changed my mind from last year." Warren then addressed the issue to which Justice Black had so strenuously objected. The Chief Justice's suggestion was simple: "Set aside the First Amendment issue." It was not necessary for decision and its resolution should be avoided. As far as the Un-American Activities Committee was concerned, Warren said, the Court should assume the validity of the congressional resolution establishing it. In addition, the questions asked were pertinent. But "we can dispose of these cases on the slipshod method of the committee in questioning."

According to Chief Justice Warren, both defendants had clearly claimed their privilege. The committee, however, did not give a clear warning of the need to answer. "The committee must clarify the claim and the contempt issue. Any indication of the claim should be enough to make the committee alert," and they must then indicate "whether they denied it or not. Here, there was a lack of direction by the committee on their duty to answer the questions."

Justice Black agreed that the Court should decide on other than First Amendment grounds. The "narrow grounds" suggested by Warren "would be enough." Justices Reed, Clark, and Minton adhered to the view they had expressed at the prior year's conference. Justice Harlan, who had taken Justice Jackson's place, also voted for affirmance. But Justices Douglas and Burton said that they agreed with the Chief Justice. That converted the prior year's six-to-two vote for affirmance into a bare majority for reversal.

Chief Justice Warren delivered the *Quinn* and *Emspak* opinions himself. His opinions for the Court stressed that a claim of the privilege did not require any special combination of the words and that, under this test, defendants *had* claimed the privilege. Warren also relied on the point raised in his second conference discussion — that the committee had failed to give a fair notice of its ruling on the privilege claim and to direct the witnesses that they were required to answer. Justice Clark, who had said that he agreed with Justice Reed at the April conference, joined the Warren opinions, giving the Chief Justice a six-to-three majority.

The grounds upon which *Quinn* and *Emspak* were decided were of less importance than the indication they gave that the Chief Justice and a majority of the Justices were now ready, as Justice Black had urged at the first *Emspak* conference, "to draw a line on the powers of the [Un-American Activities] committee . . . and keep judicial and legislative powers separate." As Justice Frankfurter wrote to Justice Harlan, "I thought and think it was right to charge those loose-mouthed, loose-mannered and loose-headed men on the Hill with a little more responsibility in the serious business of Congressional investigations. That's all the [*Quinn* and *Emspak*] requirement . . . gets down to."

The *Emspak* scenario was repeated in a case decided later in 1955 — *Toth v. Quarles,* discussed in Chapter 4. In that case, too, we saw that when the case was first considered in conference, Chief Justice Warren spoke in favor of governmental power (there the power to subject a former serviceman to court-martial jurisdiction). Though a draft opinion of the Court was again circulated by Justice Reed, *Toth* was also reargued. At the postreargument conference, Warren once more stated that he had changed his mind and spoke in favor of reversing the court-martial conviction. The Warren switch, as seen in Chapter 4, led the Court to hand down the decision now favored by the Chief Justice.

In our previous discussion, *Toth v. Quarles* was used to illustrate the Warren ability to lead the Court. Both *Toth* and *Emspak* also demonstrate how a vote switch can change the result in cases already "decided" the other way. More than that, they show how a vote switch can signal a changed course of jurisprudence, both by a Justice and by the Court itself. To be sure, outside the Court neither the Warren vote switches nor their implication for the Chief Justice's future judicial posture were known. To those in the Marble Palace, however, it was now clear that the Warren Court was about to begin a new era.

SWITCHES AND MURDERING WIVES

During the 1956 Term, Chief Justice Warren's new activist approach became publicly apparent. It was then that the Chief Justice led the Court to the first Warren Court decisions protecting individual rights. To the public and the press, the culmination of the new Warren judicial stance came on June 17, 1957, when four decisions were handed down reversing a dismissal from the State Department on loyalty grounds, as well as convictions of Communist leaders under the Smith Act, and convictions for contempt of the House Committee on Un-American Activities and a state legislature investigating subversive activities. Critics of the Court promptly dubbed the day "Red Monday."

Critics claimed that, in the words of *Nine Men against America* (a book containing a vituperative attack against the Warren Court), "on June 17, 1957, the Court really went to town — amid the cheers and hurrahs of the communist conspirators." At a Senate hearing there was the following seriocomic exchange between Senator James O. Eastland and Senator Joseph R. McCarthy:

Eastland: The Supreme Court seems to be issuing one Communist decision after another.

McCarthy: You're so right.

Eastland: What influence is there except that some Communist influence is working within the Court?

McCarthy: Either incompetence or the influence you mention.

The four Red Monday decisions did not depend upon any vote switches; from the first conferences, the Chief Justice had the votes to ensure that his view striking down the dismissal and convictions prevailed. The same was not true in *Reid v. Covert,* also decided in June 1957. Two wives of American servicemen, residing on American bases in England and Japan, were convicted of murdering their husbands by courts-martial and sentenced to life imprisonment. The Uniform Code of Military Justice subjected to court-martial jurisdiction "all persons serving with . . . or accompanying the armed forces without the continental limits of the United States." The wives claimed that this provision was unconstitutional, since they were civilians who might not be tried in military courts.

Among themselves, the Justices referred to *Reid v. Covert* as the Case of the Murdering Wives. The case had come before the Court during the previous term. It was first argued in May 1956, and discussed in conference on the following day. Chief Justice Warren began by reaffirming the strong view he had ultimately taken in the *Toth* case, discussed in Chapter 4. He pointed out that under the Uniform Code provision, even children of servicemen were subjected to military trials. "I doubt," Warren asserted, "that these youngsters are part of the Army of the U.S. It's hard to believe that a housewife and youngsters — not in the field — in England and Tokyo are members of the armed forces for military justice. The fact that they use the PX means nothing. If they are, then the Army may try them. That's not in keeping with our traditions."

Only Justices Burton and Minton spoke in favor of affirming military jurisdiction. Justice Minton said that it was hard to "get away from *{In re} Ross*" — an 1891 case that had upheld the trial of an American seaman by a consular court in Japan. "The Constitution," said Minton, "does not follow him *there.*"

On May 14, Justice Reed circulated a memorandum, which stated, "Further examination of the law and the records in *Reid v. Covert* . . . convinces me that my tentative votes in these cases were erroneous." He had now concluded that the Uniform Code provision was constitutional. "Accordingly, I wish to change my vote."

The next day Justice Frankfurter wrote to Reed, "My ears could hardly believe it when I heard you vote as you did in the case of the murdering wives. I had not the slightest doubt . . . that in due course you would vote the way I was sure you would vote, and as you have now indicated." Justice Reed had cited five cases to support his vote change. According to the Frankfurter letter, however, "the five cases which you cite . . . haven't a thing to do with our problem."

After Justice Reed switched, Justices Clark and Harlan also decided to vote in favor of military jurisdiction. This made a majority for a decision against the wives. Chief Justice Warren, and Justices Black, Douglas, and Frankfurter refused to go along. Justice Reed, the senior majority Justice, assigned the opinion to Justice Clark. His draft opinion stressed the cases like *Ross* that had upheld congressional power to set up so-called legislative courts and consular courts to try certain crimes overseas.

After he had received the Clark draft, Justice Frankfurter sent Justice Harlan a written note: "I have just read Tom's opinion . . . and I'm appalled." Frankfurter conceded that "a respectable — that is a lawyer-like opinion" sustaining the Uniform Code provision could be written. "But not this farrago of irresponsible, uncritical admixture of far-reaching needlessly dangerous incongruities." Frankfurter wrote, "I cannot believe that this opinion will be allowed to go down with your concurrence — until it does!" Justice Harlan did, however, concur, so that Justice Clark spoke for five Justices when he announced the opinion in June 1956, upholding court-martial jurisdiction over the wives.

Though the Court had announced its decision and opinion, those who disagreed were dissatisfied. Justice Black prepared a dissent, as did Justice

Frankfurter, who delivered copies to the Chief Justice and Justices Black and Douglas. In addition, the now four dissenters worked to secure a rehearing in the case. Counsel for the wives had filed a petition for rehearing after the decision against them. It is the normal practice for losing counsel in the Supreme Court to file petitions for rehearings, but they are almost invariably denied. This time the situation was different. Justice Douglas sent a note to Justice Frankfurter that he liked his dissent. "I hear," Douglas also wrote, "the majority are having conferences on the petition for rehearing. So maybe trouble for them is brewing."

In September the dissenters circulated a *Memorandum on Reid v. Covert,* drafted by Justice Black. The memo stated the issue broadly: "The issue in these cases is whether Congress can constitutionally authorize the military trial of civilians during times of peace for alleged crimes." Though the bare majority had answered this question in the affirmative, "study and reflection since the Court's decisions have strengthened our view that this Court's holdings in these cases have given the military authorities new powers not hitherto thought consistent with our scheme of government." The memo asserted, "We see no possible way to reconcile these holdings with our decision in *Toth v. Quarles.* . . . We think that either the *Toth* case should be expressly overruled or that the Court should now reverse its holdings in . . . *Covert.*"

The four dissenters now worked to win over one or more majority Justice to join them in granting the rehearing petition. The Chief Justice and Justice Frankfurter tried to convince Justice Harlan, who had never been firmly in the opposition camp. They persuaded Harlan that the technique used in the *Brown* school segregation case (where questions to be reargued were submitted by the Court to counsel) should be employed again to clarify the difficult points here. Harlan was assigned the job of drawing up questions on which counsel would be asked to reargue the case.

There is a Frankfurter memorandum to Justice Harlan which indicates that the questions on which the Court invited discussion on reargument were drawn up almost entirely by Justice Frankfurter, though submitted to the others as a Harlan draft. The four questions related to the practical necessities requiring court-martial jurisdiction over civilian dependents; the historical evidence on such jurisdiction; the distinction, if any, between civilians employed by the armed forces and civilian dependents; and that between major crimes and petty offenses.

In November 1956, the Court granted the petition for rehearing. At the reargument, counsel were "invited to include among the issues to be discussed" the four questions. Justices Reed, Burton, and Clark voted to deny the rehearing, Justice Minton having retired before the Court acted on the rehearing petition. Before the reargument in February 1957, the former majority was weakened further by Justice Reed's retirement.

At the conference after reargument, the Chief Justice began, "I come out the same as before. We can't apply *Ross* and we can't say this was a 'legislative court,' as permitted" by some cases. The decision the past June had relied on the Necessary and Proper Clause of Article I, but Warren said that he could not see that that clause "comes into the case." As the Chief Justice saw it, "the simple question is whether Congress has the right to declare these dependents a part of the armed forces of the U.S. and are subject to court-martial. This goes beyond anything; it's contrary to the history of the U.S. and England. Congress does not possess the power to declare them in the armed forces."

This time there was little discussion after Warren's forceful presentation. All except Justices Burton and Clark agreed with the Chief Justice that the wives might not be subjected to court-martial jurisdiction. Warren assigned the opinion to Justice Black.

As it turned out, though six of the eight Justices who sat (Justice Whittaker had come to the Court after the reargument and conference) voted to invalidate the court-martial of the wives, the Black opinion was joined only by Chief Justice Warren and Justices Douglas and Brennan — one fewer than a majority. It became merely a plurality opinion because of the objections of Justices Frankfurter and Harlan. On March 6, Frankfurter wrote to Warren that he could not go along with Justice Black, "whose conclusion of unconstitutionality has the farthest reach." Instead of Black's broad condemnation of court-martial jurisdiction, the opinion should follow the practice "of not deciding more than the Court has to." Justice Frankfurter urged that the Court should invalidate only the courts-martial "in these capital cases." Frankfurter then wrote his own opinion, which, he explained in a "Dear Brethren" letter in April, "is restricted to a test of constitutionality of the confined problem that these two cases raise, namely, the power of Congress under Art. I to authorize prosecution by court-martial procedure of *capital* crimes by civilian wives accompanying their service husbands."

When Justice Black delivered his opinion ruling invalid any court-martial jurisdiction over civilian dependents, Justice Frankfurter issued an opinion concurring in the result but only in capital cases. Justice Harlan wrote a similar separate concurrence. Justice Clark, joined by Justice Burton, dissented, saying that his former opinion in the case was correct.

The result, wrote Sherman Minton to Justice Frankfurter, was that, "all you succeeded in doing in Covert . . . was to turn out a couple of cold blooded murderers without the Court arriving upon any principle of law." The concurring opinions, the retired Justice went on, seem "strangely to have found some difference between Capital and other Crimes not to be found in the Constitution."

EXPATRIATION CASES

Among the cases that gave the Warren Court the greatest difficulty were the so-called Expatriation Cases, decided in 1958. The legal issue in them was as troublesome as any that came before the Court during the Warren years. Their outcome was determined by several vote switches among the Justices.

There were two Expatriation Cases: *Perez v. Brownell* and *Trop v. Dulles.* The government claimed that Clemente M. Perez had lost his citizenship by voting in a foreign election. Albert L. Trop, it was urged, had lost his citizenship because he had been convicted by court-martial of desertion from the Army in wartime. In both cases, Congress had provided for loss of citizenship for the acts done. Could Congress constitutionally provide for forfeiture of citizenship in these cases?

The Expatriation Cases had come to the Court during the 1956 Term. At the conference after the argument, Chief Justice Warren spoke strongly for reversal of the decisions in favor of the government. "Congress," he said, "has the right to provide for denationalization when he makes the claim to dual citizenship" — but not otherwise. The Chief Justice asserted that citizenship by birth could come to an end only by "renunciation." Congress could not provide "a punishment of banishment" for desertion. "Congress can't impose it as punishment." If it does, "he has the right to a jury trial. I doubt if a court-martial would be enough."

The others were sharply divided. Justice Black spoke most strongly in support of the Chief Justice, saying he had "never thought there is any constitutional power to strip a man of what's given for life." Justice Frankfurter led the opposition. To him, the key issue was that of the proper judicial posture. "The ultimate determinant," he said, "is not what we find in the Constitution, but our conception of what is the job of the judge." For Frankfurter, the governing doctrine was that of deference to the legislative judgment.

Justice Frankfurter expanded on his view in a letter on the cases that he sent to Justice Harlan a few days after the conference. The crucial question, he wrote, was "who is to judge" on denationalization, "Is it the Court or Congress? Indeed, more accurately, must not the Court put on the sackcloth and ashes of deferring humility in order to determine whether the judgment that Congress exercise, judged as it must be under the Due Process Clause, is so outside the limits of a supportable judgment by those who have the primary duty of judgment as to constitute that disregard of reason which we call an arbitrary judgment[?]"

At the postargument conference, Justices Black, Douglas, Harlan, and Brennan supported Chief Justice Warren and voted to reverse in both cases. Justices Frankfurter, Burton, Clark, and Whittaker voted the other way. The Chief Justice assigned the opinions to himself, and he circulated draft opinions of the Court delivered in his name for both cases. The principal opinion was prepared for the *Perez* case. It consisted of eighteen printed pages. The Warren draft rejected the government's contention of "a broad power in Congress, implied from the very fact of national sovereignty, to make loss of nationality follow from acts which Congress may reasonably think constitute an unwarranted participation in the sovereign affairs of a foreign nation or which are inconsistent with the gravest obligations of American citizenship. We do not believe the decisions of this Court sustain the exercise of any such broad implied power."

Warren's draft opinion of the Court in *Trop* was shorter, consisting of six printed pages. It stated that what had been said in the *Perez* draft "is largely dispositive" of the constitutional issue here. "We hold here . . . as we did there . . . that Congress has no power to prescribe loss of citizenship as the consequence of conduct inconsistent with fundamental obligations of citizenship."

Two days after he had received the Warren draft, Justice Frankfurter sent around a memorandum in which he wrote, "I regret to find myself unable to agree with it." He said that he would prepare a dissent. However, he noted, "The issues at stake are too far-reaching and the subject matter calls for too extensive an investigation, let alone the time necessary for writing an adequate opinion, that I shall not attempt the preparation of such an opinion before the Term closes. I shall content myself with noting my inability to agree and the promise of filing an opinion at the next Term of Court."

Other Justices also had misgivings about the cases. Even those in the bare majority were not wholly satisfied with the decisions and the draft opinions. In these circumstances, it was natural for the Justices to agree to hold the cases for the next term; the Court issued an order in June 1957 setting the cases for reargument in October.

In a letter a year later to five of the Justices, Justice Frankfurter explained why the reargument in *Perez* and *Trop* was scheduled: "There are situations when the feeling of a Brother that he needs the summer, as it were, to work on setting forth his views in a case should delay handing down a decision. Such a situation was presented by the *Expatriation Cases* at the end of last Term. . . . The problems there were new, difficult and of far-reaching import in our national life. More than that, not only was the Court closely divided, but within the narrow majority there were those who had doubts and uncertainties. Nothing could have been more appropriate to the circumstances of that situation than to set the cases down for reargument."

The reargument of the Expatriation Cases took place in October 1957. At the conference the next day, the Chief Justice restated his position that Congress had power to denationalize "only where there is a voluntary abandonment of citizenship." What Congress had done here, Warren went on, "is to make loss of citizenship a punishment. It doesn't have that power — no power to add to any punishment loss of citizenship. It makes no difference whether it's by a jury or administrative procedure."

Most of the others adhered to the stands they had taken the prior term. But there were important shifts. Justice Harlan said that he had found it "very difficult to vote" in these cases. Though he had voted originally to reverse, he was at present for affirmance in both cases. Justice Brennan also changed his vote. He was voting to affirm in *Perez,* though he was still for reversal in *Trop.* Justice Whittaker stuck to his vote to affirm in *Perez,* but had changed his mind and voted to reverse in *Trop.*

The conference left Chief Justice Warren with his bare majority in *Trop.* The only difference was that, since Justices Harlan and Whittaker had switched positions, the vote for reversal was now Warren, Black, Douglas, Brennan, and Whittaker, with the remaining four voting to affirm. In *Perez,* however, the decision had changed. Because Justices Harlan and Brennan had altered their votes, there was now a six-to-three decision for affirmance, with only Chief Justice Warren and Justices Black and Douglas still for reversal.

Justice Frankfurter, now senior majority Justice in *Perez,* assigned the opinion to himself and soon prepared a draft essentially similar to his final opinion in the case. During the next month Justice Whittaker again switched his vote in *Trop.* Justice Frankfurter now had a bare majority and circulated his *Trop* opinion as the opinion of the Court.

Because of the changed votes, Chief Justice Warren had to recirculate his *Perez* and *Trop* opinions as dissents. Both opinions were thoroughly redrafted, with the work done almost entirely by a Warren law clerk. The *Trop* redraft expanded on the theory expressed by the Chief Justice at the postreargument conference: that loss of citizenship was a punishment that Congress had no power to impose. The redraft was expanded to assert that taking away citizenship for Trop's desertion was to impose cruel and unusual punishment. Warren himself inserted into the new draft a statement that "The basic concept underlying the Eighth Amendment is nothing less than the dignity of man. . . . The Amendment must draw its meaning from the evolving standards of decency that mark the progress of a maturing society." This statement was to be quoted many times in later cases.

The Chief Justice's new *Trop* draft, circulated as a dissent March 14, 1958, concluded with a ringing affirmation of the superiority of civil over military power:

> Finally, wholly apart from the question of whether citizenship can ever be divested, either as punishment or otherwise, I deny that any power to denationalize may constitutionally be exercised by the military authorities. If the priceless right of citizenship is ever to be forfeited in a trial, it should be in a civilian court of justice, where all Bill of Rights protections guard the fairness of the outcome. Military courts are to try soldiers for military crimes and impose punishments that do not encroach on purely civilian rights. Who is worthy of continued enjoyment of citizenship is not the constitutional concern of the Army. Its business is to fight wars. . . . Far from keeping the military authorities within their proper bounds, this statute gives them the last word on the right to be a citizen — a right which is, or should be, peculiarly under civilian authorities and courts. Nothing in the language, history or any known purposes of our Constitution lends the slightest support to military control over the basic right of United States Citizenship.

This passage was absent from the *Trop* opinion that the Chief Justice delivered. It is unfortunate that it was omitted. One of the particular things Warren was able to accomplish was to lead the Court in limiting military jurisdiction over civilians. The Warren Court opinions on the subject were not, however, delivered by the Chief Justice. It would have been of great significance if he had been able, in his own name, to pronounce the passage on "keeping the military authorities within their proper bounds" contained in his *Trop* draft dissent.

After the Chief Justice circulated his *Trop* dissent, Justice Whittaker once more changed his vote and joined the Warren opinion. This again made a bare majority for reversal. But Warren had to recirculate his *Trop* opinion as that of a plurality (Warren, Black, Douglas, and Whittaker), since Justice Brennan wrote to him "I have tried over the past week, without success, to mesh our two opinions in *Trop*. Because I am not of the view that Congress is wholly without power to provide for expatriation of citizens in proper cases, and because my approach makes unnecessary a discussion whether expatriation as punishment violates the Eighth Amendment, I have concluded I should file my own opinion."

When Chief Justice Warren delivered the *Trop* opinion, it was joined by Justices Black, Douglas, and Whittaker. Justice Brennan concurred in the reversal, but not the opinion. He issued a separate opinion justifying the result on due-process grounds.

When his *Perez* opinion was announced by Justice Frankfurter as an opinion of the Court, it was supported by a bare majority (Frankfurter, Burton, Clark, Harlan, and Brennan), for Justice Whittaker had written to Frankfurter and switched his vote here also. He later joined the Warren dissent.

The decisions in the two Expatriation Cases thus came down only after substantial vote switching. The original votes gave Chief Justice Warren a bare majority in both cases. The majority, however, wavered sufficiently to justify a reargument. After it, Justices Harlan, Brennan, and Whittaker changed their votes. There was now a different bare majority behind the Chief Justice in *Trop*, but a six-to-three vote against him in *Perez*. Justice Whittaker then switched his *Trop* vote again, and this also made the Warren position a dissenting one. It became a majority again when Whittaker once again changed his mind and rejoined the Warren camp. Now Justice Brennan refused to join the Warren *Trop* opinion and it spoke only for a plurality. Finally, the Frankfurter *Perez* opinion became that of a bare majority, when Justice Whittaker switched his vote again and joined the Warren dissent.

Speak of vote switches! In the Expatriation Cases, the Justices' votes went back and forth like a tennis ball.

Finally, an interesting footnote to the Expatriation Cases. When the *Perez* decision was announced, Justice Frankfurter did not read the opinion, but instead stated his oral version of it. After the Justice had finished, Chief Justice Warren, miffed by the Frankfurter practice, prefaced the delivery of his dissent with the remark that his opinion was directed at the printed opinion of the Court, not the oral opinion of Mr. Justice Frankfurter. At this, Justice Frankfurter wrote on a memo pad, "Does he mean my oral was more persuasive?"

CRIMINAL CASE SWITCHES

The *Bartkus* case referred to at the beginning of this chapter made the second trial of the Los Angeles police officers who beat Rodney King possible, by diluting the constitutional guaranty against double jeopardy. Alfonse Bartkus had been prosecuted in a federal court for robbery of a federally insured savings and loan association. The jury returned a verdict of acquittal. He was indicted for the same robbery less than three weeks later by Illinois. The indictment charged a violation of the state robbery statute. This time he was convicted and sentenced to life imprisonment. He claimed that the state conviction violated the constitutional prohibition against double jeopardy. The state courts rejected his claim.

The *Bartkus* case first came before the Supreme Court during the 1957 Term. At the postargument conference, the Justices divided four-to-four (Justices Frankfurter, Burton, Clark, and Harlan voting for affirmance and Chief Justice Warren and Justices Black, Douglas, and Whittaker for reversal—with Justice Brennan not participating). In January 1958, the Court announced that it was affirming in *Bartkus* by an equally divided Court (in such a case, where the Court is equally divided, the lower court is affirmed without opinion). In May, however, a petition for rehearing was granted. The January judgment was vacated and the case set for reargument during the 1958 Term.

At the conference after the *Bartkus* reargument, Chief Justice Warren spoke strongly in favor of reversal. "The Fourteenth Amendment," he urged, "bars a retrial after the federal acquittal." He pointed out that the Court had prohibited the use of illegally obtained evidence when offered by federal to state officers. "These crimes are the same," the Chief Justice stressed.

Justice Black agreed. He stated that the Court could apply the Fifth Amendment, which contains the constitutional prohibition against double jeopardy, to the states. "It doesn't say twice put in jeopardy by the same government, but for the same offense."

Justice Frankfurter led the case for affirmance. "Both criminal justice and federalism," he said, "are involved here." To him, the case was a simple one. "The same act is a transgression against two sovereigns," and each may prosecute separately.

The vote at the conference was inconclusive. Justices Frankfurter, Clark, and Harlan were still for affirmance, and Chief Justice Warren and Justices Black and Douglas for reversal. Justice Frankfurter had tried the previous term to induce Justice Whittaker to join the vote for affirmance. Whittaker had refused, explaining, in a letter just after the prior term's four-to-four conference vote, that "after a trial in a federal court resulting in acquittal, to permit a second trial and a conviction in a state court upon precisely the same issues seems quite unfair. . . . All of this 'shocks (my) conscience' and, in my view, constitutes a denial of due process." By the postreargument conference, however, Frankfurter was able to persuade Whittaker to change his vote to affirmance.

Justice Brennan, however, now voted for reversal. Chief Justice Warren had made the point that the case for reversal was "compounded by the federal officers' acts" in participating in the subsequent Illinois conviction. To Brennan, this became the crucial factor. As described by a Justice, a "hot feud" developed between Justices Brennan and Frankfurter as to whether the state conviction was, in fact, the result of a prosecution by federal officials using the state courts. Justice Brennan believed that the second prosecution, though in form by the state, was in essence a federal prosecution and thus barred by the Constitution. As Brennan explained it in a letter to Frankfurter, "You will remember how vigorously I balk at the extent to which the Federal Government made use of Illinois officials to effect Bartkus' conviction."

With the Whittaker switch and the Brennan vote, the Justices were still divided four-to-four, since Justice Stewart (who had replaced Justice Burton) told the conference that he was not yet able to make up his mind. Soon afterwards, Justice Frankfurter circulated a memorandum rejecting what he called Justice Brennan's "surprising" approach. Frankfurter urged that the state was only "exercising its independent constitutional powers although it had evidentiary help and, if you please, encouragement from federal officials—a help and encouragement, to repeat, the desirability of which has been preached from the house tops for most of my professional life."

Justice Brennan replied by a memorandum which repeated his view, "that even though the state by 'its free will' decided to prosecute, if that prosecution is instigated by the federal government and the state case prepared and guided by federal authorities this is enough to void the state conviction. Such a situation, for all practical purposes, is one in which federal resources, federal power, and federal energies are utilized to put an accused twice in jeopardy for the same criminal conduct. I think it clear that that degree of federal participation was present in this case."

Both the Frankfurter and Brennan memos were designed to persuade Justice Stewart. A few days after the Brennan memo, Stewart made up his mind and joined Justice Frankfurter. That made a bare majority for affirmance, and the decision was so announced, with Frankfurter delivering the opinion of the Court.

Had Justice Whittaker not switched his vote, there would have been a majority for reversal, no matter how Justice Stewart would have voted. Had that been the case, it would have been unconstitutional for Bartkus to be tried by the state after his federal acquittal. Similarly, it would have been unconstitutional for the Los Angeles police officers to be tried in a federal court for the Rodney King beating after their state acquittals. Once again, a vote switch had changed the course of Supreme Court jurisprudence.

Perhaps the most significant criminal case in which vote switches determined the decision was *Mapp v. Ohio*—one of the Warren Court's famous criminal-law trilogy. As seen in our previous discussion of the case in Chapter 4, the conference had voted to decide *Mapp* as a First Amendment obscenity case. It was only because Justice Clark suggested that the exclusionary rule be made the focus of the decision that *Mapp* became the landmark decision that we know. Justice Clark, with the agreement of Justices Brennan and Black and the later approval of the Chief Justice and Justice Douglas, completely changed the decision's basis, allowing *Mapp* to become the leading case on the exclusionary rule.

Aside from *Bartkus* and *Mapp*, the most important Warren Court criminal case in which changed votes played a decisive part was *United States v. Wade* (1967). Criminal law specialists know that mistaken identification has probably been the single greatest cause of conviction of the innocent. The Supreme Court attempted to deal with the problem by its decision in *Wade* and two other cases raising the same issue, which were referred to by the Justices as the Lineup Cases. The issue was to be presented to the Burger Court as well, where, we shall see, the ultimate decision was also different from that originally voted by the Justices.

Wade had been indicted for bank robbery. Without any notice to his lawyer, he was placed in a lineup and identified as the robber. He was convicted, despite his claim that the conduct of the lineup violated his privilege against self-incrimination and his right to counsel. The court of appeals reversed.

At the February 1967 conference, Justice Black took the strongest position in favor of the defendant. The case, he declared, "represent[s] a violation of the right to counsel and the privilege against self-incrimination." Black asserted that "as soon as you utilize a man's person to get evidence from him, or take him to a place to get someone else's evidence by having him act out a crime, you must give him a lawyer because you can't compel him to be a witness against himself."

Chief Justice Warren's conference statement did not go that far. He expressed the view that "you can't take voice or writing exemplars, dress [defendant] a certain way, or act out anything. Doing these things is the equivalent of interrogation and, therefore, *Miranda* would apply." On the other hand, when he presented the case, Warren said, "If none of these things were done and it was a pure line-up, counsel can be excluded."

After extensive discussion, which centered on the Fifth Amendment privilege, the conference was closely divided. The vote was five-to-four to reverse the court of appeals. The bare majority consisted of Justices Clark, Harlan, Brennan, Stewart, and White. Justice Brennan had expressed the view that no Fifth Amendment rights were violated by placing the suspect in a lineup. On considering the case after the conference, however, the Justice became convinced that the lineup was a "critical stage" requiring the presence of counsel under the Sixth Amendment. Brennan informed the others in a Memorandum to the Conference that he had switched his vote and enclosed a draft opinion that vacated the *Wade* conviction.

The Brennan *Wade* draft rejected the Fifth Amendment claim but held that Wade had a Sixth Amendment right to counsel at the lineup. As Justice

Brennan explained it in a memorandum to Chief Justice Warren and Justices Black, Douglas, and Fortas, the draft's conclusion was that "the lineup was a critical stage of the prosecution at which Wade was as much entitled to the aid of counsel as at the trial itself."

The most important aspect of the Brennan *Wade* opinion was the holding that there was a Sixth Amendment right to counsel at the lineup. After Justice Brennan circulated his draft, there was a meeting on April 21 of Justices Stewart, Clark, Harlan, and White. What happened there was described in a Brennan memorandum to the other four Justices. Brennan wrote, "you may be interested in something Potter told me this morning. He, Tom, John and Byron had a meeting on Friday to exchange views. Potter tells me that the four of them agree with Part I [rejecting the self-incrimination claim] and where I conclude that neither the lineup itself nor anything shown by the record that Wade was required to do in the lineup violated his privilege against self-incrimination."

"However," the Brennan memo went on, "all four reject Part IV" — the part of Brennan's draft that extended the right to counsel to Wade. Justice Brennan wrote, "Potter tells me that since this is a federal case, he would be willing to put the right to counsel on the basis of our supervisory power and that he believes Tom would do likewise. He is uncertain whether that would be acceptable to John and Byron, but does not rule out the possibility."

Justice Brennan indicated in his memo to Chief Justice Warren and Justices Black, Douglas, and Fortas that he was not willing to go along with the Stewart right-to-counsel approach. "I personally am convinced that the right to counsel should be declared a constitutional right for the reasons I have stated in the opinion. But apparently there can be a Court for that disposition only if you are of that view." Justice Fortas agreed to join the Brennan opinion. His memorandum to Justice Brennan concluded, "Needless to say, on the central point I agree. I agree. I totally agree. This is critical stage. There is a right to counsel — Amendment V {sic}, Amendment XIV. Federal. State."

Justice Douglas also wrote to Brennan formally joining the *Wade* opinion, except for Part I, which rejected Wade's Fifth Amendment claim. Justice Black then circulated an opinion agreeing that there was a Sixth Amendment right to counsel at the lineup but dissenting from the view that this should affect the admissibility of the in-court identification.

This meant that getting a Court for Justice Brennan's *Wade* reversal on the right-to-counsel ground now depended on obtaining the concurrences of Justice Clark and the Chief Justice. Clark phoned Brennan that he would join him if certain changes were made in his *Wade* opinion. The next morning Clark met with Brennan and asked for the deletion of two pages about the various functions counsel could perform. Justice Brennan yielded on the point.

But now Chief Justice Warren proved more difficult. At the conference, he had indicated the view that counsel might be excluded from a line-up that required defendant only to stand and be identified. The Chief Justice still expressed difficulty with the right to counsel. What if, Warren asked, counsel was an obstructionist or he was unavailable and his presence would require a delay in the identification? Justice White now circulated a dissent on the Sixth Amendment issue that mentioned these very problems. Justice Brennan dealt with them by pointing out in a revised draft that no delay had been argued in *Wade,* leaving open the possibility of substitute counsel where delay might occur, and quoting the language Warren had used in *Miranda* that it was not to be assumed that counsel would interfere with law enforcement.

This did not, however, induce the Chief Justice to join in *Wade.* At a later conference on June 2, Warren remained silent as Brennan outlined the status of the case, even though the Justice prefaced his remarks with, "assuming I have the Chief."

At the conference, Justice Black strongly urged the Court to set the case for reargument during the following term. Justice Fortas then sent Justice Brennan a note that he was revoking his agreement to join in *Wade,* and was writing separately. As it turned out, the Fortas opinion related solely to the issue of being compelled to appear in the lineup. Fortas thus still joined Brennan's Sixth Amendment holding.

On Monday, June 5, while Justice Brennan was conferring with Chief Justice Warren on two other cases, the Chief Justice informed Brennan that he was going to join his opinion in *Wade* except for Part I, rejecting the Fifth Amendment privilege.

There was now, a week before the decisions were announced, a fluctuating majority behind all the parts of Brennan's opinion. At first, this appeared not true of Part III, which distinguished the lineup as a "critical stage" from preparatory steps such as fingerprinting, blood samples, clothing and hair analysis. Justice White's opinion, joined by Justices Harlan and Stewart, noted him as dissenting from Part III, which would have left only Chief Justice Warren and Justice Clark behind Brennan on that part. This was apparently a mistake. When Justice Brennan called this to Justice White's attention, White circulated a new printing joining in Part III.

The Court was so fragmented on the different parts of Brennan's three opinions that Justice Brennan circulated the following "score card":

June 6, 1967

Memorandum to the Conference

The following is my score card on the *"lineup cases"* that I thought I'd circulate to be sure my count is accurate:
No. 334 — *United States v. Wade*

Part I.
A Court made up of Tom, John, Potter, Byron and me; the dissenters are the Chief Justice, Hugo, Bill and Abe.

Part II.

A Court made up of the Chief Justice, Hugo, Bill, Tom, Abe and me; the dissenters are John, Potter and Byron.

Part III.

A Court made up of Bill, Tom, John, Potter, Byron and me; and I think also the Chief Justice and Abe (I say this because the Chief Justice is joining Abe's opinion and I see nothing in that opinion indicating that there is any dissent from Part III); the dissenter is Hugo.

Part IV.

A Court made up of the Chief Justice, Hugo, Bill, Tom, Abe and me; the dissenters are John, Potter and Byron.

Part V.

A Court made up of the Chief Justice, Bill, Tom, Abe and me; the dissenters are Hugo, John, Potter and Byron. . . .

On June 12, the last day of the term, the results alone were announced along the lines of the Brennan "score card." One of the Justices commented that this made "the announcement smack of a colloquy from an Abbott and Costello movie."

With the changing views expressed by the Justices — starting with the crucial switch after his February 17 conference vote by Justice Brennan, who was then to lead the Court to its Sixth Amendment right to counsel at a lineup holding — the *Wade* case proved to be one of the Warren Court's most difficult criminal decisions. As it turned out, however, *Wade* did not resolve the lineup right-to-counsel issue. The same issue came before the Burger Court in *Kirby v. Illinois* (1972) and there, too, the final decision was different from that first voted by the Justices.

More than that, as ultimately decided, *Kirby* all but overruled *Wade* — though the Justices originally voted to treat *Kirby* as a case calling for the simple application of *Wade. Wade* itself involved a postindictment lineup, but that had not been a crucial factor in the Court's decision. As Justice Brennan pointed out in his draft *Kirby* opinion, the same "hazards to a fair trial that inhere in a post-indictment" lineup are also present in a lineup before indictment.

Kirby involved just such a preindictment situation. Thomas Kirby had been arrested for robbery and taken to a police station, where the victim positively identified him. The lower court held that the admission of testimony about the identification was not error; *Wade* was not applicable to preindictment identifications.

Only seven Justices were present at the *Kirby* postargument conference (Justices Black and Harlan had resigned just before the 1971 Term). Chief Justice Burger started the discussion by indicating that he favored affirmance. "I don't have trouble with a preindictment and postindictment dichotomy" and *Wade* should be ruled applicable only to lineup-type identifications after indictment. Burger was supported by Justices Stewart and Blackmun, though the latter did say, "This leaves me with a bad taste."

Justices Douglas, Brennan, White, and Marshall favored a reversal. They were led by Justice Brennan, who strongly urged that the *Wade* reasoning applied equally to pre- and postindictment identifications. The four-Justice majority agreed that the opinion should be written by Brennan, since he had written the *Wade* opinion.

The Brennan draft opinion contained a simple and straightforward rejection of the pre- and postindictment dichotomy as the criterion upon which the *Wade* lineup right to counsel turns: "*Wade* did not turn on the circumstance that the lineups conducted were postindictment without notice to counsel who represented the accused." Instead, the test for *any* pretrial confrontation of the accused is "whether the presence of his counsel is necessary to preserve the defendant's basic right to a fair trial."

Such a test required a decision in Kirby's favor. "There plainly inheres in a showup after arrest and before indictment the hazards to a fair trial that inhere in a post-indictment confrontation." In this respect, "the confrontation after arrest differs not at all from the confrontation after indictment." The draft's conclusion was that "the principles of . . . *Wade* apply to showups conducted after arrest." Hence, Kirby's conviction must be reversed because he "had not been advised that he had the right to have counsel present at the show up."

When Justices Powell and Rehnquist were sworn in in January 1972, there was now a full Court and it was desirable to have *Kirby* decided by a majority rather than only a four-Justice plurality. The Court therefore issued an order restoring *Kirby* to the calendar for reargument. At the postreargument conference, the seven who had participated in the original *Kirby* conference took their same positions.

Chief Justice Burger again urged affirmance. "Does *Wade* . . . apply to a preindictment confrontation?" he said. "No and we don't have to overrule *Wade*." He went further and said, "I'd overrule if it were the only way to decide." But that was unnecessary here if the Court simply refused to extend *Wade* to this case.

The two new Justices were for affirmance. Justice Powell indicated that he "would not apply *Wade* to preindictment. Per se exclusionary rules should be developed with great restraint. . . . So I won't extend *Wade*." Justice Rehnquist agreed. "On the basis of no extension to punishment and that only I'd affirm."

The original four-to-three decision in Kirby's favor became a five-to-four decision the other way. The draft dissent that Justice Stewart had prepared in opposition to the Brennan draft became the prevailing opinion. It distinguished between pre- and postindictment identifications and held that there was no right to counsel until the postindictment stage.

Had the Brennan draft come down as the final *Kirby* opinion, it would have made a substantial difference to the rights of criminal defendants. Identification of suspects through confrontation with their victims is most often a part—

and a vital part—of the investigative stage. It usually occurs after the suspect is arrested and brought in for questioning. Postindictment lineups are relatively rare. To guarantee the right to counsel only for them, as the final *Kirby* decision does, is, in effect, to take away the right in most lineups.

SWITCHES AND FREEDOM OF THE PRESS

Under the First Amendment, the press is wholly free to publish any news it may gather. Yet the right to publish may be empty if the press does not have access to government information. Does the Constitution confer upon the press a judicially enforceable right of access to files, trials, and prisons?

The right of access to news was dealt with by the Warren Court in *Estes v. Texas* (1965), the first case involving the issue of television in the courtroom, and one which, we shall see in the next chapter, also turned upon a vote switch. The original draft opinions in *Estes* rejected the notion of a press right of access. Both the draft opinion of the Court by Justice Stewart and the draft dissent of Justice Clark expressly denied that the First Amendment grants the news media such a privilege. Had this remained in the final *Estes* opinions, it might have foreclosed fresh consideration by the Burger Court. Instead, the final Clark opinion of the Court in *Estes* stated only that the press was "entitled to the same rights as the general public," while the Stewart dissent contained an intimation that the First Amendment did support a right of access.

These statements were the only ones by the Court on the matter when *Houchins v. KQED* (1978) came before the Burger Court. Thomas L. Houchins was the sheriff of Alameda County, California. Television station KQED reported the suicide of a prisoner in the Greystone portion of the county jail and requested permission to inspect Greystone. After permission was refused, KQED filed suit, arguing that Houchins violated the First Amendment by refusing to provide any effective means by which the public could be informed of conditions at Greystone or the prisoners' grievances.

Houchins then announced regular monthly tours for twenty-five persons, to parts of the jail. But Greystone was not included, and cameras, tape recorders, and interviews with inmates were forbidden. The lower court enjoined petitioner from denying responsible news media access to the jail, including Greystone, and from preventing their using photographic or sound equipment or conducting inmate interviews.

The conference was closely divided. The case for reversal was stated bluntly by Justice White: "I don't see any right of access for anyone or why, if [they] let the public in, [they] must let the press in with their cameras." On the other side, Justice Stevens asked, "Can a policy denying all access be constitutional? I think not." Stevens emphasized the public interest "as to how prisons are run."

Of particular interest, in view of his position as the swing vote, was the ambivalent statement of Justice Stewart: "The First Amendment does not give [the press] access superior to that of the general public. Moreover, there is no

such thing as a constitutional right to know." Nevertheless, the Justice concluded, "Basically, I think the injunction here does not exceed [the permitted]
bounds." Stewart also noted, "If the sheriff had not allowed public tours, he did
not have to allow the press in."

The conference, with Justices Marshall and Blackmun not participating,
divided four (Justices Brennan, Stewart, Powell, and Stevens) to three (the
Chief Justice and Justices White and Rehnquist) in favor of affirmance. The
opinion was assigned to Justice Stevens who circulated a draft opinion which
contained a broad recognition of a constitutional right of access to information
on the part of the press — a right that "is not for the private benefit of those who
might qualify as representatives of the 'press' but to insure that the citizens are
fully informed regarding matters of public interest and importance."

Under the Stevens draft, "information gathering is entitled to some measure
of constitutional protection," and had it come down as the *Houchins* opinion of
the Court, it would have established a First Amendment right of access to news.
But the Stevens draft was not able to retain its majority. On April 24, 1978,
Justice Stewart, whose vote had helped to make up the bare majority for
affirmance, wrote to Justice Stevens, "Try as I may I cannot bring myself to
agree that a county sheriff is constitutionally required to open up a jail that he
runs to the press and the public. . . . [I]t would be permissible in this case to
issue an injunction assuring press access equivalent to existing public access,
but not the much broader injunction actually issued by the District Court."
This was essentially the view taken in Justice Stewart's *Houchins* concurrence.

Chief Justice Burger prepared a draft dissent which was explained in a
Memorandum to the Conference: "I have devoted a substantial amount of time
on a dissent in this case with some emphasis on systems of citizen oversight
procedures which exist in many states. . . . this approach, rather than pushy
TV people interested directly in the sensational, is the way to a solution. . . . I
agree with Potter's view that media have a right of access but not beyond that of
the public generally."

But the Burger draft was not to be a dissent. Its holding for reversal received
a majority when Justice Stewart concurred in the judgment for reversal. On
May 23, the Chief Justice sent a "Dear Potter" letter that pointed out that any
press right of access could hardly be limited to the news media: "[T]here are
literally dozens of people . . . who tour prisons. . . . Many of them write books,
articles, or give lectures or a combination. I'm sure you will agree they have the
same rights as a TV reporter doing a 'documentary.' Can they have greater First
Amendment rights than these others whose form and certainty of communications is not so fixed?"

"I do not believe," the Burger draft declared, "First Amendment rights
can be circumscribed by the scope of the audience. If so, the early pamph-
leteers who could afford only 100 sheets are 'suspect.' " On the contrary, the
Chief Justice noted, "a team of TV cameramen (camera-persons!) will tend to
produce far more disruption than the serious student or judge, lawyer, or

penologist who wants to exercise First Amendment rights with a somewhat different objective."

A second Burger draft noted, "As a legislator I would vote for a reasonably orderly access to prisons, etc., by media, because it would be useful. But that is not the issue. The question is whether special access rights are *constitutionally compelled.*" The Chief Justice answered in the negative.

The Burger opinion was joined by Justices White and Rehnquist. This made it the plurality opinion of a seven-Justice Court, as Justice Stewart's concurrence enabled the decision for reversal to come down as the majority decision. The Stewart vote switch meant that Justice Stevens's affirmation of a First Amendment right of access became the dissenting view.

The Burger Court also dealt with the press right of access to court proceedings in *Gannett Co. v. DePasquale* (1979). The decision there also ruled against the press claim — although the first draft opinion would have given a broad right of access. But a Justice changed his vote six weeks later and that opinion became the dissent.

The difficult constitutional cases are not those in which the courts are asked to vindicate a given right, but those in which conflicting rights — each by itself deserving of judicial protection — are at issue. In *Gannett,* defendants in a murder trial asserted that their right to a fair trial required exclusion of the public and press from a pretrial hearing on a motion to suppress two crucial items of evidence — a confession and a murder weapon. A newspaper claimed that the press and the public had a right of access to judicial proceedings even though the accused, the prosecutor, and the trial judge all had agreed to closure. The closure order was upheld by the highest state court.

The claims of the press rested on both the Sixth Amendment guaranty of a public trial and the First Amendment guaranty of freedom of the press. At the postargument conference Chief Justice Burger indicated that neither amendment supported a reversal. In his view, the Sixth Amendment public-trial right did not apply "because the motion to suppress [is] not part of the trial." As for the "first Amendment argument, there isn't any for me."

Justice Stewart, who ultimately wrote the *Gannett* opinion, also spoke for affirmance. "I don't think the First Amendment claim is valid, since the press has no greater rights than the public." On the Sixth Amendment issue, the Justice reached the same result as the Chief Justice. Justices Rehnquist and Stevens also were in favor of affirmance. "The Sixth Amendment," said Rehnquist, "means for me only protection for the rights of the accused. . . . [T]he Framers didn't give the public a right to access." Stevens relied on "a critical difference between seeing a live hearing and reading a transcript of it. If the public has a right of access to the live performance, we'll be holding that the electronic media must be allowed."

The other five Justices spoke in favor of reversal. They were led by Justice Brennan, who was for establishing a constitutional right of access for the press and the public. Justices White and Marshall agreed. "The public," Marshall declared, "has a right because, if the accused is done dirt, the public interest is hurt. The public is entitled to know what happens when it happens."

Of particular interest were the statements of Justice Blackmun, who wrote the first *Gannett* draft, and Justice Powell, who was ultimately the swing vote in the case. Justice Blackmun said that he agreed that the Sixth Amendment provided for the "public character of trial. . . . I think the public directly and the press indirectly have an interest in preventing the abuse of public business. I'd take the Sixth Amendment approach." Justice Powell, who was to change his mind on this point, agreed. As he put it, "This is Sixth [Amendment] and not First." In Powell's view, "the trial judge didn't do enough when he heard the accused and the prosecutor agreed to closure." The judge should also have allowed the press to be heard.

In a letter to Justice Blackmun, Justice Powell wrote that at the *Gannett* conference, "I do not think a majority of the Court agreed as to exactly how the competing interests in this case should be resolved." On the other hand, the tally sheet of a Justice present at the conference indicates that a bare majority (Justices Brennan, White, Marshall, Blackmun, and Powell) favored reversal.

The opinion was assigned to Justice Blackmun, who circulated a draft opinion of the Court which was a broadside rejection of the decision below. The draft read a broad right of public and press access to all criminal proceedings into the Sixth Amendment's public trial guaranty: "The public trial guarantee . . . insures that not only judges but all participants in the criminal justice system are subjected to public scrutiny as they conduct the public's business of prosecuting crime."

Had the Blackmun draft opinion come down as the final *Gannett* opinion, it would have completely resolved the issue of access to criminal proceedings in favor of a wide right on the part of the public and the press. But the Blackmun draft was not able to secure a majority.

Justice Stewart circulated a draft dissent which stated that the Sixth Amendment public trial guaranty is one created for the benefit of the defendant alone and was personal to the accused. Nor did the First Amendment compel a different result, since it gives the press no right superior to that of the public. "If the public," Justice Stewart wrote, "had no enforceable right to attend the pretrial proceeding in this case, it necessarily follows that the petitioners had no such right under the First and Fourteenth Amendments."

Justice Stevens also circulated a brief draft dissent, which asserted, "I do not believe the Court has the authority to create this novel remedy for a random selection of bystanders."

The general expectation in the Court was that the Blackmun draft would come down as the *Gannett* opinion. Then, on May 31, 1979, a month and a half after the drafts were circulated, Justice Powell wrote to Justice Blackmun: "I was inclined to view this case as presenting primarily a First Amendment rather than a Sixth Amendment issue. . . . I had become persuaded that my views as to the Sixth Amendment coincide substantially with those expressed by Potter. . . . I therefore will join his opinion." Justice Powell also had written a draft, originally as a dissent, which would be issued as a concurring opinion, "in which I address the First Amendment issue. I am sorry to end up being the 'swing vote.' At Conference I voted to reverse. But upon a more careful examination of the facts, I have concluded that the trial court substantially did what in my view the First Amendment requires."

The case was now assigned to Justice Stewart, whose revised version of his draft dissent was redrafted as the *Gannett* opinion of the Court. The most substantial change was pointed out in Stewart's June 7 covering memorandum. "You will note that I have unabashedly plagiarized Harry Blackmun's statement of facts in Part I and discussion of mootness in Part II. I offer two excuses: (1) the pressure of time, and (2) more importantly, I could not have said it better."

The *Gannett* decision did not, however, finally resolve the issue of access to criminal proceedings. When the Justices were again presented with the issue in *Richmond Newspapers v. Virginia* (1980), they held that the First Amendment guaranteed both press and public a right of access to criminal *trials*. However, *Richmond News* did not overrule *Gannett* so far as *pretrial* proceedings are concerned. Had the Blackmun *Gannett* draft come down as the Court's opinion, it would have confirmed a press right of access to all criminal proceedings. Because of the Powell switch in *Gannett*, the law still remains unsettled in the matter.

9

More Switches,
Near Misses, and Abortion

"Years ago," wrote an eminent constitutional law professor of the Court of the mid-thirties, "that learned lawyer John Selden in talking of 'Council' observed: 'They talk (but blasphemously enough) that the Holy Ghost is President of their General Councils when the truth is, the odd Man is still the Holy Ghost.'" In the Supreme Court decision process, the "odd men" are the Justices who switch their votes, changing the results in cases that were all but ready to go the other way.

SWITCHES AND SODOMY

The most controversial case in recent years where the decision was changed because of a vote switch was *Bowers v. Hardwick* (1986). An action was brought by a homosexual who challenged a Georgia statute criminalizing consensual sodomy. The court of appeals held that the statute violated plaintiff's fundamental rights because his homosexual activity was a private association beyond the reach of state regulation. The lower court had relied on *Stanley v. Georgia* (1969), where the Supreme Court had held that the state might not criminalize the private possession of obscene material.

The *Bowers* majority refused to follow the *Stanley* approach and reversed the lower court. At the conference on the case, however, the vote was five to four the other way. Chief Justice Burger began the conference by stressing that "only homosexual activities" were involved in the case — "no marital privacy. Georgia agrees that an expansion to marital would get them in trouble." Burger's conference statement came down strongly in favor of reversal. "Our society has values that should be protected. The teachings of history and custom frown on this and the sanction is prohibition."

Justice Brennan led the argument the other way. As he saw it, "the case implicates two firmly established lines of our cases, namely, the right to privacy . . . and secondly, those cases which recognize that the home remains a sort of a castle within our legal system." Brennan said that he wanted "to emphasize that to me, this is a case involving certain sexual conduct engaged in between consenting adults, regardless of their marital status, regardless of their gender. It is not about homosexuality, it is not about single persons. It is about sexual privacy in the home between consenting adults. The statute purports to make none of these distinctions."

The Brennan conclusion was that "an act such as this which seeks to criminalize certain sexually intimate conduct between consenting adults, regardless of the marital status or gender of the adults, within the privacy of the home, must be [ruled invalid]."

Justice Brennan's conference view was supported by Justices Marshall, Blackmun, and Stevens. Justice Blackmun emphasized, "This isn't public conduct. It's limited to the home and reaches the marital situation. . . . [M]uch of the state's argument reminds [me] of *Loving* [the 1967 decision striking down miscegenation laws] and efforts to regulate prohibition." The Justice also said that "privacy and association were upheld in *Stanley*" and he asserted that "thought control and religion [were the] underpinning here."

Justice Stevens declared, "This is a liberty interest case." It was not enough that the "condemnation was made by a majority. If it was correct, [they could] enforce this against married people. Isn't it part of liberty for everyone?"

Chief Justice Burger was supported at the conference by Justices White, Rehnquist, and O'Connor. Justice Rehnquist said, "I can't say substantive due process supports attack on the statute as limited to the home." Justice O'Connor conceded, "The right of privacy is a Fourteenth Amendment personal liberty. But," she went on, "the right is not absolute and doesn't extend to private consensual homosexuality. State legislative power to enact this is not unconstitutional as exercised."

At the conference, the key voter was Justice Powell, who started by urging, "We ought to decriminalize this conduct. The statute [has] not [been] enforced for 50 years." He then stated a view of the case that differed from the approach of the other Justices. "*Robinson v. California* [1963, invalidating a law], mandating the criminal status of drug addiction, may be relevant. It rested on the Eighth Amendment [prohibiting cruel and unusual punishment]. . . . If [we] accept the allegation that only acts of sodomy can satisfy this fellow, isn't that pertinent? I'd treat it as such and hold that, in the context of the home," the statute is invalid.

Justice Powell's stand against the statute made the conference vote five to four for affirmance. However, a few days after the conference, Powell circulated a Memorandum to the Conference telling the others that he had changed his vote:

At Conference last week, I expressed the view that in some cases it would violate the Eighth Amendment to imprison a person for a private act of homosexual sodomy. I continue to think that in such cases imprisonment would constitute cruel and unusual punishment. I relied primarily on *Robinson v. California*.

At Conference, given my view as to the Eighth Amendment, my vote was to affirm but on this ground rather than the view of four other Justices that there was a violation of a fundamental substantive constitutional right—as [the lower court] held. I did not agree that there is a substantive due process right to engage in conduct that for centuries has been recognized as deviant, and not in the best interest of preserving humanity. I may say generally, that I also hesitate to create another substantive due process right.

I write this memorandum today because upon further study as to exactly what is before us, I conclude that my 'bottom line' should be to reverse rather than affirm. The only question presented by the parties is the substantive due process issue, and—as several of you noted at Conference—my Eighth Amendment view was not addressed by the court below or by the parties.

In sum, my more carefully considered view is that I will vote to reverse but will write separately to explain my view of this case generally.

With Justice Powell's switched vote, the bare majority became one in favor of the statute. Powell issued a separate concurrence, which indicated that, while he joined the Court's opinion, he might vote differently in a criminal case in which someone had been sentenced to prison for sodomy. "In my view," the Powell concurrence stated, "a prison sentence for such conduct . . . would create a serious Eighth Amendment issue"—that is, might well constitute "cruel and unusual punishment."

The *Bowers* opinion of the Court by Justice White, on the other hand, held that the sodomy statute did not violate the fundamental rights of homosexuals. "[H]omosexual conduct is not a constitutionally protected liberty interest, and . . . homosexuality is not a suspect or quasi-suspect classification entitled to heightened scrutiny."

The White opinion justified the fear expressed in a memo by Daniel C. Richman, a Marshall law clerk, that the Justices would either forget or be ignorant of the fact that the acts prohibited were also performed by heterosexuals. Writing in capital letters for emphasis, Richman wrote, "THIS IS NOT A CASE ABOUT ONLY HOMOSEXUALS. ALL SORTS OF PEOPLE DO THIS KIND OF THING."

Critics contend that the Court's approach in *Bowers* is unduly narrow. Perhaps there is no fundamental right of homosexuals to engage in acts of sodomy, but there is a fundamental right to privacy in the home. Or so we thought after *Stanley v. Georgia*. With the Powell vote switch, however, the right of privacy gave way before the governmental interest in ensuring what Chief Justice Burger called at the *Bowers* conference societal "values that should be protected."

SWITCHES AND THE MEDIA

When the First Amendment was adopted, freedom of the press was, of course, intended to protect only the traditional print media. During the present century, the guaranty has been extended to the newer broadcast media. This does not, however, mean that freedom of the press means the same thing for broadcasters as it does for publishers of newspapers, magazines, and books. Any person can publish a newspaper without any license. But the same is not true of the broadcast media with their inherent physical limitation; no one may operate a broadcast station without a license from the Federal Communications Commission. Similarly, while government may not interfere with the editorial judgment of print publishers, the same is not as true of broadcasters.

The Warren Court itself stated that there can be no First Amendment right to broadcast comparable to the right to speak, write, or publish. Consequently its *Red Lion* decision in 1969 upheld the FCC's so-called fairness doctrine, which required broadcasters to provide reply time to personal attacks or political editorials. The *Red Lion* opinion stated that it was based on "the right of the public to receive suitable access to social, political, esthetic, moral, and other ideas and experiences." The implication is that there may be a right of individual access to the airwaves to ensure that the public right to receive diverse materials is vindicated.

The Burger Court decisions, however, refused to recognize such a constitutional right of access to the broadcast media. Nevertheless, on this matter also, Congress and the regulatory agency established by it possess authority over broadcasters which the First Amendment prohibits so far as print publishers are concerned.

This means that although, as just stated, there is no constitutional right of individual access to the airwaves, a different result may be required where Congress requires broadcasters to grant access to their facilities. Such a congressional provision was at issue in *Columbia Broadcasting System v. Federal Communications Commission* (1981). The statutory provision there authorized the FCC to revoke a broadcast license because of the broadcaster's "failure to allow reasonable access to or to permit purchase of reasonable amounts of time by a legally qualified candidate for federal elective office." The broadcast networks challenged the statute on First Amendment grounds, claiming that it unduly circumscribed their editorial discretion. The networks had sought review of an FCC order that they had violated the statute by refusing to sell time to the Carter-Mondale Presidential Committee for December 1979, which they felt was too early for the 1980 campaign.

In effect, the statute provided an affirmative right of access to the broadcast media for individual candidates for federal office. And it was a new right created by Congress. As Justice White put it at the conference, "Congress intended to change the law. The old law never allowed a candidate to do this."

The conference vote was five to four to reverse the decision below affirming the FCC order. The Chief Justice said that he had only a "skeptical confidence in the FCC." The issue was, "Could the networks' judgment as to when the campaign was in full swing be reviewed [by the FCC]? . . . I'd be inclined to sustain the network's judgment unless clearly wrong. Even if the networks made the wrong decision, in my view, to avoid censorship I'd give them the benefit of the doubt."

The view of the conference majority was best stated by Justice White, who ultimately delivered the dissent. "I think the FCC put too tight a grip on the broadcasters — particularly on the threshold issue of when the campaign began. My standard would be something like, if reasonable men could differ, the networks' decision should be sustained." Justices Powell, Rehnquist, and Stevens agreed with Justice White. As Justice Powell put it, "The Commission went beyond its authority in saying it decided when the campaign commenced."

Justices Brennan, Stewart, Marshall, and Blackmun spoke for affirmance. Their opinion was that Congress could change the law to provide for the right of access and, in Justice Blackmun's words, "I'd let the Commission decide when the campaign begins." Justice Marshall's statement was pithy: "The networks are the biggest censors of all and I don't mind the FCC censoring the censors."

Once again vote switches changed the outcome. Chief Justice Burger and Justice Powell changed their votes in favor of affirmance, so that the final decision in *CBS v. FCC* was to uphold the statute and the FCC order. The result is that, as stated by the Chief Justice at the conference, "TV has large, but not as much as the print media, discretion in editing." Congress and the regulatory agency may impinge upon that discretion in a manner not permissible for the traditional press. They may impose upon the broadcasters the kind of fairness requirement that would be unconstitutional for newspapers. Congress may even create a right of access though none is demanded by the First Amendment. Once again, however, that is true only because of the vote switches in the Supreme Court decision on the subject.

A crucial vote switch also determined the outcome in the Supreme Court's first case on a matter of great importance to the broadcast media — that of television in the courtroom. Chief Justice Warren led the Court to its decision in the case, *Estes v. Texas* (1965). Warren believed strongly that television had no legitimate place in a criminal trial. There is a memorandum by a law clerk which tells what Warren said to him about the subject while the *Estes* case was pending. It indicates that the very idea of televised trials was repulsive to the Chief Justice. If they are permitted, he told his law clerk, "we turn back the clock and make everyone in the courtroom an actor before untold millions of people. We are asked again to make the determination of guilt or innocence a public spectacle and a source of entertainment for the idle and curious."

The Chief Justice recalled for his clerk how "The American people were shocked and horrified when Premier Castro tried certain defendants in a stadium." The same thing could happen here, Warren warned his clerk: "[I]f our courts must be opened to the pervasive influence of the television camera in order to accommodate the wishes of the news media, it is but a short step to holding court in a municipal auditorium, to accommodate them even more. As public interest increases in a particular trial, perhaps it will be moved from the courtroom to the municipal auditorium and from the auditorium to the baseball stadium."

Chief Justice Warren's feelings on the matter led him to declare in an unissued draft dissent in *Estes* that to allow televising of criminal proceedings means "allowing the courtroom to become a public spectacle and source of entertainment." Estes himself was a notorious swindler, whose trial and conviction in a Texas court was a national cause célèbre. Over Estes's objection, portions of the trial proceedings were televised. In the courtroom, twelve cameramen jostled for position and bright lights and a tangle of wires and equipment, in *Time* magazine's phrase, "turned the courtroom into a broadcast studio." Despite this the Texas courts rejected Estes's claim that he was deprived of due process.

The Justices were closely divided throughout their consideration of the case. The conference after the oral argument began with a strong statement by the Chief Justice. "I think," he declared, "this violates due process. To stage a trial this way violates the decorum of the courtroom, and TV is not entitled to special treatment." Warren rejected any First Amendment claim the other way, saying he could "see no violation of [freedom of] speech or press. They may be in the courtroom, like the press, only as part of the public. The way this is set up bears on the question of fair trial."

The Chief Justice was supported by Justices Douglas, Harlan, and Goldberg. "The constitutional standard," Justice Douglas pointed out, "is a fair trial. Trial in a mob scene is not a fair trial." Here, Douglas referred to the 1936 case of *Brown v. Mississippi,* where the Court had reversed convictions because of mob violence. He said, "that was a judgment not hinged to any particular specific." Douglas seconded the Chief Justice in his objection to televised trials. "A trial," he observed, "is not a spectacle, whether he objected or not. This is the modern farce — putting the courtroom into a modern theatrical production."

Justice Harlan said that the case "comes down to the concept of what is the right to a public trial. It doesn't mean for me that the public has the right to a public performance. This goes more deeply into the judicial process than just the right of the defendant." Justice Goldberg asserted that "the shambles deprived defendant of a fair trial. In the present state of the art, this was an obtrusive intervention of the outside into this trial."

Justices Clark, Stewart, and White opposed a flat ban on television in the courtroom. Justice Clark stressed that the trial judge's finding that no prejudice had been shown was not clearly erroneous. Clark had tried to avoid the constitutional issue by urging the Justices to dismiss the case as one in which certiorari had been improvidently granted. In a later memorandum, Clark noted, "not mustering any other votes for this disposition I then voted to affirm on the narrow basis of the facts, *i.e.,* the pre-trial televising of September 23–24 indicated no prejudice; the trial on the merits in October was telecast piece-meal — only picture, for the most part, without sound; the jury was sequestered and no prejudice was shown."

Justice Brennan was not as certain in his presentation. "What," he asked, "is the concept of a fair trial? Is there a court concept independent of the individual?" He pointed out that "technology may bring this into line within the courtroom." He then referred to the trial "as theatre or spectacle that's been part of our heritage," as well as to a "legislative inquisition." Brennan stressed that "this was no sham. The jury was sequestered. There's no suggestion that the witnesses, the judge, or others were affected in a way to hurt." Brennan conceded that, in such a case, "the totality [of circumstances] might knock it down," but said that was not the case here.

Justice Black, who had spoken after Chief Justice Warren, indicated even greater doubt. As a starting point, he said, "I'm against television in courts. But this is a new thing that's working itself out." Black conceded that the case presented difficulties for his normal constitutional approach. "For me," he affirmed, "the test is, 'what is in the Constitution on which I can grasp as a handle?' On lawyers, confrontation, etc., I have no problem. I can't do this on how bad it is short of the *Brown {v. Mississippi}* test." Black concluded that "the case for me comes down to only a slight advance over what we've had before." He also noted that, "some day the technology may improve so as not to disturb the actual trial." But, even with the disturbance involved in Estes's trial, Justice Black ultimately came down on the side of affirmance.

The *Estes* vote was for affirmance by a bare majority consisting of Justices Black, Clark, Stewart, Brennan, and White. Justice Black, as senior majority Justice, assigned the case to Justice Stewart. A draft opinion of the Court was circulated. "On the record of this case . . . ," it concluded, "we cannot say that any violation of the Constitution occurred."

Once again, however, the bare majority for affirmance in *Estes* did not hold and, once again, it was Justice Clark who made the crucial shift to the Warren position. That the Chief Justice himself played a key part in the Texan's switch cannot be doubted. As seen, Warren felt strongly about the baneful effect of tele-vision on court proceedings, and this was just the sort of thing he would discuss with Clark as the two of them walked part of the way to the Court each morning.

Justice Clark circulated a Memorandum to the Conference telling of his change in position. "After circulation of the opinions and dissents, along with my interim study," Clark informed the Justices, "I became disturbed at what could result from our approval of this emasculation by TV of the trial of a case. My doubts increased as I envisioned use of the unfortunate format followed here in other trials which would not only jeopardize the fairness of them but would broadcast a bad image to the public of the judicial process."

The Clark memo stressed that the Sixth Amendment right to a public trial was granted only to the accused. "Nowhere does the Constitution say that the attendance of the public is mandatory or that that of the news media is required. The Founders spoke only of the benefit that must be accorded the accused. The presence of the public was made permissible so that Star Chamber methods might not result and the accused be unfairly condemned. It is even more certain that the news media were not in the mind of the Founders because there were few newspapers then and, of course, no radio or television." Justice Clark denied "that First Amendment freedoms grant the news media an absolute 'right' to be present and to report trial proceedings." "It appears to me," the Clark memo concluded, "that the perils to a fair trial far outweigh the benefits that might accrue in the televising of the proceedings."

Two days later, Justice Clark circulated a draft opinion reversing Estes's conviction. Though Chief Justice Warren had written a lengthy dissent that might easily have been converted into the opinion of the new majority (created by the Clark switch), the Chief Justice assigned the *Estes* opinion to Clark. The Texan promptly circulated a revision of his own draft as the opinion of the Court, which was then issued in June 1965. Justice Stewart revised his draft opinion of the Court and issued it as a dissent, joined by the other members of the former majority. The Clark switch had led to the reversal because of television in the courtroom. The Court had once again refused the press a right of access to the courtroom greater than that possessed by the public.

It is of interest to note that the Burger Court Justices were also disturbed about the televising of criminal trials. The Court did, in *Chandler v. Florida* (1981), refuse to hold that televising in the courtroom is always violative of due process. Among themselves, however, the Justices were anything but sanguine about televised trials. Thus, while *Chandler* was being considered, Justice Powell wrote to Chief Justice Burger of the "enduring concern . . . that the presence of the camera may impair the fairness of a trial, but not leave evidence of specific prejudice." Powell suggested that the Court should be "clear as to the protection that the Constitution affords a defendant who objects to his trial being televised. . . . I am inclined to think it desirable that we make explicit that the defendant who makes a timely motion to exclude the cameras, and alleges specific harms that he fears will occur, is entitled as a matter of right to a hearing."

Chief Justice Burger also indicated that he was far from approving television in every case. "For me," he wrote in a letter reminiscent of Chief Justice Warren's comment, "there *may be* a risk of due process and equal protection violations in putting a few out of thousands of trials on TV or in a 'Yankee Stadium' setting."

The others, too, were uneasy at what Justice Blackmun called "the risk of adverse psychological impact on various trial participants." In criminal trials, Blackmun wrote to the Chief Justice, "any type of media coverage is capable of creating an impression of guilt or innocence. Assuming *arguendo* that more people are likely to watch the news than read about it, the incremental risk of juror prejudice seems to me a difference in degree rather than kind."

GOLDBERG FOR FRANKFURTER

Even those uninitiated in Supreme Court mysteries now know that decisions depend as much, if not more, upon the individual Justices who sit in a case as upon legal doctrine. This truism has been apparent throughout the Court's history. Striking illustrations occurred when the Marshall Court gave way to that under Chief Justice Taney and when President Franklin D. Roosevelt was able to replace the "Nine Old Men," who had invalidated the core of the New Deal program, with Justices of his own choosing.

In our own day, the Justices appointed by Presidents Reagan and Bush have been able to remold constitutional jurisprudence in accordance with their own conservative bent. No one doubts, for example, that the Rehnquist Court would have decided many of the Warren Court decisions differently than the Justices did under Earl Warren's lead.

In the Warren Court itself, there was a striking illustration of the impact of changed Court personnel upon individual decisions during the 1961 and 1962 Terms, when Justices Felix Frankfurter and Charles E. Whittaker had to retire suddenly because of illness and were replaced by Justices Arthur J. Goldberg and Byron R. White. In particular, the replacement of Justice Frankfurter made a crucial difference in a significant number of cases.

The first such case was *Kennedy v. Mendoza-Martinez* (1963). The case involved the constitutionality of a section of the Nationality Act. Under it, loss of citizenship was imposed on Francisco Mendoza-Martinez for leaving the United States to evade military service in time of war or declared national emergency.

At the October 1961 conference on the case, there was a majority of five (Justices Frankfurter, Clark, Harlan, Whittaker, and Stewart) for reversing the lower-court decision that the statute was unconstitutional. Justice Stewart circulated a draft opinion holding that the law was validly designed for the accomplishment of legitimate objectives under the congressional war power. Justices Frankfurter, Clark, and Harlan agreed to join the draft. But then Justice Whittaker became ill and Justice Frankfurter had a stroke while working in his chambers; he was carried from the building, protesting that his shoes were being left behind. Both Justices retired and *Mendoza-Martinez* was scheduled for reargument. In the interim, Justice Frankfurter was replaced by Justice Goldberg.

During the December 1962 postreargument conference, Chief Justice Warren briefly stated the issues and said that he was for a decision of unconstitutionality. As he put it, "you can't take citizenship away without an unequivocal act of expatriation." He also asserted, "you can't 'punish' this way."

All in the room then turned to the new Justice. The Chief Justice asked, "Well Arthur, how do you vote?" Justice Goldberg said that he would vote to hold the denationalization provision invalid and gave his reasons. The Goldberg vote now made for a bare majority in favor of Warren's position. The opinion was assigned to Goldberg, and it held the statute unconstitutional because it imposed "punishment" without affording the procedural safeguards that must attend a criminal prosecution. Had Justice Frankfurter still been on the Court, the decision would have been five-to-four in favor of constitutionality.

The Frankfurter replacement by Justice Goldberg also changed the result in *Wong Sun v. United States* (1963), a criminal case with a complicated fact pattern. Federal narcotics agents in San Francisco arrested Hom Way and found heroin in his possession. Way stated that he had bought heroin from "Blackie Toy," proprietor of a laundry on Leavenworth Street. At 6 A.M., agents went to a laundry on Leavenworth Street operated by James Wah Toy. They rang the bell and, when Toy appeared, showed their badges. Toy slammed the door and ran to the bedroom where his wife and child were sleeping. The agents broke open the door and followed Toy and arrested him. Toy denied selling narcotics, but said he knew a "Johnny," who had sold heroin and described the house where Johnny lived. The agents located the house, entered it, and found Johnny Yee in the bedroom, who showed them heroin in a drawer. Yee said that the heroin had been brought to him by Toy and another known as "Sea Dog."

Toy was questioned and said that "Sea Dog" was Wong Sun. He took some agents to Wong Sun's dwelling. They were allowed in by Wong Sun's wife and found him, but no narcotics. Toy, Yee, and Wong Sun were arraigned and released on their own recognizance. Each was later interrogated by the Narcotics Bureau office. Toy and Wong Sun made incriminating statements but refused to sign English written versions.

Both Toy and Wong Sun were convicted of transporting and concealing heroin. The government's evidence consisted of (1) statements made by Toy at his arrest; (2) heroin surrendered by Yee; (3) Toy's unsigned statement; and (4) Wong Sun's similar statement. The evidence had been admitted over objections that it was inadmissible as "fruits" of unlawful arrests or of attendant searches. The court of appeals had held that the arrests were illegal because they were not based on "probable cause," but that the four items of proof were properly admitted because they were not the "fruits" of the illegal arrests.

The conference that considered the *Wong Sun* case took place on April 6, 1962. This was the last conference that Justice Frankfurter attended; later that day, he suffered his stroke. To Chief Justice Warren, the case was a simple one. When his law clerks started to discuss the technical elements involved, the Chief Justice interjected, "Now, wait a minute! This guy was a Chinaman in San Francisco, who was awakened six o'clock in the morning by a couple of guys in plainclothes. They say they're narcotics agents. He's scared, he slams the door shut, he runs back to his bedroom, standing next to his wife, who was asleep in one bed. His kid was asleep in another bed in the corner of the room. These guys start to ask him questions. And now you're gonna tell me that the statements he makes in those circumstances can be admitted in evidence against him. *You can't do that!*"

Chief Justice Warren urged reversal at the conference, saying that the lower court "was right when it found that the arrest was illegal, but wrong when it said that they could use this evidence." Justice Frankfurter argued the other way. In his view, the arrests were lawful, since there was "probable cause" to make them. The conference vote was four-to-four. The Chief Justice and Justices Douglas, Brennan, and Black voted to reverse. Justices Frankfurter, Clark, Harlan, and Stewart voted to affirm. Justice White, who took his seat on April 6, did not participate. Because of the close division and Justice Frankfurter's absence during the remainder of the term, the case was set for reargument.

At the postreargument conference the next term, the vote among the first eight Justices was four (Chief Justice Warren and Justices Black, Douglas, and Brennan) to four (Justices Clark, Harlan, Stewart, and White). That left the decision once more up to Justice Goldberg, who again voted with the Chief Justice. He thought that the statements made by Toy and Wong Sun were fruits of illegal arrests. "You can't distinguish," the junior Justice asserted, "between statements and tangible objects as fruits."

Had Justice Frankfurter still been on the Court, the *Wong Sun* decision would have been five-to-four for affirmance. With Justice Goldberg voting in his place, the vote was five-to-four to reverse, and that was the holding in the opinion of the Court delivered by Justice Brennan. There was a strong dissent by Justice Clark.

There is an amusing footnote to Justice Clark's *Wong Sun* dissent. In his first draft, Clark chided the majority for its "total lack of acquaintanceship with the habits and practices of Chinatown," which would enable the officers to know about the identity of a person described as "Blackie Toy." Justice Clark did not realize that Toy's laundry on Leavenworth Street was nowhere near Chinatown, but was instead on Russian Hill, in an area notable for the absence of Chinese residents. Justice Brennan went to the Clark chambers armed with a map, and pointed out the error in geography. Justice Clark revised his dissent to point out only that the Toy arrest was "by officers familiar with San Francisco and the habits and practices of its Chinese-American inhabitants."

In terms of their potential impact, the most significant cases where the replacement of Justice Frankfurter by Justice Goldberg made the difference were two cases growing out of southern efforts to curb the National Association for the Advancement of Colored People. The NAACP Legal Defense Fund had been the catalyst for civil-rights suits; most desegregation cases could not have been brought without the financial help, moral assistance, and legal counsel provided by the NAACP.

Because of this the NAACP became the favorite bête noire to much of the white South. As the poet Langston Hughes put it, "the southern states [have] been busy since 1954 . . . seeking 'legal' ways of putting the NAACP completely out of business." Laws were passed throughout the South to harass and intimidate the organization and its members. It was not until the most extreme of them were invalidated by the Supreme Court that the NAACP was able to operate freely in the desegregation effort.

Even in the Warren Court, the key decisions on the southern attempts to put the NAACP out of business almost went against the organization. Only chance, in the form of the illnesses that forced the retirement of Justices Frankfurter and Whittaker, led to the final decisions in favor of the NAACP.

In *NAACP v. Button* (1963), indeed, the Court had already "decided" the case against the NAACP just before Justice Frankfurter's stroke. The NAACP had challenged a Virginia statute that amended the laws on improper solicitation of business by attorneys to include agents for an organization that retained a lawyer in connection with an action to which it was not a party and in which it had no pecuniary interest. The Virginia Supreme Court had included the NAACP's activities within the statutory ban on improper solicitation of legal business. If upheld, this would have ended the NAACP's legal role in desegregation cases.

At the conference in November 1961, both the Chief Justice and Justice Black led the argument for reversal. The latter stressed that "this is but one of a number of laws passed as a package designed to thwart our *Brown* decision — a scheme to defeat the Court's order." However, despite the fact that the law's purpose was, in the Warren phrase, "to circumvent *Brown* obviously," the conference voted five to four to uphold it. The majority accepted the argument made by Justice Frankfurter. "I can't imagine a worse disservice," he declared at the conference, "than to continue being the guardians of Negroes." He argued that the statute was a valid exercise of the state's regulatory power over the legal profession. "There's no evidence here," Frankfurter asserted, "that this statute is aimed at Negroes as such."

A few weeks later, Justice Frankfurter circulated an opinion of the Court affirming the Virginia court. Justice Black wrote a dissent stressing that the statute's legislative history showed that it had been enacted with the racially discriminatory purpose of precluding effective litigation on behalf of civil rights. Though the case had thus been "decided" during the 1961 Term, before the decision could be announced Justice Whittaker retired because of ill health and Justice Frankfurter became incapacitated after his stroke. The case was then set down for reargument in the next term.

At the October 1962 conference after the reargument, Justices White and Goldberg, who had replaced Justices Whittaker and Frankfurter, voted to strike down the law. This changed the final decision to one in favor of the NAACP.

There was a similar scenario in *Gibson v. Florida Legislative Investigation Committee,* also decided in 1963. The committee was set up by the Florida legislature to investigate the Miami NAACP branch. Theodore R. Gibson, president of the branch, was ordered to appear and bring with him records of members and contributors. At the committee hearing, the chairman said that the inquiry was into Communist infiltration into the NAACP. Gibson refused to produce the records. He was adjudged in contempt and sentenced to six months' imprisonment and a twelve-hundred-dollar fine.

At the December 1961 conference, the vote was once more five to four to affirm the conviction, with Justices Frankfurter, Clark, Harlan, Whittaker, and Stewart for affirmance. But again Justice Whittaker's retirement and Justice Frankfurter's collapse caused the case to be set for reargument in the 1962 Term. At the October 1962 conference after the reargument, the Chief Justice and the others who had participated in the earlier conference voted as they had the first time. Justice White, who had taken the Whittaker seat, voted for affirmance. However, Justice Goldberg, the Frankfurter successor, voted the other way. That made the final decision a bare majority for reversal. Justice Goldberg was assigned the opinion and it held that the committee had failed to show any substantial relationship between the NAACP and subversive or Communist activities. Justice Harlan dissented, joined by Justices Clark, Stewart, and White. If Justice Frankfurter had cast the decisive vote, the decision would have been the other way.

The Supreme Court thus ultimately rebuffed the Southern efforts to bar the NAACP from its crucial role in desegregation cases. The *Button* and *Gibson* decisions allowed the Legal Defense Fund to continue its support in cases like the *Swann* school busing case discussed in Chapter 6. But it was a close-run thing. Had Justices Frankfurter and Whittaker been able to cast the deciding votes, both decisions would have gone the other way.

LEGISLATIVE APPORTIONMENT

Had a vote switch come earlier in one of the Warren Court's landmark cases, it would have made an important difference in the law. Chief Justice Warren wrote in his *Memoirs* that *Baker v. Carr* (1962), holding that the federal courts may review legislative apportionments under the Equal Protection Clause, "was the most important case of my tenure on the Court." The case arose out of a suit by Charles W. Baker, a Tennessee voter who challenged the 1901 law under which seats in the state legislature were apportioned. He claimed that voters from urban areas had been denied equal protection "by virtue of the debasement of their votes," since a vote from the most populous county had only a fraction of the weight of one from the least populous county. The population ratio for the most and least populous districts was over nineteen-to-one.

Baker v. Carr presented two principal issues: the first of jurisdiction and the second of the merits of the constitutional claim. The lower court dismissed Baker's complaint, relying on *Colegrove v. Green,* the leading pre-Baker case, which had dismissed an action challenging a legislative apportionment on the ground that the case presented a political question. It was the *Colegrove* opinion that made the oft-quoted statement: "Courts ought not to enter this political thicket."

At the April 1961 *Baker* conference following argument, Chief Justice Warren stated, "I think the case ought to be reversed on the Solicitor-General's argument. But I think he was too cautious. I don't see why we should say merely that there is jurisdiction. I'd say the case stated a cause of action [and] I'd let the Court determine the remedy."

The Chief Justice was strongly supported by Justices Black, Douglas, and Brennan, and was vigorously opposed by Justice Frankfurter. One of the Justices who was present recalled, "Frankfurter unleashed a brilliant tour de force, speaking at considerable length, pulling down reports and reading from them, and powerfully arguing the correctness of *Colegrove*." Justices Clark and Harlan agreed with Frankfurter. Justice Whittaker had been uncharacteristically vigorous in questioning the claim of lack of jurisdiction during the argument. "If there is a clear constitutional right being violated . . . ," Whittaker had interrupted counsel at one point, "is there not both power and a duty in the courts to enforce the constitutional right?" At the conference, Whittaker disagreed with Frankfurter on the question of jurisdiction. However, since he thought that *Colegrove* should not be abandoned by only a bare majority, he was voting with Frankfurter.

With Justice Whittaker's vote the conference was divided four-to-four. That put the matter up to Justice Stewart, who felt unable to decide and wanted the case to go over. At his urging, the case was put over for reargument during the next term.

In his *Autobiography,* Justice Douglas stated that the conference vote was five-to-four in favor of reversal, with Justice Stewart, tentatively at least, one of the five. Insofar as he implied that this was true of the first conference, his recollection was mistaken. The contemporary notes of those present indicate that Stewart did not vote. A Douglas Memorandum to the Conference also confirms this. According to it, "In *Baker v. Carr* last Term, JUSTICE STEWART was undecided in his view. Hence we put the case down for reargument and we have recently reheard it. This is as it should be. . . . When opinions have jelled, the case is handed down. When jelling is not finished, the case is held."

The *Baker v. Carr* reargument took place in October 1961. From the discussion and vote at the first conference, it looked as though Justices Stewart and Whittaker would be the key Justices in the case. After the reargument, Justice Harlan, who had strongly supported the Frankfurter position, wrote to Justices Stewart and Whittaker. He was writing, said Harlan, because, "Unless I am much mistaken, past events in this case plainly indicate that your votes will be determinative of its outcome." Harlan maintained that "from the standpoint of the future of the Court the case involves implications whose importance is unmatched by those of any other case coming here in my time (and by those in few others in the history of the Court, not excluding the *Desegregation* case). I believe that what we are being asked to do in this case threatens the preservation of . . . the independence of the Court."

"The only sure way of avoiding this," Justice Harlan wrote, "is to keep the gate to the [political] thicket tightly closed. Politics being what they are it seems to me that it would be almost naive to blink the dangers of this situation. [Now] the responsibility is entirely in our laps, and to me it would be a sad thing were we by our own act to plunge this institution into what would bid fair, as time goes on, to erode it[s] stature."

Justice Stewart had, however, made up his mind to vote for reversal before he had received the Harlan letter. The notion that the courts were without jurisdiction over apportionments even in the face of patent violations of the Equal Protection Clause had increasingly troubled him after the first conference.

The conference following reargument made known Justice Stewart's decision to vote with the Warren wing of the Court. At the conference, Chief Justice Warren reaffirmed that the district court had jurisdiction. He also asserted, "This is a violation of equal protection," though he also conceded, "we don't have to say that the state must give complete equality."

As at the first conference, the Chief Justice was supported by Justices Black, Douglas, and Brennan. "I still feel," stated Justice Black, "as I did in my dissent in *Colegrove v. Green.* I think *Colegrove* is a weak reed on which to hang the notion of a settled rule of law." Black discussed the classic 1849 case of *Luther v. Borden,* where the Court refused to decide which of two competing governments was the legal government of Rhode Island. "I think *Luther* was right," Black declared. "Two factions claimed to be the state. It wasn't a dispute over a law passed by a state, but which was the state." He referred to another case that held that it was for Congress to decide whether a state had a republican form of government. "But it's different," he said, "when you attack a law that's not an attack on the state's form of government. Here it's simply a question of whether the law passed bears so unequally, capriciously, as to deny equal protection."

Justice Douglas noted that "the Equal Protection Clause was not designed for Negroes," and he asserted that "the difficulties of the judiciary doing anything about it, great as they are, can't deter us from doing our job." Justice Brennan stressed that, whatever might be true in other cases, here the apportionment defied rational explanation, and it had to be reversed.

This time the case in opposition to reversal was stated primarily by Justice Harlan. Usually the most restrained of the Justices, Harlan argued with intense emotion, as he sought to show the undesirable results he expected to flow from a reversal in the case.

Justice Clark indicated that he, too, was firmly in accord with the Frankfurter view. "Even if there was jurisdiction," he said, "I wouldn't exercise it. But there are a dozen cases since 1932 where the Court has stayed out of this problem." Clark also pointed out that Baker had "failed to show [he] had exhausted other avenues to relief"—a point that was to be the one on which the Texan's ultimate vote in the case was to turn. Clark added that what really was at stake here, at least in the South, was the white control of the power structure.

Justice Whittaker again voted as he had at the April 1961 conference, saying that, though he disagreed with the Frankfurter view on jurisdiction, he was not prepared to vote that way, with the Court so closely divided. That made the vote once again four-to-four and left the matter up to Justice Stewart, who, as the junior Justice, spoke last.

Justice Stewart started by telling how he thought, as Justice Brennan had stated, that this case presented a malapportionment so extreme it could not have a rational basis. In such a situation, Stewart declared, "the district court did have jurisdiction." Stewart thought the case did not involve "a so-called 'political question,' in the sense of a question which the Constitution precluded" the courts from answering. Nor, in his view, did the case raise "a republican form of government issue." Since he thought the district court had jurisdiction, Stewart said he would vote to reverse. That made the conference vote five-to-four for reversal.

However, Justice Stewart went out of his way to emphasize that he would agree only to decide that the district court had jurisdiction. "I can't say," he said, "whether we can or can't frame appropriate relief. On the merits, I couldn't say that equal protection requires representation approximately commensurate with voting strength. So the state doesn't have to justify every departure from a one-man vote basis."

Baker v. Carr directly illustrates the importance of the Chief Justice's opinion assigning power, as well as the crucial role of Justice Brennan in the Court. Chief Justice Warren devoted much effort to the question of the opinion assignment. He considered Justices Black and Douglas, because they had dissented in *Colegrove v. Green* and had consistently expressed disagreement with that case. But assigning the opinion to either of them might have lost Justice Stewart's vote and the Chief Justice soon decided that the assignment had to go to either Justice Brennan or Justice Stewart. This was the kind of close case where the Chief Justice would often turn to Brennan. In addition, Justice Douglas had indicated to him that he would be unable to join a Stewart opinion. Chief Justice Warren conferred repeatedly on the matter, particularly with Justices Black and Douglas. Then, two weeks after the conference, the Chief Justice came to see Justice Brennan early in the morning, and assigned the opinion to him.

We are, however, interested in *Baker v. Carr* here because it dramatically illustrates the "might have been" in Supreme Court jurisprudence. Justices Black, Douglas, and Brennan, with Chief Justice Warren's support, wanted to go beyond the jurisdictional issue. They also wanted to decide the merits and hold that the Tennessee apportionment law violated the Equal Protection Clause. Their view was that, as Justice Frankfurter summarized it in a letter to Justice Stewart, "the Fourteenth Amendment . . . requires what Hugo called 'approximately fair' distribution or weight in votes."

Justice Stewart, however, would vote for reversal only if the decision was limited to the holding that the district court had jurisdiction to entertain Baker's complaint. Since Justice Stewart's vote was then necessary for the bare majority in favor of reversal, the Chief Justice and the other three agreed that Justice Brennan would limit his draft opinion to the jurisdictional issue.

Justice Brennan's draft *Baker v. Carr* opinion was circulated at the end of January, 1962. A few minutes after he received his copy, Justice Frankfurter dropped into Justice Clark's chambers to announce, "They've done just as I expected." Frankfurter told Clark that he was circulating his dissent without delay. He did so the next day.

After he read it, Justice Clark wrote to Justice Frankfurter, "Your dissent is unanswerable, except by ukase." Clark also wrote, "As you suggested by telephone, I will prepare something on failure to exhaust other remedies."

On the same day, Justice Clark wrote to the others that he was going to have to delay the decision because he was going to write something in dissent in addition to Justice Frankfurter's opinion. Since Justice Clark, the Chief Justice, and Justice Brennan were leaving for ten days to attend a judicial conference in Puerto Rico, this meant that the decision would not be announced for some weeks. "We leave for 'sunnier' climes . . . ," Justice Clark wrote, in his letter, "so I shall have to set the task aside until I return. In light of the waiting period Tennessee has already experienced I hope my delay will not too long deprive it of a constitutional form of government, *i.e.,* control by the 'city slickers.' "

After the Chief Justice and Justices Clark and Brennan returned from Puerto Rico, there was a wait of three weeks while Justice Clark worked on his expected dissent. It was generally thought that Clark would say that Baker had not exhausted his other remedies. Instead, Justice Clark surprised everyone by changing his vote.

On March 7, Clark wrote to Justice Frankfurter: "Preparatory to writing my dissent in this case, along the line you suggested of pointing out the avenues that were open for voters of Tennessee to bring about reapportionment despite Its Assembly, I have carefully checked into the record. I am sorry to say that I cannot find any practical course that the people could take in bringing this about except through the Federal courts." Therefore, Clark wrote, "I am sorry to say that I shall have to ask you to permit me to withdraw from your dissent."

The day before, Justice Clark had sent to Justice Brennan a typed copy of an opinion "concurring in part and dissenting in part." It concluded: "My difference with the majority, therefore, narrows down to this: I would decide the case on the merits. Instead of remanding it for the District Court to determine the merits and fashion the relief, I would do that here. There is not need to delay the merits of the case any further."

After he received the Clark draft, Justice Brennan conferred with the Texan. He persuaded Justice Clark to issue his opinion only as a concurrence. As issued, however, Clark's concurrence did state that he would have invalidated the Tennessee apportionment law on the merits. Clark had tried to persuade Brennan to change his opinion to strike down the Tennessee law. Brennan had refused, saying that he had given an undertaking to Justice Stewart that he would not do so.

Needless to say, Justice Clark's switch brought jubilation to the majority Justices. When the Chief Justice received Clark's concurring opinion, he called

Justice Brennan at home. During the first minutes of the call, Warren just laughed with joy. When he was able to get down to serious discussion, the Chief Justice said that, in spite of the fact that Justice Stewart was no longer indispensable, he also believed that the majority opinion should not be changed unless Stewart agreed. The next day, Justice Stewart indicated to Justice Brennan that he would not agree to any changes of importance. In a memorandum to Chief Justice Warren and Justices Black and Douglas, Justice Brennan informed them that he and Justice Stewart had discussed the changes requested by Justice Clark. "Potter felt that if they were made it would be necessary for him to dissent from that much of the revised opinion. I therefore decided it was best not to press for the changes."

When Justice Brennan announced the decision, the opinion of the Court was substantially that which Justice Stewart had joined before Justice Clark changed his vote. While the opinions were being read, the Chief Justice wrote a note to Brennan. As originally written, it read, "It is a great day for the Irish." Before passing the note, Warren crossed out "Irish" and substituted "country."

If Justice Clark had switched his vote earlier and been with the majority at the postreargument conference, that would have made for a majority without Justice Stewart's vote. That majority would have voted not only to exercise jurisdiction but also to decide the merits of the challenge to the apportionment law.

If that had happened, it would have meant a different rule of equality in apportionments than that ultimately enunciated in *Reynolds v. Sims,* as discussed in Chapter 4. At the time of *Baker v. Carr,* those who favored the requirement of what Justice Black called "approximately fair" weight in votes were willing to apply that requirement to only one house of the legislature. Chief Justice Warren, in particular, was swayed by the situation in California where only the Assembly was apportioned by population, while the Senate represented counties equally, regardless of population.

Thus, if the merits had been decided in *Baker v. Carr,* the Court would have held that only lower-house apportionments not based upon equality of population were invalid. They would have upheld unequal apportionments, based for example upon geographical areas such as counties, for the upper houses of state legislatures. This would have made for a substantial difference in apportionment law and, through it, the distribution of political power in state legislatures. Instead of the transfer of power to urban and suburban areas that has occurred under the *Reynolds v. Sims* one-person–one-vote rule, there would still be ample room for rural dominance of state senates. The *Reynolds v. Sims* political death warrant for countless rural legislators, whose seats have been reapportioned out of existence, would never have been issued. In the hunting trip with state senators referred to at the end of the Chapter 4 *Reynolds v. Sims* discussion, Chief Justice Warren would not have had to worry, "All those *senators?* With *guns?*"

NEAR MISSES

According to the famous epigram, "God looks after fools, drunkards, and the United States" — and, one is tempted to add, the U.S. Supreme Court. One who has access to what goes on behind the Court's red velour curtain is struck by the cases in which the cooperative decision process has saved the Court from legal blunders it was about to commit. In recent Courts, that has been true even in some of the most significant decided cases. The outstanding example of such a case in the Warren Court was *Bolling v. Sharpe* — a companion case to *Brown v. Board of Education,* the most important case decided during the Warren tenure, if not during the entire century.

The *Brown* case itself was one of several cases challenging school segregation that had come to the Supreme Court during the 1952 Term. The cases involved schools in four states and the District of Columbia. As seen in Chapter 4, the first draft of the *Brown* opinion was written by Chief Justice Warren himself. The original manuscript, in pencil in Warren's writing on nine yellow legal-size pages, is in the Warren papers at the Library of Congress. In the draft the four state segregation cases and that from the District of Columbia were dealt with together. This was shown by the draft's opening sentence: "These cases come to us from the States of Delaware, Virginia, Kansas and South Carolina and from the District of Columbia." The Warren draft went on to say that, though they were separate cases, "the basic law involved in their decision is identical to the point that they can on principle properly be considered together in this opinion."

In treating the state and D.C. cases together, the Warren draft was making a legal mistake. The rationale for striking down segregation in the states cannot be used to reach that result in Washington, D.C. The state action in *Brown* was invalidated under the Equal Protection Clause of the Fourteenth Amendment. Yet that amendment is binding only on the states, not the Federal Government. The latter is bound by the Fifth Amendment, which contains a Due Process Clause, but no requirement of equal protection. Obviously, the Court would not decide that the states could not have segregated schools, while the District of Columbia could. But the result had to be reached by due process rather than equal protection analysis.

After he had finished his *Brown* draft and had it typed, Chief Justice Warren called in his three law clerks and told them that the decision in *Brown* was to strike down segregation, and that the decision was unanimous. He enjoined them to the strictest secrecy, saying that he had not told anyone outside the Justices what the decision was — not even his wife. The Chief Justice asked all three clerks to write drafts based on his own draft opinion.

Following the example set in Warren's draft, the three law clerks dealt with the state and D.C. cases together in their drafts. However, in the covering memorandum to the Chief Justice attached to his draft, Earl Pollock, the clerk primarily responsible for helping on the *Brown* opinion, indicated that this was not the proper approach. Pollock stated that his draft was "along the lines of your memo of last week. Like the memo, this draft covers all five cases in one consolidated opinion." Pollock then wrote, "I am inclined to think, however, that the District of Columbia case should be treated independently in a short, separate opinion accompanying the other one. . . . The material relating to the equal protection clause of the 14th Amendment has no direct relevance to the District of Columbia case, which, of course, is based primarily on the due process clause of the 5th Amendment."

"In short," the Pollock memo concluded, "the legal problem in the states and the legal problem in the District are different and require somewhat different treatment. For the sake of clarity, a short, separate opinion in the District case is recommended."

Chief Justice Warren accepted this suggestion, and the details of the legal theory underlying the D.C. case were worked out by the other two Warren clerks, William Oliver and Richard Flynn. They also drafted the separate short opinion delivered in the case. It held that racial discrimination could be so arbitrary that it constituted a denial of due process, and that was true of school segregation in the nation's capital.

One shudders at what might have happened had the original Warren approach treating the state and D.C. cases similarly been followed in the final *Brown* opinion. The landmark decision would have suffered from a crucial legal defect and the Court's error would quickly have been spotted by the press and the public. Imagine the field day that the critics of *Brown* would have had if the Court had ruled that D.C. segregation, like that in the states, had violated the Equal Protection Clause, which is binding only upon the states, not the Federal Government. At a 1956 Senate hearing, Senator Joseph R. McCarthy of Wisconsin complained (quite unfairly in view of Warren's extensive legal experience as a district attorney and state attorney general), "We made a mistake in confirming as Chief Justice a man who had no judicial experience and very little legal experience." Think of what the Senator could have said if the blunder in the original *Brown* draft had not been corrected.

In the Burger Court, an important near miss occurred in *Goldwater v. Carter* (1979). Nine senators and sixteen members of the House sought declaratory and injunctive relief against President Carter after he announced that he was going to terminate the mutual defense treaty with the Republic of China (Taiwan). The President had recognized the Peking government as the legal government of China. At the same time, he gave Taiwan the one-year notice that the termination clause of the treaty required.

A majority at the *Goldwater v. Carter* conference in December 1979 agreed that the complaint should be dismissed. Chief Justice Burger and Justice Stevens thought that there was no standing—that is, the plaintiffs did not show that they were personally injured by the treaty termination; Justice Powell urged that the case was not ripe for review; Justice Rehnquist argued that the case presented a "political question" not subject to judicial review. Justice

Stewart also said that "the case is nonjusticiable." In addition, Justice Brennan would have decided in favor of the President under his authority to recognize foreign governments, while Justices Blackmun and White would have set the case for oral argument and full consideration.

The consensus among the conference majority was to issue an order stating the holding of the Court in skeleton fashion and remanding for dismissal. After the conference, the Chief Justice and Justice Stevens circulated a proposed order. It was summarized in a "Dear Chief" letter the next day by Justice Powell: "The order as now drafted holds that the petitioners have no standing. This theory reflects the Wright-Tamm concurrence [in the lower court] which stated that a congressman is not injured unless Congress is injured, and that Congress is not injured unless its will has been ignored."

Had the proposed order been issued, it would have constituted another judicial blunder, since it was contrary to the leading case on the subject. This was pointed out a few days later in a Rehnquist Memorandum to the Conference. In it Justice Rehnquist stated that, "as I read the case of *Coleman v. Miller,* 307 U.S. 433 (1939), five out of the nine Justices who participated in that case thought that the 20 Kansas state senators who voted against ratification of the Child Labor Amendment had standing in this Court sufficient for Article III case or controversy purposes to question the ratification by Kansas of that amendment."

Now the Burger-Stevens draft order contained a contrary holding—and without any supporting reasoning or citation of authority. Such an order, Justice Rehnquist wrote, troubled him. "It seems to me that a per curiam of this sort which not only does not cite the authorities upon which it relies for reversal, but seems (at least to me) to run counter to an authority of this Court which has never been overruled, might be thought to give the appearance of 'brute force' and would surely be subject to very valid criticism."

At the conference on the case, several Justices had referred to the "political question" issue. The Rehnquist memo now proposed decision on that ground. "I would simply invert the language of the proposed per curiam, and assume that there is standing but hold that the issue decided by the Court of Appeals and by the District Court is a 'political' question. . . . at least in the field of foreign affairs, the authority of the President to act is a 'political' or 'non-justiciable' question, and Art. III courts are not empowered to pass judgment on it."

The approach Justice Rehnquist suggested was adopted by the Court. *Goldwater v. Carter* thus stands for the proposition that termination of a treaty presents a nonjusticiable political question. Had the Rehnquist memo not pointed out the manifest error in the Court's proposed order on standing, the order might well have been issued—inconsistent though it was with the leading case on the subject and without any explanation of why that case had been ignored. In his letter to the Chief Justice, Justice Powell, if anything, understated the effect of the proposed order when he wrote, "But with no explanation, a flat holding here on standing could create trouble for the future." Such a holding would, as indicated, have been a judicial error that, in the words of the Rehnquist memo, at the least "would surely be subject to very valid criticism."

Still another near miss occurred in *New York Times Co. v. Sullivan* (1964), one of the most important cases decided by the Warren Court. In Chapter 7, we saw how Justice Brennan led the Court in that case to rule that a libel action by a public official against a critic of his official conduct could not be sustained without a showing that the critic's statement was not merely false and defamatory, but "was made with 'actual malice' — that is, with knowledge that it was false or reckless disregard of whether it was false or not."

Justice Brennan's draft opinion reversed the libel judgment in the case and held in Part III that "a new trial under the correct rule would not be warranted in this case since the evidence submitted was insufficient to establish actual malice." The draft then analyzed the evidence to demonstrate that insufficiency. Justice Harlan sent Justice Brennan a letter which stated, "While I agree that there should not be a new trial, I would not feel able to join Part III of your opinion as presently written without writing something in addition by way of elaboration."

Justice Harlan offered a proposed revision of Part III that dealt specifically with the question "whether we should leave the way open for a new trial or should terminate this litigation." It urged the latter course, relying on 28 U.S.C. § 2106, which authorizes a federal appellate court to "direct the entry of such appropriate judgment, decree, or order . . . as may be just under the circumstances." Harlan analyzed the evidence presented and found it insufficient to show malice or defamation of plaintiff. His draft then stated that no new trial would be warranted "on the basis that respondent would be afforded an opportunity to adduce further and sufficient evidence."

The reasons given by Justice Harlan were that the question of whether the advertisement that had allegedly defamed plaintiff really referred to him had been a hotly contested issue at the trial and "we may reasonably assume therefore that he had no evidence of different and more substantial quality to offer," and, as to the malice requirement, that Alabama law required evidence of malice to establish punitive damages, and plaintiff accordingly had tried to prove malice, and had failed. Thus the draft concluded, "the reasons favoring a retrial are unreal," and none could be had.

Though Justice Brennan was not satisfied that the Harlan approach was preferable, he thought that he needed the support of the Justice and those who might follow him. Hence the Harlan revision was substantially incorporated in Part III of a later draft of Justice Brennan's opinion.

However, it was not realized that there were major difficulties in the Harlan approach. Section 2106 of the Judicial Code had never been applied to a case from a state court, and its application to prevent the Alabama courts from allowing a new trial might exceed the constitutional limits of the Supreme Court's appellate jurisdiction. This was pointed out in a note from Justice Black to Justice Brennan. "I do not see," wrote Black, "how John could possibly adhere to that position on more mature reflection. I can think of few things that would more violently clash with his ideas of 'federalism'. . . . Construing the statute as authorizing our Court to *overrule* state laws as to a right to a new trial would undoubtedly raise constitutional questions, some of which I recall were discussed in the famous *cause célèbre, Cohens v. Virginia*" — a famous 1821 decision of the Marshall Court.

Because of the Black letter, Justice Brennan removed the portions of Part III that had been based upon the Harlan revision. Instead, his final opinion eliminated the statements barring a new trial and said instead only that the proof presented was constitutionally insufficient. Once again the Court had been saved from an error that would have exposed it to strong criticism. Once again also, it was a near miss; had Justice Black not caught the error, it would probably have remained an important part of the Brennan opinion, contrary though it was to the established principles governing Supreme Court appellate jurisdiction.

NEAR MISS ON ABORTION

Perhaps the most important case in which the Court was saved from a judicial blunder was *Roe v. Wade* (1973) — probably the most controversial Supreme Court decision during the last half century. Few decisions ever handed down were more bitterly attacked. "It is hard to think of any decision in the two hundred years of our history," declared Cardinal Krol, the president of the National Conference of Catholic Bishops, "which has had more disastrous implications for our stability as a civilized society." Condemnatory letters were sent to the Justices in unprecedented volume, particularly to Justice Blackmun, the author of the opinion. Even today, says Blackmun, so many years after the decision, antiabortion pickets continue to show up at his speeches.

Justice Blackmun himself has termed *Roe v. Wade* "a landmark in the progress of the emancipation of women." But that could hardly have been said had Justice Blackmun's original draft come down as the opinion of the Court. That draft did not go nearly as far as the final opinion. On the contrary, although the draft did strike down the abortion statute before the Court, it did so on the ground of vagueness and not because it restricted a woman's right to have an abortion. The draft expressly avoided the issue of the state's substantive right to prohibit abortions or "imply that a State has no legitimate interest in the subject of abortions or that abortion procedures may not be subject to control by the state."

Had the original Blackmun draft come down as the Court opinion, the case would not have dealt with the constitutional merits of state abortion prohibitions, but would have been only a narrow decision striking down a state law for vagueness. The subsequent schism that has been a major factor in American life might have been postponed or avoided — or possibly mitigated by its relegation to political rather than legal resolution. More than that, however, the vagueness ground upon which the Blackmun draft was based was so weak, legally speaking, that it would have subjected the Court to severe criticism for dealing so ineffectively with so controversial an issue.

Roe v. Wade itself was as activist a decision as any rendered during this century. During the conference on the 1965 *Griswold* right of privacy case discussed in Chapter 7, Chief Justice Warren had stated that he could not say that the state had no legitimate interest, noting that that could apply to abortion laws—implying that he thought that such laws were valid. Those who expected the Burger Court to be less activist than its predecessor relied upon false hopes. It was under Chief Justice Burger that the right of privacy was extended to include the right to an abortion. As a Burger Memorandum to the Conference put it, "This is as sensitive and difficult an issue as any in this Court in my time."

At issue in *Roe* were Texas statutes that prohibited abortions except to save the mother's life. As characterized by the final *Roe v. Wade* opinion, "The Texas statutes under attack here are typical of those that have been in effect in many States for approximately a century." A pregnant woman sought a judgment that the Texas laws were unconstitutional. At the postargument conference in December 1971, Chief Justice Burger said, "The balance here is between the state's interest in protecting fetal life and the woman's interest in not having children." In weighing these interests, the Chief Justice concluded, "I can't find the Texas statute unconstitutional, although it's certainly archaic and obsolete."

Justice Douglas, who spoke next, declared categorically, "The abortion statute is unconstitutional. This is basically a medical and psychiatric problem"—and not one to be dealt with by prohibitory legislation. Douglas also criticized the statute's failure to give "a licensed physician an immunity for good faith abortions." Justice Brennan, who followed, stressed even more strongly the right to an abortion, which should be given a constitutional basis by the Court's decision. The *Roe* statute, he urged, was clearly invalid; it did not even allow an abortion for a twelve-year-old or a woman who had been raped.

Justice Stewart, next in order of seniority, stated, "I agree with Bill Douglas." He did, however, indicate that there might be some state power. "The state can legislate, to the extent of requiring a doctor and that, after a certain period of pregnancy, [she] can't have an abortion."

Justice White said, "On the merits I am on the other side. They want us to say that women have a choice under the Ninth Amendment." White said that he refused to accept this "privacy argument." Justice Marshall, on the other hand, declared, "I go with Bill Douglas, but the time problem concerns me." He thought that the state could not prevent abortions "in the early stage [of pregnancy]. But why can't the state prohibit after a certain stage?" In addition, Marshall said that he would use " 'liberty' under the Fourteenth Amendment as the constitutional base," since " 'liberty' covers about any right to have things done to your body."

Justice Blackmun, then the junior Justice, spoke last. Blackmun displayed an ambivalence that was to be reflected in his draft *Roe v. Wade* opinion. "Can a state properly outlaw all abortions? If we accept fetal life, there's a strong argument that it can. But there are opposing interests: the right of the mother to life and mental and physical health, the right of parents in case of rape, the right of the state in case of incest. I don't think there's an absolute right to do what you will with [your] body." Blackmun did, however, say flatly, "This statute is a poor statute that . . . impinges too far on her."

The conference outcome was not entirely clear because the tally sheets of different Justices do not coincide on the votes. What was clear, however, was that a majority was in favor of invalidating the statute: five (Justices Douglas, Brennan, Stewart, Marshall, and Blackmun) to two (the Chief Justice and Justice White) in the tally sheet made available to me — but four to three (with Justice Blackmun added to the dissenters) according to a Douglas "Dear Chief" letter to Burger. Despite the fact that he was not part of the majority, the Chief Justice assigned the opinion to Justice Blackmun.

Roe v. Wade now depended upon the draft opinion being prepared by Justice Blackmun. In a letter to Justice Douglas, Justice Brennan had written, "I appreciate that some time may pass before we hear from Harry." Justice Blackmun was known as the slowest worker on the Court. The abortion case was his first major assignment, and he worked at it during the next few months, mostly alone and unassisted in the Court library; he was still working on his draft as the Court term wore on. It was mid-May 1972 before he felt able to circulate anything. Finally, on May 18, 1972, Justice Blackmun sent around his draft *Roe v. Wade* opinion. "Herewith," began the covering memo, "is a first and tentative draft for this case. . . . [I]t may be somewhat difficult to obtain a consensus on all aspects. My notes indicate, however, that we were generally in agreement to affirm on the merits. That is where I come out on the theory that the Texas statute, despite its narrowness, is unconstitutionally vague.

"I think that this would be all that is necessary for disposition of the case, and that we need not get into the more complex Ninth Amendment issue. This may or may not appeal to you. . . . I am still flexible as to results, and I shall do my best to arrive at something which would command a court."

There was, however, a serious legal difficulty in the Blackmun draft's holding that the Texas abortion law was unconstitutionally vague. In *United States v. Vuitch,* decided only the year before, the Court had upheld a similar District of Columbia abortion law against a vagueness attack. The Blackmun draft distinguished *Vuitch* on the ground that the statute there prohibited abortion unless "necessary for the preservation of the mother's life or health," while the Texas statute only permitted abortions "for the purpose of saving the life of the mother." Thus *Vuitch* "provides no answer to the constitutional challenge to the Texas statute."

In the Texas statute, the Blackmun draft noted, "Saving the mother's life is the sole standard." According to the draft, this standard is too vague to guide a physician's conduct in abortion cases. "Does it mean that he may procure an abortion only when, without it, the patient will surely die? Or only when the odds are greater than even that she will die? Or when there is a mere possibility that she will not survive?"

After posing other questions which, in Justice Blackmun's view, were not definitely answered, the draft reached its conclusion: "We conclude that Art. 1196, with its sole criterion for exemption as 'saving the life of the mother,' is insufficiently informative to the physician to whom it purports to afford a measure of professional protection but who must measure its indefinite meaning at the risk of his liberty, and that the statute cannot withstand constitutional challenge on vagueness grounds."

In his *Liberty and Sexuality,* David J. Garrow called the Blackmun *Roe* draft "an almost wholly unremarkable document." More than that, Justice Blackmun's vagueness analysis was extremely weak. If anything, the "life saving" standard in the *Roe v. Wade* statute was more definite than the "health" standard upheld in *Vuitch.* But the draft's disposition of the case on vagueness enabled it to avoid the basic constitutional question. As the Blackmun draft stated, "There is no need in Roe's case to pass on her contention that under the Ninth Amendment a pregnant woman has an absolute right to an abortion, or even to consider the opposing rights of the embryo or fetus during the respective prenatal trimesters."

Indeed, so far as the draft contained intimations on the matter, they tended to support state substantive power over abortions. "Our holding today," the draft noted, "does not imply that a State has no legitimate interest in the subject of abortions or that abortion procedures may not be subjected to control by the State." On the contrary, "We do not accept the argument of the appellants and of some of the amici that a pregnant woman has an unlimited right to do with her body as she pleases. The long acceptance of statutes regulating the possession of certain drugs and other harmful substances, and making criminal indecent exposure in public, or an attempt at suicide, clearly indicate the contrary." This was, of course, completely different from the approach ultimately followed in the *Roe v. Wade* opinion of the Court.

Had the Blackmun draft come down as the final *Roe v. Wade* opinion, the last twenty years in American life and politics might have been quite different. Instead of the flat prohibition against state interferences with the right to abortion, there would have been only a weak decision that implied that the states did possess substantive authority over abortions. In addition, the Blackmun vagueness holding itself was plainly inconsistent with the *Vuitch* decision only a year earlier. The draft made no effort to overrule *Vuitch,* but only an ineffective effort to distinguish it.

The patent inadequacy of the Blackmun vagueness holding was made clear to the Justices when Justice White circulated a three-page draft dissent that effectively demonstrated the weakness of the Blackmun approach. Referring to the *Vuitch* decision that a statute that permitted abortion on "health" grounds was not unconstitutionally vague, the White draft declared, "If a standard which refers to the 'health' of the mother, a referent which necessarily entails the resolution of perplexing questions about the interrelationship of physical, emotional, and mental well-being, is not impermissibly vague, a statutory standard which focuses only on 'saving the life' of the mother would appear to be a fortiori acceptable. . . . [T]he relevant factors in the latter situation are less numerous and are primarily physiological."

Despite the weakness of the Blackmun draft, it was supported by the Justices who favored striking down the abortion law. The conference minority Justices who had voted to uphold the Texas statute now sought to delay — and perhaps reverse — the abortion decision. *Roe* had come before a seven-Justice Court. The two vacancies were not filled until Justices Powell and Rehnquist took their seats in January 1972. After the Blackmun drafts were circulated in May, the Chief Justice led an effort to secure a reargument in the case, arguing that the decision in such an important case should be made by a full Court.

The Burger move to secure reargument was opposed by the Justices who favored striking down the abortion laws. They feared that the two new Justices would vote for the laws. In addition, the White draft dissent might lead another Justice to withdraw his support from the Blackmun *Roe* draft — maybe even Blackmun himself, whose position had been none too firm. The view of the conference majority was expressed in a Brennan letter to Justice Blackmun: "I see no reason to put these cases over for reargument. I say that since, as I understand it, there are five of us (Bill Douglas, Potter, Thurgood, you and I) in substantial agreement with [the opinion] and in that circumstance I question that reargument would change things."

The White draft dissent had, however, given the coup de grace to the Blackmun *Roe* draft. It convinced Justice Blackmun himself that his draft was inadequate and that the decision should be postponed. At the end of May 1972, Blackmun circulated a Memorandum to the Conference: "Although it would prove costly to me personally, in the light of energy and hours expended, I have now concluded, somewhat reluctantly, that reargument in *both* cases at an early date in the next term, would perhaps be advisable. . . . I believe, on an issue so sensitive and so emotional as this one, the country deserves the conclusion of a nine-man, not a seven-man court, whatever the ultimate decision may be."

Justice Douglas replied in a letter to Blackmun, "I feel quite strongly that [the case] should not be reargued." Instead, wrote Douglas, "it is important to announce the [decision], and let the result be known so that the legislatures can go to work and draft their new laws."

The next day, June 1, an angry Douglas wrote to the Chief Justice, "If the vote of the Conference is to reargue, then I will file a statement telling what is happening to us and the tragedy it entails."

Despite the Douglas threat, the Justices did vote to have *Roe v. Wade* reargued. The decisive votes were cast by the two new Justices — Powell and

Rehnquist—who joined the Chief Justice and Justices White and Blackmun in voting for the reargument.

Justice Douglas then prepared a draft dissent that was largely a diatribe against Chief Justice Burger. It began: "I dissent from the order putting these cases down for reargument." It then pointed out that *Vuitch,* an equally troublesome abortion case, had been decided in three months, while six months had now gone by since the *Roe* argument. The draft then repeated the language, already quoted on page 46, objecting to the Burger assignment of the opinion even though the Chief Justice had been in the *Roe* minority—including the assertion that because of the Burger "control [of] the assignment, there is a destructive force at work in the Court. When a Chief Justice tries to bend the Court to his will by manipulating assignments, the integrity of the institution is imperilled."

The Douglas draft dissent then asserted, "Perhaps the purpose of The Chief Justice, a member of the minority in the *Abortion Cases,* in assigning the opinions was to try to keep control of the merits." Nevertheless, the draft went on, an opinion striking down the abortion law had "been circulated and each commands the votes of five members of the Court. Those votes are firm. . . . The cases should therefore be announced."

According to the Douglas draft, "The plea that the cases be reargued is merely strategy by a minority somehow to suppress the majority view with the hope that exigencies of time will change the result. . . . But that kind of strategy dilutes the integrity of the Court and makes the decisions here depend on the manipulative skills of a Chief Justice."

"This is an election year," the draft pointed out, and abortion had been made a political issue. "We sit here," Douglas wrote, "not to make the path of any candidate easier or more difficult." The implication was that the Burger effort to secure reargument was an attempt to aid the Republican campaign effort. Indeed, the draft asserted, "To prolong these *Abortion Cases* into the next election would in the eyes of many be a political gesture unworthy of the Court."

A direct attack on the Chief Justice followed: "Each of us is sovereign in his own right. Each arrived on his own. Each is beholden to no one. Russia once gave its Chief Justice two votes; but that was too strong even for the Russians."

The draft dissent again referred to the fact that "Five members of the Court have agreed on a disposition of the [case]." Therefore, the decision "should come down forthwith."

"I dissent," the Douglas draft concluded, "with the deepest regret that we are allowing the consensus of the Court to be frustrated."

Such a bitter dissent, with its acid attack upon the Chief Justice, had never been issued in the history of the Court. It could not but have a baneful effect upon the Court's reputation. Justice Brennan particularly was disturbed about the impact of such a public outburst. He pleaded with Douglas not to issue the draft. Though Douglas at first resisted, he eventually gave in and withdrew the dissent. When the Court announced the order setting *Roe* for reargument, there was added only the simple statement, "Mr. Justice Douglas dissents."

As it turned out, however, Justice Douglas and the others who favored invalidating the abortion laws secured the advantage from the reargument. Chief Justice Burger had hoped to gain the votes of the two new Justices and then persuade Justice Blackmun himself to switch. Instead, he got a split vote from the new Justices and a vastly stronger *Roe* opinion.

The abortion case was reargued in October 1972. At the conference, the Justices who had participated in the earlier conference took the same positions as before. The two new Justices took opposing positions. Justice Powell said that he was "basically in accord with Harry's position," while Justice Rehnquist stated, "I agree with Byron [White]" — who had declared, "I'm not going to second guess state legislatures in striking the balance in favor of abortion laws."

Justice Blackmun told the conference, "I am where I was last Spring." However, he made a much firmer statement this time in favor of invalidating the abortion laws. Most important of all, Justice Blackmun announced to the conference, "I've revised . . . the [opinion] of the last term." During the summer, Blackmun had devoted his time to the abortion opinion and had completely rewritten it. On November 21, he circulated a completely revised draft of his *Roe v. Wade* opinion. "Herewith," began the covering memo, "is a memorandum (1972 fall edition) on the Texas abortion case."

Justice Blackmun's second *Roe* draft expressly abandoned the vagueness holding on which his first draft had turned. The holding on the constitutional merits, the new draft states, "makes it unnecessary for us to consider the attack made on the Texas statute on grounds of vagueness."

The new Blackmun draft contained the essentials of the final *Roo v. Wade* opinion. Now there was a flat ruling that the Texas abortion law violated the constitutional right of privacy. The new draft also adopted the time approach followed in the final opinion. However, it used the first trimester of pregnancy alone as the line between invalid and valid state power. The draft stated that, before the end of the first trimester, the state "must do no more than to leave the abortion decision to the best medical judgment of the pregnant woman's attending physician."

Later drafts refined this two-pronged time test to the tripartite approach followed in the final *Roe* opinion. This led to a criticism in a "Dear Harry" letter from Justice Stewart: "One of my concerns with your opinion as presently written is the specificity of its dictum — particularly in its fixing of the end of the first trimester as the critical point for valid state action. I appreciate the inevitability and indeed wisdom of dicta in the Court's opinion, but I wonder about the desirability of the dicta being quite so inflexibly 'legislative.' "

This has, of course, been the common criticism that has since been directed at *Roe v. Wade* — that the high bench was acting like a legislature; its drawing of lines at trimesters and viability was, in the Stewart letter's phrase, "to make policy judgments" that were more "legislative" than "judicial." Justice Stewart worked on a lengthy opinion giving voice to this criticism, but in a later letter he informed Blackmun that he had decided to discard it and "to file instead a brief monograph on substantive due process, joining your opinions."

According to Justice Blackmun's covering memorandum transmitting his second *Roe v. Wade* draft, "As I stated in conference, the decision, however made, will probably result in the Court's being severely criticized." Just before he circulated the final *Roe v. Wade* draft, Justice Blackmun sent around a Memorandum to the Conference, which began, "I anticipate the headlines . . . when the abortion decisions are announced." Because of this, the Justice was enclosing the announcement from the bench that he proposed to read when the two cases were made public. With this announcement, the memo expressed the hope that "there should be at least some reason for the press not going all the way off the deep end."

The Blackmun announcement did not, of course, have the calming effect for which its author hoped. On the contrary, the scare headlines and controversy were, if anything, far greater than anything anticipated by the Justice and his colleagues. All that would have been avoided had the original Blackmun *Roe v. Wade* draft come down as the final Court opinion. Instead of a cause célèbre, *Roe* might then have been a constitutional footnote used by law professors to illustrate how the Court can evade important legal issues.

But the case would also have been used to illustrate how the Court can base its decision upon a patent error of law. Commentators would surely have seized upon the White dissent (which its author would presumably have issued to counter the Blackmun vagueness opinion) to show how the Court had blundered in its vagueness holding. All this was avoided because the White dissent convinced Justice Blackmun that his draft's reasoning would not stand up and that he should back the motion for reargument—the motion strongly opposed by the proabortion Justices.

Yet, in one of those tricks legal history sometimes plays, it was Justice Douglas and the other proponents of invalidating the abortion laws who gained the most from the order for reargument. Had Douglas won his battle to prevent reargument, the original Blackmun draft would have remained the final *Roe* opinion.

For the antiabortion Justices, *Roe v. Wade* was, indeed, a near miss. Had they succeeded in their effort to prevent reargument, they would have gotten a decision so weak that it would only have sent the legislatures scurrying to enact new abortion laws. Their loss of the reargument battle enabled them to secure the vastly improved *Roe* opinion, with its broadside confirmation of the constitutional right to an abortion.

10

Civil Rights and
Other Rehnquist Court Switches

One who has read the first chapter realizes that the Rehnquist Court's decision process has been similar to that of its predecessors, as described in the last few chapters. Both the *Webster* and *Hodgson* cases discussed in Chapter 1 showed the Justices as "nine little law firms" — each having its own approach to the issues presented. They come together to discuss and vote; their vote, however, is anything but etched in gold. Both *Webster* and *Hodgson* (and the survival of *Roe* in consequence) were determined by vote switches that prevented putative opinions of the Court from coming down as such. Outsiders may not realize it, but the *Webster* and *Hodgson* decision process was as typical of the Rehnquist Court as it was of other Courts. In addition, the inability of the Chief Justice to work his will on overruling *Roe* was not that unusual either in the Rehnquist Court or to one familiar with what happened during the decision process in earlier Courts.

REHNQUIST AND CIVIL RIGHTS LAWS

Among the most controversial Rehnquist Court decisions have been those dealing with civil rights. Not coincidentally, it was a dispute over his civil-rights stance that was the chief obstacle to Justice Rehnquist's confirmation as Chief Justice. After he had graduated from Stanford Law School, Rehnquist served as a Supreme Court clerk to Justice Robert H. Jackson. Rehnquist wrote a memo on the *Brown* segregation case, urging that the separate-but-equal doctrine, under which segregation had been upheld, was "right and should be affirmed."

The memo became an important factor in the Senate confirmation hearings on the nominations of Rehnquist, first to the Supreme Court and then as Chief Justice. Rehnquist maintained that the memo "was prepared by me at Justice

Jackson's request; it was intended as a rough draft of a statement of *his* views at the conference of the justices, rather than as a statement of my views." Rehnquist's version is inconsistent with a draft concurrence in the Jackson papers in the Library of Congress that Justice Jackson prepared but never issued in *Brown*. In it, Jackson declared categorically, "I am convinced that present-day conditions require us to strike from our books the doctrine of separate-but-equal facilities and to hold invalid provisions of state constitutions or statutes which classify persons for separate treatment in matters of education based solely on possession of colored blood." Would Jackson have written this if he had held the view stated in the Rehnquist memo?

Justice Rehnquist stated in a 1985 *New York Times* interview that his views have probably changed and that he accepts *Brown* as the law of the land. But his votes in cases involving civil rights clearly place him in the right wing of the Court on civil rights issues.

What is not known outside the Marble Palace is that Chief Justice Rehnquist has urged even more extreme views within the Court than have appeared in his published opinions. A major part of contemporary civil-rights litigation has been based upon laws enacted during Reconstruction. Among them is an 1866 statute that provides, in its second section (now 42 U.S.C. §1982), "All citizens . . . shall have the same right, in every State and Territory, as is enjoyed by white citizens thereof to inherit, purchase, lease, sell, hold and convey real and personal property." In the 1968 case of *Jones v. Alfred H. Mayer Co.*, the Court held that section 1982 prohibits racial discrimination in the sale or rental of property. As such it forbids a private development company to refuse to sell a home to someone because he is black.

A 1976 case, *Runyon v. McCrary*, dealt with section 1 of the 1866 law (now 42 U.S.C. §1981). It provides that all persons "shall have the same right in every State and Territory to make and enforce contracts . . . as is enjoyed by white citizens." *Runyon* ruled that this statute prohibits racial discrimination in the making and enforcement of private contracts. The Court found that a private school's denial of admission on racial grounds violated the statute. The relationship the pupils' parents had sought to enter into was contractual in nature and by denying them the right to enter into the contracts, the school had discriminated contrary to the statute.

In the 1989 case of *Patterson v. McLean Credit Union*, the Court heard argument on "Whether or not the interpretation of §1981 in *Runyon v. McCrary* . . . should be reconsidered." At the postargument conference, Chief Justice Rehnquist declared that *Runyon* was wrong and that Justice White was correct in his dissent in that case. Therefore, he urged, the Court should overrule *Runyon*.

The Chief Justice did not, however, stop with his recommendation to overrule *Runyon*. He also told the *Patterson* conference that the Court should overrule *Jones v. Alfred H. Mayer Co.* as well. The Rehnquist position in this respect was not a new one, though it was unknown outside the Court. The

Chief Justice had written an April 7, 1987, letter to Justice White on a 1987 case involving section 1981 in which he stated, "I once again question the soundness of our opinion in Jones v. Alfred H. Mayer Co., . . . which held that this class was protected not merely against state action but against action by other private individuals."

Justice Powell sent a letter two days later to Justice White, stating, "I . . . share the reservation expressed by the Chief Justice in his join note of April 7. In retrospect, I think our cases following Jones v. Alfred H. Mayer Co., . . . misconstrued 1981 and 1982." Justice O'Connor also wrote to Justice White that she "shared [the] reservations about the Court's construction" of the 1866 law.

After these 1987 notes were circulated, Justice Blackmun, who had authored the lower court opinion in the *Jones* case, wrote to Justice White: "I am somewhat amused at the exchanges in the correspondence concerning Jones v. Alfred H. Mayer Co. . . . My amusement is due to my personal involvement in the case. If one just hangs on long enough, he may see almost anything happen."

CIVIL RIGHTS AND STARE DECISIS

Despite the last Blackmun comment, what did not happen was the overruling of either *Jones* or *Runyon*. *Jones* itself was not questioned in any published opinion, and, in *Patterson v. McLean Credit Union*, the Court expressly refused to overrule *Runyon v. McCrary*. In *Patterson*, even the Justices who agreed with the Rehnquist view that *Runyon* had been wrongly decided refused to go along with the Chief Justice and overrule that case. Their view was that stated a few years earlier by Justice Powell in his quoted April 9, 1987, letter: "if the 'slate were clean' I would be inclined to agree with your view." The Powell letter "went on to say, however, that it was 'too late' to reexamine the prior precedents. John . . . also stated that he thought these precedents were 'incorrectly decided,' but he concluded that it would be inadvisable to overrule Jones and its progeny."

Perhaps the best statement of the reasons why *Jones* and *Runyon* should not be overruled is contained in the draft opinion of the Court prepared by Justice Brennan in the *Patterson* case. It is far more complete than the treatment of the subject in either the ultimate opinion of the Court or the final Brennan dissent in *Patterson*. It is a pity that it was never published, for it contains a discussion of stare decisis and the exceptions to its doctrine that merits comparison with the already-classic analysis of stare decisis in the joint opinion of Justices O'Connor, Kennedy, and Souter in the 1992 case of *Planned Parenthood v. Casey* (which, by the way, was the portion of the *Casey* opinion drafted by Justice Souter).

My summary of the Brennan draft on stare decisis will focus upon those portions not contained in the Justice's published *Patterson* dissent. The draft starts with a typical judicial encomium to stare decisis: "it serves important societal interests in fairness, stability, and predictability in the law . . . and in efficient judicial decisionmaking. Through adherence to *stare decisis*, 'we ensure that the law will not merely change erratically, but will develop in a principled and intelligible fashion.'"

Nevertheless, "we have identified circumstances in which we will recognize an exception to that doctrine." That is the case because "the alternative to a somewhat relaxed doctrine of *stare decisis* is stagnation, or at least an unsatisfactory resort to drawing ever finer lines of distinction." Stare decisis, however, remains the rule. "It remains . . . the heavy burden of a litigant urging that we overrule a precedent to demonstrate that it falls within the scope of [the] exceptions to *stare decisis*."

In *Patterson*, the Brennan draft goes on, "Considerations of *stare decisis* . . . require that we defer to our prior and now long-standing interpretation of §1981, absent compelling reasons not to do so." There is no "special justification" for a departure from *Runyon*. To be sure, "*Stare decisis* will not save a statutory precedent that is without foundation." But *Runyon*'s interpretation of the statute, "though disputable, lies well outside these exceptions to *stare decisis* recognized for inadequately considered or patently unfounded decisions." Indeed, Justice Brennan affirms, the *Runyon* interpretation was "based upon a full and considered review of the statute's language and legislative history, assisted by careful briefing, and . . . this interpretation, though not inevitable, is by no means an implausible one."

The Brennan *Patterson* draft not only holds that stare decisis required the reaffirmation of *Runyon*. It also goes out of its way (in more detail than in the published Brennan dissent) to find that *Jones v. Alfred H. Mayer* was correctly decided. The draft specifically agrees with *Jones* "that Congress said enough about the injustice of private discrimination, and the need to end it, to show that it did indeed intend the [1866] Civil Rights Act to sweep that far." In fact, the Brennan analysis leads the draft to state, "In sum, although *Jones* and *Runyon* both resolved what are assuredly close questions of statutory interpretation, we are unable to conclude that either the decision in *Jones* that . . . the 1866 Act was intended to reach private discrimination, or the decision in *Runyon* . . . was patently wrong and thus within the acknowledged exception to *stare decisis* that allows us to correct past errors." A contrary result would defeat the very goal of stare decisis. "The entire purpose of the policy of *stare decisis* . . . is to avoid the uncertainty that would result from our intermittent reconsideration of such questions. We do not believe our long-standing interpretation of §1981 to prohibit private discrimination has been shown to be so dubious as to trigger an exception to this sound policy."

Finally, in a draft section paralleled by a shorter treatment in the final Brennan dissent, the Justice declared, "We are equally unpersuaded that *Runyon v. McCrary* falls within the exception to *stare decisis* for precedents that have proved 'outdated, . . . unworkable, or otherwise legitimately vulnerable to serious reconsideration.'" The draft notes that, "With the passage of time, a statutory precedent sometimes becomes so problematic as to appear ripe for reconsideration. The Court has in those circumstances recognized an exception to the dictates of *stare decisis*." The following examples are given: "The Court has overruled statutory precedents because the premises underlying a decision have been rendered untenable by subsequent congressional or judicial action . . . . ; because a decision has come to appear inconsistent with another line of authority . . . ; and because experience has shown a precedent to be seriously at odds with congressional policy. . . ."

However, the Brennan draft states, "None of these considerations is present here. On the contrary," the draft concludes, in language similar to that in Justice Brennan's published dissent, "*Runyon* is entirely consonant with our society's deep commitment to the eradication of discrimination based on a person's race or the color of her skin. . . . In the past, this Court has overruled decisions antagonistic to our Nation's commitment to the ideal of a society in which a person's opportunities do not depend on her race . . . , and we decline now to abandon a statutory construction so in harmony with that ideal."

RESTRICTING CIVIL RIGHTS LAWS

In *Patterson v. McLean Credit Union*, Chief Justice Rehnquist definitely lost his battle to have the Court overrule the *Jones* and *Runyon* cases. Despite this, the Chief Justice has generally prevailed in the civil rights cases decided by the Rehnquist Court. In accordance with Rehnquist's view, the Court has narrowed the scope of civil rights statutes in a number of decisions and has also limited the power of the states to enact such laws.

However, Chief Justice Rehnquist's approach almost lost a Court in one important civil rights case — *Patterson v. McLean Credit Union* itself. At issue in *Patterson* was more than the question of whether *Runyon v. McCrary* should be overruled. Once the Court decided that *Runyon's* holding should remain as governing law, it had to deal with the merits of the case. Petitioner, who had been employed by respondent credit union for ten years, brought an action under section 1981 alleging that respondent had harassed her, failed to promote her to an intermediate accounting clerk position, and discharged her, all because of her race. The lower courts ruled in favor of respondent. Certiorari was granted by an eight-Justice Court, with Justices Brennan, White, Marshall, and Stevens voting to grant, and the Chief Justice and Justices Blackmun, O'Connor, and Scalia to deny.

We have seen that Justice Brennan prepared a draft *Patterson* opinion of the Court. That was true because the conference on October 14, 1988, voted by a bare majority (Justices Brennan, Marshall, Blackmun, Stevens, and Kennedy, appointed after the cert vote) to reverse. The Justices not only rejected the Chief Justice's plea to overrule *Runyon*; the conference majority also refused to accept his interpretation that racial harassment was not actionable under the statute. Three days later, Justice Brennan, senior in the majority, assigned the opinion to himself.

Justice Brennan circulated a draft opinion of the Court on December 3. We have already dealt with its discussion of the stare decisis issue. On the merits, the draft found for petitioner and vacated the decision below. The key issue, as stated in the draft, was "whether a plaintiff may state a cause of action under §1981 based upon allegations that her employer harassed her because of her race. The Court of Appeals held that claims of racial harassment, as opposed to allegations of discriminatory hiring, firing, or promotion, are not cognizable under §1981, because racial harassment does not go to 'the very existence and nature of the employment contract,' . . . and hence cannot abridge the right to make and enforce contracts free of discrimination. We disagree."

The Brennan draft asserted "that in granting the freedmen the 'same right . . . to make and enforce contracts' as white citizens, Congress meant to encompass post-contractual conduct demonstrating that a freedman had not been accorded the right to enter a contract on the same terms as white persons." Hence, "the equal right to make and enforce contracts protected by §1981 is not limited in scope to a right to overtly equal treatment at the time of entering into and ending a contractual relationship."

The draft concludes, "Racial harassment severe enough to amount to a breach of contract as a matter of state law is certainly cognizable . . . , for an employer's discriminatory failure to abide by the terms of a black employee's contract constitutes a denial of contractual opportunities as surely as does the initial offer of different employment terms to blacks and whites, or a race-based discharge." Nor need the "term breached by the racial harassment . . . be an explicit one." On the contrary, "it may be the implied covenant of good faith and fair dealing often supplied and given content by state law." Racial harassment that amounts to a breach of contract violates the statute, if it was racially motivated.

Nor, under the Brennan draft, is a breach of contract itself necessary. "Even if it does not breach an express or implied contract term, however, harassment is actionable . . . if it demonstrates that the employer has sought to evade the statute's strictures concerning contract formation." In such a case, where an employee makes a claim under the statute alleging racial harassment and alleges no breach of contract, the question is "whether in nature and extent the acts constituting harassment were sufficiently severe or pervasive as effectively to belie any claim that the contract was entered into in a racially neutral manner." Thus, "Where a black employee demonstrates that she has worked in conditions substantially different from those enjoyed by similarly situated white employees, and can show the necessary racial animus, a jury may infer that the black employee has not been afforded the same right to make an employment contract as white employees." When "the different contractual expectations are unspoken, but come clear during the course of employment as the black employee is subjected to substantially harsher conditions than her white co-workers," it cannot "be said that whites and blacks have had the same right to make an employment contract."

In *Patterson* itself, Justice Brennan's draft concludes, petitioner's harassment claim came within the scope of the statute. "On the basis of the evidence at trial, the jury might have concluded that petitioner was subjected to such serious and extensive racial harassment as to have been denied the right to make an employment contract on the same basis as white employees of the credit union."

BRENNAN'S DRAFT REJECTED

Justice Brennan's draft *Patterson* opinion refused to limit section 1981 to the formation of a contract. Instead, it held that the statutory scope extended to conduct by the employer after the contract relation had been established, including racially motivated breach of the contract's terms or the imposition of discriminatory working conditions. Had the draft come down as the opinion of the Court, it would have made for a broadside interpretation of the statute that could have made it a general proscription of racial discrimination in all aspects of contract relations. More specifically, the statute could prohibit all racial discrimination in employment, even that practiced long after the making of the employment contract.

That result was, however, avoided by the ultimate disposition of the *Patterson* case. Once again the conference majority did not hold. Of course, the Justices who had voted the other way at the conference did not join the Brennan opinion. Thus, Justice O'Connor sent a December 7, 1988, "Dear Bill" letter: "While I agree that Runyon v. McCrary should not be overruled, I do not think I agree with your treatment of the merits, and I will await further writing or circulate something myself in due course." O'Connor meant, of course, that she would wait for a dissent on the merits or, if none was forthcoming, draft one herself.

On January 12, 1989, Justice White circulated an eight-page printed draft, which concurred in the decision not to overrule *Runyon*, but dissented on the merits. On the first point, White wrote, "Though I dissented in *Runyon*, and continue to believe the Court was wrong in that case, no arguments have been presented here that merit reversing that decision, particularly in light of our rule 'that considerations of *stare decisis* weigh heavily in the area of statutory interpretation.'"

On the merits, Justice White asserted, with regard to Justice Brennan's draft, "It is difficult to understand this holding. Either a contract contains, or does not contain, racially-discriminatory terms." It follows that "the ultimate issue in such a case is—and must be—whether there has been intentional discrimination in the 'making or enforcement' of the contract. . . . Racial harassment may 'show' that such discrimination exists, but—and this is critical—it is not *itself* such discrimination." In a case such as this, the White draft concluded, "where there is no allegation that an employment contract contains racially-discriminatory terms, and no allegation that there has been racially-discriminatory enforcement of the employment contract, racial harassment is not actionable under §1981."

The White draft was caustic in its condemnation of Justice Brennan's approach: "To hold otherwise, as the Court does, divorces the interpretation of §1981 from the statute's language. The words of limitation in the statute guarantee equal rights only to *make and enforce* contracts;' the Court's interpretation of the law — holding that it forbids all racially-discriminatory acts (beyond a certain threshold of egregiousness) by parties in a contractual relationship — renders irrelevant this limiting phrase, or at the least, rewrites it substantially. . . . Consequently, I cannot accept the Court's judicial alteration of this century-old civil rights law."

The White draft dissent made the *Patterson* decision process "boil like a pot." What happened was described by Justice Stevens, in a May 22, 1989, letter to Justice Brennan. "On December 5, 1988," Stevens wrote, "when I joined your proposed majority opinion, I thought your draft expressed a position on the racial harassment issue that had been adopted by four other Justices at Conference — indeed, the portion of your opinion discussing harassment that amounts to a breach of contract was also endorsed by Byron. . . . In the intervening months, further study has convinced at least three members of the present majority to modify their views — and, in one case, his vote. I have no quarrel with this process (having done so a number of times myself, this Term as well as in the past)."

In *Patterson*, the process described by Stevens took place after the White draft dissent was circulated. The key development occurred when Justice Kennedy sent around an eleven-page printed draft dissent on April 17, which began its discussion of the merits: "I agree with JUSTICE WHITE's basic approach to interpreting the scope of §1981." This meant that Justice Kennedy had changed his conference vote on the case.

The Kennedy draft, however, took an even more restrictive view of the reach of section 1981 — in effect adopting the confined conference view asserted by Chief Justice Rehnquist. "I disagree . . . ," stated the Kennedy draft, "with the dictum in JUSTICE WHITE's opinion, also found in JUSTICE BRENNAN's opinion, stating that §1981 applies to racially-motivated conduct amounting to a 'breach' of the terms or conditions of an employment contract."

The Kennedy draft contained somewhat different language than the Justice's final opinion in the case. "By its plain terms," the draft points out, "the relevant provision in § 1981 protects . . . 'the same right . . . to make . . . contracts'." The protection here "extends only to the formation (*i.e.*, 'mak[ing]') of the contractual relation, and not to problems that may arise later from performance of the contract. . . . But the right to 'make' contracts does not comfortably extend to conduct by the employer after the contractual relationship has been established, including breach of the terms of the contract or discriminatory working conditions. Such post-formation conduct does not involve the right to 'make' a contract, but rather involves the performance of contractual relations already established and the conditions of continuing employment, matters more naturally governed by state contract law."

"Nor," according to Justice Kennedy's draft, "does §1981's guarantee of 'the same right . . . to . . . enforce contracts' cover conduct amounting to a breach of the terms of a nondiscriminatory contract or to discriminatory working conditions in the employment context. A guarantee of 'the same right . . . to enforce . . . contracts as is enjoyed by white citizens' constitutes protection of a legal process, and of a right of access to legal process, that will address and resolve contract-law claims without regard to race."

Both the Brennan draft opinion of the Court and the White draft dissent had interpreted the statute more broadly. Their language, asserts the Kennedy draft, "assuming that §1981 extends coverage to discriminatory conduct amounting to a breach of contract adds a third right to that provision's protections, one that is simply not in the statute. An allegation that the employer has for racial reasons breached an implied or express term of the contract does not state a claim for the impairment of either the right to 'make' or the right to 'enforce' a contract."

Nor, Justice Kennedy declared, can it be said that "a claim that the employers conduct amounts to a breach of contract alleges that the plaintiff's right to 'enforce' his contract has been impaired. To the contrary, conduct amounting to a breach of contract under state law is precisely what the language of §1981 does not cover."

The Kennedy draft thus rejected the holding of the Brennan draft opinion of the Court, as well as the assumption in Justice White's draft dissent, "that §1981 applies to post-formation conduct by the employer amounting to a breach of contract." In fact, Justice Kennedy declared in his draft, "Interpreting § 1981 to cover discriminatory breach of contract is not only inconsistent with a fair reading of that provision, but it would also produce undesirable results."

Specifically, the draft states, "because § 1981 covers all types of contracts, such an interpretation would federalize all state-law claims for breach of contract where racial animus is alleged." This would go counter to one of the themes of Rehnquist Court jurisprudence — that, as summarized in the Kennedy draft, "we should be and are normally 'reluctant to federalize' matters traditionally covered by state common law."

In addition, the Kennedy draft asserts, "It would . . . be no small paradox that under the interpretation of § 1981 offered by the dictum in the opinions of JUSTICES BRENNAN and WHITE, the more a state extends its own contract law to protect employees in general and minorities in particular, the greater would be the potential displacement of state law by § 1981. I do not think § 1981 need be read to produce such a peculiar result." At any rate, the Kennedy draft dissent concludes, "I join with JUSTICE WHITE and THE CHIEF JUSTICE in concluding that racial harassment *itself* is not actionable under 1981." Even if "racial harassment may serve as evidence to show either that the contract was made on discriminatory terms or that the plaintiff's right to enforce her contractual rights has been impaired . . . such racial harassment is not itself cognizable divorced from the more specific claim that the employee's right to enforce the contract was impaired."

Justice Kennedy's draft dissent meant that there was now a bare majority to hold for the employer on the claim that the alleged racial harassment violated section 1981. This was recognized by Justice Brennan himself, when he wrote to the other Justices who had joined his draft *Patterson* opinion, "Dear Thurgood, John, and Harry: Tony's dissent leaves me without a Court on Part II of my opinion in this case, dealing with the harassment claim."

Though the Kennedy switch changed the *Patterson* result, the new majority was divided on the scope of the statute in such a case — with different views on the subject stated in the White and Kennedy draft dissents. The matter was, however, resolved when Justice White sent a May 17 note to Justice Kennedy: "Dear Tony, I am withdrawing my prior circulation in this case and have decided to join you. I shall circulate a few words of my own shortly."

Justice Kennedy could now issue his opinion as the opinion of the Court, which he announced on June 15, 1989. Justice Brennan had to redraft his opinion as one "concurring in part and dissenting in part." His emotion at losing his Court on the merits is shown by the language at the beginning of the Brennan dissenting redraft: "What the Court declines to snatch away with one hand, it steals with the other." The redraft refers to "The Court's fine phrases about our commitment to the eradication of racial discrimination." However, it asserts, "When it comes to deciding whether a civil rights statute should be construed to further that commitment, the fine phrases disappear, replaced by a formalistic method of interpretation antithetical to Congress' vision of a society in which contractual opportunities are equal." (The underlined phrases were eliminated in the published Brennan dissent.)

Thus, *Patterson* came down as a victory for the more restricted Rehnquist interpretation of the civil rights statute. As in *Webster*, however, the final outcome was brought about only by a vote switch — this time by Justice Kennedy. Had the switches not occurred, both *Webster* and *Patterson* would have been decided differently. Without a doubt, they would have been landmarks in Rehnquist Court jurisprudence, but they would have stood for exactly the opposite doctrines than those decisions stand for today.

CRIMINAL CASE SWITCHES

The cases discussed in this and the first chapter show that vote switches have been as significant in the Rehnquist Court jurisprudence as they had been in that of its predecessors. The remainder of this chapter will discuss other Rehnquist Court cases in which vote switches played a crucial part, starting with criminal cases that might have become leading cases had key Justices not changed their votes.

Missouri v. Blair came before the Court during the 1986 Term — the first Rehnquist term as Chief Justice. A murder had been committed in Kansas City. The only clue was a palm print in the victim's truck. An informer implicated respondent. The police did not arrest respondent for homicide because of lack of probable cause. They knew, however, that a municipal court had issued a bench warrant for her arrest in connection with a traffic violation. They arrested her, informing her that they were arresting her on the municipal warrant. She was taken to the police station and her finger and palm prints were taken. Respondent posted bond and was released. After it was found that her palm print matched that taken at the scene, respondent was again arrested and, after interrogation, confessed to the murder. The Missouri courts granted a motion to suppress, on the ground that the arrest on the traffic warrant was a mere subterfuge and that the palm print and the statements taken from her were the fruits of an illegal arrest for homicide and should accordingly be suppressed.

The Justices voted to reverse by a bare majority, with Justices Brennan, Marshall, Powell, and Stevens dissenting. The opinion was assigned to Justice White, who circulated an eleven-page draft opinion of the Court on January 9, 1987. After stating the facts and the holding below, the draft stated, "the issue comes down to whether the police violated Blair's Fourth Amendment rights when they acquired her palm print to investigate the killing of Carl Lindstedt. We hold that they did not."

Though the police lacked probable cause to arrest respondent for homicide and take her to the station house and secure her palm print, she was, according to the White draft, "the subject of a valid bench warrant issued by the municipal court and authorizing her custodial arrest at any time." Had respondent "been arrested and booked on that warrant, independently of any desire to investigate the homicide, the Fourth Amendment would not forbid taking her finger and palm prints and retaining them in police files." Indeed, the White draft concludes, "Had Blair's palm print been taken in this manner, its use in the homicide investigation would have raised no question under the Fourth Amendment."

Such would be the case, Justice White's draft goes on, even if the palm print had been taken at the request of the homicide unit. As the draft puts it, "The testimony was that such requests were honored while traffic arrestees were in custody, and since the State in such cases would be doing no more than the Constitution allowed, there would be no occasion to apply the exclusionary rule, which is designed to deter unconstitutional conduct."

Nor would the result be changed "if Blair's arrest on the traffic warrant was triggered by the need to get her palm print to investigate the homicide." Even in such a case, the White draft asserts, "There would have been a valid arrest, a valid temporary custody and the taking of identifying prints in connection therewith, which is no more than the Constitution permits."

The basic principle, according to the White draft, is that, "When a valid custodial arrest occurs and the police take fingerprints or gather other evidence incident to that arrest that proves relevant in investigating another crime, the

Federal Constitution does not forbid using such evidence for that purpose, even if it could be proved that the impetus for the immediate arrest was the interest in investigating the other crime. The Fourth Amendment does not require inquiry into the motives of the police officers in such situations." In this case, "assuming a valid arrest on the traffic warrant, taking Blair's palm print was legally permissible and consistent with standard procedures when a request for a palm print is made."

After the White draft was circulated, a twelve-page printed draft dissent was sent around by Justice Powell (whom Justice Brennan joined) and a two-page dissent by Justice Stevens (whom Justice Marshall joined). The dissenters urged that respondent had really been illegally arrested on the homicide charge and that the traffic arrest was a mere pretext. As the Powell draft dissent put it, "the police arrested respondent Zola Blair on a municipal parking warrant and took her palm print solely because they lacked probable cause to arrest her on a charge of murder. . . . In my view, the police conduct was not objectively reasonable and was undertaken to evade constitutional restraints otherwise applicable to their conduct."

According to Justice Powell, the police conduct here was both objectively unreasonable and a mere pretext to evade the constitutional requirement: "the police arrested Blair on the parking violation warrant for the sole purpose of discovering incriminating evidence of a completely unrelated crime. Such pretextual conduct flouts the limits established by the Fourth Amendment on police investigative abilities."

The Powell draft concluded, "the police relied on a theretofore unexecuted municipal parking violation warrant as a pretext to arrest Blair for the sole purpose of obtaining evidence of the homicide. In my view, this was a clear violation of the Fourth Amendment. Accordingly, I dissent."

Once again, however, the bare majority did not hold and, as in *Webster*, the key vote switch was by Justice O'Connor. On January 27, 1987, she sent a "Dear Byron" letter. "This has been a difficult case for me," O'Connor wrote. "You have written as well as could be done in support of the State's position, but I find myself at the end of the day agreeing with Lewis that the judgment should be affirmed."

The O'Connor letter went on, "I disagree with Lewis, however, that it is open in all cases to explore the subjective motives of the police. In my view, if an officer's actions are objectively reasonable and in accordance with standard procedures, the accused has not suffered any additional invasion of privacy by reason of the improper motivation and there has been no Fourth Amendment violation. I agree with Lewis that the officers' actions in this case were not objectively reasonable." Justice O'Connor wrote that she would circulate her own opinion "concurring in part with Lewis' dissent in due course."

The promised O'Connor opinion was sent around on February 17. It disagreed with the White conclusion that "the police officers' conduct is supported by the municipal traffic warrant." Instead, Justice O'Connor found that the officers' conduct was objectively unreasonable. The facts here, O'Connor concluded, "belie any claim that the evidence in this case was seized as a bona fide step in the execution of a traffic warrant. . . . The evidence was taken incident to an unlawful homicide arrest, and the police would not inevitably have discovered it by some other means."

With the O'Connor switch, there was now a bare majority to affirm the suppression of the evidence. But the Justices were unsatisfied with that result as well. As Justice Blackmun wrote to Justice White, "I continue to rest uneasy about this case." Blackmun noted, "You will recall that I so expressed myself at conference and that I then stated that I could go along with a DIG" — that is, a decision to dismiss as improvidently granted.

This was the solution ultimately adopted. On March 25, 1987, the Court issued a per curiam (drafted by the Chief Justice) stating simply, "The writ of certiorari is dismissed as improvidently granted." Instead of the important Fourth Amendment case it would have been had the White draft come down as the opinion of the Court, *Missouri v. Blair* became not even a footnote in recent Supreme Court jurisprudence.

Another case where vote switches prevented the Court from handing down an important criminal law decision was *Tompkins v. Texas*, decided in 1989. Tompkins had been found guilty of an intentional killing during a robbery and kidnapping and been sentenced to death. As stated in Justice Stevens's draft opinion of the Court, "His case gives rise to two questions: (1) whether it was constitutional error for the trial judge to grant only one of petitioner's three requests for instructions on lesser included, noncapital offenses; and (2) whether the lower court erred when it affirmed the trial judge's determination that the prosecutors' use of peremptory challenges to exclude all blacks from the jury was based consistently on 'neutral, relative, clear and legitimate' reasons and 'was not racially motivated.' "

Tompkins came before an eight-Justice Court, Justice O'Connor having recused herself. The conference voted five-to-three to affirm on the first issue and reverse on the second. Justice Stevens prepared a lengthy draft opinion of the Court in which he ruled that defendant was entitled "to have the jury instructed regarding not only capital murder and acquittal, but also one lesser included, noncapital offense suggested by the evidence at trial."

Defendant had argued that he had a constitutional right to have the jury instructed on *every* lesser included, noncapital offense that might be supported by the evidence. The Stevens draft rejected this claim. "It may," Justice Stevens wrote, "well be sound policy to instruct the jury on every lesser included offense supported by the evidence. But the Constitution requires no such rule. It mandates only that a jury be given a means to avoid a Hobson's choice between acquittal and capital murder. Because the instructions in this case afforded the jury such an option, they did not offend the Constitution."

The second *Tompkins* question gave rise to what the Justices themselves called "the *Batson* issue." The 1986 case of *Batson v. Kentucky* had invalidated the use of peremptory challenges by the prosecution to exclude blacks from a jury. Tompkins claimed that *Batson* had been violated in his case. He was black. All the jurors were white; the thirteen blacks on the venire from which the jury had been chosen had all been excluded — eight by challenges for cause and five by peremptory strikes. The Texas court had accepted the prosecutors' testimony of a neutral, nonracial reason for each of the peremptory challenges. As that court saw it, the finding of the trial judge, "which is supported by sufficient evidence, comports with that of a rational trier of fact."

According to the Stevens draft, the Texas court's "application of a sufficiency-of-the-evidence standard inadequately protected the important interests at stake." Hence, "Today we reject the Texas criminal appeals court's standard for reviewing *Batson* claims." As the Stevens draft saw it, "The Texas court's sufficiency-of-the-evidence standard erodes *Batson*'s protection. Allowing reversal only when 'no rational trier of fact' would have ruled against a defendant asserting a *Batson* violation narrows the scope of review to a point that is virtually meaningless."

Instead, the trial court's decision must be reviewed under the clearly erroneous standard that normally governs appellate review in federal courts. As Justice Stevens explained it, "the clearly erroneous standard requires the appellate court, after locating record support for an explanation, to decide separately whether the trial judge was mistaken. . . . This extra step mandates more careful examination of the record and more considered evaluation of the validity of the trial court's findings. Thus a standard no less protective than clearly erroneous is essential to the faithful application of *Batson*."

"In this case," the Stevens draft concluded, "the process by which petitioner's *Batson* claim was assessed by the trial court and the Court of Criminal Appeals of Texas was inadequate." That was true because the Texas courts "seem to have assumed that any neutral explanation would suffice as long as the trial judge believed the prosecutor's testimony that the neutral reason prompted the peremptory challenge." However, the draft asserted, "In addition to overlooking our admonition that the neutral explanation must be case-related, their assumption provides no protection against the danger that a facially neutral explanation may be nothing more than a proxy for racial bias, conscious or subconscious."

Also, "neither court heeded our admonition to 'consider all relevant circumstances.'" In particular, the Texas courts "made no comment on the dubious character of the questions put to the black venirepersons." As stated in the Stevens draft, "Courts must make sure that prosecutors are not permitted to circumvent our holding in *Batson* by requiring black venirepersons to demonstrate an understanding of areas of the law — such as the 'law of parties' — that have no special relevance to the case at hand. Consideration of all relevant circumstances should encompass whether similar questions were propounded to white venirepersons and whether accepted jurors' answers differed significantly from those of the excused black jurors."

Soon after the Stevens draft was circulated, Justice White sent around a draft opinion concurring in the affirmance on the jury instruction issue, but dissenting on the reversal on *Batson* grounds. Under the majority approach, White wrote, "The Constitution is said to bar Texas' sufficiency of the evidence standard in favor of a clearly erroneous standard which would give appellate courts more room to find error in the trial courts' findings. . . . this is an extraordinary imposition on the state courts." Since "the Court [has] proceeded with such evident gusto to invalidate the traditional standard of review used in Texas, what the Court does is quite unacceptable to me."

"As I understand *Batson*," the White draft stated, "the accused has the burden throughout of proving deliberate discrimination. The prosecutor in response must do more than assert his good faith and absence of discriminatory intent. But it suffices if he puts forth a believable, neutral explanation for his strikes. . . . In *Batson*, the Court emphasized that this was the extent of the prosecutor's duty."

In this case, "The majority now, however, insists not only that the prosecutor do more but also requires that the trial judge and the appellate courts second-guess reasons for removing jurors, even if these courts credit the prosecutor's honesty." The majority is subjecting the trial court's judgment to "appellate review on a cold record . . . by judges sitting in Washington, D.C."

Justice White concluded, "Rather than subject peremptories to the regime the Court imposes today, it would be more straightforward to hold that when a black is on trial in a criminal case, peremptory challenges by the prosecution are unconstitutional because they pose an unacceptable risk of racial discrimination in the selection of jurors. With all due respect, I dissent."

Justice Blackmun also circulated an opinion, concurring in part and dissenting in part. However, he concurred on the *Batson* issue and dissented on the jury instruction holding.

The Stevens draft could have become a leading case on application of the *Batson* rule, had it come down as the *Tompkins* opinion of the Court. But the five-to-three majority in its favor became a four-to-four vote on the issue when Justice Kennedy, in the phrase of a law clerk memo to Justice Marshall, "jumped ship and voted to affirm on the *Batson* issue." The Kennedy switch was announced in a May 16, 1989, letter to Justice Stevens. "I tentatively voted at Conference," Kennedy noted, "to vacate the judgment of the Texas Court of Criminal Appeals and remand for further consideration of the trial court's findings on the *Batson* issue." Justice Kennedy had, however, now changed his mind. "As I understand *Batson*," Kennedy wrote, "where there is a prima facie case of discrimination in jury selection, the prosecution bears the burden of coming forward with a neutral, case-related explanation for its actions. In my view, the State has done so here, and the trial court's findings to support the State's showing are not clearly erroneous."

The Kennedy letter concluded, "Since the prosecutors' explanations for their use of peremptory challenges against black venirepersons are neutral, case-related, and supported by the evidence, I believe the trial court did not err in finding that no *Batson* violation was committed. For these reasons, I cannot join Part II of your opinion. My vote is to affirm the conviction."

This now made for a four-to-four division on the *Batson* issue. In addition, Justice Stevens had concluded that he had been wrong on the jury instruction issue. He had circulated a new draft opinion of the Court on May 17, 1989, deleting the *Batson* discussion. Then, two days later, Stevens sent a "Dear Chief" letter stating, "After further reflection, I have decided to change my vote on the [jury instruction] issue in this case." This meant a four-to-four division on that issue also. This led Justice Stevens to conclude, in his letter to the Chief Justice, "I am now persuaded that the best disposition of the entire case . . . is a simple affirmance by an equally divided Court." On June 5, 1989, the Justices issued a per curiam affirming in *Tompkins* by an equally divided Court.

Justice Kennedy's switch in *Tompkins* made a difference in the application of *Batson*. In 1991, the Court dealt with the issue again in *Hernandez v. New York*. This time Justice Kennedy announced the principal opinion. It substantially followed the approach of Justice White's draft *Tompkins* dissent. Instead of the stricter standard that would have been adopted under the Stevens draft *Tompkins* opinion of the Court, *Hernandez* stated the lesser holding that, as summarized by the Stevens *Hernandez* dissent, "a defendant's *Batson* challenge fails whenever the prosecutor advances a nonpretextual justification that is not facially discriminatory."

This is true, according to *Purkette v. Elem* (1995), the most recent case on the matter, even where the prosecutor's reason is "silly or superstitious." Justice Stevens dissented in both *Hernandez* and *Purkett*. Had his stricter *Tompkins* standard retained its majority, both *Hernandea* and *Purkett* might have been decided differently.

A TAX CASE SWITCH

The 1991 case of *Ford Motor Credit Co. v. Department of Revenue* well illustrates the often tortuous Supreme Court decision process. In that case, the judicial mountain truly labored, and all that it brought forth was the mouse of an affirmance by an equally divided Court.

At issue in *Ford Motor Credit* was one of the most difficult constitutional questions — that of the power of the states to tax interstate commerce. Florida taxed intangible personal property, such as accounts receivable and shares of stock, at one-tenth of one percent of the assessed value of the property. The tax was imposed on "any person, regardless of domicile, who owns or has management, custody, or control of intangible property that has acquired a business situs in this state." Ford Motor Credit Co. (FMCC) was a Delaware corporation that provided financing in Florida for dealers and consumers to purchase Ford automobiles. Could the Florida tax be imposed on FMCC without unconstitutionally burdening interstate commerce?

At the conference on the case, the Justices voted six-to-two to uphold the tax, with Justice O'Connor not participating. However, according to a December 7, 1990, Blackmun Memorandum to the Conference, "According to my notes, the Conference discussion on this case was indecisive and tentative, and the voting was far from firm." As summarized by Justice Blackmun, "Thurgood and Tony were to reverse. Sandra is 'out.' John would affirm for lack of standing. Nino 'did not understand' John's explanation and would affirm by refusing to apply the internal consistency test [to be discussed later] to property taxes; if, however, that test does apply, he would reverse. David leaned toward affirmance so long as there was as yet no actual imposition of a duplicative tax. . . . The Chief initially passed, stating that he had been in dissent in this area, but, after the discussion, leaned toward affirmance. Byron stated that he 'never did understand' the internal consistency test and was inclined, 'some way or another,' to affirm."

The Chief Justice had assigned the opinion to Justice Blackmun, but the Justice added to the confusion by changing his vote. As his memo explained it, "After again reviewing the Court's recent cases, I have come to the conclusion that we cannot affirm here without overruling established precedent. I have not understood my assignment as being one to overrule. Thus, the proposed opinion is to reverse."

The Blackmun memo was accompanied by a seven-page printed draft opinion of the Court, which invalidated the tax. The draft stated the governing rule in such a case as follows: "In reviewing a state tax alleged to violate the Commerce Clause, this Court has upheld the tax if it 'is applied to an activity with a substantial nexus with the taxing State, is fairly apportioned, does not discriminate against interstate commerce, and is fairly related to the services provided by the State.' . . . If the challenged tax fails any one of these four conditions, the tax is unconstitutional."

The apportionment requirement, Justice Blackmun went on, ensures "that each State is permitted to tax only its fair share of an interstate transaction." The Court has not required any specific apportionment formula. "Instead . . . we have held that a tax is fairly apportioned if it is internally and externally consistent." In this case, the Blackmun draft stated, "we conclude that the tax challenged here is not internally consistent." Justice Blackmun explained that "A tax is internally consistent if no multiple taxation would result from every other State's imposing an identical tax."

According to the Blackmun draft, "Florida's intangible tax scheme fails this test. . . . If every State were to adopt the Florida tax, Company A, an entity domiciled in Florida but owning intangible property with a business situs in Georgia, would pay two taxes on the same intangible property—a domiciliary tax to Florida and a business situs tax to Georgia. This inevitable multiple taxation renders the Florida intangible tax scheme internally inconsistent."

More than that, the draft explained, "If one extends the hypothetical somewhat, it demonstrates that the Florida tax scheme discriminates against interstate commerce. Under the challenged tax, Company B, domiciled in Georgia and doing business exclusively in Georgia, would be subject only to a single tax on a loan made on a car sale in Georgia, while Company A would be subject to the double tax noted above on the same car loan. Thus, the intangibles tax disadvantages an interstate business competing with a wholly intrastate entity for the same market."

The Blackmun draft was the first opinion to apply the internal consistency test to an intangible property tax. But the draft itself was not to come down as the opinion of the Court, since it was contrary to the conference vote. As Chief Justice Rehnquist put it in a December 7 "Dear Harry" letter, "your proposed opinion in this case has come out to 'reverse,' rather than to 'affirm,' which as you point out in your memo of December 7th was the tentative Conference vote." Because of this, the Chief Justice reassigned the case to Justice Stevens on January 4, 1991.

Justice Stevens circulated a new thirteen-page printed draft opinion of the Court on February 26, which affirmed the state court decision upholding the tax. The Stevens draft, like that which Justice Blackmun had prepared, recognized that the Florida tax "is not internally consistent. For if every State were to replicate Florida's scheme, finance companies would be taxed twice on their out-of-state receivables — once by their home State and once by the situs State — whereas their in-state receivables would be taxed only once."

Nevertheless, the Stevens draft did not conclude from this that the tax was invalid. Florida had argued "that there is no constitutional requirement that property taxes must pass the internal consistency test." Justice Stevens did not deal with this argument. Instead, his draft followed the view stated by him at the conference — that FMCC, a nonresident, did not have standing to avoid the application of the tax to its Florida intangibles because the statute arguably discriminated against Florida domiciliaries. As the Stevens draft concluded, "To the extent that Florida has elected to discriminate against its own residents, FMCC has no standing to vindicate their rights. The strength of the attack a resident may make on the state and the fashioning of an appropriate remedy if such an attack should succeed must be considered in litigation brought by a different taxpayer."

On March 20, 1991, Justice Blackmun wrote to Justice Stevens that he could not join his opinion and would be circulating a dissent. On April 2, Blackmun sent around a seven-page printed draft dissent, which was quickly joined by Justices Marshall and Kennedy. The Blackmun draft dissent urged that, so far as standing was concerned, FMCC "is in a position no different, and no less strong, from that of the Florida resident whom the majority names as the proper party to raise the challenge." The draft dissent also repeated (though in shorter form) the holding in the Blackmun draft opinion of the Court "that the Florida intangibles tax is internally inconsistent and therefore is in violation of the Commerce Clause."

However, on May 9, the decision to affirm the tax unraveled, as Justice Souter changed his vote. In a letter on that date to Justices Blackmun and

Stevens, Souter wrote, "Because John's opinion comes out to where I hoped to be when we voted on this, I feel a little bit of a rotter in joining Harry's dissent. But so I believe I must do." Though the Souter explanation was ambivalent, the Justice had definitely switched his vote. This made for a four-to-four division. This was pointed out in a May 9 "Dear Chief" note from Justice Scalia, who wrote, "I had intended to write a few words separately but since it now appears that the decision below will be affirmed by an equally divided Court it would be a waste of time to circulate anything."

The next day, May 10, Justice Stevens wrote to Chief Justice Rehnquist, "Since David and Nino have now voted, and since I have established such an enviable record at writing majority opinions that end up in a tie, cf. *United States v. France*, I propose that we enter the attached order on Monday."

The order mentioned by Justice Stevens was a per curiam drafted by the Justice which affirmed the decision upholding the Florida tax by an equally divided Court. (Parenthetically, the *France* case referred to in the Stevens letter was another 1991 case in which Justice Stevens had also written a draft opinion of the Court, only to see his majority disappear, with the case likewise ultimately decided without opinion by an equally divided Court.)

Had the Blackmun draft opinion of the Court come down as the *Ford Motor Credit* opinion, it would have answered the question of whether the internal consistency test applies to intangible property. As it turned out, however, the vote switches in the case prevented the question from being answered. Therefore, the lacuna in this highly technical area of constitutional law that would have been filled by the Blackmun opinion still remains.

11

Apotheosis of Mediocrity?

Just before his death in 1971, Dean Acheson wrote that "our age might be called the apotheosis of mediocrity." The history of the Supreme Court affirms that this is true of our highest tribunal as well. Not since pre–Civil War days has the caliber of the Justices been so ordinary. Yet even the Taney Court had two outstanding Justices: The Chief Justice himself and his archrival, Justice Curtis. As the recently released papers of Justice Thurgood Marshall show, the Justices today are meticulous in their devotion to their work. As a commentator in the *American Bar Association Journal* put it, "What can be found [in the papers] is thoughtful analysis, concern, and . . . deference between justices on opposite sides of an issue." Yet one is reminded of what Justice Holmes once wrote about a colleague: "he was a very honest hard working Judge [but] He had not wings and was not a thunderbolt." Even our inferior Supreme Courts have had their Justices who soared and thundered.

Alas, that is not true today. Perhaps it would be extreme to say, with John Randolph of Roanoke, "Never were abilities so much below mediocrity so well rewarded; no, not when Caligula's horse was made Consul." The most remarkable thing about the Justices today is that, in James Bryce's phrase, "being so commonplace they should have climbed so high."

Not only has the caliber of the Justices declined; it is most unlikely that, with the recent politicization of the appointing and confirmation process, a nominee with the potential for greatness could be approved. The prime attribute of the ideal Supreme Court nominee now seems to be the absence of a "paper trail": strong views publicly expressed are more disqualifications than indices of the ability needed to serve on the highest bench. Greatness in the Court, as in other areas of public life, seems out of place in an age in which the world of law, like that of physics, is perceived only as the relativity of one value compared with another. In such an age, we seem to be (as in *Twelfth Night*) "afraid of greatness." Could judges such as Holmes, Brandeis, or even Douglas successfully run the Senate gauntlet today?

Recent developments lend emphasis to the decline of competence in the Court. Despite a continuing increase in its calendar, the Court has been deciding fewer cases during its latest terms. It began the 1994 term with the lowest number of scheduled arguments in years. In the 1993 term, it issued signed opinions in only eighty–four cases — 40 percent fewer than it did ten years earlier. And this even though the number of cases on the Court's docket had increased by over 50 percent during the period, reaching 7,786 in the 1993 term.

Even more important is the fact that there is now one great defect in the Supreme Court's operation that, if not corrected, threatens to weaken both the effectiveness of our high tribunal and the public confidence on which the Court ultimately depends.

JUNIOR SUPREME COURT

"It is often suggested," Justice Robert H. Jackson wrote in 1955, "that the Court could create a staff of assistants like those of administrative tribunals to take much of the drudgery of judicial work from the Justices." In Chapter 2, we saw that the law clerks have developed into such a staff, designed to aid the Justices in their work. But the clerks are no longer merely a "staff of assistants." Instead, they have evolved into what Justice Douglas called a "Junior Supreme Court," which performs a major part of the judicial role delegated by the Constitution to the Justices themselves.

The greatest deficiency in the Supreme Court's decision process has been the increasing delegation — if not abdication — of key elements of the deciding function to the law clerk corps within the Court. There is, in the first place, the selection of cases, where, as seen in Chapter 2, the Justices have all but ceded their power to the clerks. As it was described in a 1993 *Wall Street Journal* article by Judge Kenneth W. Starr: "The justices themselves rarely read the certiorari documents that parties go to great trouble and expense to prepare; the law clerks do that for them. Like congressmen, justices have learned to rely on staff."

The situation has gotten worse since the establishment during the 1972 Term of the cert pool. Under it, Judge Starr tells us, "No matter how complex the case, a single law clerk writes a single memo on any given certiorari petition."

The problem has been compounded by expansion of the cert pool. In an August 2, 1991, letter to Justice Kennedy, Chief Justice Rehnquist pointed out that "the number of Justices who participate in [the cert pool] grows. As originally conceived by Lewis Powell, all members of the Court would have participated; but when it actually did get started, there were only five. By a process of accretion it has grown to seven, and as you point out, that number could increase to eight if our new colleague decides to participate." The new colleague, Justice Clarence Thomas, did agree to participate, so that the situation became that described in an August 6, 1991, "Dear Chief" letter by Justice Blackmun: "It seems that every time a new Justice arrives he almost automatically is assigned to the Pool. So long as there are four or three not in the Pool, there was a brake against errors that might be committed by Pool writers. Now John Stevens is the only non-participant."

The weakness of the cert pool is that there is no independent review of its work. This led Justice Kennedy to propose to Chief Justice Rehnquist, in a letter of August 1, 1991, that "we alter the system so that in each case one pool member does not receive the pool memo but instead performs an independent review of the petition by whatever in-chambers system he or she selects. To insure review isolated from the memo, perhaps the exclusion rotation should be designed so a clerk for the excluded judge has not prepared the memo for that case."

Mere tinkering with the cert pool is, however, scarcely enough. Judge Starr's solution "is simple: Disband the cert pool." That would be an improvement, but it would still leave the dominant role in the cert process to the clerks in the individual chambers, who had been doing almost all the work in selecting cases before the cert pool was set up. In those days, the practice was for the clerks in a Justice's chambers to divide up the cert petitions among themselves and prepare cert memos on all the cases, which would summarize the facts and issues and recommend how the Justice should vote on whether the Court should hear the cases. In the vast majority of cases, the Justices' knowledge of the petitions and the cases they presented was based on their clerks' cert memos, and they would normally vote in accordance with the memos' recommendations. Sheer volume, if nothing else, made this the normal practice.

In a 1975 article on "law clerks' influence," Justice Powell asserted, "The Court simply could not function without the assistance of these extremely bright and dedicated young lawyers." At the same time, in Judge Starr's words, "The function of selecting 100 or so cases from the pool of 6,000 petitions is just too important to invest in very smart but brand-new lawyers."

Yet, if their cert role is to be taken from the law clerks, the question posed in the Starr articles arises: "how to do this without driving the justices blind, crazy, or both, from overwork?"

An answer was given in a 1972 report by a seven-member blue-ribbon committee, headed by Professor Paul A. Freund, that was appointed by Chief Justice Burger to study the problem. The Freund Committee recommended creation of a new National Court of Appeals to "screen all petitions for review now filed in the Supreme Court." The proposed court was to exercise the Supreme Court's certiorari jurisdiction to determine which cases would be considered by the highest tribunal.

The Freund Committee proposal was never adopted—in large part because of the opposition of Earl Warren. The recently retired Chief Justice reacted with uncharacteristic vehemence to the Freund Committee recommendation. After he read a *Washington Star* article describing the new court proposed by the committee, Warren sent a letter to a former law clerk on the Freund panel. "To put it mildly," Warren wrote, "I was shocked to read in the Sunday Star that you and the committee of which you are a member are expected to advance a scuttling of the Supreme Court. I can think of few things which could throttle the Court to a greater extent in its avowed purpose of establishing 'Equal Justice under Law.'" Warren also sent a memorandum to all his former law clerks strongly opposing the proposed court.

Warren's opposition to the Freund proposal continued literally until the end of his life. Justice Brennan, who saw Warren on his deathbed, recalls, "I last saw him only two hours before his death. He wouldn't talk with me about his health. He wanted an update on the status of the proposal to create a National Court of Appeals. He strongly opposed the proposal. Its adoption, he was convinced, threatened to shut the door of the Supreme Court to the poor, the friendless, the little man."

The sitting Justices also found ways to make known their hostility to the Freund Committee proposal. They indicated that the new screening court would undercut the Supreme Court by transferring the Justices' essential power to decide what cases to decide to another panel. Combined with the Warren opposition, this argument against the proposed court ensured that the Freund proposal would remain stillborn. The reality of the cert decision process today, however, makes one wonder if the Supreme Court would not be better off if the decisions to grant or deny certiorari were made by experienced federal judges, subject to review by the Justices, instead of by a pool of neophyte lawyers who have never practiced law or otherwise been involved outside the academy.

As we saw in Chapter 2, the Justices' delegation to their law clerks is not limited to the certiorari screening process. As federal Judge Richard A. Posner points out in his 1995 book, *Overcoming Law*, only a "handful of judges . . . today still write their own opinions." By now, it is widely known among students of the Court that opinions are drafted by the clerks, though it may still not be realized by the general public how common the practice has become. "By 1959," Posner tells us in his book, "a majority of the Supreme Court's opinions were being written by law clerks; today, a judge–written opinion . . . is rare." Posner uses a striking analogy to indicate what this means: "It is a little as if brain surgeons delegated the entire performance of delicate operations to nurses, orderlies, and first–year medical students." The situation is summed up in David G. Savage's 1992 book on the Rehnquist Court, "The clerks draft most of the majority and dissenting opinions for most of the justices." The extreme recent example was Justice Marshall, who completely left opinion writing to his clerks, at least in his later years on the Court. Savage cites Marshall law clerks who told him, "He didn't write anything my year."

Yet, as Savage points out, "Marshall practiced only an extreme version of the common pattern at the Court." Opinions are almost always more the handiwork of the clerks than of the Justices in whose names they are issued. In the present Court, all the Justices (except for Justice Stevens) are editors rather than authors. Supreme Court opinions are now almost as much ghost-written as presidential speeches. In the Court as in the Government, the bureaucracy has triumphed.

The clerks themselves, according to Mary Ann Glendon's 1994 book, *A Nation Under Lawyers*, are amazed at the responsibility handed to them. She quoted one law clerk: "You go back to your office, you stare at your computer screen, and you go, 'Holy shit, I'm going to write the law of the land.' "

To those who criticize the present situation, the stock answer is that the Court's workload makes it impossible for the Justices to do all of the work themselves. That, however, scarcely justifies the present virtual abdication of what many consider the Justices' most important function — that of explaining their decisions to the profession and the public.

In addition, one may question the common assumption that, in Alexander M. Bickel's phrase, the Justices' "burden is crushing." We need not agree with Justice Douglas's assessment in a *New York Times* interview, "It's about a four–day–a–week job," leaving "three days with nothing to do much except take a walk, go out West on a trek, . . . fly down to Knoxville for three days in the Smokies." Still, the reality of the judicial workload is closer to that stated by Judge Posner, "judges on average do not work as hard as lawyers of comparable age and ability. I believe that this is true, at least of appellate judges."

It is not that judges, including those on the highest court, do not have the time to write their own opinions. With the almost total surrender of the cert function, indeed, one is tempted to wonder whether Justice Douglas was that far from the truth — particularly since he was noted for writing his own opinions.

Not too long ago, the Justices wrote their own opinions, using their law clerks only to aid in their research. Certainly that was true a century ago when the law clerk system was in its infancy. It will be said to this that the Court caseload was much lighter in those days. That may be true as far as the docket was concerned; but it was not true of the opinions issued by the Justices. In fact, as then Justice Rehnquist informed us in a 1973 article, "The number of signed opinions handed down by the 1889 Court compares favorably with most later courts. With virtually no assistance from law clerks, its justices managed to turn out 265 signed opinions during this term. Now, with three law clerks for each associate justice and four for the chief justice, the Court turns out in the neighborhood of one hundred twenty–five or one hundred thirty signed opinions each year. I am willing to treat this as being pure coincidence, rather than any reflection on law clerks."

It is, of course, a reflection not on law clerks, but on the Justices themselves. Today, to quote Judge Posner again, "most judges . . . are happy to cede opinion–writing to eager law clerks, believing . . . that the core judicial function is deciding, that is, voting, rather than articulating the grounds of the decision." Nor can the present renunciation by the Justices of their opinion-writing function really be justified, whether because of the workload or because so many recent Justices suffer from what Justice Frankfurter once called "pen paralysis." The function of a Supreme Court Justice is not only to decide but to explain the reasoning behind the opinion. Too many Justices are not only unwilling but unable to perform the latter function. For them the law clerk system is a godsend; but for the law it is a disaster, since it will inevitably lead to a dilution not only in the quality but also in the reputation of the Court.

In 1963, Justice Frankfurter received a letter from Sir Owen Dixon, the Chief Justice of Australia, about our Supreme Court: "during recent years as the advance sheets have come to me, I got the impression that the quality of the work of the Court was badly falling off. This was a hasty and too shallow a passing impression, so I decided the other day to take on the bound volumes of your Court's opinions during the last four or five Terms and to my great disappointment I had to conclude that the craftsmanship of the Court had become sloppy. You know the feelings I have always entertained for your Court and you therefore can understand some measure of the sadness with which my honesty compels me to write this."

Now that the law clerk system has become solidly entrenched, Sir Owen's comment is even more appropriate. As the country learns that this is true, there are bound to be unfortunate consequences. Here, as in other areas, there is a Gresham's law that will have an unfortunate effect upon the Supreme Court's prestige itself.

SHOOTING THE PIANO PLAYER?

In a 1988 case, Justice Scalia wrote an opinion of the Court which reversed a decision by the U.S. Court of Appeals for the Ninth Circuit granting certain naturalization petitions. The report of the case noted that Justice Blackmun concurred in the result. Blackmun explained his action in a letter to Scalia stating that "the tone of the opinion" had disturbed him. "I am frank to say," Blackmun wrote, "that what concerns me is the repeated criticism of the Ninth Circuit and its Judges. As the old saying goes, 'Don't shoot the piano player; he is doing the best he can.'"

Perhaps what Justice Blackmun said about the piano player should be said about my criticism of the role of the law clerks. After all, the Justices, too, are only "doing the best [they] can." One may, however, wonder whether that should suffice to shield them from otherwise deserved censure. If I am accused of being hypercritical, I can only refer to what Salman Rushdie once wrote: "it always matters to name rubbish as rubbish; . . . to do otherwise is to legitimize it."

The development of the law clerk corps as a crucial factor in the Court's decision process has had a baneful effect that may ultimately result in the loss of public confidence in the Supreme Court itself. The Court as an institution has always enjoyed the highest reputation among the American people. Americans today are still adherents of the view expressed almost a century ago in *The Education of Henry Adams*: "he still clung to the Supreme Court, much as a churchman clings to his bishops, because they are his only symbol of unity; his last rag of Right. Between the Executive and the Legislature, citizens could have no Rights; they were at the mercy of Power. They had created the Court to protect them from unlimited Power."

Will the same be true when the public fully realizes that Supreme Court opinions are now largely the handiwork of an anonymous minibureaucracy composed of neophyte lawyers without training or experience outside academe? Or that the decisions on what cases the Court should consider have also been largely delegated to the same junior court?

In a 1957 letter to Justice Harlan, Justice Frankfurter noted: "beginning with the Dred Scott decision — and this is the 100th anniversary of a decision that we do not celebrate — this Court gets into hot water about every twenty years." *Roe v. Wade* supports the Frankfurter thesis in the years since he wrote. If the thesis is valid, the Court may be due for another immersion. Is it going too far to suggest that this time, it will be caused by the loss of public confidence as realization of the role of the law clerks becomes widespread?

How important will such a loss be? It should not be forgotten that the Court is, to quote Alexander Hamilton once more, "the weakest of the three departments." The authority of the Court is moral, not physical. The Justices themselves have recognized this. "The Court's power," states a 1992 opinion, "lies . . . in its legitimacy, a product of substance and perception that shows itself in the people's acceptance of the Judiciary as fit to determine what the Nation's law means and to declare what it demands." The Justices must depend on public support for the ultimate efficacy of their judgments. "Like the character of an individual," according to the 1992 opinion, "the legitimacy of the Court must be earned. . . . If the Court's legitimacy should be undermined," the effectiveness of the Court itself will be seriously impaired.

"John Marshall has made his decision, now let him enforce it" — Andrew Jackson is supposed to have said. More recently, the *Economist* summarized the 1952 decision invalidating President Truman's seizure of the nation's steel mills: "All observers of the American scene should have noted, with respect, the most impressive fact. This is that the Supreme Court, although it does not possess and never has possessed any means of enforcing its decisions, has once more brought to heel the mighty: the President, the union, the industry, and Congress. All that was needed to produce this effect was the knowledge that the Court had seen and was ready to do its constitutional duty."

Will the same be true if the public loses trust in the Court as an institution?

Table of Cases

Index